CAMPAIGNING FOR HEARTS AND MINDS

STUDIES IN COMMUNICATION, MEDIA, AND PUBLIC OPINION

A series edited by Susan Herbst and Benjamin I. Page

Campaigning for Hearts and Minds

How Emotional Appeals in Political Ads Work

TED BRADER

The University of Chicago Press   CHICAGO AND LONDON

TED BRADER is assistant professor of political science and faculty associate at the Center for Political Studies of the Institute for Social Research at the University of Michigan.

The University of Chicago Press, Chicago 60637
The University of Chicago Press, Ltd., London
© 2006 by The University of Chicago
All rights reserved. Published 2006
Printed in the United States of America

15 14 13 12 11 10 09 08 07 06   1 2 3 4 5

ISBN: 0-226-06988-5 (cloth)
ISBN: 0-226-06989-3 (paper)

Library of Congress Cataloging-in-Publication Data

Brader, Ted.
    Campaigning for hearts and minds : how emotional appeals in political ads work / Ted Brader.
        p.   cm. — (Studies in communication, media, and public opinion)
    Includes bibliographical references and index.
    ISBN 0-226-06988-5 (cloth : alk. paper) — ISBN 0-226-06989-3 (pbk. : alk. paper)
        1. Political psychology. 2. Advertising, political. 3. Communication in politics. 4. Persuasion (Psychology) 5. Emotions and cognition. I. Title. II. Series.
    JA74.5.B69 2006
    324.7'3—dc22

                                    2005009159

For my parents, Jeanine and Jim Forney
and
in memory of my father, Kenneth

Contents

Tables and Figures

Tables

Figures

Acknowledgments

As snow falls on another winter morning in Ann Arbor, Michigan, my mind willingly wanders to the distant time and place where this project began. Man and nature were in greater harmony, as they are wont to be, on the lush hillsides overlooking the Connecticut River in Hanover, New Hampshire. Over the course of many warm and quiet summer afternoons, I started to ponder the connections between how politicians campaign for office and how our brains make sense of the world. The impetus for this somewhat unconventional line of thinking was a book, recommended by a former teacher of mine, that described new research on the role of emotion in human reasoning and behavior. The relevance of what I was reading to the way voters choose candidates and candidates try to influence those choices seemed obvious, nowhere more clearly than in the realm of political advertising. I thought there might be an opportunity to bring our current understanding of how campaigns appeal to emotions, whatever that was, into line with the latest research from neuroscience. But when I returned to my graduate training that fall, I was surprised to discover there was hardly any current understanding at all. Politicians appeal to emotions? Sure, everybody knew that, and yet they were silent on why and how it mattered. My efforts to break that silence turned into a dissertation and eventually this book.

I am blessed with many friends, colleagues, and mentors who have aided me in this pursuit. So it has been for the entire decade over which this project has evolved. I welcome this opportunity to thank you for all of the advice, support, and encouragement I have received.

I should begin with Roger Masters, the mentor who recommended that book and helped plant the idea for the entire project. From my years at Dartmouth College onward, Roger inspired me with his commitment to interdisciplinary thinking and his gift for boldly connecting distant ideas. He kindled my interest in neuroscience and psychology, opened my eyes to the critical link between science and values, and provided my first exposure to experiments as both subject and investigator. His knack for reaching across disciplines extends to financial resources, as he helped this young political scientist secure support from as unlikely a source as an evolutionary biologist. Of course, the boldness of the connections Roger makes can attract many doubters. I hope to repay a small part of my intellectual debt to him by demonstrating in these pages how such connections improve our ability to see the world right in front of our faces.

As the idea developed into a dissertation at Harvard University, I was fortunate to have the wisdom, confidence, and healthy skepticism of my committee. Mo Fiorina served as the principal advisor and role model. From him I learned to appreciate good social science, clear writing, and fine wine (though not nearly enough of the latter). He helped me to secure funding, insisted that I keep making progress, and was open to the possibility that emotion might matter even to a rational choice theorist. I always suspected this was somehow linked to those teary-eyed reflections on what the Proposition 13 campaign had meant to a young professor and California homeowner years earlier. I am especially grateful for his hospitality, which took many forms, during the final memorable months of writing at Stanford University.

Steve Ansolabehere was essential to the project. I simply could not have run experiments without his experience and creativity. During hour-long meetings, my hand literally cramped trying to write quickly enough to record the flood of suggestions he generously poured out. As I worried about the design and the headaches of data collection, Sid Verba shared comforting stories with lessons about resourcefulness and perspective. His gentle doubts also elicited constructive anxiety as he first worried the experiment was too subtle and then worried the effects were too big.

My debts extend well beyond the primary circle of advisors. For advice on the project at various stages, I thank Chris Achen, John Brehm, Ann Crigler, Alan Gerber, Marty Gilens, Doris Graber, Don Green, Vince Hutchings, Shanto Iyengar, Marion Just, Jon Krosnick, Russ Neuman, Pippa Norris, Vincent Price, Sam Popkin, Wendy Rahn, Paul Sniderman, Walt Stone, and Bill Zimmerman. I am very grateful for the feedback I received from those who read earlier drafts of this work in whole or in part, including Nancy Burns, Don Kinder, Skip Lupia, Mike MacKuen, George Marcus, Liz Suhay, Nick Valentino, and anonymous reviewers.

Several contributions deserve further recognition. John Aldrich is well known as the very model of collegiality and I too have benefited from his kindness through the years. I am particularly indebted for the timely and invaluable moment of clarity he brought as I worked out the experimental design. David Brady provided advice, meals, money, laughs, his unique brand of tough love, and a spacious office at Stanford with a lovely view of orange trees and other beautiful sights. I'm not sure many scholars look back on their final months of dissertation writing as paradise; thanks in part to David, I can. George Marcus, who has done more than anyone to pioneer the place of emotion in political science, displayed extraordinary generosity from the beginning, setting aside time at conferences, responding to email messages promptly, and reading everything I sent his way. In many respects, this book builds on and validates his hard work and devotion to the field. Don Kinder made critical suggestions that fundamentally changed the way I presented the evidence in this book. I didn't take every piece of his advice, but I know the book would be even better if I had. Nick Valentino has been a tireless cheerleader for the project and helped assemble the ads and coding procedures for the content analysis of campaign ads in the penultimate chapter (though he bears no blame for the analysis).

This project required a large investment of time, skills, labor, and money, and much of each was provided by others. Vic Mendiola lent his skills and sacrificed his time, just two weeks before his wedding, to shepherd me through production of the videos for the experiments. For this, I also owe my thanks to his wife Lisa Mendiola. Gina Petrocelli and Dave Campbell volunteered their services on countless summer days to administer the experiments at my side (and sometimes in my absence). I would not have been able to collect the data without their amazing generosity. I thank Marvin Kalb for lending his voice to the narration of the ads and the several libraries and churches in eastern Massachusetts that allowed me to use their buildings as a research site. Kanchan Chandra, Julie Granof, Bert Johnson, Felicia Mebane, Bonnie Meguid, Rob Mickey, Andy Rudalevige, and Rob Van Houweling also lent a hand on the experiments. For research assistance on the content analysis of political ads, I thank Antoine Banks, Whitney Crutchfield, Roei Davidson, Sarah Dobson, Eakta Khangura, Charyl Kirkland, Joey Litman, Baylee Miller, Stefanie Peppard, Jamey Schey, and Madhuri Singh. I also appreciate the assistance of Eric Groenendyk in compiling the ads. Over the course of working on this project, I received financial support through Mellon fellowships from Harvard's Department of Government; two grants from Edward O. Wilson and the Green Fund at Harvard; a Goldsmith Research Award from the Joan Shorenstein Center on Press, Politics, and Public Policy at the John F. Kennedy School of Government; a Graduate Research Fellowship and Dissertation Improvement Grant (SBR-9632565) from the National Science Foundation; and a grant from the Howard R. Marsh Center for the Study of Journalistic Performance at the University of Michigan. Maureen Connors at Harvard worked patiently with me to file all grant-related paperwork for the experiments, and Steve Baker stepped in with funds from the Department of Government to cover a shortfall from NSF.

I feel fortunate this book has found a home at the University of Chicago Press. As an avid collector of books, I have long admired its craftsmanship. And the heritage feels right—Chicago's backlist reads like the intellectual family tree of this book, and it is company I am humbled to keep. Most importantly, working with the press means working with John Tryneski and his excellent staff. John's enthusiasm and patience have been fantastic. I can't imagine entrusting the book to anyone else.

The book and I made it this far only with the help of friends and family. In graduate school, I was privileged to be part of group of remarkable classmates who met regularly to comment on one another's projects: Jacques Hymans, Aaron Lobel, Andy Rudalevige, Ken Scheve, Mike Tomz, and Josh Tucker. For additional help along the way, I thank Andrea Campbell, Tracy Gleason, Yoi Herrera, Anne Joseph, David Kaiser, Kathleen O'Neill, and my colleagues at the University of Michigan. I am especially obliged to Rob Van Houweling, who offered daily pep talks in Cambridge, Palo Alto, Ann Arbor, and many places in between. Another friend, Jill Hopper, passed away unexpectedly as I began to write the dissertation. She and I had spurred each other on through foreign studies, senior theses, and doctoral research for nearly a decade. I miss her counsel and friendship dearly.

The love and encouragement of my family has sustained me through the years. I dedicate this book to my parents, Jeanine and Jim, and to the memory of my father, Kenny. Needless to say, they have done more than anyone to shape my own heart and mind. I am profoundly grateful for all that they have sacrificed on my behalf, particularly my mother, without ever losing faith in me.

Finally, I thank my wife, Valerie. No one has suffered more to see this book reach publication, except perhaps me, and probably not even me. She read the entire manuscript, typed footnotes, cross-checked references, debated word choice, forwarded articles, freed me from other duties, and promoted the work shamelessly. She showed tremendous patience and believed in both this project and me. But more precious than all of those things, she has bestowed on me her priceless intellectual and emotional companionship.

Appealing to Hopes and Fears

All sorts of propaganda rely on emotional appeals to get their message across. . . . In 1940, such [appeals] were found in virtually every sentence of campaign propaganda.

Paul Lazarsfeld, Bernard Berelson, and Hazel Gaudet (scholars, 1944)

[M]ost ads — political and otherwise — are designed to appeal more to your emotions than your intellect. They have become the prime forum in which candidates attack and respond, convey image and information, and woo voters. . . . Ads that provoke fear, anxiety, disgust are part of the political stock-in-trade.

Patricia Lopez Baden (journalist, 1998)

"It's morning again in America."

The words are simple and yet, for some, they call forth a kaleidoscope of colorful landscapes filled with smiling, industrious, and patriotic citizens. They also may summon buried feelings of nostalgia, or perhaps revulsion. Not everyone reacts this way, of course. You had to have been alive, mildly invested in the political future of the United States, and inclined to watch television in 1984. President Ronald Reagan ran for reelection on a theme of "morning in America" that was memorably conveyed in a series of television ads throughout the year. The message of the ads was not difficult to grasp: The country is doing better than it was four years ago, so you should stick with "leadership that's working." It is a lucid and sensible argument for reelection.

A bigger mystery, given what political scientists know about the effects of political ads, is why the Reagan campaign felt compelled to package such a clear message in a gloss of music and pictures. Reagan, a gifted communicator, could have delivered the words effectively himself; the simplicity of the message surely suited his plain-spoken manner. As it is, the narrator's voice blends into the visual and musical rhythms of the ads, inviting viewers to absorb the message more as a feeling than as an argument. If there were little evidence to support the claims the ads make, their goal could be distraction and deception. This does not appear to be the case. There were indications at the time of an improving economy and restored public morale consistent with the conditions that generally forecast success for incumbent politicians. So why not dispense with all the hoopla and just say it?

This book offers an answer. Contemporary political advertising is saturated with emotional appeals, and the consultants who make the ads believe these appeals matter. As I show in the chapters that follow, the motivational and persuasive power of campaign advertising depends considerably on whether an ad appeals to fear or enthusiasm. But the effects are more complicated than conventional notions of positive and negative ads imply. We must understand the psychology underlying the responses of viewers to appreciate how such appeals work. This book offers a theoretical account of the way in which campaign ads use images and music to trigger emotions, along with an empirical demonstration that these cues indeed influence the participation and choices of citizens. With that in mind, I also explore how often and in what circumstances politicians target emotions with their ad campaigns.

The notion that politicians routinely appeal to the emotions of voters when they campaign for public office is unlikely to be controversial. Journalists, political consultants, politicians, scholars, and ordinary citizens all seem to take this for granted. But many would be surprised to discover that we know almost nothing about how emotions figure into the effects of campaign advertising. There has been a *sense* that emotion matters, but little effort to back this up with evidence. From the 1950s to the 1970s, two intellectual trends conspired to foster this neglect at roughly the time that televised advertising was on the rise in politics. First, students of politics and communication concluded that mass media and election campaigns exert minimal influence on citizens. Second, the cognitive revolution in psychology deemphasized the role of "affect" in human decisionmaking, and social scientists of all stripes largely left emotions out of their explanations.[1] All the while, political ads relying heavily on emotional appeals were steadily becoming the dominant tool in most major election campaigns.[2]

By the 1980s, emotionally laden advertising was a centerpiece in campaign strategies (Kern 1989), and ambitious new research began reversing both intellectual trends from preceding decades. Scholars launched a new wave of research into the effects of the media. By drawing on a wider range of theories and methods, they were able to uncover compelling evidence that the priorities and evaluations of citizens can be significantly altered by what they see on television (Kinder 2003). New studies testifying to the effectiveness of political advertising followed in the 1990s. Meanwhile, psychologists had "rediscovered" emotions and were inspiring others to follow suit. By the late 1990s, political scientists had assembled considerable evidence that public opinion is shaped by the moods, feelings, or emotions of citizens (Marcus 2000). All of this recent work laid a promising foundation for explaining the role of emotions in campaign communication.

But why should we bother? First, it is difficult to imagine that something so widely and evidently a part of everyday politics is inconsequential. Although politicians execute their plans with varying degrees of success, they seem to regard as self-evident that effective political appeals are also emotional appeals. In the 2004 election, candidates and groups were at it again, although the dominant emotions were markedly different than they had been twenty years earlier. Howard Dean's campaign for the Democratic nomination and the unprecedented advertising campaigns of liberal "527" groups focused on fomenting anger toward President George W. Bush for the war in Iraq. In the general election, Democratic candidate John Kerry and the president both appealed heavily to fears over issues such as outsourcing of jobs, rising health care costs, the possibility of a draft, and especially terrorism. Journalists and other observers judged it to be the most emotional and fear-driven campaign in decades. A mid-October *New York Times* report headlined "Scary Ads Take Campaign to a Grim New Level" noted these tactics were not limited to the presidential race. Political scientist and commentator Darrell West remarked, "I'm not sure we've seen a campaign with so many explicit plays to emotion. What we're seeing this year are direct plays to fear and anxiety."[3] Students of politics are obliged to ascertain whether something so commonplace as attempts to stir emotion matter—that is, the extent to which these emotional appeals actually influence citizens.

Second, the practice of appealing to emotions raises normative questions for democratic politics. Where emotional appeals are used, there too we can find criticism of politicians for "preying on the hopes and fears" of the public. Observers condemn such appeals as manipulative and view emotion as an inferior basis for decisionmaking. Critics often reserve their greatest scorn for fear appeals like those that pervaded campaigns in 2004, saying they are "unworthy of the men who would call themselves our leaders."[4] These objections have deep cultural roots in the idea that people ought to suppress emotion in favor of logic and reason. Recently, scholars of emotion have challenged these traditional views (Damasio 1994; Marcus 2002). Our judgments concerning what is right or wrong about appeals to emotion should be based on scientific knowledge regarding their effects on the process of political communication. While normative questions require more than empirical answers, our capacity to apply our values properly depends on a solid understanding of the facts, which in this case amounts to an understanding of how emotional appeals work (Masters 1994).

In this book, I present results from the first systematic study to test the effects of emotional appeals in campaign advertising. Before outlining the book's plan, I should clarify precisely what I mean by "emotional appeals."

The Primacy of Packaging

Political ads almost always contain simple messages. They typically recite a brief list of reasons to back up their main argument, which amounts to: "You should vote for this candidate, not the other guy." One of the principal ways in which the ads differ is the extent to which they focus on reasons for supporting a candidate, opposing a candidate, or both. They also vary in what sorts of reasons are mentioned—policy positions ("issues"), leadership qualities ("character"), performance in office ("the record"), relevant experience, and endorsements. Most studies of political advertising have focused on these sorts of differences in the tone and verbal messages.

But political ads, like product commercials, usually contain more than words. They are full of pictures, sounds, and music. Why are simple messages packaged with this nonverbal fanfare? It could be that these features make ads more entertaining and thus encourage an otherwise disinterested public to watch. Even so, it is doubtful that people who are not already political junkies find much entertainment in political ads. The music and images accomplish something more than merely enhancing the pleasure of the viewing experience. They make the ad compelling by eliciting specific emotions and, in doing so, change the way viewers respond to the message of the ad.

This attempt to stir the feelings of the audience while delivering a political message is what I refer to as an "emotional appeal." The overall emotional impact of the ad is produced by the conjunction of words, music, and images in a narrative structure. The words are nearly indispensable to the message because they more sharply delimit its meaning, but the music and images are meant first and foremost to stir emotions. Imagery and music do not compete with or substitute for the verbal message, but they sharpen its effectiveness by altering how the message is received.

This study is particularly concerned with the impact of those emotionally evocative, nonverbal elements of campaign ads. Before describing that study, I want to remind readers of how these emotional ads look and sound. Although similar advertising styles characterize almost all major state and federal elections (Kern 1989), the following discussion draws examples from presidential ad campaigns because they provide a model that others follow and a greater proportion of readers will have had an opportunity to see these ads for themselves at one time or another. I focus on ads that may be considered archetypes of two common types of appeals at root in the contrast between the reelection campaigns of 1984 and 2004. The first are ads that appeal to hope and enthusiasm, the second are ads that appeal to fear. We should also consider how these sorts of ads differ from those that appeal only weakly, if at all, to emotions. In making these distinctions, I am not offering an exhaustive typology of emotional appeals. Ads can and do appeal to other emotions (e.g., anger, pride, sympathy, amusement) that may or may not be similar in their appearance and impact to those already mentioned. As a first step, however, my focus here and more generally in this book is on appeals to enthusiasm and fear.

I also want to clarify at the outset how I am using emotion labels such as "enthusiasm appeal" and "fear ad" throughout this book. An emotion is not technically a property of an ad, but rather a response that the ad may or may not elicit from those who view it (see chapter 3). In many cases, a single ad may elicit more than one emotion from a single person (e.g., fear as well as anger) or different emotions from different people (e.g., enthusiasm from some people, disgust from others). In both everyday language and scholarship, however, there is a convention of using labels to describe the emotion that something conveys or elicits in its intended audience—for example, fear appeals, sad music, sympathy cards, horror movies, and hopeful signs. In an effort to make this book more widely accessible, I follow the standard practice by labeling ads, appeals, and audiovisual cues according to the emotion(s) they seem primarily aimed to evoke in the target audience. Nonetheless, we must take care to distinguish this labeling convention from the actual emotional impact of the ad.

Feel-Good Ads: Appeals to Hope and Enthusiasm

Ads in the *Morning in America* campaign represent a common form of advertising often called "feel-good" spots by consultants. As this name implies, feel-good spots try to shape reception of the ad's message by eliciting positive emotions such as hope, enthusiasm, and perhaps even pride. It is commonly held that such ads aim to win the affection of voters for the sponsoring or supported candidate. But matters are not that simple. In fact, as we shall see later, feel-good ads—or "enthusiasm ads," as I label them—can be just as effective at driving opposing viewers away in disgust. Their true power lies in stoking the desire to get involved and reinforcing existing loyalties.

How do these ads stir hope and enthusiasm? They rely principally on music and images to generate an emotional response.[5] Ads in the *Morning in America* series are accompanied by a piano and orchestra playing a soft, uplifting tune. It is the kind of music one expects from a movie soundtrack that invokes sentimental or nostalgic themes (e.g., *Field of Dreams* or *A River Runs Through It*). Images from an idyllic "town not too far from where you live" serve as the primary backdrop for the ads. Men and women go to work in fields and factories, displaying pride in what they accomplish. A young couple is getting married, as an older couple walks hand-in-hand down Main Street sharing an ice cream cone. Families are moving into new homes and buying new cars. Children line a parade route waving American flags. Flags in fact are everywhere, and smiling faces too.

Morning in America set the standard for enthusiasm-eliciting political advertising and remains largely unparalleled for its combination of evocative symbolism and minimal discussion of politics. However, this general style of ad is extremely common and has been mimicked by presidential candidates and those pursuing other offices ever since. Figure 1.1 shows just a few examples of the images frequently used in feel-good or enthusiasm ads. The musical score is invariably uplifting, whether it strikes chords of sentimentality or patriotism. Other sound effects occasionally appear in the form of laughter, applause, or even the roar of a jet in ads emphasizing military strength. Visuals are typically rich in color with warm light and soft edges. Scenes portray happy families and economic prosperity against the backdrop of picturesque landscapes. National pride is cued not only through flags but also by people in uniform, navy vessels and military aircraft, political and natural monuments, and ceremonies honoring fallen soldiers.[6]

Fear Ads

Although the *Morning in America* spots are considered classics of political advertising, they are neither the best known among all ads nor even the most memorable from the 1984 election campaign. The distinction in each case falls to a dramatically different sort of ad. Perhaps the most (in)famous ad ever is the *Daisy* ad aired by President Lyndon Johnson's reelection team in 1964, which sought to stoke fears of nuclear war. Similarly, the most memorable spot of the 1984 election, according to polls at the time, was the *Bear* ad, which also struck a Cold War theme by suggesting that a strategy of deterrence through military strength was the best way to deal with the risk of Soviet aggression.

Fear ads of this sort are another staple of modern election campaigns. Although they are not necessarily more common than feel-good spots, they often garner more attention. Their purpose is just as clear—namely, to awaken or fuel the anxieties of the viewing public. Some observers believe the goal of fear ads is to cause voters to associate their fears and disgust with the opponent. This conventional notion makes sense only for "attack ads," a

FIGURE 1.1 Feel-Good Ads Reassure and Inspire Voters with Uplifting Tunes and Colorful Images of Family, Country, and Prosperity

Ronald Reagan's *Morning in America* Ad Campaign (1984)

Other Examples of Feel-Good Ads

Bill Clinton, *I Have Done My Best* (1996)   Bill Clinton, *Accomplishment* (1996)

George W. Bush, *Whatever It Takes* (2004)   George H. W. Bush, *Future* (1988)

particular type of negative ad devoted to criticizing the opposing candidate. Although a large proportion of attack ads use fear appeals, not all fear ads explicitly criticize an opponent. Regardless, the conventional view proves too simplistic for fear ads as well. As new evidence reveals, their true power lies in stimulating attentiveness to relevant information and encouraging people to rethink their choices.

As with feel-good spots, fear ads do not merely deliver a worrisome message, but also rely heavily on images, music, and sound effects to make voters uneasy. The way that emotional appeals work is more or less the same in each case, though the types of cues utilized in the ads are obviously quite distinct. Figure 1.2 shows images from recent and classic fear ads.

The *Daisy* ad generated more controversy than any political advertising before or since, despite airing only once. The sixty-second ad juxtaposed the image of a small child and a nuclear explosion. Its "attack" on Johnson's opponent in the upcoming election, Republican Barry Goldwater, was only implicit, seizing on public awareness of his earlier statements without actually referring to him or his statements directly. The ad begins with a young girl standing in a field and counting to ten as she picks petals off of a flower, accompanied only by the bucolic sounds of birds and a gentle breeze blowing through the grass. By the time her count reaches nine, however, an ominous voice initiates a ten-second countdown as the camera zooms in on a frozen image of the girl. When the screen is filled with the black of her pupil and the countdown reaches zero, a nuclear bomb explodes. Images of a mushroom cloud fill the screen for the rest of the ad, as President Johnson's voice delivers a solemn warning over the rumbling roar of the cloud, concluding that "we must either love each other, or we must die."

The 1984 *Bear* ad took a more subtle, though equally symbol-driven, approach. It touched on a second theme in Reagan's reelection campaign—namely, that his strong defense policies had made the country "prepared for peace." However, the narrator mentions neither defense policy nor the election explicitly:

There is a bear in the woods. For some people, the bear is easy to see. Others don't see it at all. Some people say the bear is tame. Others say it's vicious and dangerous. Since we can never really be sure who's right, isn't it smart to be as strong as the bear . . . if there is a bear?

The entire script is a metaphorical reference to the Cold War standoff with the Soviet Union (the bear is a traditional symbol of Russia). Like *Daisy,* the *Bear* ad counts on viewers to fill in what is missing. The audiovisual packaging of the ad does nothing to help clarify the message. For nearly thirty seconds, a bear lumbers over rocks, through bushes, and into streams, until

FIGURE 1.2 Fear Ads Stir Anxiety among Voters with Ominous Music and Dark Images of War, Crime, Pollution, and Other Threats

Lyndon Johnson's *Daisy* Ad (1964)

From Ronald Reagan's *Bear* (1984) to George W. Bush's *Wolves* (2004)

Other Examples of Fear Ads

NAACP, *Byrd I* (2000)

George H. W. Bush, *Revolving Door* (1988)

George H. W. Bush, *Harbor* (1988)

George H. W. Bush, *Arkansas* (1992)

finally meeting a man with a gun atop a grassy ridge. At first, the bear walks directly toward the man but then pauses several feet away and takes a step back. The ad never cuts away to images of Soviet tanks, missiles, or other visual evidence that might help viewers who miss the point.[7] Just as the *Morning in America* ads use a sentimental tune to elicit an emotional reaction from viewers, the *Bear* ad uses disquieting string chords with the "thump-thump" of a drum at regular intervals.

Although reliance on metaphor alone is extremely rare in political advertising, fear ads that use similar nonverbal cues to stir anxiety are not. In 2004, the reelection campaign of George W. Bush borrowed from the Reagan playbook by producing the *Wolves* ad to stress that Americans are no longer threatened by a strong lumbering superpower but instead by packs of lurking terrorists. The ad leaves less to the imagination, however, by telling viewers explicitly that John Kerry represents weakness in the face of terrorism and that "weakness attracts those who are waiting to do America harm." Fear ads emphasize domestic dangers such as crime, unemployment, and pollution, as well. In general, the soundtrack of fear ads features tension-raising instrumentals full of minor chords, ominous rhythms, and discordant tones. Sound effects such as sirens, crying infants, and howling wind punctuate the visual storyline. These ads use grainy, black-and-white images or dark and muted colors. They show scenes of war, violence and crime, drug use, desolate landscapes, sewage, poverty, and death.[8]

What Does an Ad Lacking in Emotion Look Like?

We realize the extent to which we expect televised political messages to be accompanied by emotionally evocative images and music when we encounter ads that don't meet those expectations. "Unimpassioned ads," as I shall call them, largely eschew dramatic depictions and emotional appeals in favor of argument and information. They also are exceptions that prove the rule. Generally speaking, unimpassioned ads are not the ones people talk about during the election, remember after the election, or spotlight in political analyses. Although they are less daring and therefore less risky, analysts tend to see these "informational" ads as less effective (Kern 1989; Perloff and Kinsey 1992). Their one advantage is that they are likely to stand out for their novelty amid the stream of other political and commercial spots inundating television viewers. If an understated video production style and a "just the facts" posture also dovetail nicely with an outsider campaign theme, then unimpassioned ads may even be the best option for a particular politician.

This was probably the case for the 1992 presidential campaign of independent candidate H. Ross Perot. Ads that use little in the way of music, evocative symbols, and colorful backdrops are especially difficult to find in presidential races. But most Perot ads, including his sixty- and thirty-second spots, as well as his half-hour infomercials, were of the unimpassioned variety. Their goal was to convey a verbal message full of factual claims and arguments. For example, during the ad *Trickle Down,* the narrator criticizes the economic policies of the Bush administration and suggests that Perot is the sensible alternative. As shown in figure 1.3, the entire script scrolls steadily up the screen in fragments as the narrator speaks. Although there is a tone of contempt for the incumbent's positions, the message is not delivered with much emotion. At the same time, *Trickle Down* also reinforces the general rule regarding political ads because it is not entirely devoid of symbolic images and music. The backdrop remains fixed on a dark, rain-speckled pane of glass, with an occasional raindrop trickling down the screen. The musical score features slightly tense orchestral chords that are later enhanced with the soft heralding call of trumpets, as the narrator makes the case for choosing Perot. Nonetheless, these cues strike dreary or somber notes more than alarm or unease.

There are other styles of ads we might classify as unimpassioned. Some throw selected words from the script on the screen to highlight sound bites against a monochrome backdrop. They occasionally use such graphic devices as tables and charts to emphasize a point. Perhaps the most common form of unimpassioned ad is the "talking head," which features a candidate speaking directly to the camera. In many cases, the ads still pose the candidate in a mildly evocative manner such as sitting in a colorful political office flanked by flags or standing among attentive family members or voters. However, both Perot in 1992 and Jimmy Carter in 1976 aired talking-head ads with a plain black or brown backdrop. Some ads use the same visual style of talking-head spots but feature testimonials from everyday members of the public rather than comments by the candidate.

In general, ads are almost never stripped completely of emotional content. Verbal messages can and do stir emotions (Crigler, Just, and Neuman 1994). Nonverbal facial displays and body language, especially from powerful political leaders, have considerable capacity to evoke an emotional reaction (Sullivan and Masters 1988). We might question whether it is even possible to create a purely unemotional ad. For that reason, I use the term "unimpassioned"—it suggests the ad does not make a particularly impassioned appeal, but it does not imply that passion is altogether absent. In this sense, ads classified as unimpassioned comprise those at the low or weak end of the spectrum for a number of emotional appeals (e.g., the faintest of appeals to fear, hope, anger, etc.), rather than as a distinct category of advertising as such. Unimpassioned ads are simply those that adopt a less evocative style of presentation.

FIGURE 1.3 Unimpassioned Ads Stand Out as Exceptions that Prove the Rule by Stressing Words, While Still Using Mildly Evocative Sounds and Images

Ross Perot's *Trickle Down* Ad (1992)

Other Examples of Unimpassioned Ads

Ross Perot, *Best Person* (1992)

John Kerry, *Paperwork* (2004)

People for the American Way, *Sure* (2000)

Ronald Reagan, *Headley* (1984)

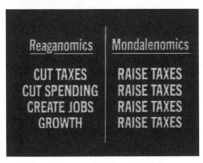

Ronald Reagan, *Reaganomics* (1984)

RNC, *Gore-gantuan* (2000)

The Impact of Emotional Appeals

Studies of the *content and history* of televised political advertising have explored the audiovisual style of campaign ads and only occasionally have touched on the apparent importance of stirring emotions. Studies of the *effects* of televised political advertising have focused primarily on the tone and content of information the ads contain. Very few have tried to test the impact of musical and visual cues, and none have tried to test the impact of appealing to specific emotions.

This book takes up the long overdue task of determining whether and how campaign ads affect voters by appealing to their emotions. I argue that campaign ads use symbolic images and evocative music to trigger an emotional response in viewers. By appealing to different emotions, ads can influence the participation and choices of viewers in distinct ways. Recent advances in psychology reveal the central role emotions play in reasoning and social behavior. I borrow these insights to predict the consequences of emotional appeals in political advertising and test the predictions with a series of experiments during an on-going election. The results show that the audiovisual "packaging" of ads may be paramount to their effectiveness. In addition, consistent with theoretical expectations, enthusiasm appeals motivate viewers to get involved and act on existing loyalties, while fear appeals provoke viewers to seek out new information and reconsider their choices. As a result, we should not be surprised that politicians rely heavily on emotionally laden advertising, but we should expect the circumstances in which they find enthusiasm and fear ads advantageous to differ. I present systematic evidence from recent ad campaigns to demonstrate the extent to which politicians use appeals to fear, enthusiasm, and other emotions, and how this varies across electoral settings. In sum, I argue that politicians frequently make appeals to voter emotions through televised advertising and that these appeals greatly shape their ability to sway the electorate.

This argument is developed fully in the pages that follow. Chapter 2 explains what we *believe* and what we *know* about the effects of political advertising campaigns and the role of emotion generally in political communication. Over the past half century in American politics, television ads have become the principal tool of contemporary electioneering. Spending on ads accounts for the largest share of the budget for almost all presidential, gubernatorial, and congressional campaigns. I investigate what political consultants, journalists, academics, and others think about the role of emotion in campaigning and discover widespread agreement about the practices of selling candidates. These political observers believe that emotional appeals are powerful staples of campaign advertising, embedded in music and images, that manipulate uneducated and uninformed voters. This contrasts

sharply with research by social scientists: out of hundreds of studies of televised political advertising, not one examines the effects of emotion. Recon-
ciling this gap between political "science" and political "art" is the central
goal of the book.

In chapter 3, I lay out a partial blueprint for this reconciliation by offering a theoretical account of the political psychology underlying responses to
emotional appeals. Conventional explanations for the role of emotion tend
to treat emotionality in one of three ways: (1) as epiphenomenal; (2) as a matter of valence (i.e., positive versus negative affect) that can be transferred to
the sponsoring or opposing candidate; or (3) as a matter of arousal or vividness that determines the entertainment value and thus attention-grabbing
powers of the ad. Drawing on psychological theories of emotion and their
recent application to public opinion, I argue that campaigns ads have the
capacity to affect political behavior by triggering specific emotions such as
enthusiasm or fear with audiovisual cues. Ads capitalize on learned associations between particular stimuli and expected outcomes. Basic emotional
systems monitor incoming information for its significance to our goals and
well-being, allowing us to adapt our behavior accordingly. In addition, the
power of emotions stems from the way our brains often identify cues and respond to them without our awareness. This perspective enables us to explain
the potency of music and symbolic images and to generate distinct predictions for the consequences of enthusiasm and fear ads.

Chapters 4–6 are concerned with presenting empirical evidence on the
impact and use of emotion in campaign advertising. Chapters 4 and 5 report
results from a pair of experiments designed to test the effects of televised
emotional appeals on the voting behavior of ordinary citizens. The experiments were carried out during an actual gubernatorial election and simulated the way in which citizens are incidentally exposed to campaign ads
while watching other programs. The first experiment sets up a comparison
between exposure to an unimpassioned positive ad and the identical ad with
enthusiasm-evoking images and music. The second experiment sets up a
comparison between an unimpassioned negative ad and the identical ad
with fear-evoking images and music. This design allows us to look past the
positive or negative tone of the script and focus on the effects of stirring specific emotions with the nonverbal cues.

Chapter 4 also examines the role emotional appeals play in drawing citizens into electoral politics or pushing them away. I find evidence that enthusiasm ads possess broad motivational power. In contrast to recent discussions about the demobilizing impact of political ads, attempts to stir
hope and enthusiasm inspire greater interest in the election and stimulate
the desire to volunteer and vote. I find that fear ads can motivate involve-

ment as well, but this potential is more narrowly limited to those with higher levels of civic competence. On further inspection, the evidence also reveals that these "sophisticated" citizens tend to be more responsive to emotional appeals of either type. Finally, despite a few suggestive findings, I find little evidence that emotional appeals either strengthen or undermine civic attitudes such as trust in the political process and citizens' confidence in their own ability to make a difference.

The results presented in chapter 5 primarily concern attitudes toward the candidates and the choice made between them. Enthusiasm spots reinforce prior convictions, leading to greater certainty and loyalty in voting decisions. As a result, these warm, uplifting ads ironically polarize the electorate, rallying supporters and hardening the commitment of the opposition. Fear ads are more persuasive, improving the sponsor's standing in relative assessments of the candidates and increasing the likelihood of winning converts or softening electoral support for the opponent. In essence, these appeals stimulate a reassessment of political options. When an ad appeals to voter anxieties, it weakens reliance on prior dispositions and strengthens the salience of new information and contemporary evaluations in candidate choice. I also consider the impact of emotional appeals on attention, learning, and information seeking. Despite their motivational impact, there is little evidence to suggest that either type of appeal greatly improves learning from the ad itself. However, fear appeals seem to motivate vigilance in the form of a search for related information and a desire to learn more. Once again, I find that it is the attitudes, choices, and information seeking on the part of knowledgeable citizens that are most readily influenced. Taken together with the findings on motivation from the preceding chapter, these results upend traditional views about who is most susceptible to "manipulation" by emotional appeals.

In chapter 6, the perspective shifts from the effects of campaign ads to the conduct of advertising campaigns. The chapter describes a systematic content analysis of more than fourteen hundred campaign ads from elections during 1999 and 2000, undertaken to discover how and when politicians appeal to emotions. The results confirm that most ads appeal to one or more emotions and that enthusiasm and fear ads are indeed common. Ads appealing to enthusiasm and fear use music, imagery, and other audiovisual elements in distinct ways—distinctions that correspond to the sorts of cues theories of emotion lead us to expect. In addition to enriching our general impression of how campaign ads cue emotions, the data shed some light on the strategic use of emotional appeals. Consistent with expectations, political challengers are more likely to produce fear appeals than incumbents, and front-runners are more likely to produce enthusiasm appeals. Moreover, in state elections, candidates are more likely to appeal to enthusiasm when their party has the advantage among voters statewide, and are more likely to appeal to fear when the opposing party has the advantage.

Finally, in chapter 7, I put into perspective the progress the book makes in explaining the role of emotion in televised campaign advertising. This book continues the efforts begun by others to bring an appreciation for the importance of emotion to the study of politics. In trying for the first time to provide a theoretical account and empirical test of the effects of two common types of emotional appeals, the research reported here is more of a beginning than an end. Many questions remain.

The findings of this study also have implications for our empirical and normative understanding of election campaigns. The final chapter reflects on how the manner in which politicians choose to communicate can shape the very temper of citizenship in the mass public. It also reconsiders complaints that politicians prey on the hopes and fears of voters in light of a more theoretically and empirically grounded account of the role of emotions in the process of political communication.

2

The Art and Science of Campaigning

[T]elevision spots . . . create auditory and visual stimuli that can evoke a voter's deeply held feelings. . . . The real question in political advertising is how to surround the voter with the proper auditory and visual stimuli to evoke the reaction you want from him.

Tony Schwartz (political consultant, 1973)

Symbolic manipulation through televised political advertising simply does not work. Perhaps the overuse of symbols and stereotypes in product advertising has built up an immunity in the television audience. Perhaps the symbols and postures used in political advertising are such patently ridiculous attempts at manipulation that they appear more ridiculous than reliable. Whatever the precise reason, television viewers effectively protect themselves from manipulation by staged imagery.

Thomas Patterson and Robert McClure (scholars, 1976)

At the time of the country's founding, American leaders initiated a bold experiment that made government accountable to the people through regular elections. Their boldness, however, extended only so far. Although they expected a measure of electoral competition, the Founders took a dim view of candidates campaigning for public office through direct and public appeals to the citizenry (Schudson 1998). Politicking for votes was not just unseemly, it was dangerous. The Founders worried that ambitious men would seek office by arousing the "passions" of the people and, in so doing, encourage the "intolerant spirit" of political parties to endure.[1] The country's second generation proved them right, as vigorous election campaigns and organized political parties emerged side-by-side as a staple of American politics (Aldrich 1995). Citizens today are besieged by election campaigns almost continuously, thanks to the vast number of elected offices, staggered election cycles, primary contests, increased use of ballot propositions, and lengthening of the campaign process. This chapter reviews what practitioners, scholars, and other observers believe about the influence of such campaigns on popular passions.

My central argument in this book—namely, that politicians, by appealing to specific emotions, can change the way citizens respond to political messages—concerns the role of emotional appeals in political communication generally. Although context and medium may alter the ease with which particular emotions are elicited, the nature of the impact should be the same for emotions evoked by ads, speeches, news coverage, debates, or direct mailings. However, my focus here is on explaining the role of emotion in campaign advertising. Much of the effort to motivate and persuade citizens occurs during election campaigns and takes the form of commercials on television. In addition, observers understand campaign ads to rely heavily on emotion, perhaps to a greater extent than other forms of communication. Campaign ads are an appropriate medium on which to focus an initial study of the impact of emotional appeals.

In this chapter, I begin that investigation by identifying several beliefs about the role of emotion in selling candidates that are widely held by the political consultants who make ads, the journalists who cover campaigns, and the scholars who study campaign communication. I also review what scholars have learned about the role of emotion in political communication. These explorations reveal a clear contrast between the art and science of campaign advertising. Much of the conventional wisdom about the role of emotion remains untested by systematic research, leaving a significant gap between what practitioners consider central to their craft and what scholars have included in their models. Related research on the expressive behavior of leaders and the use of evocative words or pictures in printed leaflets is promising, but no one has yet undertaken systematic study of emotional appeals where they are most prominent—in campaign ads on television.

The Principal Tool of Contemporary Campaigns

I begin by considering the place of advertising in contemporary elections. Throughout most of the nineteenth century, political parties practiced a vigorous style of campaigning designed to mobilize supporters and, at times, deter opponents (Aldrich 1995; Altschuler and Blumin 2001). Local clubs formed, members sang and drank at raucous events, parades marched from town to town, candidates made a few appearances, and local partisan newspapers embellished the events in their reporting. Even when progressive reforms weakened parties in the early decades of the twentieth century, candidates continued to rely on state and local party machines to spread the word and turn out likely supporters on Election Day. In the years after World War II, however, the focus of political campaigns shifted from parties to candidates (Wattenberg 1992) and from door-to-door to mass-mediated mobilization techniques (Ansolabehere, Behr, and Iyengar 1993; Norris 2000). "Media politics" did not entirely displace "party politics" as an organizing force in public affairs, but it transformed the manner in which politicians campaign for public support (Zaller n.d.).

Candidates now form personal campaign organizations charged with getting their message out to potential voters, while parties and interest groups pursue their broader agendas with parallel efforts. Options for communicating with the public often are divided into two categories: free media and paid media. The main source of free publicity is news coverage, and campaign activities such as local rallies and national party conventions often are designed to "make the news." The downside of free media for politicians is that they cannot control the message. Journalists increasingly seek to reshape the messages politicians try to convey through them (Zaller n.d.). The other option is paid advertising, which comprises posters and buttons, direct mail, and radio and television spots. While this approach is costly and lacks an aura of neutrality compared with news coverage, politicians can use ad campaigns to control the amount and content of the information conveyed to the public.[2]

Many observers implicate television in the transformation to candidate-centered campaigning, both fueling and reflecting it. Although other media play a part, the ubiquitous TV set sits at the center of modern mass-mediated elections (Ansolabehere, Behr, and Iyengar 1993; Graber 2001; McCubbins 1992). There is an enduring fascination with television that often leads observers to assign it credit or blame for important changes in society. While the evidence for actual influence has often been thin, several features of the medium do lend it the potential for considerable power. TV does not require its audience to be literate nor even to expend the effort of reading. The combination of moving images and sound provides a window into distant places and events in such a way that they feel "real," as if the viewer were "there" in some sense, lending an aura of truth or authenticity to what is seen and heard (Barry 1997). Some have remarked on the apparent intimacy conveyed by transporting speakers and events into the viewer's living room (Hart 1999). Others argue that TV confers an advantage to charismatic leaders that harks back to premodern times, because it partially restores the communicative power of nonverbal behavior that is so important in everyday social interactions (Masters 1991).[3] Whether due to its seeming authenticity, intimacy, or simply the combination of two sensory channels (image and sound), many suggest that TV has greater emotional power than other sources of political information (Graber 2000). While the political consequences of the television era are still debated (Norris 2000), perhaps its largest impact on society has been to recenter the average American's life around televised entertainment (Putnam 2000).[4]

The nature of TV viewing helps to shape the potency of campaign ads as a source of political information. Exposure to ads is a by-product of watching other programs. The relatively passive viewing experience usually requires serial attention to a stream of audiovisual signals (i.e., it is more difficult for the viewer to selectively attend to information). In this way, advertising reaches people who are not necessarily seeking news about politics. The fact that Americans spend more time watching TV for entertainment and less time watching it for "hard" news increases the relative importance of advertising as a source of information (Putnam 2000).

Televised campaign advertising has become the principal tool of politicians in major elections. Presidential candidates were the first serious political advertisers on TV, but today candidates for Congress, many statewide offices, and some municipal elections make heavy use of television ads. Interest groups also devote substantial resources to airing ads to influence candidate elections, ballot propositions, and even policy debates outside of elections. What began with a modest splash in the 1950s has grown to an electronic flood in recent decades.

Television advertising is the primary cause of the upward spiral in campaign spending, as most candidates for major offices devote a greater proportion of their budget to airing ads than to any other type of expenditure. The second largest campaign expense often is fundraising to collect the money needed (largely) for ads. In developing ads and strategies for airing them, some candidates have taken a "Madison Avenue" approach by enlisting the help of companies experienced at product advertising. During the 1980s and 1990s, however, increased reliance on ads fueled the rise of political consulting as a profession, complete with a trade association and industry publications.[5] Campaign ads have since become more sharp-edged and more slickly packaged.[6]

Styles and Functions of Campaign Advertising

Campaigns seek to increase the number of supporters for their candidate and to encourage those supporters to be politically active. Therefore, the primary goals of political advertising are to persuade and to motivate. In pursuit of these goals, ads seek to shape the impressions voters form of the candidates, including providing information about who they are (name recognition), what they have done (experience and record), what they stand for (issue positions), and whom they represent (group ties). Politicians also use ads to shape perceptions of policy issues and current conditions, not only to make their arguments more convincing, but also to motivate involvement by altering how citizens perceive the stakes.

Scholars have categorized ads in a number of ways. They have developed categories based on the predominant type of information presented, such as biography, issues, or character. Other categories have to do with presentation style (e.g., "talking head," "testimonial," "image"). Perhaps most commonly, scholars have characterized ads as either positive or negative according to the "tone" of the information given. This categorization has been drawn so broadly, however, that it obscures differences in the *ways* an ad can be positive or negative, differences that may have implications for the ad's effectiveness and perceived ethical status. In its most popular usage, tone refers to the type of arguments made about the candidates: negative or "attack" ads criticize the opponent, positive or "promotion" ads praise the sponsor, and "comparison" spots contrast weaknesses of the opponent with strengths of the sponsor. Nonetheless, the tone of an ad may come across as negative or positive for other reasons, such as the way in which current conditions are discussed or the mood suggested by the images and music. For example, while it is not uncommon for negative ads to cast a pall over the opponent's stance on the issues, some negative ads scarcely mention the opponent at all, as was the case in the *Daisy* and *Bear* ads discussed in chapter 1.

Emotion is notably absent from most of these classification schemes. While I just suggested that one might define the tone of an ad according to the mood struck by its imagery and music, few scholars do. They conceptualize and operationalize tone primarily in terms of informational content, not emotional appeal. But this has not always been true in the study of political communication. An old line of research at the intersection of psychology and communication categorizes propaganda according to whether it makes an appeal to emotions or to what is variously termed "logic," "reason," or "rationality" (Bauer and Cox 1963; Hartmann 1936; Pallak, Murroni, and Koch 1983; Rosselli, Skelly, and Mackie 1995). In making such a distinction, this body of work in turn draws on the importance assigned to both logic and emotion in the venerable study of rhetoric dating back to Aristotle and Cicero (Aristotle 1991; Jamieson 1988; Pratkanis and Aronson 1992). Most of these studies remain broadly focused on contrasting emotional and logical appeals and do not further examine distinctions based on the specific emotions to which communicators appeal (but see Roseman, Abelson, and Ewing 1986). Although its impact on the scientific study of political advertising has been minimal, this research tradition has significantly shaped popular and professional understanding of political communication. The same categories that are largely missing from scientific studies seem to play a tremendous role in organizing everyday interpretations of campaign ads, even among the scientists.

Common Beliefs about the Role of Emotion

What do people think about the role of emotion in political advertising? If scientific studies have been largely silent on the topic, public and professional discussions have not. "Emotions" and "emotional appeals" emerge as central concepts for interpreting the goals and impact of political ads across an array of observers. They appear in the casual observations of ordinary citizens and journalists who follow campaigns, the advice and explanations of political consultants who make the ads, and even in the descriptions and functional interpretations of scholars. In short, for creators and viewers of political ads alike, thinking about what those ads are trying to accomplish leads ineluctably to the role of emotion.[7]

Most readers are unlikely to be surprised by that claim precisely because the link between political ads and emotional appeals is so commonplace in everyday discussions. In light of this, my focus is not on documenting the frequency with which the concept of *emotion* arises in popular and professional discourse about political ads, but rather on considering *how* people talk about the role of emotion. With rare exception, people do not engage in extensive or systematic discussion of the subject. However, I believe we can use more-or-less casual observations to discern the beliefs or assumptions about the role of emotion shared both by many ordinary citizens and by elite political actors.

My efforts to cull the conventional wisdom on emotional appeals draws from a number of sources. I have examined the comments of citizens, academics, journalists, and consultants in hundreds of articles and opinion pieces appearing in English-language newspapers and news magazines over the past twenty-five years. Dozens of articles from trade publications for the advertising, public relations, journalism, and political consulting professions have shed further light on the beliefs of elite practitioners. Finally, I have examined scholarly books and papers to glean the perspectives of the authors as well as of those they interviewed for their projects. If the central aim of this book were to understand how people think about emotional appeals, I would want to go a step farther and try to distinguish whether people are expressing their own beliefs or simply parroting the conventional wisdom as they see it. But that is not my goal here. My goal is to identify the conventional wisdom regarding emotion in political advertising, as a prelude to systematically assessing what role emotional appeals play. I focus below on six sets of beliefs about which there is considerable, though not complete, consensus. A selection of these views is highlighted in figure 2.1.

Belief 1. Politicians Routinely Appeal to the Emotions of Voters, Especially in Campaign Ads

Politicians routinely appeal to the emotions of citizens. I suspect this claim meets with little controversy and perhaps universal agreement. Why then is it worthy of our attention? If this facet of political life is obvious, it should sharpen our surprise that political scientists have offered little explanation of the nature and frequency of these appeals or their impact on the political process. It is possible that the role of emotional appeals is so self-evident as to require no investigation. That posture, however, seems both unlikely and antithetical to the aims of scientific inquiry. Scholars have on occasion found conventional wisdom severely wanting, if not plain wrong. Moreover, in some cases, they have pointed to an element of received wisdom that turns out, on closer inspection, not to have been so widely received. It is worth verifying not only the veracity of conventional wisdom regarding emotional appeals, but also its existence.

The view that politicians try to stir popular emotions indeed appears to be shared by observers of all stripes. Respected journalist David Broder describes contemporary campaigns as "costly distractions, designed to stir [voters'] emotions."[8] Reporters often claim that candidates stress specific issues to "play to emotions," "touch the deepest emotions," or because the issues have "emotional resonance."[9] Prominent political consultants concur about the nature of campaigns. Republican consultant Robert Goodman sees voting as "an emotional act," and Democratic consultant Frank Greer contends that campaigning is "an emotional endeavor" rather than "an intellectual exercise."[10] Some consultants for grassroots campaigns advocate a "clear message that plays on people's emotions," while other activists complain about this tendency to use "appeals to emotion rather than reason."[11]

When it comes to televised advertising, the consensus is even stronger. News coverage of elections is replete with references to "sophisticated commercials that play on emotions" and ads variously described as "emotion-laden," "designed to push emotional buttons," "aimed at evoking voters' emotions," engaged in "subtle emotional hype," or "stuffed with emotion."[12] In an adwatch featuring citizen commentary, a local teacher had this to say: "The established strategy of TV ads is effectively used here. Start with an emotionally credible attention grabber that zeroes in on a powerful fear, then offer an attractively simple solution."[13] As this comment implies, some

FIGURE 2.1 Conventional Wisdom about Emotional Appeals

How Prevalent Are Emotional Appeals?

"[Politicians] manipulate people's weakest and worst emotions for political gain." (Tom Klein, resident of Omaha, NE, 10/15/00)

"[M]ost ads—political or otherwise—are designed to appeal more to your emotions than to your intellect." (Patricia Lopez Baden, *Minneapolis Star Tribune*, 9/27/98)

"This is a medium where you are trying to sell people and emotions. It's not toothpaste we're selling. People need to connect to the emotional content of your ad." (Kim Alfano, Republican political consultant, 9/99)

"In these kinds of ads, the main tool is an emotional appeal." (Lewis Mazanti, curator for Julian P. Kanter Political Commercial Archive, 1/12/04)

How Do Ads Appeal to Emotions?

"[Politicians] know that emotionally charged pictures and the manipulation of symbols that touch our core beliefs make it possible to appeal to our emotions and bypass our intellect." (Rose Elizabeth Bird, former Chief Justice of California Supreme Court, 6/12/90)

"With the advent of television, where pictures and emotion rule over rational discourse, the power of imagery has become even more important." (Alexandra Marks, *Christian Science Monitor*, 4/11/00)

"From the first known campaign advertisement on television, musics have proven themselves to be crucial to persuasion through the communication of emotion." (John Nelson & G. R. Boynton, *Video Rhetorics*, 1997)

Are Emotional Appeals Legitimate?

"[Banning political ads] would do away with the visceral emotional impact of negative advertising that subverts political discourse." (Gerald Mooney, resident of Dobbs Ferry, NY, 3/26/90)

"On both sides of this campaign there has been too much pandering to image and emotion." (Richard Nixon, former president of the United States, 10/23/88)

"From the perspective of critics, however, campaign ads that appeal by emphasizing emotions inherently depreciate rational processes." (F. Christopher Arterton, dean of the Graduate School of Political Management, 1992)

Why Appeal to Emotions?

"The beauty of successful advertising is that it . . . circumvents our best efforts at critical thinking. It creates a feeling, a subtle but powerful emotion. Most of us respond to these gut reactions whether we realize it or not." (Diane Carman, *Denver Post*, 12/3/98)

"Emotions are basic. An emotional ad or story is always more interesting than a straightforward presentation of the facts." (Peter Bynum, Democratic political consultant, 6/92)

"To hook most voters . . . architects of modern campaigns know that victory is more likely attained through an appeal to the heart and emotions than to the brain." (Richard Scher, *The Modern Political Campaign*, 1997)

How Do Emotional Appeals Work?

"Positive ads are designed to push their own buttons. . . . The good feelings generated by the ad are supposed to transfer to the candidate." (Patricia Lopez Baden, *Minneapolis Star Tribune*, 9/27/98)

"They create a frightening scenario then make a simplistic association between it and [the opponent]." (Kathleen Hall Jamieson, Annenberg School of Communications, 9/8/96)

"[W]hen a speaker stands in front of a huge flag, an emotional association is transferred to the speaker." (Garth Jowett & Victoria O'Donnell, *Propaganda and Persuasion*, 1999)

Who Is Affected by Emotional Appeals?

"Negative ads in newspapers are rarely tried—people who can read are more readily swayed by logic than emotion." (David Childs, resident of Omaha, NE, 11/9/94)

"The consultants have decided that the intelligent, educated people already made up their minds. And people have got to get that kind of dumb group—and they exist—who don't think very hard about things, who are easily emotionally swayed." (Burt Manning, ad agency executive, 11/4/96)

"[T]his expectation nicely conforms to a commonplace of contemporary opinion—namely, that the more ignorant and less sophisticated tend to lean on their emotions." (Paul Sniderman, Richard Brody, and Philip Tetlock, *Reasoning and Choice*, 1991) observers tend to associate emotional appeals primarily with negative advertising.[14] Critics accuse "fright mongers" of airing "scare" ads that make "raw, emotional appeals to voters' fears" or "flagrantly exploit emotional fears."[15] But journalists also recognize that positive ads appeal to emotion. These ads usually bear the label of "feel-good" spots or "warm and fuzzy" ads.[16]

Political consultants see emotional appeals as central to their craft. Goodman says "touching those emotions in such a way that a voter feels attracted to a particular candidate is a campaign media person's job."[17] In *Campaigns & Elections,* a trade magazine for consultants, Richard Schlackman and Jamie Douglas advise admakers to "keep it inherently emotional" and to "excite the emotions."[18] Republican consultant Kim Alfano counsels that people "need to connect to the emotional content of your ad."[19]

Academic research into the views of consultants and journalists reinforce these impressions. Drawing on numerous interviews with political consultants, Montague Kern (1989) identifies the "emotional school" as one of three prominent approaches to political advertising in the 1980s, but contends that all of the approaches are essentially emotion-oriented. In a rare effort to survey consultants and journalists, Richard Perloff and Dennis Kinsey (1992) find considerable agreement among the two groups of professionals that people vote on "gut feelings," ads are more concerned with "conveying feelings" than issues, and "negative ads are more likely than positive ads to stir people's deepest emotions." Figure 2.2 summarizes the views of journalists and consultants on emotion-related aspects of political advertising.

Communication scholars do not merely relay the views of political professionals, but also offer their own similar take on campaign ads. Kern (1989, 7) argues that "appeals to basic human emotions" are common to both positive and negative ads. Lynda Lee Kaid claims "there is a lot of emotional appeal in ads," even when they focus on issues.[20] Gary Copeland says ads work by "tugging on viewers' emotions more than appealing to their intellects."[21] In their history of political advertising, Edwin Diamond and Stephen Bates (1992, 109) observe that by 1964 the "latest 'reality in advertising' was emotion" and this "soft-sell" emotional approach has been used in campaigns ever since. Psychologists have a similar view of ads. Seymour Epstein believes that "political ads appeal to emotion, not reason."[22] Eugene Borgida contends that negative ads in particular are "designed to affect people's emotions."[23] Finally, political scientists also see ads as infused with emotion. Drawing on case studies of three ad campaigns, Dorothy Davidson Nesbit (1988, 27) concludes: "Affective strategies are extremely common and used throughout the campaign. If the truth of the ad is in the feelings evoked, then all commercials, to some extent, must evoke emotions." Glenn Richardson (2001, 215) observes that "while an ad can be seen as 'negative' because of the way it manipulates emotion, 'positive' ads can be quite emotional too."

FIGURE 2.2 Consultant and Journalist Opinions about Emotions and Campaign Advertising

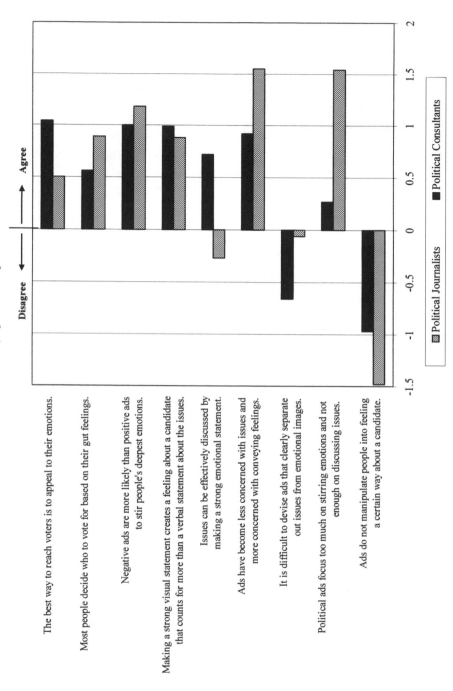

Note: Adapted from findings reported by Perloff and Kinsey 1992. Source of the data is a 1989 survey of 150 political consultants and 185 political journalists.

Emotional appeals and recognition of their centrality to campaigning predates the age of TV ads. Even when campaigns consisted largely of political stump speeches, Kathleen Hall Jamieson (1996, 20) notes that "[o]ratory was an appeal primarily to the emotions." In 1928, Frank Kent, a journalist for the *Baltimore Sun,* wrote a book aimed at identifying the principles underlying contemporary political practices in the United States. On the subject of election campaigns, Kent observed that candidates must face the "basic fact" that in contested campaigns "the real appeal has to be an emotional appeal and not a rational one" (1928, 105–6). In their classic study of voter decisionmaking during the 1940 presidential campaign, sociologists from Columbia University noted that "[a]ll sorts of propaganda rely on emotional appeals to get their message across" and that in 1940 "[s]uch appeals . . . were found in virtually every sentence of campaign propaganda" (Lazarsfeld, Berelson, and Gaudet 1944, 119).

In sum, observers and practitioners seem to agree that emotional appeals have long been a staple of campaign politics and that this holds especially true for televised political ads.[24] When examining scholarly histories, case studies, and other texts, as well as comments of scholars quoted in the press, we can clearly see that researchers across a variety of academic disciplines also regard emotional appeals as prevalent in campaign advertising. Their acknowledgement of this fact, however, has for the most part not led them to incorporate emotion into systematic analyses of political advertising.

Belief 2. Emotional Appeals Strengthen the Power of Campaign Ads to Sway Voters

A second common belief holds that the power of ads to influence voters depends to a large extent on their ability to elicit emotions. This may seem to follow rather directly from the preceding belief. Why would politicians rely so heavily on emotional appeals if they were ineffective? The answer is that it is possible that the emotional aspects of TV ads merely constitute rhetorical window dressing that at best makes ads more entertaining to watch or modestly boosts attention and memory, without significantly altering political choices or behavior. Nonetheless, popular discourse demonstrates a clear belief in the potency of emotional appeals. In fact, many people seem to regard emotion as the key to what makes ads work.[25]

Some people simply equate the emotionality of an ad with its power or likelihood of success. Commentators refer to "emotionally powerful spots," or describe the "emotional message" of ads as "powerful."[26] One journalist advises advocacy groups cynically that if "your emotional triggers are stronger than their emotional triggers, my vote is yours."[27] GOP consultant Douglas Bailey believes the attempt to play on voters' fears "certainly works" and the "emotional content" of ads is "where the power of TV is."[28] In a letter to the editor, Arthur Cole, a resident of Northborough, Massachusetts, claims that "[s]ome of the most successful political ads in the past worked on raw emotional response."[29] Al Davidson, a Colorado resident, complains that an antitrapping ballot initiative was passed by voters "who were swayed by emotional political ads."[30] Psychologist Michael Milburn (1991, 155) speculates that the 1988 ad campaign of George Bush succeeded because it relied on "emotional activation," while the opposing campaign of Michael Dukakis was "unable to develop any powerful emotional messages." Ironically, according to Michael Barone, some Dukakis ads satirizing the Bush ad campaign portrayed voters as "easily duped . . . because of their emotional response," yet the Dukakis ads themselves were ineffective because they failed to capitalize on this insight.[31] Indeed, as the survey results in figure 2.2 suggest, most journalists and consultants believe that the "best way to reach voters is to appeal to their emotions."

In some cases, belief in the efficacy of emotional appeals is implied by claims of manipulation and often linked closely to negative ads. David Broder calls on fellow journalists to remind voters at the start of each election how their "emotions were manipulated by negative ads in the last campaign."[32] J. Gordon, a New York resident, expresses concern that ads manipulate the public with images "known to elicit an emotional reaction," typically "fear, anguish, and anxiety."[33] Consultants Schlackman and Douglas contend that "it's much easier and more effective to persuade with the heart than the head alone. Fear, anger, envy, indignation, and shame are powerful emotions in the political arena."[34]

On occasion, journalists or other observers make contrary claims, suggesting that emotion-laden ads are ineffective, but these claims tend to come in the form of transparent flattery to the wisdom of the people. One is left with the impression that the commentator hopes to diminish the power of emotional appeals simply by asserting their impotence. Others recognize our desire to believe we are not affected by such tactics, but nonetheless feel it important to remind us that we may be fooling ourselves. Journalist Patricia Lopez Baden advises readers of the *Minneapolis Star Tribune* this way: "If you're like most folks, your opinions of the candidates will be shaped by those ads, perhaps to a greater extent than you realize. That's because most ads—political and otherwise—are designed to appeal more to your emotions than your intellect."[35] Similarly, Diane Carman of the *Denver Post* suggests the "beauty of successful advertising" is that it "circumvents our best efforts at critical thinking" by eliciting a "subtle but powerful emotion." She concludes, "Most of us respond to these gut reactions whether we realize it or not."[36]

In discussions of political ads, scholars seem equally ready to believe in the power of emotional appeals. Jamieson (1992, 105) notes "what televised ads are best at is flooding our consciousness with emotionally compelling data." Ken Goldstein says ads engage viewers by packaging information in an "easy-to-swallow emotional coating."[37] L. Patrick Devlin (1995, 203) claims that "because the best television ads are emotional ads, political ads that convey in an emotional way stands on issues, or accomplishments, or personal qualities are often the best political ads." When conducting scientific research into the effects of political ads, however, scholars make little room for emotion in their studies.

Belief 3. Much of the Emotional Power of Campaign Ads Derives from Images and Music

The third common belief concerns the source from which ads are assumed to derive their emotional power. What makes an advertising appeal more or less emotional? What elements of an ad shape the particular emotion it elicits? When thinking of any form of communication, whether it is a speech, TV ad, or direct-mail solicitation, people are likely to think its capacity to arouse an emotional reaction comes both from what is said and how it is said. In other words, both content and delivery seem to matter. A speech would be nothing without the words, and yet we must admit that the ability to *move* people with those words often depends greatly on such nonverbal mannerisms as vocal timbre, volume, pace, facial expressions, and gestures. One can be stirred simply by reading quietly to oneself the text of a speech by Martin Luther King Jr. The goose bumps may be heightened if one recalls the words as spoken by King, that is, if one imagines his voice. However, the impact reaches its zenith when one listens to or watches a recording of King delivering the speech. In each case, the words are the same but their impact changes. Similarly, the simple messages contained in political ads may spark an emotional response, but the ads are assumed to derive the bulk of their emotional power from something other than the words. As with ordinary product ads, people indeed believe that nonverbal elements, especially images and music, are particularly important in shaping the emotional impact of political ads.[38]

Observers clearly think that, when it comes to eliciting emotions, pictures are as potent as the cliché suggests. Carey Cramer Sr. advises fellow consultants to "use the emotional appeal. Pictures are worth a thousand words; make sure they convey an emotional story that motivates."[39] Journalists, consultants, and others frequently refer to visual aspects of political ads as "feel-good pictures," "emotion-laden pictures," "emotional images," "powerful images," and "emotionally-charged pictures."[40] In noting the link between product and political ads, one journalist claims the use of familiar images "provides a shortcut to voters' emotions."[41] Consultant Whit Ayres remarks that "[m]ost media consultants admit that their ads have not only a direct message but also an implied message designed to elicit an emotion in the viewer, often communicated more through pictures than words."[42] Susan Hendrix, another consultant, acknowledges the way words and pictures work together, implying an ad needs just enough of the former to help the latter carry the day: "But a television spot should use just enough well chosen words to define the message and underscore the images on the screen. It's the right verbal and visual alchemy that gives a television spot its true potential to spark the viewer's emotions."[43]

As figure 2.2 shows, both consultants and journalists concur that visuals matter more than words in creating a feeling about a candidate. Those with a distaste for these ads seem to agree. Curtis Gans, an election reform advocate, has proposed requiring politicians to use only "talking heads" ads that would "enable voters to focus on the candidate's words rather than on emotional images."[44] Media watchdog Robert Lichter believes "[r]eading is interpreting, but seeing looks like raw reality. No intervention, no thinking, from screen to the brain. . . . Video has unique emotional power."[45]

Many people think music is equally important. In 1990, a writer for an advertising trade magazine contended that one reason why political ads are less "emotionally involving" than product ads is that the former "lag behind" the latter in the use of music.[46] Nonetheless, several commentators have noted the rise of "emotional music" or "music that summons emotions" in political advertising.[47] Consultants appear to be the strongest believers in the emotional power of music. Known for his love of jingles, Robert Goodman argues that "music and words and visuals are all part of the action. . . . I'm talking about a business called feelings."[48] Consultant Dean Rindy believes the soundtrack, "the emotional message of the music," can be the key to what makes an ad work.[49] Ron Faucheux, editor in chief of *Campaigns and Elections* magazine, contends "music is crucial to the overall emotional appeal."[50]

Consultants believe that, by combining these various modalities, television is uniquely powerful in appealing to emotions.[51] "[I]t's such a powerful medium," Paula Tait claims. "There's something about television that creates a powerful visceral response in the viewers. With the exception of personal appearances, no other medium is going to present such a powerful emotional appeal to voters."[52] Ed Baches agrees that TV is the most powerful means of "winning the hearts and minds," and contends the "visceral qualities of TV ads" can "convey a significantly greater amount of emotion" than print ads or direct mail, because of the power of music and imagery.[53] Similarly, European consultant Rolf Pfleiderer (2002, 178) contends that "the visual, aural, and dynamic nature of television makes it especially effective in addressing the audience's emotions, whereas complicated content and lengthy explanations are more suited to print advertisements." Journalists appear to see it the same way. Columnist Anthony Lewis writes: "Television has an emotional power, an immediacy that the written word can hardly match. . . . Television goes right through to your emotions."[54] Lynda Taylor of the *Pittsburgh Post-Gazette* says that "while the printed word relies on reason to score points, television evokes a lot of emotion."[55] Some consultants believe the emotional power of TV is so great that it warrants caution in designing ads:

TV is a visual medium. . . . TV is supremely intimate. . . . The press doesn't notice it, but political campaigns are actually much nastier in direct mail and radio ads. That's because there's more emotional distance between those mediums and the audience. TV is stark reality. It's like having a Teamster kick open the door to your mind and whack you with a tire tool.[56]

When journalists and consultants talk about ads, they often mention the specific kinds of images and music they believe are most emotionally evocative. Positive ads feature "softly lighted hometown vignettes, romantic landscapes, and stirring patriotic imagery."[57] The sponsor appears in "brightly colored and patriotic settings with an American flag" and the music is "soothing."[58] Negative ads make heavy use of "grainy black-and-white footage," "raw sewage," "menacing visuals" from crime scenes, and "chilling footage" simulating hate crimes and stalking.[59] For a soundtrack, these ads use "low-toned ominous music," "baleful chords" out of horror films, "wailing sirens," "sharp blasts of percussion," and "eerily repetitive piano notes."[60] Observers believe ads picturing ordinary people—senior citizens, crime victims, welfare recipients, immigrants, unemployed workers—can heighten the sense of authenticity, identification, and emotional impact.[61] One ad-maker notes that "there is no better way to get a very poignant and emotional message across than with a child."[62]

In their descriptions of ads, scholars echo the beliefs of consultants and journalists. For example, Jamieson (1992, 51) claims the "evocative power of television's visual grammar couples with its use of music to invite strong emotional reactions to what is seen in ads." She goes on to say that "in the contest between evocative pictures and spoken words, pictures usually win" (103). Darrell West (2001), in a textbook on political advertising, agrees that the "visual aspect of advertising is the most important part of commercials. . . . Pictures carry an emotional impact that is much more powerful than the spoken word" (6–7). He also contends that "music sets the tone for the ad" (8) and describes how images have been "accompanied by music that enhanced the emotional impact of the ad" (9). In discussing the power of

TV generally, Doris Graber (2001) argues that "visuals excel in emotional arousal compared to most nonvisual stimuli" (35) and "sound amplifies the emotional impact created by pictures" (39).[63]

Scholars identify the same types of visual and audial cues as underlying emotional appeals. Kern (1989) describes the use of scenic vistas, images of hometown and family life, the American flag, bright colors, and "swelling" symphonic music in ads appealing to hope and reassurance. In ads appealing to fear, she observes harsh pictures, dark colors, sound effects like howling wind, and "doomsday music." In a review of presidential ads, Susan Sherr (1999, 57) reports that images of children are often used for "the purpose of eliciting fear" or conveying "hopefulness."

In sum, political observers and practitioners share a strong belief that the audiovisual nature of TV lends it special emotional power and much of this power in political ads is borne by the imagery and music. This belief is predicated on a mix of conventional wisdom, personal experience, and actual research. Although there is almost no research on the impact of emotionally evocative images and music in political advertising, psychologists have amassed a fair amount of evidence about the emotional impact of pictures and sounds more generally. Some of this research is discussed in chapter 3.

Belief 4. Emotional Appeals Influence Voters by Getting Their Attention and Evoking Emotions That Will Then Be Associated with a Candidate

A fourth common belief concerns the impact of emotional appeals. What is the nature of their influence on voters? Of the six beliefs reviewed in this chapter, this one regarding specific effects seems to be the least widely shared. Given the premise of this chapter, namely that one can find plenty of casual observation about emotional appeals but little scientific research on them, we should not be surprised that people rarely voice beliefs about precise effects. Indeed, the weakness of conventional wisdom on the subject owes more to the absence of beliefs (or at least any expression of beliefs) than to disagreement. Most observers simply assert that emotional appeals work but do not specify how. The sense that they work may seem obvious from personal experience, but ideas about specific effects requires something closer to theory. In this light, it is easy to see why scholars have been most likely to venture claims about the effects of advertising. Consultants generally focus on the end result:

As might be expected, while political managers are anxious to know what works in influencing voting decisions, they are not very interested in *how* these communications work. They rarely take time to contemplate systematic theories of communication or persuasion. . . . They concentrate on the effects produced by their messages, not on explanations of how their results are achieved. (Arterton 1992, 96)

Some consultants approach their craft as not amenable to systematic explanation because "each candidate and campaign is unique."[64] Even so, as this is their life's work, many consultants have ideas and occasionally express them as general propositions. With these limitations in mind, we can identify something like conventional wisdom—less a belief than a set of beliefs—about the effects of appealing to emotions.

One cluster of beliefs suggests that emotional appeals, in one way or another, enhance viewer reception of the ad's message. For example, there is a notion that the use of music and images to stir emotions makes ads more "entertaining" or "attention-getting" (Jamieson 1992; Nelson and Boynton 1997; Sabato 1981; Scher 1997).[65] In a world in which TV ads are often dismissed as an intrusion on one's preferred viewing, admakers must try to keep viewers' eyes and ears focused attentively on the TV even after they realize it is a political ad.

As we saw earlier, however, there is a sense that the impact goes deeper than merely capturing the attention of viewers. Because few people say precisely in what way the ads are effective, we might infer that they believe emotional appeals simply make the message of the ad more compelling. Drawing this conclusion requires us to read beyond the statements as given, but, absent further elaboration, I think it is a fair reading of general claims that emotional appeals are "the best way to reach voters." In other words, emotionally evocative images and music reinforce the positive or negative message of the ad, making it "resonate" more with viewers, and thereby increase its ability to motivate and persuade. From this perspective, the effect of emotional appeals is to increase not only the chances a viewer receives the message, but also the chances she accepts the message as well.

A somewhat more specific notion of resonance emerges from the writings of Tony Schwartz, one of the only political consultants to spend time theorizing about media effects. As the epigraph at the beginning of this chapter suggests, Schwartz agrees that the goal of advertising is to use audiovisual cues to evoke emotional responses from viewers. However, his emphasis is on tapping existing emotions rather than generating reactions "from scratch." He argues that "television is an ideal medium for surfacing feelings voters already have, and giving these feelings a direction by providing stimuli that may evoke the desired behavior" (Schwartz 1973, 92). Resonance, therefore, means increasing the salience of existing hopes or fears in relation to an issue or candidate so that these feelings play a greater role in a voter's decision.[66] Although Schwartz stresses the role of emotions, his conception of resonance is not specific to emotional appeals, but rather applies to appeals in general. For example, he suggests that ads should also capitalize on existing attitudes and beliefs (92–96). In fact, the most prominent application of Schwartz's view to research on advertising focuses on how issue content and advertising tone (attack versus advocacy) resonate with the partisan beliefs of viewers (Ansolabehere and Iyengar 1995). The notion of resonance, as conceived by Schwartz, is not so much a belief about the impact of eliciting emotions as a belief about when it is or is not possible to do so.

Drawing on interviews with consultants, Kern (1989) sees Schwartz as the originator of a broader approach that also specifies what happens to the feelings evoked by an ad:

> [H]e was an innovator . . . in the sense not just of seeking to tap preexisting feelings about a particular candidate but of seeking to *transfer* or *refer* positive and negative affect evoked by means of sight and sound from emotionally laden symbols to the candidate and his opponent. (32, emphasis in original)

Kern calls the idea of using emotionally evocative content to transfer feelings from that content to a candidate "referential advertising." Although the effects of political ads are rarely discussed with such specificity in newspapers, a reader may occasionally come across remarks about the way music and images are used to "associate" candidates with the emotions evoked.[67] More often, there are merely vague references to the way ads used these techniques to generate good feelings about the sponsor and bad feelings about the opponent.[68]

The notion of transferring feelings from symbolic ad content to candidates clearly has roots in the psychological theory of classical conditioning (Petty and Cacioppo 1981) and is mentioned more frequently in academic writings than in news stories. Jamieson (1996) argues that political ads use "visual association" by juxtaposing highly evocative images with images of candidates to solicit a "visceral response" (521). Garth Jowett and Victoria O'Donnell (1999) make a similar claim about the use of visual symbols in propaganda: "For example, when a speaker stands in front of a huge flag, an emotional association is transferred to the speaker" (293). In describing the techniques used by consultants, Sabato (1981) says that "[c]andidates are also 'improved' by association with symbols of desired qualities or favored groups. . . . To stress a candidate's power or patriotism, the emotion-laden symbols of democracy (the White House, Capitol Hill, monuments of various descriptions, the seals of office, and the ubiquitous flag) are made to order" (146). According to West (1999), "[a]ds can be used for a variety of purposes, from undermining political opponents by associating them with unfavorable visual images to enhancing the candidates' appeal by associating them with positive images such as flag and family" (27). West (2001) also extends this associative logic to color: "Media consultants use bright colors to associate their candidates with a positive image and grayish or black and white colors to associate opponents with a negative image" (8). Kern (1989) concludes that all schools of political advertising use referential techniques to "transfer affect-laden meaning to the candidate from a symbol that already has meaning to the viewer" (208).[69]

Although most observers are silent on the topic of how emotional appeals work, we can find a few ideas that are shared by a number of scholars, consultants, and journalists. These views do not constitute a single common belief, but we might take them collectively as the conventional wisdom on the topic, as the speculations do not appear inconsistent with one another. To summarize, I suggest that people believe ads elicit emotions in order to attract the attention of viewers and entertain them, to increase the persuasive power of ads by reinforcing the message and making it more compelling, or to transfer the feelings to the sponsor or her opponent. Except for the last idea, which is the most specific and has roots in the theory of classical conditioning, beliefs about the impact of emotional appeals are quite vague.

Belief 5. Campaign Ads That Rely on Emotional Appeals Are Manipulative, Lacking in Substance, and Antithetical to Reason or Rationality

There is no shortage of opinions on the normative value of emotional appeals. The conventional wisdom holds that their use is morally suspect. There is a fairly broad consensus among observers that the tactic manipulates voters, supplants substantive discourse, disrupts reason or rationality, and is generally harmful to democracy. This set of beliefs is grounded in a venerable cultural tradition of contrasting emotion as a powerful but inferior rival to reason, rationality, logic, or intellect (Marcus 2002). The latter are the prized attributes of the modern educated thinker and the ideal democratic citizen. Not surprisingly, one group of people stands apart from this consensus—the consultants who make ads. Even among their ranks, however, there are those who take a dim view of emotional appeals or at least equivocate on the matter.

Many of the comments already discussed imply, if not explicitly state, that appealing to emotions is an ethically questionable practice. In letters to the editor, citizens criticize ad campaigns that rely on emotion for striving to "manipulate the individual" and doing "nothing to stimulate thinking" or "the ability to reflect, analyze, or draw a conclusion."[70] Journalists suggest that "pictures and emotions rule over rational discourse" on TV, emotional ads circumvent "our best efforts at critical thinking," and reporters must expose how ads appeal to emotions to "give your intellect a fighting chance."[71]

In the words of yet another journalist, "the people who run today's political campaigns do not want to stir rational thought. They want to stir irrational emotion."[72] Columnist George Will stressed the incompatibility of emotion and serious issues when describing Steve Forbes's 1996 presidential ads as having "high informational, as opposed to emotional, content."[73] In that same year, John Hagelin, Natural Law candidate for president, said his own campaign "isn't about emotional appeal. It's about substance."[74]

As with attributions of effectiveness, some observers put negative appeals in a special category, claiming that "[i]f you have an appeal to fear, then voters will be tempted not to make intellectual, rational choices."[75] Editors of the *Montreal Gazette* argue that some negative advertising is acceptable, but not ads appealing to emotions: "This is not to say that all attack ads are necessarily bad. A spot that accurately and level-headedly tackles a politician's record, without use of demagogy or emotion-pumping tricks, is quite capable of bringing welcome substance to an election campaign."[76] Other journalists contend that "positive commercials can be just as manipulative" by relying on "music that summons emotions and images stripped of context."[77] Political scientist Glenn Richardson (2001) concurs: "Distortion, emotional appeals, and one-sidedness rightly warrant academic attention and public condemnation, but they can be found in positive ads as well, and can be effectively cleaved from 'negativity'" (215).[78]

One can regard emotional appeals as evading rationality, logic, and intellect and yet not necessarily see them as unethical or dangerous. Consultants like Bill Hillsman, the inventive Minnesota admaker for Paul Wellstone and Jesse Ventura, take this view.[79] However, it seems that most observers intend to denigrate emotional advertising with such labels, and some explicitly condemn this style of campaigning as subversive of democracy. Columnist William Pfaff proposes banning political ads, not because of the negativity or pandering, but rather due to the "general substitution of irrelevant emotional appeals for debate."[80] One citizen, in a letter to the editor, writes that emotional ads are

an insult to American democracy, for they attempt to rob the individual of the right to decide, to push him in a direction without giving him time to think. . . . Appealing to [fear] in American citizens can hardly further the cause of democracy, or inspire the civic evolution of the voting public.[81]

In his 2002 bid for the U.S. Senate, Lindsey Graham aired commercials attacking his opponent's ads as "bogus appeals to emotion that are trying to scare us all to death."[82] In a rare academic discussion of the ethics of political advertising, Lynda Lee Kaid (1991) briefly addressed the topic of emotional appeals with a tone of disapproval, yet with limits:

It is easy to condemn the gratuitous use of emotion in political advertising. When emotion is used for no purpose other than to elicit fear or to create unthinking allegiance, it has no defensible place in a democratic society. Examples of such usage in political ads abound. . . . There may, however, be times when valid issues have strong emotional content, and the melding of emotion with issue content in such cases is not necessarily unethical. (149)

Consultant Charles Guggenheim is undoubtedly not alone in defending his approach to advertising with the claim that "feelings play a legitimate role in elections" (Diamond and Bates 1992, 312). The survey results in figure 2.2 indeed indicate that consultants are far less likely than journalists to accuse emotional appeals of driving issue content out of ads. A different survey of consultants, however, reveals considerable ambivalence about the use of one type of emotional appeal—namely, scare tactics. Although 97 percent find nothing wrong with "going negative" in ads, only 37 percent find the use of scare tactics "acceptable," while 46 percent say it is "questionable," and 14 percent agree it is "clearly unethical" (Thurber and Nelson 2000).[83] Those who work in related professions are sometimes critical of political consultants for their emotional approach. For example, critics among public relations professionals charge that consultants use "sophisticated polling techniques to find emotional levers that can manipulate the behavior of voters, avoiding intellectual stimulation as much as possible."[84] A writer in the commercial advertising business claims that many political ads "flagrantly exploit emotional fears. . . . Audiences are confused, misled, and misinformed."[85] Joe Napolitan, a founder of the professional organization for consultants, draws a line between legitimate attacks on opponents' records and "insidious attacks designed to appeal to the voters' worst instincts in a highly emotional way."[86] Another consultant, Victor Kamber, wrote a book condemning these practices:

The problem with negative ads is not that they are manipulative, but that they often appeal to emotion instead of reason, and those emotions appealed to are often our darker ones. Attack ads that seek to persuade voters from the baser motives of fear, hatred, greed, and prejudice are what is wrong with our political discourse. Television is what gives those appeals emotional power, but the fault lies not with the medium, but with the message. (1997, 36)[87]

In sum, there is widespread agreement, even shared by a number of consultants, that emotional appeals are unethical because they discourage reasoning, promote superficiality, and manipulate the public. This is not to say the consensus is complete. Many consultants and a few scholars see it differently. These "contrarians" tend to view emotions, as well as logic and rationality, as a legitimate basis for decisionmaking. They also are more likely to believe that an ad can simultaneously appeal to emotions and raise in the public's mind important issues.

Belief 6. Emotional Appeals Are Most Effective at Influencing Uninformed or Uneducated Voters

The sixth common belief emerges in the context of asking on whom emotional appeals exert the greatest influence. The answer, according to conventional wisdom, may seem an obvious corollary to the preceding belief. If emotion is opposed to intellect, then emotion must hold greater dominion over those who lack intellect. If emotion supplants serious discussion of issues, then emotional appeals must be aimed at those who avoid such discussions. The nation's Founders worried that demagogues would stir the passions of the "masses" (Hamilton, Madison, and Jay 1999 [1787–88]); this belief seems to presume the "masses" are vulnerable to such stirring, whereas the "elite" are not. Observers today who suggest that emotional appeals work better on some people than others reflect such centuries-old presumptions.

Some observers merely imply a difference in susceptibility by suggesting that education, experience, or sophistication bring resistance to emotional appeals. While maintaining that people are in fact fooling themselves, one reporter observes that "most of us probably would say we're much too sophisticated to be swayed" by "simple-minded messages" that elicit "a subtle, but powerful emotion."[88] A letter writer from Ithaca, New York claims emotional appeals are "elementary psychological tricks" and an insult to intelligence.[89] According to political scientist Larry Sabato, current advertising practices work because of a "lack of education in politics. People are satisfied with a discussion of symbolic issues which taste great and are less filling."[90] A British journalist expresses skepticism that Britons have yet become a "mature electorate tired of playground politics" in which voters "desire information and facts instead of a one-dimensional, emotional approach in political ads."[91] Another journalist concludes that British political parties "treat voters as bored children, who need to be entertained and emotionally manipulated."[92] Bob Beauprez, Republican candidate for Congress in 2002, accused his opponent of using ads to "whipsaw emotion, to scare people. It's playing with emotion and trying to play on people's lack of intelligence, perhaps, on this question, of hoping to incite emotion that will win an election."[93] In a 1932 radio address, Franklin Roosevelt claimed that, "with the spread of education, with the wider reading of newspapers," public discourse and opinions will be shaped less by "mere emotion" (Jamieson 1996, 20).

Others express the conventional wisdom directly. Burt Manning, an ad agency executive, claims political consultants do not target "intelligent, educated people" but instead go after "that marginal kind of dumb group—and they [*sic*] exist—who don't think very hard about things, who are easily emotionally swayed."[94] Education reform advocate Diane Ravitch argues that "without historical perspective, voters are more likely to be swayed by emotional appeals, by stirring commercials, or by little more than a candidate's good looks and charisma."[95] In one news story, a teacher complains that students should not be allowed to vote on sensitive issues because they are "easily swayed by emotions," presumably due to their incomplete education.[96] Some people use newspaper readership to draw the line, suggesting that "readers of the quality press" are "less readily swayed by emotional" appeals or, conversely, that "people who can read are more readily swayed by logic than emotion."[97] In a letter to the editor, an Ohio resident writes that wildlife management issues should be decided by "trained professionals" and not by "voters swayed by emotion but possessing little or no real knowledge of the issue."[98] Similarly, a journalist argues against pursuing social reform through litigation because citizens serving on juries are "often poorly educated and easily swayed by emotion."[99] A legal consultant who writes about jury selection indeed claims that the "defense must find jurors easily swayed by emotion. They don't want brainy types who collect data from the prosecution, store it and hold onto it."[100] Finally, Paul Sniderman and colleagues (1991) call attention to "a commonplace of contemporary opinion—namely, that the more ignorant and less sophisticated tend to lean on their emotions, using them as a crutch" (22).[101]

Journalists, consultants, and scholars often talk about the power of emotional appeals without suggesting that they affect certain kinds of people more than others. But when such a suggestion is made, there is nearly complete consensus on who is vulnerable—the uneducated, uninformed, unintelligent, illiterate, immature, or unsophisticated masses. This view appears to be related to the belief that emotions stand in opposition to reason and substance. In sum, although little research has been done on the design and impact of emotional appeals in political advertising, people of all stripes commonly talk about emotion as an integral part of campaign ads and their effects.

What We Know about the Design and Impact of Campaign Ads

Given the impression one gets from reading the comments of consultants, reporters, and scholars, it is not surprising that, when I tell people I study the role of emotion in campaign advertising, they ask: "Don't we already know about that?" The strength of conventional wisdom on the topic far exceeds the evidence gathered by social scientists. In some fields, weakness of the evidence stems from conflicting findings or the inability to turn up conclusive evidence. When it comes to the impact of emotional appeals, the weakness instead arises simply from a lack of research.

A Brief History of the Study of Campaign and Media Effects

In a history familiar to many readers, research on the effects of mass-mediated campaigns evolved unevenly over the past sixty years. After an ambitious period in the mid-twentieth century, scholars concluded that elections are decided by long-term social forces embodied in individual predispositions and by short-term responses to current conditions, but not by mass-mediated candidate messages (Berelson, Lazarsfeld, and McPhee 1954; Campbell et al. 1960; Key 1966; Lazarsfeld, Berelson, and Gaudet 1944). As a result, they turned away from research on media effects. In a review of the emerging communications field, Joseph Klapper (1960) implicitly reinforced the wisdom of this shift, noting that studies had produced little evidence of persuasion or motivation at the hands of mass communication.

Almost none of the work at the time explicitly considered emotional aspects of media messages. The exception was the start of a research program on fear-arousing messages in public health or other educational campaigns. Initial experiments confirmed that mildly and moderately threatening messages were persuasive (Hovland, Janis, and Kelley 1953; Janis and Feshbach 1953). Klapper, however, chose to highlight the fact that extremely threatening messages were not persuasive and ignored the persuasive power of mild and moderate fear appeals relative to the control group (1960, 117–18).

By the 1960s, candidate-centered campaigns began to displace traditional party politics and TV was bringing presidential debates, the civil rights movement, and the Vietnam War into 90 percent of American households. Observers began to attribute many of the changes in U.S. politics to the persuasive power of TV and televised ad campaigns (Agranoff 1972; Edelman 1964; Lang and Lang 1968; McGinnis 1969; Nimmo 1970). Prompted by these attributions and the absence of any research on how TV affects voters, Thomas Patterson and Robert McClure (1973, 1976) conducted a seminal study arguing that the power of TV, whether through news coverage or paid advertising, is a myth. Their two principal findings flew in the face of popular beliefs: (1) voters learn little about the candidates from TV and what they learn comes from ads instead of news; and (2) neither news nor ads shape images or evaluations of the candidates due to the preexisting biases of voters.

Patterson and McClure recognized the centrality of "imagery and emotion" (1976, 95), as well as "issues and reason" (102), in ads at the time:

The critics claim that the same advertising strategies and techniques that sell soft drinks also are used to sell Presidents. According to them, televised political ads contain several parts emotional gimmickry for each part of useful information (94). . . . Both [product and political ads] aim at people's hearts more than their heads. Most product advertising is based on a simple assumption about consumer buying habits— people make purchases for emotional, not cerebral, reasons. Efforts at candidate image-making rest on a similar assumption. (101)

Despite this recognition, Patterson and McClure did not explicitly study the emotional qualities of ads, yet nonetheless claimed that "symbolic manipulation" or "staged imagery" in political ads "simply does not work" (1976, 115–16). Their conclusion rests solely on the *kinds* of effects they observe from self-reported exposure to ads—namely, heightened awareness of issue positions but no consistent shift in candidate images, by which they mean assessments of the candidate leadership traits.

By the late 1980s, scholars began to reverse the "minimal effects" view that had come to dominate earlier decades. This renaissance was fueled by an emphasis on a more subtle array of effects and a methodological shift toward careful tracking of media content and opinion change as well as tightly-controlled experiments. These studies provide support for the impact of news coverage on policy opinions, political knowledge, issue priorities, and the criteria of political judgment (Graber 1988; Iyengar and Kinder 1987; Neuman, Just, and Crigler 1992; Page, Shapiro, and Dempsey 1987). Aggregate-level studies of opinion demonstrate the potential for broad campaign effects as well (Bartels 1988, 1993; Zaller 1992, 1996). In recent years, we have seen mounting evidence on the impact of campaign events (Holbrook 1996; Shaw 1999; Shaw and Roberts 2000), nonpartisan canvassing (Gerber and Green 2000a, 2000b), framing of political issues (Cappella and Jamieson 1997; Iyengar 1991; Nelson, Clawson, and Oxley 1997; Nelson and Kinder 1996), source cues (Druckman 2001; Kuklinski and Hurley 1994; Lupia and McCubbins 1998), and visual cues to race or gender (Gilens 1999; Gilliam and Iyengar 2000; Kahn 1996; Mendelberg 2001; Valentino 1999). During this time, scholars also began to show renewed interest in studying the content and effects of campaign advertising.[102]

Contemporary Research on Advertising Content and Effects

As the new wave of research on media effects was gaining momentum, two studies of advertising content stressed that, if we wish to understand the impact of political ads, we must recognize the importance of emotion. In the first study, Montague Kern (1989) argues that "emotional advertising is a basic part of the campaign advertising arsenal" (39) and that "understanding the theory of emotional appeals is thus a key to understanding media strategies" (30). Her conclusions are based on interviews with dozens of consultants, several campaign case studies, and content analysis. For the latter, she examines 122 ads that aired late in the 1984 election, in order to "start the process of building a typology of ads that use sound and symbols intended to appeal to positive and negative feelings or affect" (71). Kern finds that ads targeting reassurance, hope, and pride are common and use symbols of family, place, and nation, while ads targeting anxiety and anger are also common and rely on symbols of "harsh reality" and death. Perhaps her most striking but understated conclusion is that only a trivial fraction of ads were categorized as "neutral," by which she means they failed to appeal to any emotion.

The second study appeared two years later and arrived at a similar conclusion. John Boiney and David Paletz (1991) did not intend to focus specifically on emotions. Their study sets out to compare the *explicit models* of voter decisionmaking offered by political scientists with the *implicit models* apparently held by consultants, as revealed through the content of ads. Using a sample of 196 ads from the 1984 election, their major finding is that ads reveal one type of appeal absent from most political science models: emotion. As a result, Boiney and Paletz call on researchers to investigate the use and effects of emotion in political advertising more systematically:

One point that emerges vividly from the publications containing consultants' comments on their means and motives, tactics and techniques, is that advertising targets viewers' emotions. . . . Ads are designed for the client's benefit in a wondrous variety of ways to manipulate viewers' actual and latent emotions. The power of these appeals and the reason political scientists have not yet adequately attempted, let alone succeeded, in capturing and quantifying their influence, lies in the ways the ads tap and use emotions nonverbally. Particularly through visual images, sound tracks, camera angles, editing, and colors, advertisers consciously attempt to paint a picture, tell a story, create a feeling with which many viewers can resonate or, even better, identify. The intent is to give each ad a "feel" to which the voter can emotively react; which capitalizes on voters' emotions in ways benefiting the candidate. . . . Finally, and most importantly, emotion clearly fulfills an integral function for political advertising. Political ads can be remarkably clever and complex in invoking emotion, yet researchers and practitioners understand surprisingly little about the process. Research devoted to assessing the prevalence and targeting of emotion in ads, categorizing emotional appeals, identifying patterns of usage, and trying to determine effects is vital. (21–24)

These pleas for attention were well-timed to influence the burgeoning research agenda on mass media. Remarkably, they did not. Most systematic studies of content and especially of effects pay little attention to emotion. Following in the steps of Patterson and McClure (1976), many researchers have focused heavily on the issue and candidate "image" content of ads (Garramone 1983; Johnston and Kaid 2002; Joslyn 1980; Just et al. 1996; Shyles 1983, 1984; Thorson, Christ, and Caywood 1991; West 2001). Controversy over the implications of negative advertising messages has produced a tremendous body of work (Geer 2003; Jamieson, Waldman, and Sherr 2000; Kahn and Kenney 2004; Kaid and Johnston 2001; West 2001). The resulting avalanche of studies, however, has been frustratingly inconclusive as to the impact of negative versus positive ads on a variety of attitudes and behaviors (Ansolabehere et al. 1994; Ansolabehere and Iyengar 1995, 1999; Basil, Schooler, and Reeves 1991; Finkel and Geer 1998; Freedman and Goldstein 1999; Garramone et al. 1990; Goldstein and Freedman 2002a; Kahn and Kenney 2000, 2004; Lau et al. 1999; Meirick 2002; Schenck-Hamlin, Procter, and Rumsey 2000; Wattenberg and Brians 1999). Researchers also have begun to look at how ads activate or neutralize group stereotypes (Gordon, Shafie, and Crigler 2003; Kahn 1996; Valentino, Hutchings, and White 2002; Valentino, Traugott, and Hutchings 2002) and the interaction between ad campaigns and their context as defined by news coverage and other ads (Ansolabehere and Iyengar 1994; Basil, Schooler, and Reeves 1991; Simon 2002). Most of these studies focus on the verbal content of ads rather than on the symbolic elements most closely associated with emotional appeals, such as music and images (but see Thorson, Christ, and Caywood 1991; Valentino, Hutchings, and White 2002).

Limited Forays: Emotions and the Effects of Televised Political Ads

Although the mainstream literature has largely eschewed the role of emotional appeals in election campaigns, there have been limited forays into the domain of emotion and televised political ads. By "limited," I mean to say the inquiries have been both few in number and circumscribed in their reach. More precisely, since 1990, four laboratory studies report on attempts to measure the impact of the emotion-eliciting qualities of political ads on TV viewers.[103] This number, taken by itself, might suggest emotional appeals are a low priority for the field but not utterly neglected. However, none of the studies directly examines whether political ads can use emotional appeals to motivate or persuade voters during an election. In fact, they each have a different research goal in mind. Nonetheless, these studies serve as valuable points of reference for their efforts to link emotion-eliciting aspects of political ads to viewer responses.[104]

Two of the studies appear in a single volume on psychological dimensions of political advertising (Lang 1991; Newhagen and Reeves 1991). Both compare the impact of positive and negative ads on memory for the verbal and visual content of the ad, and both conduct the research using real candidate ads from earlier elections. The fact that the ads are not meaningfully tied to an on-going election is not necessarily a liability in this case, given the focus on memory rather than candidate evaluations and vote intentions. Like other scholarship on advertising tone, emotion is conceptualized in terms of "valence" (i.e., positive or negative). Unlike other research, coders classified the ads as positive or negative on the basis of the feelings the ads evoked. One study showed thirty residents of the local community a series of twenty-eight ads, each thirty seconds in duration (Newhagen and Reeves 1991), while the other showed sixty-seven undergraduate students a total of eight thirty-second ads mixed in with "distractor" clips from a variety of TV programs (Lang 1991). Both studies find that ads evoking negative emotions improve memory, especially for visual images.[105]

Jacqueline Hitchon and colleagues (1997) examine how gender-stereotyped expectations regarding the use of emotional appeals affect viewer reactions to political ads. They used ads from earlier elections, not presently relevant or familiar to participants. Positive ads showed a candidate with family and friends, negative ads attacked the opponent and featured negative visuals, and neutral ads presented a candidate's issue positions or record in an unemotional manner. Seventy-two students watched six political ads, one each from the male and female competitors in three races. After each ad, subjects stopped to assess its perceived effectiveness and rate their own attitudes toward the ad and candidate. Consistent with the authors' predictions about the role of gender stereotypes, they find viewers respond most favorably when women do not appeal overly to emotions and least favorably when women appeal to negative emotions.[106]

Finally, Wendy Rahn and Rebecca Hirshorn (1999) investigate the impact of advertising tone on the political orientations of children (ages eight to thirteen). They focus on the use of advocacy or attack arguments, not on emotional appeals. Their goal is to determine what residual effects ads may be having on a future generation of voters. Emotion enters the picture through the concept of *public mood,* an individual's current feelings *as a member of a community with which one identifies.* Rahn and Hirshorn hypothesize that the tone of ads influences public mood about America in a negative or positive direction, which in turn sours or sweetens one's image of the government. In the study, sixty-nine children watched either four positive or four negative ads from an earlier election. The authors find ads can indeed affect public mood among children and changes in public mood mediate changes in evaluations of government.

These studies do not tell us whether politicians can use emotional advertising appeals to influence voting behavior. Their ability to answer the questions of this book is simply limited by their design and scope. The researchers had other objectives in mind. While they characterize the tone of ads in emotional terms, they do not seek to distinguish the emotional appeal of ads from informational content or forms of argument. The studies do not try to simulate the impact of ads during elections and, for the most part, do not even measure the key variables campaigns seek to influence—namely, candidate preference and intention to vote. Subjects were asked to self-consciously watch and think about ads featuring candidates who were unfamiliar and not currently competing in an election. Nonetheless, these studies demonstrate that positive and negative ads can evoke distinct emotions and that such differences can affect memory, perceptions of social desirability, and nascent political orientations. In doing so, they suggest that emotional appeals could be potent tools for motivating and persuading voters.

Close Encounters: Emotions and the Effects of Printed Leaflets and TV News

Given the unabashedly emotional nature of much political advertising, it is somewhat surprising that the studies most closely related to the present inquiry concern the impact of emotion in printed propaganda or televised news. Scholarship on these topics is hardly vast, but a handful of studies in each area provide further clues to suggest that emotionally evocative messages or imagery may play a role in shaping political attitudes and behavior.

In the 1930s, George Hartmann (1936) conducted a field experiment by randomly distributing campaign leaflets across wards of Allentown, Pennsylvania in his run as a Socialist Party candidate for municipal office. Depending on the ward, volunteers went door-to-door one week prior to the election delivering either leaflets that made an "emotional" appeal or leaflets that made a "rational" appeal; in one ward no leaflets at all were delivered. Relative to the previous election, the Socialist Party vote across these wards increased 50 percent, 35 percent, and 24 percent, respectively. The results suggest the emotional leaflets were most effective at winning votes. However, critics later called these provocative findings into question because the "rationality" and "emotionality" of the appeals was tied to the linguistic content and style of the leaflets and, thus, impossible to disentangle from the quality of the argument (Bauer and Cox 1963).

Two laboratory studies have examined emotional appeals in printed political communication.[107] In the first, researchers found some support for the notion of resonance (Roseman, Abelson, and Ewing 1986). Students read a series of statements from interest groups that had been coded as appealing to anger, hope, fear, or pity. Appeals to anger or pity improved attitudes toward the group when the subject reported feeling that emotion often in everyday life. However, fearful subjects responded more favorably to hopeful appeals. Unlike earlier work, the second study circumvents the potentially confounding influence of message content or argument quality by focusing on the emotional appeal of pictures rather than words (Huddy and Gunnthorsdottir 2000). Students read a flyer from a fictitious environmental group that either favored or opposed action to save a fictitious animal in Central America. Researchers manipulated the emotional appeal of the flyers by including an emotionally evocative image of a cute or ugly animal or no image at all. They find no support for a simple *affect transfer* hypothesis, but instead argue that emotion and cognition interact to determine the response. When a pro-wildlife group uses a cute image, pro-environmentalist students become more supportive; when a group opposed to saving the animal uses the same image, these students are more willing to oppose that organization. In other words, the positive emotional appeal produces a stronger reaction, but whether the reaction is support or opposition is still shaped by the relationship between individual predispositions and message content.[108]

Several studies suggest the emotion-eliciting qualities of news can influence political attitudes, especially the nonverbal behavior (e.g., facial displays) of political leaders as seen on TV. Human faces excel at communicating emotion, often unintentionally, and the interpretation of emotion from body language plays a large role in social behavior (Ekman and Rosenberg 1998). Researchers have applied these insights to show that politicians' nonverbal displays elicit distinct emotional responses and can shape attitudes toward those politicians (Bucy 2000; Glaser and Salovey 1998; Lanzetta et al. 1985; Masters and Sullivan 1993; McHugo et al. 1985; Sullivan and Masters 1988).[109] Happy/reassuring displays from prominent leaders exert a strong effect on Americans (Masters and Sullivan 1989) and, in competitive contexts, can polarize viewers on the basis of prior attitudes (McHugo, Lanzetta, and Bush 1991). In another blow to the idea of affect transfer, when presidential images are paired with subliminal anxiety-inducing images, opposing partisans describe both the president's and their own emotions in negative terms but evaluate the president more favorably (Way and Masters 1996a, 1996b).[110]

Whereas the nonverbal studies emphasize the power of images, other researchers underscore the importance of combining images and sound in news reports. For example, one study of TV news about public affairs finds that sound alone is as effective at communicating information as the full audiovisual version, but the combination of sound and imagery produces greater emotional arousal (Crigler, Just, and Neuman 1994). In another study, a combination of pictures and audio clips from news stories about the September 11 terrorist attacks elicited strong emotional responses (Lerner et al. 2003). Different excerpts could predictably evoke anger or fear, with very different consequences for the outlook and policy opinions of viewers. Anger-evoking stimuli increase optimism and support for punitive policies; fear-evoking stimuli increase pessimism and support for precautionary policy measures.[111]

* * *

In sum, existing research tells us almost nothing about whether emotional appeals in political ads persuade or motivate voters, but it offers us a reason to suspect they might. A few studies show that political ads can elicit strong emotional reactions and, in doing so, influence memory, perceptions of social desirability, and the blossoming political orientations of children. But none of this work cleanly separates the tone of information from the emotional appeal, focuses on the attitudes and behavior targeted by campaigns, or simulates the natural viewing conditions with an audience to whom the ads are meaningful (i.e., relevant to an actual upcoming decision about whether and how to vote). Studies of printed leaflets and TV news also demonstrate the emotion-eliciting potential of political communication and show that emotionally evocative messages can influence citizen evaluations and involvement. These are promising indications about the impact of emotional political ads, especially if we assume TV has greater emotional power than print and ads appeal more overtly to emotions than the news.

Reconciling Art and Science

A tremendous gap exists between what most people believe about the importance of emotional appeals in political advertising (the "conventional wisdom") and what is actually known about these appeals. Consultants think of their work creating ads as an *art,* a practice guided by principles and experience for sure, but shaped by skill, intuition, and cleverness in recognizing the largely unique demands of each new election and new constituency. They, as well as many other observers, view the ability to elicit emotions as a crucial component of the advertising craft. Political scientists and other scholars believe that the use and effects of campaign ads, like much else in politics, can be understood as a *science,* as a set of relationships governed by regularities in cause and effect, albeit without denying a place for chance or idiosyncrasy. Their scientific inquiries have focused on the substantive content, styles of argumentation, and references to groups in political ads, but steered clear of emotion. This book seeks to reconcile the gap between the art and science of campaign advertising by investigating how ads appeal to emotions and to what effect.

3

The Political Psychology of Emotional Appeals

Emotional occasions ... are extremely potent in precipitating mental rearrangements. The sudden and explosive ways in which love, jealousy, guilt, fear, remorse, or anger can seize upon one are known to everybody. ... And emotions that come in this explosive way seldom leave things as they found them.

William James (1902)

There are no end of things which can arouse the emotion. ... For you can associate an emotion, say fear, first with something immediately dangerous, then with the idea of that thing, then with something similar to that idea, and so on and on.

Walter Lippmann (1922)

What theory should guide an investigation into the effects of emotional appeals? Major research traditions in political science offer little guidance. This is not to say that political scientists have entirely ignored emotion. Our everyday observations about politics include a healthy dose of emotional appellations. We speak of euphoric supporters, angry voters, and proud citizens, as well as of ethnic hatred, economic anxieties, and politicians who are "running scared." These colorful words decorate otherwise drab academic prose. In contrast to the richness of our vocabulary, however, scholarship on the role of emotions has been conceptually impoverished. As noted in chapter 2, until recently, few studies ventured to say what systematic role, if any, emotions play in their empirical theories of politics.

Three major approaches have dominated the study of political behavior, but none of them has offered a clear conception of emotion or given it full explanatory force (Kinder 1994). The world according to political scientists has been inhabited either by cold-hearted citizens, for whom emotion is inconsequential, or hot-headed citizens, in whom emotion is a vague non-rational force behind their attachments and oppositions. The hot-headed citizens are children of the behavioral approach, which is rooted in social psychology and especially concerned with the study of political attitudes and group identities. In this vein, scholars have defined attitudes or identities as "affective," meaning little more than that they embody a person's positive or negative feelings toward an issue, person, or group. Beyond this, their references to enthusiastic partisans or angry voters are purely descriptive. For example, the definition of party identification as an "affective orientation" (Campbell et al. 1960) conveys that identifiers feel one way or another about a party and perhaps that it is a deeply held product of socialization; but how emotion contributes to that socialization and depth of commitment is left a mystery. Its presence seems either banal or rhetorical (i.e., it lends realism without advancing the explanation).

Cold-hearted citizens are the children of political psychology and rational choice theory. Either by cognitive processing of information or calculation of costs and benefits, these citizens perceive, reason, choose, and act without the help or hindrance of emotion. Researchers in both traditions have regarded emotion as an idiosyncratic facet of life that is best excluded from efforts at systematic explanation. When they do make space for an "affective" component in decisionmaking, emotion is again merely a label on attitudes (e.g., "feeling thermometers") or a "read" on the citizen's utility function.[1]

Although these various approaches have greatly advanced our understanding of political choices and participation, they seem ill equipped to explain how emotional appeals in political advertising might work. If they lead us to expect anything, it is the *null* hypothesis: emotions are epiphenomenal and thus the effectiveness of campaign ads does not hinge on appealing to them. Many political scientists would feel quite comfortable claiming that the symbolic imagery, stirring rhetoric, and musical anthems that draw the attention of journalists and historians are simply so much "sound and fury" in the conduct of contemporary campaigns.

What about the producers of all that sound and fury? As we just saw in chapter 2, campaign consultants who use emotional appeals naturally believe in their effectiveness and have at least an inkling of how they work. Based on the review in that chapter, we can translate their intuitions into the following rough "predictions": (1) ads that appeal to emotions are more attention-getting and memorable; (2) emotions elicited by ads are transferred to the candidate portrayed in the ad; (3) ads persuade by tapping and amplifying preexisting feelings (i.e., the idea of resonance); and (4) ads that appeal to fear are most effective. Nonetheless, consultants' professional intuition does not translate into a coherent theory and even arriving at the preceding "hypotheses" requires some creative license. Practitioners wish to find appeals that resonate with voters in the current election, but they are not interested in constructing "systematic theories of communication and persuasion" (Arterton 1992, 96). Indeed, by social science standards, consultants operate with little more than impressionistic or anecdotal evidence about "what works."

Over the past twenty-five years, however, psychologists have taken impressive strides in learning more about the causes and consequences of emotions. After years of neglect, research on emotion has flourished (Cacioppo and Gardner 1999; Damasio 2000; Zajonc 1998). This surge of interest was predicated on the belief that the rise of cognitive psychology had led to an overemphasis on information processing (LeDoux 1996). The research has also been fueled by advances in psychophysiological measurement and the growth of neuroscience (Lane and Nadel 2000; Panksepp 1998; Rolls 1999). All of the excitement in psychology has proven contagious and new work on emotion has sprung up across the social sciences and humanities.[2] Applying insights from psychology, scholars have begun to uncover strong relationships between emotions and public opinion (Marcus 2000). Taken together, these developments provide a solid foundation on which to build an explanation for how political advertising uses emotional appeals to affect the actions and choices of voters.

In this chapter, I explain the political psychology underlying citizen responses to emotionally evocative political ads. This task requires that I introduce readers to how contemporary researchers on the mind and brain think about emotions.[3] I argue that we can best explain responses to emotional appeals by understanding emotions, as neuropsychologists do, as fundamental systems in our brain that detect the significance of external events and prepare our minds and bodies to act accordingly. Marcus and colleagues (2000) have applied this perspective to the realm of politics with their theory of *affective intelligence* and formulated predictions about the impact of enthusiasm and fear on political attitudes and behavior. For the most part, I adopt their predictions as my own and focus on the same two emotions, although many of the hypotheses are consistent with a range of existing psychological work. I also draw selectively from the research literatures on appraisal theory, mood and information processing, and fear appeals to explain how campaign ads cue emotions and why and how this is likely to affect voters.

Psychological Perspectives on Emotion

People use a wide variety of words to describe both specific emotional experiences and emotional phenomena generally. Although our language is rich in this way, it is also imprecise. For example, few people distinguish "emotions" from "feelings," and while some people use "anxious" to mean worry or stress, others treat it as synonymous with eager. Scientific research benefits from greater precision in the use of terms, and psychologists have shown that the preceding examples are distinctions that matter. However, even when borrowing ideas from the burgeoning science of emotion, confusion is possible as the use of particular terms has scarcely been consistent (Ekman and Davidson 1994).

Therefore, I begin by clarifying my own use of several key terms. This book is principally concerned with the role of emotions. *Emotions* are specific sets of physiological and mental dispositions triggered by the brain in response to the perceived significance of a situation or object for an individual's goals (up to and including survival). I flesh out this conception further in the pages that follow. Given their frequent use as synonyms, it is especially important to distinguish emotions from feelings. *Feelings* are the subjective awareness and experience of emotions (Damasio 2000). Fear is the collection of responses to a threat, but the feeling of fear is what those responses literally "feel like" to the person being threatened. For example, a person can experience an accelerated heart rate and heightened neural processing in the amygdala but never sense these reactions or feel scared.[4] Feelings then are potential, but not necessary, consequences of emotions. In addition, where emotions are *discrete* responses to specific stimuli, *moods* are diffuse positive or negative states that last for longer periods of time. Finally, *affect* is an umbrella term referring to an entire class of phenomena that is often taken to include not only emotions, feelings, and moods, but also pain, pleasure, and basic human drives.

Psychologists have focused increasingly on the constituent processes that define an emotion. Despite differences in emphasis or categorization, there is a fairly broad consensus on these components (Adolphs and Damasio 2000; Clore and Ortony 2000; Frijda 1999; Lazarus 1991). Emotions consist of (1) the perception that a stimulus holds a particular significance for a person's goals; (2) a set of physiological changes that may include visceral responses, arousal of the autonomic nervous system (which controls breathing, heart rate, etc.), and activation of the central nervous system to prepare for action; (3) changes in cognitive activity such as attention, memory, and thought processes that may be critical to adapting plans to new circumstances; (4) an *action tendency,* which is an inclination to act in a certain way (e.g., freeze, avoid, attack, comfort, proceed, take, withdraw, etc.); and (5) often the subjective experience of all of the preceding components. This last component is what I have labeled "feelings." Treating them as a product rather than core component of emotions serves as a reminder that shifts in mental and behavioral tendencies do not depend on feelings.

Structures and Models of Emotion

Much of what political scientists and social psychologists have written on the role of affect focuses on the gross distinction between positive and negative reactions (Lerner and Kelter 2000; Marcus 2000). This emphasis is rooted in an early, influential conceptualization of affect as consisting of two qualities or dimensions (Bradley and Lang 2000; Osgood, Suci, and Tannenbaum 1957): The first is *valence* and reflects the extent to which one regards a stimulus as pleasant or unpleasant. Valence is generally considered to be the defining feature of affective phenomena (Ellsworth 1994b; Zajonc 1998). The second quality or dimension is most commonly called *arousal* and captures the intensity or energizing nature of the response (Ferguson 2000). In the classic view of emotions as motivating either approach or avoidance behavior (Zajonc 1998), the valence and arousal dimensions of an emotional response indicate its direction and vigor, respectively (Bradley and Lang 2000).[5]

Social psychologists have offered competing views on the structure of emotion (Marcus 2003; Scherer 2000). Some conceptualize emotion as falling along a single bipolar dimension running from negative to positive (valence) with increasing intensity (arousal) as one moves from the center toward the poles. This conception underlies most contemporary studies of attitudes, in which emotion or affect reflects the evaluative component of social judgment (Eagly and Chaiken 1993; Fiske and Taylor 1991; McGuire 1985; Schwarz and Bohner 2001). This is a reasonable way to think about the way people divide the world into "likes" and "dislikes."

However, others argue that, by focusing exclusively on valence and summary judgments, we are likely to overlook the distinct and powerful role of specific emotions (Plutchik 1980). Fear, anger, and disappointment are all negative reactions to politics or other aspects of life, yet common sense tells us that these three emotions are very different from one another and imply more than simple dislike. We might say the same for positive emotions such as enthusiasm, sympathy, and serenity. This focus on discrete emotions is reflected in two major approaches to the study of emotion, one emphasizing cognition and the other emphasizing physiology (Scherer 2000).

Many leading discrete emotion theories fall under the *cognitive appraisal* approach that emphasizes the role of the perceptual component of emotion (Ellsworth 1994a, 1994b; Frijda 1986; Lazarus 1991; Oatley 1992; Ortony, Clore, and Collins 1988; Roseman 2001; Roseman and Smith 2001; Scherer 1994c; Scherer, Schorr, and Johnstone 2001). Lazarus (1991) defines appraisal as "a continuing evaluation of the significance of what is happening for one's personal well-being" (144) and regards it as the key mediating variable between a stimulus and emotional response. The appraisal determines the kind of harm or benefit presented by a situation, yielding a particular emotional response. For example, the loss of something valued produces sadness, while the imposition of some injustice, injury, or obstacle produces anger.[6] Other discrete emotion theories stress the existence of a few neural systems that have evolved to facilitate adaptive responses to the environment and give rise to a specified number of basic emotions (Ekman 1992; Ekman and Rosenberg 1998; Gray 1987; Izard 1991; Izard and Ackerman 2000; Panksepp 1994a, 1994b, 2000). Scholars in this tradition emphasize not only the biological mechanisms, but also the ways in which emotions occur outside of awareness and control.

Finally, some psychologists believe that a bipolar valence model is inadequate, but claim that emotions are more highly structured than discrete models imply (Marcus 2003). They conceptualize all emotional experiences as falling somewhere within a space defined by a limited number of dimensions (Plutchik 2003). One such model lays the classical dimensions of emotion—valence and arousal—at right angles to form this two-dimensional space (Russell 1980). For example, enthusiasm would fall in the quadrant between the high arousal pole and the positive valence pole, while fear would fall in the quadrant between high arousal and negative valence. Other scholars have argued for the separability or independence of positive and negative affect (Cacioppo and Bernston 1994; Cacioppo, Gardner, and Bernston 1997). One can turn the two-dimensional valence-arousal model forty-five degrees in order to form separate positive and negative axes that each run from low to high arousal (Watson, Clark, and Tellegen 1988), with enthusiasm and fear now falling at the high arousal endpoints of these two dimensions. Marcus (2003) observes that the dimensional models do a good job of capturing most of the variation in self-reported emotional reactions to a wide range of stimuli, but do not move beyond the description of structure to provide a theory about the origins and consequences of those emotions. For such a theory, one needs to draw on the cognitive and/or neurophysiological approaches.

Although my argument emphasizes the specificity of emotions, valence and arousal remain significant concepts because they form a basis for prominent lay theories concerning the impact of emotional appeals in advertising. In addition, because I focus on two emotions—one negative (fear), one positive (enthusiasm)—this study does not truly test among competing models of emotion that posit specific dimensional structures or emphasize discrete emotional responses. By chapter's end, however, I hypothesize that fear and enthusiasm produce distinct patterns of effects that are not only asymmetrical, but also are sufficiently complex that they cannot be characterized in simple, oppositional terms. As a result, to the extent evidence supports these hypotheses, this study provides stronger validation for rich (dimensional or discrete) accounts of emotions than for simple valence models.

Cognition and Emotion

In the wake of the cognitive revolution in psychology since the 1970s, appraisal models of emotion flourished. Their emphasis on cognition has been challenged by Robert Zajonc (1980), who argues that affect and cognition are separable processes and that affect can arise without cognitive input. His claims rest on evidence that people can experience an affective reaction or develop a preference for an object even when unaware of their reaction or its source (Murphy and Zajonc 1993; Zajonc 1998). These findings call into question the idea that emotions must be preceded by an explicit recognition of a stimulus and evaluation of its relevance. In this vein, some scholars focus on the way nonconscious or preconscious "emotional processing" shapes subsequent judgments or behavior (Damasio 1994; LeDoux 1996; Panksepp 1998).

Following a vigorous debate over the primacy of affect versus cognition (Lazarus 1981, 1982, 1984; Zajonc 1984, 2000), most psychologists agree that the relationship between the two depends on how one defines cognition (Clore and Ketelaar 1997; Cornelius 1996; Ekman and Davidson 1994; Ellsworth 1994a; Leventhal and Scherer 1987). An emotion occurs only when the brain assesses that something a person has encountered holds significance for her well-being. If we label this preconscious processing of sensory information as cognition, then cognition is indeed a precursor of emotion. If we define cognition as pertaining to higher reasoning functions and/or conscious thoughts, then cognitive activity is a sufficient but not necessary cause of emotion.

Although some of the preceding distinctions may seem esoteric, they can prevent confusion about the causes and effects of emotions. This is especially important because of a long tradition of contrasting emotional appeals with "cognitive" or "rational" appeals (Hartmann 1936; Jamieson 1988; Roseman, Abelson, and Ewing 1986), in which the latter rest implicitly on the second definition of cognition just given.[7] Once we understand such distinctions, we can more easily grasp critical points of consensus on how emotions work. There is wide agreement that both appraisal and arousal can occur outside of conscious awareness (Clore 1994; Damasio 1994; Frijda 1994a; Izard 1994; Lazarus 1991, 1994a; LeDoux 1994b; Zajonc 1994). Thus, we can experience an emotional reaction to an object in our environment without realizing the object is there, that we have judged its significance, or that we feel a particular way about it. Many psychologists also concur that emotion and cognition are conceptually distinct yet thoroughly intertwined (Aldophs and Damasio 2001; Damasio 1994; Frijda 1994a; Lazarus 1991; LeDoux 1989, 1994a; Panksepp 1994c; Plutchik 1980). On the one hand, appraisals initiate all emotions and conscious thoughts can generate new emotions or reshape old ones. On the other hand, emotional responses form the bases of judgments, consciously and unconsciously influence thinking, and turn thoughts into action.

Psychologists of emotion differ mostly in which aspect of the emotional process is at the center of their research (Scherer 2000). Cognitive appraisal theorists tend to study the subjective experience of emotions (i.e., feelings) and the specific patterns of appraisal that generate distinct emotions. Other scholars, especially neuropsychologists, focus on the behavioral function of emotions and the links between proximate stimuli, physiological responses, and effects on judgment and behavior. Both lines of research inform the investigations in this book. Neuropsychological approaches provide a useful framework for understanding how and why the images and music in televised political ads can subtly but dramatically alter the way in which citizens respond to a politician's message. Appraisal theories lend some clarity to the task of drawing meaningful distinctions among emotions and shed light on the types of situations or cues that may give rise to different emotions.

Emotions as Fundamental Systems for Adapting Behavior

I now turn to the specific propositions from psychological theories of emotion that guide this investigation. What can we learn by studying emotions that we can't learn by studying cognition? First, let's consider what sets emotions apart. The terms "cognition" and "affect" both refer to major categories of psychological phenomena that are interdependent, but the two are distinct in a number of ways (Zajonc 1998). Affect includes not only emotions, but also moods, feelings, preferences, and direct sensations such as pain and pleasure. Cognition includes thoughts, beliefs, inferences, and application of rules such as those governing mathematics and language.[8] When most people reflect on what distinguishes emotions (and other types of affect) from cognition, they probably first think of how they experience emotions. We become aware of emotions as feelings, but we do not "feel" our thoughts or beliefs.

Emotional Processing: Detective and Directive Functions

Although feelings are the most distinctive quality of emotions in phenomenological terms, two other defining features hold the key to grasping the importance of emotions and emotional appeals. The first is that emotions function as *relevance detectors* (Frijda 1986) that provide feedback on the significance of internal and external stimuli for a person's goals (Damasio 1994; Lazarus 1991; Scherer 1994a, 2000). Thus, "emotions are a fairly good index of how conducive the environment is to one's well-being" (Damasio 2000, 19). The second defining feature is that emotions serve a *directive function* that often interrupts current activity and prepares the mind and body to respond to new circumstances (Damasio 1994; Frijda 1999; LeDoux 1996; Scherer 1994a). Detection of relevance and preparation for response occur automatically. We have little control over the occurrence of emotions.[9]

Emotions arise from brain processes that provide continuous feedback on the relationship between an individual and her environment. The brain uses that feedback to adapt mental and physical activity to cope with the significance of that relationship for the person's goals and well-being (Damasio 1994; Lazarus 1991). How do emotions assist in that process? Emotions are in large part physiological responses, a constellation of changes in breathing, heart rate, muscle tension, and body chemistry. Although they do not require us to think first, the complete set of responses occur at the level of the mind as well as the body.[10] Attention, perception, motivation, and thought processes shift along with physiology. Emotions produce shifts in thought and action that help a person respond appropriately to changing circumstances. An individual may sense these internal changes as a feeling, or she may never be fully aware of the changes even though she has modified her behavior in response to them.

Emotional systems allow us to respond efficiently to a flood of sensory information pouring in from the world around us. Research in political psychology has made the concept of *information processing* familiar to many political scientists. The study of emotion expands our notion of what happens when people process information. Sensory data is channeled simultaneously along parallel pathways in the brain, enabling both cognitive and emotional processing of information. Data travels to the emotional centers of the brain directly as well as indirectly by way of those areas responsible for "higher" cognitive functions. These dual pathways allow the brain to detect the emotional significance of a stimulus quickly and then revise the initial reaction on the basis of further analysis (Cornelius 1996; LeDoux 1996). The "quick and dirty" pathway primes the reception of subsequent information concerning a stimulus delivered through the slower cognitive channels (LeDoux and Phelps 2000). When something triggers an emotion, it affects the way in which information is processed along the cognitive pathways. Because emotional systems process information more quickly, the precious resources of attention and reasoning can be allocated more efficiently to salient features of the environment. Without emotions operating in the background, we would be endlessly distracted and overwhelmed sorting through information and weighing the options that confront us (Damasio 1994).[11]

Enthusiasm and Fear as Systems for Monitoring Success and Threat

There is no single system in the brain responsible for all emotions. Psychologists have identified distinct emotional processes that serve as "special purpose" systems shaping responses to situations commonly encountered by humans and other animals (Damasio 1994; Gray 1987, 1994; LeDoux 1996; Ochsner and Barrett 2001; Panksepp 1998, 2000; cf. Buck 2000). Although the enumeration and labeling of these systems differs, there is considerable consensus on the importance played by two fundamental systems in the decisionmaking and behavior of everyday life. The first involves detection and response to success and, when activated, corresponds to enthusiasm or joy. It directs behavior into those pursuits that prove reliable sources of reward. The second involves detection and response to threat and, when activated, corresponds to the emotion of fear or anxiety. It redirects behavior to enable a person to deal appropriately with potential danger. These positive and negative emotions are not opposites; they are distinct responses to a specific set of cues.[12] Despite divergent views on many aspects of emotion theory, neuropsychologists and social psychologists demonstrate broad agreement on the causes and effects of these two fundamental emotions.

The *enthusiasm system* monitors an individual's progress toward her goals or the goals of a group with which she identities.[13] We experience enthusiasm (or hope, elation, joy, etc.) when we process signals from the environment that we deem to have positive implications for our pursuits or, in other words, we acquire new evidence that we "are making *reasonable progress toward the realization of our goals*" (Lazarus 1991, 267, emphasis in original). Enthusiasm whets the appetite to seek what we desire; it is as much a "psychic energization" as a state of physical arousal (Panksepp 1998). The responses sustain or even strengthen our drive to pursue our goals and the present plans for achieving them (Lazarus 1991; Oatley and Jenkins 1996; Roseman 2001). Throughout much of our lives, we act on the basis of learned routines or habits. Neuropsychologists argue that the enthusiasm system facilitates development of these dispositions, by implicit and explicit learning of what works and what fails, and encourages their use (Damasio 1994; Gray 1987; Panksepp 1998). Similarly, researchers have found substantial evidence that people rely on heuristics and the "peripheral processing" of information when they are in happy or positive mood states (Bless 2000, 2001; Eagly and Chaiken 1993; Fiedler 2001; Hertel et al. 2000; Martin and Clore 2001; Schwarz 2000). If signals suggest we are not achieving our goals, the result is sadness or disappointment and a diminishing drive for present pursuits. We lose spirit and find it hard to continue.

The *fear system* monitors the environment for signs of threat. When the brain receives indications of potential danger, we experience fear (or anxiety, worry, unease, etc.). This is a "system of defensive behavior" concerned with maximizing "the probability of surviving a dangerous situation in the most beneficial way" (LeDoux 1996, 128). Uncertainty about both the extent of a threat and the likelihood of coping with it plays a large part in anxiety, making heightened vigilance an adaptive response. Fear breaks us out of habitual routines (Gray 1987, 1994) and directs our attention to relevant portions of the environment and any information that may help address the threat

(Mogg and Bradley 1998; Öhman 2000; Oatley and Jenkins 1996; Roseman 2001). It activates thinking about alternative courses of action as we try to decide what—if anything—we should do next (Izard 1991). Similarly, researchers find that fear or negative mood states encourage systematic evaluations and "central" processing of information (Öhman 2000).[14] Absent indications of threat, we feel calm and our behavior is governed by routines.

Although there is little doubt that fear motivates increased vigilance for a time, the role of fear in motivating other changes in behavior is more complicated. Where routine behavior is concerned, fear generally inhibits activity (Gray 1987), yet even in such cases fear generates a high level of readiness for further action (Gray 1994). Scholars have understood fear to simultaneously prepare an individual to act in one of several ways, including to freeze and hide, flee to safety, or fight off danger, depending on what the circumstances allow. These are prototypical reactions to imminent physical danger, though the full activation of the "fight or flight system" is only infrequently experienced by most people. However, many researchers agree that milder, everyday forms of fear in response to more remote threats involve similar neural processing and patterns of denial, avoidance, prevention, or confrontation (LeDoux 1996; Panksepp 1998). Lazarus observes that such anxiety is often regarded as "a primary, often *the* main, motivating force in human affairs" (1991, 234, emphasis in original).[15]

In the case of fear, the trickier issue is whether people are motivated to take more or less constructive forms of action. For example, when a "moment of truth" looms, anxiety sometimes leads us to "avoid" the danger by throwing ourselves into diversionary projects; on other occasions it may energize us to "avoid" the danger by preparing ourselves to meet the challenges ahead. When do people run away from a perceived threat and when do they face it? Lazarus (1991) suggests that knowledge and certainty about what is happening helps some people deal with anxiety by taking concrete action, but much of the recent research on the psychology of fear remains silent on this question.

We can find some answers in the separate and surprisingly far-removed field of research on fear appeals. For fifty years, scholars have been conducting empirical studies of the effects of threatening or fear-arousing communications, largely focused on health and safety campaigns (Beck and Frankel 1981; Hovland, Janis, and Kelley 1953; Janis and Feshbach 1953; Mulilis and Lippa 1990; Rippetoe and Rogers 1987; Sutton 1982; Sutton and Hallet 1989).[16] The accumulated research strongly indicates that fear appeals are successful in persuading recipients to take recommended actions to prevent whatever danger is being discussed (Witte and Allen 2000). Investigators have also found that the success of fear appeals in bringing about a desired change in attitudes and behavior depends on the perceived efficacy of the proposed response (Rogers 1975, 1983; Witte and Allen 2000; cf. Bandura 1977). In other words, people are more likely to face their fear and address the threat when they judge the available or recommended course of action as likely to be effective *(response efficacy)* and see themselves as capable of taking that action *(self-efficacy)*. When fear is strong and perceived efficacy is low, individuals are more likely to engage in defensive behavior such as denial or avoidance (Witte 1992, 1998).

The enthusiasm and fear systems help to regulate much of human behavior. Many psychologists believe these emotions help individuals to respond in an adaptive manner as they interact with the world around them (Damasio 1994; Lazarus 1991). Operating in the background, so to speak, the first system translates feedback about success into appropriate levels of enthusiasm and motivation for continuing the tasks at hand, while the second system interrupts to refocus attention and thinking only when signs of threat warrant a potential change of plans. These two systems taken together allow us to keep tabs on our environment without requiring a lot of attention and thinking on our part. Faced with more information and potential choices than the human mind can remotely attend to, the enthusiasm and fear systems monitor our circumstances for signs of success and threat, so that we can go about our business with reasonable efficiency. Their joint activity conditions the focus of attention, the use of higher cognitive functions, and the motivation for pursuing goals.

Emotions in the Realm of Politics

The preceding description of enthusiasm and fear may fit more or less comfortably with what you recognize in your own experiences. But responding to a bear in the woods is one thing, while watching a bear in a political commercial on your living room TV is another. Should we really expect people to respond similarly in these situations? Yes, as it turns out, at least if we assume that the bear reflects a potential threat, whether concrete or symbolic, in both contexts. While it is easier to visualize our reaction to a real bear, research shows that identical processes, albeit less amplified, can occur in response to very subtle signals. Recall that mild episodes of emotions such as fear often arise without our conscious awareness. Although ordinary democratic politics typically elicits anxieties of the modest sort and is probably not the peak source of enthusiasm in most people's lives either, the emotions are every bit as real and produce the same general patterns of response. Indeed, even since I began work on this book, there has been growing evidence that the view of emotion sketched above can be usefully applied to study the way citizens form opinions and evaluate leaders in politics. Before discussing how symbolic threats in political communication trigger emotions, I first consider how these propositions about emotions can be and have been applied to the study of political behavior.

Renewed interest in studying the emotional reactions of citizens has led scholars to borrow from a variety of approaches, including appraisal theories (Abelson et al. 1982; Conover and Feldman 1986; Kinder 1994; Roseman, Abelson, and Ewing 1986), dimensional theories of affect or mood (Huddy and Gunnthorsdottir 2000; Isbell and Ottati 2002; Ottati and Wyer 1993; Rahn 2000; Rahn, Kroeger, and Kite 1996), and neuropsychological theories (Marcus and MacKuen 1993, 2001; Marcus et al. 1996; Masters 2001; Masters and Way 1996; Way and Masters 1996a, 1996b).[17] This burgeoning research has left no doubt that affect is a distinct and important determinant of political attitudes.

Marcus, Neuman, and MacKuen (2000) have pushed farthest in constructing a full-scale model to explain the role of emotion in political behavior. They place enthusiasm and fear at the center of their theory by extending the insights of Gray's (1987) neuropsychological theory and Watson's (Watson, Clark, and Tellegen 1998) dimensional model. Their theory of *affective intelligence* posits that two fundamental systems operate in parallel to produce emotional appraisals that in turn shape the choices and actions of citizens. The disposition system generates enthusiasm/satisfaction or depression/frustration as incoming information reports that the execution of one's plans either matches or does not match expectations (of success). The surveillance system generates anxiety/unease or relaxation/calm as incoming information suggests it is either safe or potentially unsafe to go about one's business as usual. Marcus and colleagues argue that these systems affect the extent to which individuals engage in one of two distinctive modes of political judgment. The disposition system regulates a person's relative motivation to act on the basis of enduring political habits (e.g., partisanship, prejudice, social identity). When triggered by a potential threat, the surveillance system interrupts this reliance on habit and encourages greater attentiveness and reasoned consideration of choices.

Drawing primarily on the biennial surveys of the National Election Studies (NES), Marcus and colleagues find considerable support for their theory in the relationship between self-reported feelings about presidential candidates and patterns of campaign behavior. Overall levels of both enthusiasm and anxiety seem to be correlated with interest in the campaign, caring about who wins, and following campaign coverage in newspapers and magazines. However, panel data show that enthusiasm predicts *increases* in interest and caring, while anxiety predicts *increases* in media attention. Anxious citizens also call to mind more reasons for liking or disliking candidates and display greater knowledge of where candidates stand on the issues. Consistent with their predictions, enthusiasm is linked to involvement and anxiety is linked to attentiveness and learning. Although both enthusiasm and anxiety are associated with increased participation in the campaign, anxiety predicts considerably higher levels of participation than enthusiasm. Marcus and colleagues attribute this to the fact that the surveillance system sends "more urgent signals" (90), but the relatively weak findings for enthusiasm seem surprising in light of the energizing role that the disposition system is supposed to play, especially if it serves as a basis for the politics of mobilization (52–53).

Evidence on the relationship between candidate feelings and political judgment is perhaps even more supportive of the theory. Responses from the disposition system contribute to candidate evaluations in a direct and unsurprising fashion, such as when higher levels of enthusiasm for Pat Buchanan translated into more support for Buchanan over Bob Dole in the 1996 Republican primary. Responses from the surveillance system affect evaluations indirectly, by altering the bases of evaluation. Anxious partisans are more likely to defect and vote for the other party's candidate, but anxiety provides the biggest boost to defection rates when partisans actually prefer the policies of the opposing candidate. This lends credence to the view that activating the surveillance system not only decreases reliance on habit, but also increases reconsideration of choices on the basis of contemporary information. In general, anxiety alters the salience of particular factors in the voting decision, decreasing the role of partisanship and increasing the role of issue positions and personality traits. Finally, Americans who positively assessed U.S. performance in the 1991 Gulf War were more likely to change their views to support the intervention policy if they had been anxious about the war and were *only* likely to change their views to support President Bush if they had been anxious.[18]

Using an early elaboration of the affective intelligence model as a point of departure (Marcus and MacKuen 1993), two other studies contend that the impact of anxiety on political behavior is conditional. A study of French-speaking students in Quebec finds that anxiety about the future of the French language increases learning about the issue only among those have some expectation (hope) of success in the fight to preserve the language (Nadeau, Niemi, and Amato 1995).[19] This is consistent with the notion that the motivational effects of fear depend on efficacy, though the measure in the Quebec study does not allow us to distinguish response efficacy from self-efficacy. A second study provides clearer evidence of an interaction between anxiety and self-efficacy, or what political scientists call *internal political efficacy,* the sense that one can understand and participate effectively in politics. Revisiting Marcus and MacKuen's (1993) analysis of 1980 NES panel data, the researchers show that anxiety does increase interest in the campaign but only among those scoring high in political self-efficacy (Rudolph, Gangl, and

Stevens 2000). At the same time, they confirm that the positive impact of enthusiasm on campaign interest is not moderated by feelings of efficacy.

In sum, there is a good deal of evidence that enthusiasm and fear affect political evaluations and behavior in the manner predicted by psychological theories of emotion. Enthusiasm motivates involvement in politics in accordance with the dictates of one's existing goals and predispositions. In contrast, fear calls into question one's standing decision, focuses attention on new information, and invites reconsideration of the options. It facilitates reflection and acts of political defection. From this perspective, we can begin to see how emotion causes citizens to lead a double life, sometimes practicing a politics of habit and at other times exercising political judgment to choose among alternatives. This integration of predisposition, rational calculation, and emotional response in sensible ways is what Marcus and colleagues (2000) dub "affective intelligence."

In the conclusion of their book, Marcus and colleagues claim that we must revise our understanding of the "causal dynamics" of elections by recognizing that campaign communication cues the affective intelligence of citizens. However, as some critics have observed (Isbell and Ottati 2002; Joslyn 2001), almost all of the research on emotion and politics to date, including the work on affective intelligence theory, relies on survey data and correlational analysis. Therefore, emotions could be the cause of observed behavior, the consequence of that behavior, or simply another outcome of whatever did cause the behavior. More generally, we have no evidence that campaign communications can elicit these emotions and change behavior as a result. In order to test the claim that campaign ads trigger the affective intelligence of voters, we must ascertain precisely how campaign ads cue enthusiasm and fear.

Emotional Cues

Perhaps the most critical goal of this chapter is to explain how televised messages can use imagery and music to trigger emotions and thereby influence the political behavior of viewers. In order to explain the impact of emotion in political communication, we must consider (1) how specific pieces of music, sounds, images, or other phenomena go from being just another bit of sensory data to being *emotional cues;* (2) why we respond to mass-mediated cues that are symbolic or abstracted from the contexts that originally made them concrete signs of success or threat; (3) why emotional appeals can be effective even if, or especially if, people do not pay close attention to the music, images, or even the ad itself; and (4) what sorts of cues from the political context, and especially among those typically used in political advertising, might elicit enthusiasm and fear. I take up each of these issues in turn.

Sorting the Good, the Bad, and the Ugly

Emotions are responses to cues from the world around us, and any piece of information or sensory data can become an emotional cue. When the emotional machinery of the brain evaluates objects and situations for their relevance, these appraisals have two components that we can distinguish conceptually, even though they do not necessarily constitute distinct operations. In a sense, the detection systems ask:

> Is this relevant to my goals/plans?
> If so, in what way is it relevant?

In the dimensional view of emotion, we might see the answers to these questions as determining arousal and valence, respectively. In the view I have espoused here, there are multiple emotional systems asking these questions independently and simultaneously (LeDoux 1996; Panksepp 1998). If none of these systems answers "yes" to the first question, no emotion is triggered. When the enthusiasm system finds that information is relevant to ongoing plans, it also evaluates whether the information portends success or failure. Enthusiasm or disappointment ensues. When the fear system finds that information is relevant to well-being, it also determines whether the information indicates a situation that is threatening or safe. As a result, a person is made anxious or relaxed. Other systems appraise other sorts of relevance and, if activated, yield other emotions. But how do emotional systems make these appraisals?

Emotional appraisals rely on a store of innate and learned *associations* of the significance of stimuli and their contexts. The brain sorts through the sensory data for signals associated with success or failure (the enthusiasm system) and data associated with threat or a trouble-free environment (the fear system). LeDoux (1996, 127) argues that select classes of stimuli are "natural triggers" that have associations hard-wired by evolution, but that most emotional cues are "learned triggers" whose associations have been acquired through personal experience. Similarly, Damasio (1994) claims that people may be predisposed to respond with one of several "primary emotions" to certain types of stimuli, but that most emotional reactions are triggered by *"systematic connections between categories of objects and situations, on the one hand, and primary emotions, on the other"* (131–34, emphasis in original).[20] Our brains record these connections in associative memory. Over the course of our entire lives, we generate and update the associations automatically (i.e., without intention or conscious effort) in light of new experiences. It is these associations that allow our brains to translate new sensory information into cues that trigger an emotional response.[21]

Anything can acquire emotional significance and, for each individual, a vast number of things eventually do (Damasio 2000; Zajonc 1998). Emotional cues may be colors, sounds, smells, bodily sensations, patterns of movement, people or other living creatures, objects, places, symbols, or words. Nature provides nearly everyone with the same basic machinery of emotion, but experience fills in most of the details. "Your experience may be at subtle or at major variance with that of others; it is yours alone. Although the relations between type of situation and emotion are, to a great extent, similar among individuals, unique, personal experience customizes the process for every individual" (Damasio 1994, 136–37). As a result, there is remarkable heterogeneity in reactions to specific stimuli *and* considerable commonality as well. Emotional cues are likely to be shared across some community or category of persons to the extent that group of persons has similar experiences with the stimuli in question (Ellsworth 1994b; Frijda 1994b; Lazarus 1994b; Scherer 1994b). Flags offer a simple example. National flags elicit strong emotions in many people around the world. We can predict fairly well who will respond with pride or loathing to a specific flag, so long as we can differentiate who strongly identifies with the nation in question, who identifies strongly with "rival" (i.e., antagonistic) nations, and who identifies strongly with neither. To take a second example, many people respond with joy at the sight of a puppy, though a small number respond with fear and there are some who respond with disgust. Finally, in what may be a largely innate response, women and men around the world tend to find the shrieking cry of an infant unpleasant and often alarming, initiating a powerful drive to make the crying stop. Regardless of whether the boundary is drawn by species (in the case of "universal" antecedents), culture, or externally constructed categories (e.g., dog lovers), similarity of experience holds the key to understanding variation in emotional responses to a particular class of stimuli.

Automaticity and Imagination: "Better Safe Than Sorry"

People respond not only to concrete stimuli, but also to the abstract or symbolic representation of those stimuli. Commercial and political advertisers insert flags, puppies, shrieking infants, and many other affective stimuli into their ads, even when they are not trying to sell you flags, puppies, shrieking infants, or products or services for dealing with them. Of course, it is the central claim of this book that such representations are used as emotional cues to influence reception of political ads, and the ultimate goal of this book is to submit that claim to empirical investigation. I suspect that most readers already *believe* that these sorts of televised images and sounds in political ads can elicit emotions, even though the empirical evidence to date has been slight, because it is consistent with their own experiences in living rooms and movie theaters. However, in developing a theory, my goal is to explain precisely why representations can evoke the same emotions as the concrete stimuli they portray. *Why* should we be frightened by fictional sharks, angered by fictional wrongs, inspired by fictional achievements, or saddened by the loss of fictional lives?

Part of the answer lies in *automaticity* (cf. Bargh and Chartrand 1999), the way that stimuli are perceived and emotions are triggered automatically, prior to activation of the cognitive faculties that allow us to contextualize and "reappraise" a situation. Recall that the purpose of fundamental emotional systems is to generate a quick, crude reaction that will facilitate an adaptive response to important changes in our environment (LeDoux 1996). Our brains develop associations like SHARK = THREAT (or LARGE GRAY FIN = THREAT) so that we can respond with potentially life-saving speed when we encounter a possible predator. It is better to make a cautious mistake (e.g., seeking safety only to discover the fin belongs to a playful dolphin) than to strive for accuracy at the cost of foreclosing options (Öhman 2000). Therefore, people do not tend to form distinct associations for "real shark" and "moving picture of real shark." If this is true, then why don't people run screaming from the living room or theater during the movie *Jaws?* Leaving aside the fact that some people come close to doing just that, the perspective-providing process of reappraisal does not take long to kick in and override the emotional response. Having said that, the bodily changes that constitute emotions do not end as abruptly as they begin, but instead fade away once the triggering stimuli are gone (Panksepp 1998). An accelerated pulse, muscular tension, and slight feelings of unease linger even as a moviegoer "laughs off" his fright reaction with friends.[22] The ability to imagine ourselves in the situations we are watching and identify with characters also enhances the emotional impact by narrowing our perceptual focus to the action on the screen instead of the larger context of our viewing experience (Gaut 1999).

Even abstract representations in our mind can elicit emotions. Our brain conjures up representations of objects or situations when we imagine, remember, or think through them. In doing so, these cognitive processes can trigger emotional responses or make us feel as if we are experiencing an emotional state (Damasio 1994). This has a range of disadvantages from the serious effects of traumatic emotional memories to the "hang-ups" of a vivid imagination, such as when children and even adults shy away from the dark or the ocean after seeing a scary movie because they can imagine encountering what might lurk there. But there are also advantages. Even though emotions often arise automatically, the interaction of cognition and emotion enables us to consciously consider the source of our feelings, and feelings allow us to generalize across groups of stimuli, attach significance to contexts, and communicate our experiences with others (Damasio 1994; LeDoux 2000). We can play and replay scenarios in our mind, endowing our behavior with greater flexibility and the capacity for strategy.

Automaticity and the Implicit Appeal of Soundtracks and Imagery

Automaticity ensures that our brains pay attention to what's happening around us even when "we"—that is, our conscious selves—do not. We recognize and respond emotionally before even realizing the cues are there and often without ever knowing we reacted to them. In preparing for special occasions, people frequently employ music, fragrances, specific colors of decoration or dress, changes in lighting, and other techniques to "set the mood." These details usually are not intended to attract attention, but rather are designed to influence emotions in subtle ways that enhance the purpose of the event. Indeed, when such preparations go unnoticed, hosts and event planners often regard it as the hallmark of success.

Some of the true power of television lies in its ability to use visual and aural cues to similar effect. As Darrell West (2001) has observed, the function of most music and imagery in TV ads is also to set the mood. While critics and the public were captivated at one time by the potential impact of subliminal cues (Sears and Kosterman 1994), which by definition escape conscious perception, it is likely that the most effective cues in television and movies are readily detectable.[23] Images and music are there for us to see and hear but may still go largely unnoticed. In this way, they have an opportunity to work their influence without us knowing they are "working." Regardless of whether they are noticed, the congruent use of musical soundtrack and imagery strengthens the communication and arousal of specific emotions (G. Smith 1999; J. Smith 1999).

What about verbal messages? Individual words or short phrases, whether written or spoken, can have symbolic value and affective associations. Beloved names, racial slurs, and terms signifying historical events such as "Holocaust" or "9/11" are just a few examples. However, longer verbal statements of the sort that make up arguments, description, and dialogue require more elaborate cognitive processing. Their meaning is comprehended only as the brain decodes the series of words according to the previously learned rules of language and relevant contextual clues. Once comprehended, verbal statements can and often do have implications that produce emotional reactions. This "high road" to emotional response is slower, though it still occurs very rapidly by ordinary standards of time (LeDoux and Phelps 2000). For purposes of studying the effects of advertising, the more critical difference is that emotions elicited by comprehending the meaning of verbal statements cannot fall outside our awareness and are likely to be heavily shaped by the sorts of biased processing known to be prevalent in political cognition (Iyengar and McGuire 1993; Sniderman, Tetlock, and Brody 1991). If emotional appeals are intended to influence a viewer's receptiveness to the information in ads, then advertisers cannot rely on that same information to elicit the desired emotions. The implicitness of emotional appeals embedded in the soundtrack and background imagery enables the ad to trigger a "mood" or emotional response prior to and during the time when an individual is processing its verbal message.[24]

A Political Consultant's Cache of Cues

In chapter 2, I briefly discussed the sorts of cues used to fashion emotional appeals in political advertising. We can now begin to consider these cues in light of the psychological mechanisms they are likely to trigger. Images, sounds, and words that individuals associate with success or danger should elicit enthusiasm or fear, respectively. Because political campaigns tend to target broad audiences, they must rely on emotional cues that correspond to fairly common and similar experiences within the population in question. Reliance on widely shared affective associations is especially important for television advertising, which is relatively indiscriminate in reaching large segments of the public.

Having said that, campaigns may use TV ads, as well as other forms of communication, with more specialized cues when targeting a particular group (e.g., working mothers, veterans, or Texans). The notion of targeted political messages is hardly new (West 2001), but the visual and musical "packaging" of ads should be as likely to reflect that targeting as the verbal message content. A particular set of cues may elicit an emotional response from one group but not another; it is also possible for the same cues to elicit distinct emotional responses from different groups. For example, images and sounds of an angry crowd chanting "no justice, no peace" in Los Angeles may evoke fears of racial discord and urban riots among whites, while evoking frustration and anger among blacks.

For general advertising purposes, political consultants can draw on an extensive cache of cues in their effort to appeal to enthusiasm or fear. For enthusiasm, they can place the ad against a backdrop of picturesque landscapes, familiar skylines, sunrises, beautiful neighborhoods, stately office buildings, national monuments, and flags. Scenes of people are likely to feature smiling faces, children playing, family togetherness, lovable animals, productive and satisfied workers, the purchase of new homes and cars, affectionate couples, men and women in uniform, weddings, and parades. For fear, consultants can utilize bleak and desolate landscapes, filth and pollution, buildings in disrepair, dark streets and alleyways, stormy weather, prisons, and the devastation of war. Scenes might include menacing faces, frightened children, loneliness, dangerous animals, victims of disease or war, acts of violence and crime, unemployed workers, terrorists or rival nations preparing for attacks, and symbols of death.

Psychologists have accumulated substantial evidence that pleasant and unpleasant images with these sorts of themes arouse the expected emotions (Bradley et al. 2001; Bradley, Cuthbert, and Lang 1996; Bradley and Lang 1999; Lang, Newhagen, and Reeves 1996; Patrick and Lavoro 1997). As we saw in chapter 2, political scientists have demonstrated that the emotional expressions of leaders can shape emotions in response to TV news (Sullivan and Masters 1988) and that pictures of cute or repulsive animals can influence emotional reactions to interest group flyers (Huddy and Gunnthorsdottir 2000). Colors also differ in their affective associations: dark colors like gray and black elicit negative emotions; bright colors, especially blue, green, and red, elicit positive emotions; and "neutral" colors such as brown and white elicit very few and balanced emotions (Hemphill 1996; Valdez and Mehrabian 1994). Although there is considerably less research on the emotional impact of sounds, evidence suggests that desirable and threatening noises (e.g., laughter, cheers, a crying infant, or gunfire) work in much the same way as pictures (Bachorowski and Owren 2001; Bradley and Lang 2000). Finally, people have long recognized music's ability to communicate and arouse emotions (Juslin and Sloboda 2001). Discordant music in minor keys can increase anxiety, while melodic passages in major keys can increase enthusiasm (Juslin 2000, 2001; J. Smith 1999).

Political consultants typically do not rely on a single type of imagery or choose between using imagery or music. Most of the time, their ads contain multiple cues with similar affective properties. Images, music, sound effects, and color not only fit the promising or threatening message of the ad, but also dovetail to send a consistent audiovisual signal. This increases the "volume" of the emotional appeal and provides greater assurance that an audience with diverse individual experiences will react with the same emotion. *Redundancy of cues* allows consultants to "more predictably gain access" to the emotions of viewers (G. Smith 1999).

Emotional Appeals in Campaign Advertising

The foregoing observations bring us at last to a series of hypotheses about the effects of emotional appeals on the motivation and choices of citizens. We can apply the understanding of emotional cues discussed above to predict the consequences of appealing to enthusiasm or fear with music and imagery in political advertising. For the purposes of this study, I define an *emotional appeal* as any communication that is intended to elicit an emotional response from some or all who receive it. First, I reiterate some of the prevailing notions of how emotional appeals influence viewers and then proceed to enumerate several hypotheses based on affective intelligence theory and the view of emotions presented in this chapter.

Conventional Explanations for the Impact of Emotional Appeals

We face a somewhat peculiar situation in trying to pin down the conventional wisdom on the impact of emotional appeals. On the one hand, as we saw in chapter 2, there is no shortage of observers who believe that political ads are designed to influence voters by arousing their emotions. On the other hand, there is no prevailing theory for explaining the impact of these efforts. Most social science proceeds from the presumption that a relationship does not exist until its existence has been scientifically demonstrated. This is the null hypothesis. In this case, it states that emotional appeals, regardless of whether they actually trigger emotional responses, should not be thought consequential for voting behavior because emotion itself is epiphenomenal or at best idiosyncratic in its effects. Nonetheless, this is not a satisfying alternative hypothesis in light of widespread belief that emotion matters.

Therefore, I formulate hypotheses based on the popular beliefs uncovered in the preceding chapter and try to give them some foundation in psychological theory or research.[25] First, some believe that positive and negative appeals work by "building up" the sponsor or "tearing down" the opponent. The *affect transfer* hypothesis states that political ads "transfer" positive or negative affect triggered by the music and images to the sponsor or opponent. In the same way that situations and objects become emotional cues through learned associations, citizens may associate candidates with positive or negative feelings aroused during ads.[26] The affect transfer hypothesis draws on the traditional ideas of approach and avoidance, emphasizing valence as the key dimension of emotionality. This notion has a strong grip on conventional thinking about advertising.

Second, some people stress the importance of emotional appeals in grabbing the attention of viewers and making the ad memorable. In other words, imagery and music primarily make an ad entertaining. The *entertainment value* hypothesis predicts that evocative images and music increase the intensity of the viewer's emotional experience and thereby increase the likelihood that she receives the ad's message. In this view, emotional appeals enhance effectiveness *not* because they trigger specific emotions, but because audiovisual cues make ads more interesting. This perspective stresses the second dimension of classic emotion theories: arousal. We might also see it stemming from the psychological view that certain stimuli are more attention-getting because of their inherent vividness. Research on arousal indeed finds that emotional or dynamic imagery in ads can increase viewer attentiveness (Geiger and Reeves 1991; Lang 1991). However, research has generated mixed results and little confidence in claims concerning vividness (Fiske and Taylor 1991; Frey and Eagly 1993; Iyengar and Kinder 1987).[27]

Cueing Enthusiasm, Fear, and Affective Intelligence

We can now articulate several hypotheses about the impact of emotional appeals based on the notion that certain types of cues trigger the specialized systems responsible for fear and enthusiasm. For the most part, we can see these hypotheses as extensions of the theory of affective intelligence (Marcus, Neuman, and MacKuen 2000) to the field of political communication.[28] Ads using music and images associated with success or desirable outcomes should elicit higher levels of enthusiasm. In contrast, ads using music and images associated with threat should elicit higher levels of fear.

The first set of hypotheses concerns the motivation to take part in the election either psychologically, as an engaged and concerned spectator, or physically, as a participant in political activities:

MOTIVATION HYPOTHESES: *Enthusiasm appeals should increase interest in the election campaign and the desire to participate in related political activities. Fear appeals have the capacity to increase the desire to participate as well as to encourage withdrawal from activities.*

In this regard, I part ways somewhat from proponents of affective intelligence theory, at least in their characterization of the evidence, if not the theory itself (Marcus, Neuman, and MacKuen 2000). I posit that enthusiasm appeals possess a broader, more universal power to motivate involvement, while the motivational impact of fear should be more circumscribed, albeit quite powerful at times. Fear appeals increase the readiness to take action in response to potential threats, but the prediction for actual behavior is more tenuous. People can respond to threats by distancing themselves from the threat or by acting to remove it. As discussed earlier, research on public health campaigns suggests that these divergent responses may depend on an individual's perception of competence or self-efficacy. The same body of research suggests that the impact of fear appeals is also moderated by response efficacy, or the perception of a reasonably evident course of action that might remedy the threat. In campaign advertising, this almost always comes in the form of recommending that the viewer vote for or against a candidate (Kern 1989).[29] Therefore, while the primary expectation about the impact of fear appeals on motivation for involvement is ambiguous, we can articulate a corollary prediction based on individual differences:

FEAR AND COMPETENCE COROLLARY: *Fear appeals are most likely to motivate the desire to participate among highly competent or efficacious citizens. In contrast, fear appeals are most likely to motivate disengagement from the election among citizens who lack such feelings of competence.*

The second set of hypotheses concerns the motivation to pay attention to the election campaign. Regardless of whether ads affect a broad desire to be involved, they may influence the desire to learn more about the candidates or issues. In this case, the clearest predictions concern appeals to fear:

VIGILANCE HYPOTHESIS: *Fear appeals should steer attention to relevant information.*

Although greater attention and searching for information do not necessarily lead to greater knowledge or improved memory, we might expect some positive correlation between the former efforts and the latter mental attributes.[30] There is little doubt that emotion can affect learning and memory, but the relationship has been more widely investigated for traumatic rather than everyday emotions (LeDoux 1996).[31]

A third set of hypotheses concerns the formation of preferences, evaluation of candidates, and political choice. The enthusiasm and fear systems promote distinct modes of information processing and judgment. Enthusiasm reinforces the value of present activities, while fear signals the need to rethink existing choices:

CONFIDENCE HYPOTHESIS: *Enthusiasm appeals should increase an individual's confidence in his or her "standing decision," while fear appeals should increase uncertainty about that decision.*

Furthermore, the two emotions trigger different ways of approaching the decision itself:

JUDGMENT HYPOTHESES: *Enthusiasm appeals should encourage loyalty to initial preferences and strengthen reliance on prior preferences and relevant predispositions (or heuristics) in political choice. Fear appeals should decrease reliance on prior preferences and relevant predispositions in political choice, while increasing reliance on new information and contemporary evaluations.*

One of the key differences in decisionmaking is the role of existing preferences and predispositions. As a result, we expect that an ad's impact on a viewer's evaluation will stem from an interaction between the type of emotional appeal and the viewer's prior commitments. Supporters and opponents will respond differently. This brings us to two corollary predictions that follow from the preceding hypotheses:

POLARIZATION COROLLARY: *By activating predispositions, enthusiasm appeals should polarize voters — attracting already supportive citizens to "rally behind" the sponsor of the ad and repulsing citizens who are inclined to oppose the sponsor further into the arms of his or her opponent.*

PERSUASION COROLLARY: *Fear appeals should increase the probability that an individual will change her or his mind consistent with relevant information in the environment and, thus, also increase the probability that she or he is persuaded by the message of the ad.*

The final hypothesis concerns individual differences in susceptibility to emotional appeals. Popular belief holds that politicians use emotional appeals to sway uneducated, disinterested, and poorly informed voters. Savvy citizens are shielded by their knowledge of politics and see through such manipulative efforts. Even political scientists have argued that affect is more likely to guide the least sophisticated members of the electorate (Sniderman, Brody, and Tetlock 1991; Sullivan and Masters 1988; but cf. Rahn et al. 1990). As much as this constitutes common sense in thinking about politics, it seems at odds with the psychological theories of emotion presented in this chapter. If emotions are triggered by "relevance detectors," then cueing emotions in a political context may have its largest effect on those for whom politics is most relevant. I propose that it is time to reconsider the conventional wisdom on this matter:

RELEVANCY HYPOTHESIS: *Emotional appeals are more likely to affect individuals for whom politics holds greater relevance, such as those who are more interested and knowledgeable about politics.*

In sum, activation of the enthusiasm (disposition) system should encourage pursuit of existing political goals, promote reliance on political habits, and motivate interest and participation in the election. Activation of the fear (surveillance) system should motivate attentiveness and a search for relevant information, suspend commitment to current goals, promote consideration of contemporary information, and increase the likelihood of persuasion. These predictions involve the central aspects of citizen behavior over which campaigns typically seek influence: interest and participation, attention and learning, candidate evaluation and choice. I now turn to testing the hypotheses.

4

Emotion and the Motivational Power of Campaign Ads

Campaigns must mobilize the less interested. . . . Before we attempt to take the pas-
sions and stimulation out of politics, we ought to be sure that we are not removing the
lifeblood as well. The challenge to the future of American campaigns, and hence to
American democracy, is how to bring back the brass bands and excitement in an age
of electronic campaigning.

Samuel Popkin (scholar, 1992)

The public's fickle attentiveness to politics is well documented (Delli Carpini and Keeter 1996; Ferejohn and Kuklinski 1990; Kinder 1998). When it comes to public affairs, the average U.S. citizen cares little, knows little, and participates little. This disinterested posture may well be rational in the ordinary course of democracy (Downs 1957). Walter Lippmann (1922) even admonished us to set aside as perverse our progressive expectations for a highly engaged citizenry. Such observations, however, have failed to deter a relentless wringing of hands at the low levels of participation that typify contemporary U.S. elections, especially local races, nomination campaigns, and off-year election cycles (Dalton and Wattenberg 1993; Patterson 2002; Powell 1986; Rosenstone and Hansen 1993; Teixeira 1992). Although election campaigns occasion high tides in the ebb and flow of political interest, those who wish to motivate greater interest and participation in elections have their work cut out for them.

Candidates may have the most direct stake in encouraging (or discouraging) citizens to get involved (Aldrich 1993). To win elections, a candidate needs voters: eligible citizens must find their way to the voting booth and choose him or her over the opponent. Therefore the primary goals of electioneering are motivation and persuasion (Arterton 1992). These two functions clearly operate in tandem, but they are also distinct (e.g., some people vote in every election but their support must be earned anew each time, while others remain steadfastly loyal to one party but must be convinced to show up on election day). In keeping with most research in political science, I discuss motivation and persuasion separately, in this chapter and the next.

We know a great deal about the personal characteristics and circumstances that promote political participation. Decades of research have revealed numerous long-term and short-term factors disposing citizens to participate. An individual's level of political activity stems in large part from the resources, skills, and motivations she possesses (Verba, Schlozman, and Brady 1995). These, in turn, are often shaped by social processes in such a way that political participation is linked to income and education (Wolfinger and Rosenstone 1980), religion (Leege and Kellstedt 1993), race (Dawson 1994), gender and occupation (Burns, Schlozman, and Verba 2001), and a socialized sense of civic duty (Verba and Nie 1972).[1]

As a result of the preceding body of research, we can make some pretty good guesses about who is and who is not likely to vote on Election Day. However, we know far less about what candidates can do, especially in the months and weeks before the election, to motivate (or demotivate) citizens. Candidates try to find ways to stir the interest of potential supporters and spur them to vote on Election Day. But this task is more difficult now than it was in earlier periods of American history, when the mass mobilization efforts of political parties were key to high levels of campaign activity and voter turnout (Aldrich 1995; Rosenstone and Hansen 1993). Progressive reforms have diminished the ability and incentive for parties to mobilize reluctant citizens (Schudson 1998). Some observers argue that an era of adversarial journalism and televised "ad wars" has made citizens even more reluctant to volunteer and vote (Patterson 2002; Putnam 2000). Today, candidates may find it difficult to motivate psychological, let alone actual, involvement in politics (Doppelt and Shearer 1999; Eliasoph 1998).

On top of all of this, some campaigns seek to depress turnout among the likely supporters of their opponent. Although the strategy is not especially new, the past decade has witnessed frequent allegations that one or another campaign is using tactics, including advertising campaigns, designed to turn voters away from the polls. Setting aside the serious ethical and legal issues, are such strategies a more viable way to win elections these days than the conventional mobilization approach? While this alternative tack may seem promising on a sea of political apathy, a strategy of demobilization might not offer candidates a better guarantee of smooth sailing. The typical citizen may be equally disinterested in either type of appeal and instead follow her habit. If some citizens are largely "unreachable" by political appeals in an era of mass-mediated politics, then campaigns may have to settle for motivating those citizens already disposed to get involved, what some call a "strategy of activation" (Schier 1999). If personalized contact and inducements facilitated high participation in the eras of mass party campaigns and machine politics (Aldrich 1995), then what, if anything, puts the capacity to motivate participation in the hands of candidates in an age of mass-mediated campaigns? Can they use their principal tool, televised advertising, to accomplish this goal and, if so, whom can they reach with these appeals?

While early research focused on the informational quality and persuasive power of political ads (Patterson and McClure 1976), a recent debate has flourished about how the tone of advertising affects turnout. In particular, scholars offer competing evidence and rationales to argue alternatively that negative advertising demobilizes (Ansolabehere et al. 1994; Ansolabehere and Iyengar 1995), mobilizes (Finkel and Geer 1998; Goldstein and Freedman 2002a), or does not affect the electorate (Lau et al. 1999). The debate remains unresolved, but further insight is likely to depend on clarifying what is meant by "negative" or "positive" advertising, as well as on attending to situational differences that may moderate the effectiveness of these advertising styles. Research on the motivational power of campaign ads to date has been dominated by a focus on advertising tone to the near exclusion of anything else. Although this chapter does not enter squarely into the debate on negative advertising, future elaboration and resolution of the controversy might benefit from understanding the contribution of emotion.

In this chapter, I test whether campaign ads can motivate popular involvement in elections by appealing to the emotions of viewers. *Affective intelligence* theory leads us to expect they can. I hypothesize that ads attempting to elicit enthusiasm by using cues associated with success and the "good life" will stir greater interest and participation in the election campaign. The expectation for ads attempting to elicit fear is less straightforward. Fear has the potential to motivate action, but it is also known to produce indecision or withdrawal. Previous research suggests that responses to fear may depend on personal characteristics, such that the individuals most likely to respond constructively are those who possess greater knowledge and confidence in the domain in which they are threatened. Therefore, I hypothesize that ads seeking to elicit fear by using cues of danger and conflict will increase participation primarily among citizens who are politically sophisticated. Finally, emotional appeals may have unintended consequences. Efforts to stir up enthusiasm or fear in connection with politics may boost or undermine, respectively, voters' faith in elected officials, political institutions, or even their own ability to make a difference.

Experimental Tests of the Effects of Enthusiasm and Fear Appeals

I set out to test the effects of emotional appeals by conducting a pair of experiments during an actual gubernatorial election. Scholars have used a wide range of methods to study media effects (Iyengar and Simon 2000; Kinder 2003). The utility of any particular method depends on the kinds of questions we wish to answer; each method offers a valuable perspective on the larger puzzle. My primary question in this book is whether politicians can influence the political behavior of citizens by cueing emotions in campaign ads. Experiments are the best method for testing such causal relationships (Kinder and Palfrey 1993; Lupia 2002). They permit stronger causal inferences by allowing the researcher to rule out potential confounds through tight control over conditions and random assignment of subjects to exposure.

Experiments are especially appropriate for the study of emotion in political communication (Glaser and Salovey 1998; Isbell and Ottati 2002). Emotions, properly conceived, are not characteristics individuals possess once triggered, but rather are temporary responses to an external stimulus, which in turn determine the nature of a person's response to that stimulus. Because emotions are short-term responses that often escape awareness, their effect on attitudes occurs "on-line" (i.e., as information is perceived and processed; see Lodge, McGraw, and Stroh 1989), making it difficult to discern their contribution once they have subsided. For this reason, observation in close proximity to when emotions are triggered is desirable.

The Setting: Presenting Participants with a Real Choice

I situated the experiments during an ongoing state election. Although contrived conditions offer researchers considerable freedom in setting the parameters of an experiment (Lau and Redlawsk 1997; Lupia and McCubbins 1998), I wanted to pose meaningful choices to subjects in order to more faithfully reconstruct the process by which citizens make up their minds (Ansolabehere and Iyengar 1996). In such cases, the effects of new information are realistically constrained by prior knowledge about the candidates and the full interplay of predispositions. When asked about an election in which they must soon decide whether to vote and for whom, subjects are more likely to treat the questions seriously and offer a sincere response.[2]

Tying the experiments to a real, ongoing election has an additional advantage for a study of emotion. Recall that emotions like fear and enthusiasm are defined as responses to the relevance or meaning that external stimuli hold for an individual. Subjects may think a fictitious candidate *could* worry or excite them, without necessarily experiencing these emotions. A choice between actual candidates and the reality of an approaching election ensure that campaign ads have the potential to elicit genuine emotions.[3]

I situated the experiments in the context of the 1998 Democratic primary race for governor in Massachusetts.[4] Several candidates had their eyes on the nomination, but two well-known politicians dropped out before the campaign really got going. Congressman Joseph Kennedy bowed out in 1997 after a number of personal and family scandals came to light. Ray Flynn, the flamboyant former Mayor of Boston, switched over to the crowded race for the Eighth Congressional District in the spring of 1998. However, Scott Harshbarger, the incumbent attorney general, led each of these candidates in the polls prior to their departure. While the absence of Kennedy and Flynn did not necessarily affect the outcome of the primary, it may have diminished some of its interest for the public and the press. Although others competed, the race primarily pitted Harshbarger against Patricia McGovern, a prominent former state senator. Harshbarger won the primary decisively and voter turnout was reported to be just over 26 percent. Taxes, a budget surplus, and education were the main issues of the season. By the middle of summer, education had become *the* central issue of the year, spurred on by the failure of over half the state's teachers to pass a new statewide competency exam.

Given the presence of a primary contest and the likelihood of a competitive general election, the campaign was impressively lackluster.[5] Verbal exchanges between the candidates were constrained by a minimum of substantial policy differences. All was fairly quiet on the advertising front as well. The Republican candidates sniped the summer away in a series of negative ads for their primary, and the ten-candidate race for the Eighth District dominated Boston airwaves. In the Democratic gubernatorial primary, however, only Harshbarger ran ads for much of the summer, ads aimed primarily at his anticipated opponent in the fall. McGovern had less money and finally aired two different ads in the closing weeks of the campaign. Even though many voters were unlikely to have strong opinions about the candidates, polls showed little movement during the campaign.

As a result, the 1998 gubernatorial primary provides a fairly favorable context in which to observe campaign effects. If candidates can ever sway the electorate, then they ought to be able to do so in an election without incumbency, without an unbeatable frontrunner, and without entrenched commitments. However, with a strong economy, declining crime rates, and (relatively) colorless candidates, the conditions are considerably less ripe for stirring emotions. Thus, compared to circumstances in which ads tap deeply rooted sentiments such as partisanship or racial resentment, this election offers a fairly demanding test case for the ability of campaign ads to elicit enthusiasm, fear, or any other emotion.[6]

The Sample: Recruiting Real Voters

In line with my desire to provide a meaningful choice to participants, I also decided not to rely on college students, but rather to seek out a diverse sample of potential voters. I set eligibility requirements to match those of the Massachusetts electorate: subjects had to be residents of the state, U.S. citizens, and eighteen years of age or older. However, participants were free to come with friends, spouses, or children.

With the help of several assistants, I conducted the experiments over the last ten weeks of the primary campaign, from early July until September 15. We set up thirteen research locations in eleven communities of eastern Massachusetts (see appendix A). Research sites were open on Saturdays and Sundays, as well as weekdays, and during morning, afternoon, and evening hours. We recruited subjects in a variety of ways. Some read announcements in community newspapers or heard them on local radio stations. Others came across signs posted in public places near the research sites and saw them taped in the windows of local businesses. During busy periods at lunchtime and at the end of the business day, we distributed flyers to pedestrians. A few subjects scheduled appointments but most simply walked in off the street. Flyers, signs, and announcements invited people to participate in a study of "news and public opinion," but there was no mention of campaign ads.

Over the course of the summer, we recruited 286 eligible subjects.[7] While the subjects did not constitute a random sample of the population, they closely resembled the electorate in a number of ways and reflected a broad range of the population. To achieve such diversity, I chose research sites that ranged from upper-class suburbs like Wellesley, where 74 percent of residents had a college degree and enjoyed a median household income of $79,100, to working-class Lowell, where only 35 percent were college-educated and the median income was $29,400. Subjects themselves represented an even broader set of fifty towns and cities, from the old mill town of Lawrence to the resort communities of Falmouth and Hyannis on Cape Cod. The average subject was slightly poorer but better educated than the typical Massachusetts resident.[8]

The sample closely matched the state population in gender balance, racial composition, and median adult age (see appendix A). On other dimensions, the sample cut a broad swath through the population. Although most held jobs outside the home, nearly a third of participants were retired, unemployed, disabled, enrolled in school, or self-described homemakers. Workers were employed in administrative work (13 percent), sales and service (12 percent), education (6 percent), business professions (6 percent), or legal and medical professions (7 percent), while the remainder worked in a variety of skilled and unskilled trades. One in four subjects had children under the age of eighteen. The sample consisted mainly of "locals": the median participant had lived in the state for twenty-five years, and only 20 percent had lived there five years or less.

Finally, the sample mirrored the skewed political dispositions for which Massachusetts is well known. Based on the standard National Election Stud-

ies (NES) measure of party identification, 46 percent of the sample were Democrats, 9 percent were Republicans, and 45 percent Independents or
third-party identifiers. We can compare this to the party enrollment of registered voters: 38 percent of registrants were Democrats, 13 percent were
Republicans, and 49 percent "unenrolled" with a party. Although registration is not strictly the same as self-identification, the similarity of the two
distributions suggests that the partisanship of the sample and the population were not far apart.[9]

The Procedure: Incidental Exposure to Campaign Ads While Watching the News

Participation in the experiments involved three stages. When a subject arrived at one of the public libraries, meeting halls, churches, or other buildings that served as sites for this study, one of my assistants or I welcomed her
and confirmed her eligibility. The subject signed a consent form and received assurances that her answers would remain confidential. We then es-
corted the subject into a room, invited her to take a seat at a table, and
handed her a questionnaire. She could read on the first page that the purpose of "The Study of Press, Politics, and the Public" was to learn what different people take away from television news.[10] In filling out this *pretest*
questionnaire, the subject answered questions about her background, news
consumption, knowledge of politics, issue positions and priorities, attitudes
about politicians, party identification, and economic views. Only a small
number of questions, however, asked about the election.[11]

Once the subject signaled that she had completed the questionnaire, we
led her to a different room and invited her to take a seat on one of the chairs
or couches arranged around a television set. We selected a videotape at random and inserted it into the VCR,[12] informing the subject that the tape contained part of a local news program that had been recorded earlier that summer and saying that we would return in twelve to fifteen minutes when the
tape was over. We then pressed play and left the room. Sitting alone or with
others, the subject watched the first half of the 6 P.M. news broadcast by
WCVB-TV (Channel 5), the Boston ABC affiliate.[13] She heard reports on
controversy over the retirement age for state police officers, the release of a
sex offender from prison, the incumbent governor's response to sex offender
release laws, the arrest of a student who threatened to explode pipe bombs
at his high school graduation, and a lawsuit against actor Woody Harrelson
for punching a paparazzi photographer. During a commercial break, she
saw ads for Boston Market, Maxwell House, and Toyota. In most cases, she
also saw a campaign ad in support of either Scott Harshbarger or Patricia
McGovern sandwiched between the coffee and the car commercials. She
then watched news reports on a restaurant smoking ban in Boston, the U.S.

Navy's decision to scrap plans for allowing the U.S.S. *Constitution* to sail on tour, and mention of a new scholarship program for elementary school students that would be covered more fully later in the broadcast.

When the news segment ended, we brought the subject back to a table in the first room and asked her to fill out another questionnaire. The *posttest* began by inviting the subject to recall in her own words the news stories she had seen, to identify any issues she would like to hear more about, and to reflect on the current and future course of the country. The subject then answered the remaining questions about interest in various types of TV news, name recognition and attitudes for a number of public figures, trust in various institutions, beliefs about politics, plans to participate in the election, and evaluations of the candidates. When that was done, we thanked the subject for participating, paid her in cash, debriefed her about the true purpose of the research, and showed her to the door.[14] The typical subject spent between forty and sixty minutes participating in the study.[15]

I designed the procedures to reflect, as much as possible, the manner in which citizens come across political ads in their everyday lives. People usually see campaign ads, like other commercials, as a by-product of turning on their TV to watch something else, such as the news, a sporting event, or a favorite show. I simulated the incidental nature of exposure by focusing participants' attention on the news and saying nothing about ads. This aspect of the design heightens realism not only because it prevents an unnatural focus on the ad itself, but also because the ad delivers its message amid a stream of other related and unrelated information. In addition, participants saw campaign ads promoting and attacking real candidates who were currently competing for political office in the state. They answered questions about real choices they faced as eligible voters in a matter of weeks or even days.

Finally, although subjects were not in their own homes, they watched TV in comfortable rooms without the supervision of researchers. They were free to read, write, talk, or even sleep during the video. For better or worse, some subjects exercised their freedom liberally. Friends, family, and coworkers watched TV together and chatted during both the news and commercials.[16] Parents tried to watch while keeping track of their children, who played with toys, drew pictures with crayons, or ran about the room. At least one older gentleman dozed during a portion of the tape. Efforts to mitigate artificially high attentiveness were perhaps too successful at times. A grueling summer of data collection reached its height of folly one afternoon in Lowell. Two women, a senior citizen and an unemployed thirty-something, arrived separately but were shown in to watch TV together. Afterward, the younger woman hurriedly finished the second questionnaire, collected her money, and left. A short time later the older woman approached the researchers with a concerned look. She had arrived at the final page of the questionnaire and found several questions about TV ads (see the manipulation check below). She whispered, "I'm not sure what you want me to do, but that other woman got up and fast-forwarded through the commercials." We had unexpectedly discovered the experimental equivalent of a kitchen or bathroom break.

The Stimuli: Manipulating Emotion via the Visual and Musical Cues in Campaign Ads

In order to test the impact of specific emotional appeals, I varied exposure to campaign ads that had been specially created for this study. Each subject saw only one of these ads or none at all, and the experimental conditions differed only in terms of which ad was embedded in the news program. My goal in designing the ads, or *experimental stimuli,* was to manipulate the extent to which they targeted a specific emotion in voters (i.e., fear or enthusiasm). How did I achieve this? Earlier studies found it impossible to establish whether differences in the impact of "emotional" (versus "rational") political arguments stemmed from the use of emotional language or from the fact that this language produced a higher quality argument (Bauer and Cox 1963; Hartmann 1936; Roseman, Abelson, and Ewing 1986). In this study, therefore, I sought to manipulate the emotionality of the ad without changing its informational content or the quality of its verbal argument. I accomplished this by packaging the same script (narration) with two different sets of audiovisual cues, one set chosen for its potential to evoke the emotion in question and the other chosen for its relatively unevocative nature. By comparing ads in which only the nonverbal features differ, we can avoid the pitfalls of earlier research. Although the verbal message may also be capable of evoking emotion, we only risk understating the total impact of emotion by treating the script as a baseline.[17] This approach has another virtue: it mirrors the way in which real-world consultants use music and imagery to heighten the emotional impact of a political ad (see chapter 2).

Although I carried out the experiments simultaneously, you should think of them as two distinct but related tests in order to keep the relevant comparisons clearly in mind when we get to the results. The first experiment tested the impact of cueing enthusiasm and the second tested the impact of cueing fear. Each experiment required different baseline scripts, because there had to be a reasonable fit between the message of the ad and its audiovisual cues. Enthusiasm-evoking cues only make sense with a script that has a generally positive message, whereas fear-evoking cues are plausible only with a generally negative message.[18] Therefore, ads in the two experiments were distinguished by the valence or tone of the message. Within each experiment, then, the critical test came in manipulating the emotionality of imagery and music. The enthusiasm experiment set up a comparison between two ads in which the narrator claims progress on education and safety bode well for children. One of the ads contained hopeful imagery and music designed to amplify its enthusiasm-eliciting potential, the other ad contained less evocative imagery that did little to enhance the emotional power of the message itself. The fear experiment set up a comparison between two ads in which the narrator claims crime and failing schools threaten children. One of the ads contained menacing imagery and music designed to magnify its fear-eliciting potential, while the other ad contained less evocative imagery unlikely to have strengthened the emotional force of the message.

Even though the experimental tests are distinct, we may wish to compare how fear and enthusiasm cues alter the effectiveness of their respective scripts. In order to make such comparisons more tenable, I designed the ads in both experiments to be as similar as possible in all other ways. The ads followed a similar narrative structure: the narrator first put a positive or negative spin on the status quo and then contrasted the strengths of the sponsor to weaknesses of the opponent. Thus, all ads in this study were "comparison spots" that included elements of both attack and self-promotion. Scripts varied in the extent to which they emphasized crime or education, though all of the ads contained references to crime, drugs, and children. For fairness and balance, each of the two candidates was portrayed as the sponsor of roughly half of the ads. Otherwise identical versions promoted Harshbarger or McGovern by switching the names of the sponsor and opponent. This also allows us to examine more fully the interaction between advertising exposure and initial preferences. For any given emotional cue manipulation, ads contained identical music and imagery regardless of sponsor or issue emphasis.

I produced the ads using a state-of-the-art digital editing lab.[19] As a result, the production value of the ads was comparable to the quality of ads being aired in local and statewide races at the time.[20] Award-winning journalist Marvin Kalb provided the narration for the ads.[21] What did the ads look like? Figure 4.1 provides a sense of what was seen and heard in the enthusiasm experiment by showing a sample script along with several visual scenes from each version of the ad.[22] If we were to watch the less evocative ad (left side of the figure), we would see a series of images, each fading slowly to black before the next one appears. We would pass slowly through a sequence of scenes that includes an aerial view of a New England town, a brick school with an empty schoolyard, young children playing soccer, the Massachusetts statehouse, a school bus being driven up a road, a brick public building, and another shot of the statehouse. We would see few people and would be unable to make out their faces or expressions. The colors are dull or muted like an overcast day, and there is no music but rather silence under the narrator's voice.

If we were to watch the more evocative ad appealing to enthusiasm, we

FIGURE 4.1 Script and Visual Images for Campaign Ads in the Enthusiasm Experiment

Less Evocative Visual Images	Positive Script	Hopeful Visual Images
	There's good news in your neighborhood. The future looks bright for a generation of young people.	
	The threat of violence and drugs is being erased.	
	Children are better protected from crime than ever before.	
	While Scott Harshbarger pursued tougher sentences for violent criminals, Patricia McGovern opposed them.	
	While Scott Harshbarger led efforts to protect our children, Patricia McGovern did nothing.	
	Scott Harshbarger's record has been praised by law enforcement officials.	
	Massachusetts needs a governor like Scott Harshbarger.	

would hear the identical narration but this time with music and a dramatically different set of images (right side of figure 4.1). The ad opens on a playground where children are sliding, swinging, and climbing, as the camera shows numerous close-ups of smiling faces. Next we would see children run out of a school underneath a sign that reads "Drug Free School Zone," while another set of children is pledging allegiance to the flag in their classroom. In the final sequence, a smiling girl lets go of three brightly colored balloons in a sunny green meadow, and the balloons sail over a well-groomed neighborhood as young boys play baseball in the yard. These scenes are bathed in bright colors, and the camera lens is adjusted to make the images look soft and warm. We would hear the sentimental, stirring symphonic music of John Williams in a "Hymn for New England," performed by the Boston Pops.

Figure 4.2 displays a sample of what we would see and hear in the fear experiment. The unevocative imagery is the same as in the other experiment. For the fear appeal, however, we would see and hear something quite different. The camera cuts rapidly from scene to scene, opening with images of police officers who have their guns drawn and who escort hand-cuffed suspects while sirens flash. We would then see drugs on a table, the door of a jail cell slamming shut, and paramedics lifting a covered stretcher into an ambulance. Next, we would witness a woman entering her apartment door only to be attacked from behind by a hooded intruder who drags her inside. After this, teenagers sell drugs near a school, a boy turns in surprise on an empty schoolyard, the camera zooms on a lit crack pipe and then pans down a desolate street. Finally, we would see a close-up of a revolver being fired, a police car racing up an urban street, and a gavel swinging down as the narrator concludes. The images, mostly in black and white, have a grainy texture. From the outset, we would hear high-pitched, dissonant instrumental chords pulsating beneath the narration.[23]

Manipulation Check: Did the Ads Cue the Intended Emotions?

The music and images in the experimental ads are very similar to those commonly used by consultants. In chapter 6, evidence from recent ad campaigns confirm that the same sorts of cues appear in actual ads that observers judge to be appealing to enthusiasm or fear. In fact, I collected most of the visual scenes from product ads or campaign ads that had been used in other elections. For example, many of the scenes of children with drugs are from Bob Dole's presidential campaign in 1996. Classroom images had appeared in the 1992 reelection campaign of President George H. W. Bush. I pulled some of the crime scenes from Pete Wilson's gubernatorial ads in California and the happy playground images from a local race in the same state.

But did the ads elicit the intended emotions? The study did not take

FIGURE 4.2 Script and Visual Images for Campaign Ads in the Fear Experiment

Less Evocative Visual Images	Negative Script	Fearful Visual Images
	It's happening right now in your neighborhood. A generation of young people is in danger.	
	Violence and drugs threaten to destroy their future.	
	More children are victims of crime than ever before.	
	Scott Harshbarger supports tougher sentences for violent criminals. Patricia McGovern opposes them.	
	Scott Harshbarger has a plan to protect our children. Patricia McGovern has no plan.	
	McGovern's record has been criticized by law enforcement officials.	
	Massachusetts cannot afford a governor like Patricia McGovern. Vote for Scott Harshbarger.	

direct measures of emotional response at the time of viewing, because this would have compromised both the realism for which I was striving and my ability to mask the purpose of the study.[24] In order to obtain a check on the validity of the manipulations, however, the study employed *cued recall:* on completion of the posttest, we asked subjects whether they had seen an ad and, if so, the extent to which it made them feel anxious, excited, and hopeful. These questions cannot reliably measure the mediating emotional response (i.e., the actual emotions generated by the ad that in turn caused changes in attitudes and behavior), because they were asked *after* the attitudinal and behavioral questions the emotions are hypothesized to influence. However, the cued recall questions can tell us whether subjects saw the ads as distinct in their emotional intensity.[25]

Figure 4.3 shows the mean values of each emotion across treatment conditions. Looking only at the fear experiment, menacing music and imagery strengthened reactions of fear and anxiety to the negative message ($t = 1.91$, $p < .030$). Looking only at the enthusiasm experiment, cheerful imagery and music produced a stronger reaction of hope and excitement to the positive message ($t = 1.34$, $p < .093$). Comparing responses across the two experiments, fear ads elicited the highest levels of anxiety ($F = 4.82$, $p < .003$), and enthusiasm ads elicited the highest levels of both hope ($F = 5.61$, $p < .001$) and excitement ($F = 2.69$, $p < .048$). There is also little doubt, when compared directly to one another, fear and enthusiasm ads cued distinct levels of anxiety ($t = 3.62$, $p < .001$), hope ($t = 3.32$, $p < .001$), and excitement ($t = 2.71$, $p < .004$). In short, the ads seem to cue the intended emotions, adding to our confidence in the internal validity of the experimental tests (i.e., the ads differ in ways consistent with the inferences we wish to draw by comparing experimental groups).

How Appeals to Emotion Affect the Desire to Get Involved

The remainder of this chapter considers the effect of advertising appeals on the extent to which individuals become psychologically caught up in an election, as well as on ways people may choose to get involved in the election by volunteering or voting. We know that levels of self-reported political participation and self-expressed willingness to participate are notoriously inflated by Americans' desire to appear to be "good citizens." The purpose of this study, however, is not to estimate actual levels of participation, but rather to monitor short-term changes in motivation. The impact of social desirability on overestimating one's likely participation should be constant across the experimental conditions. In addition, we can take advantage of pretest measures to use a person's initial predisposition toward involvement as a baseline in order to observe individual-level change more precisely.

FIGURE 4.3 Self-Reported Emotional Reactions to the Campaign Ads

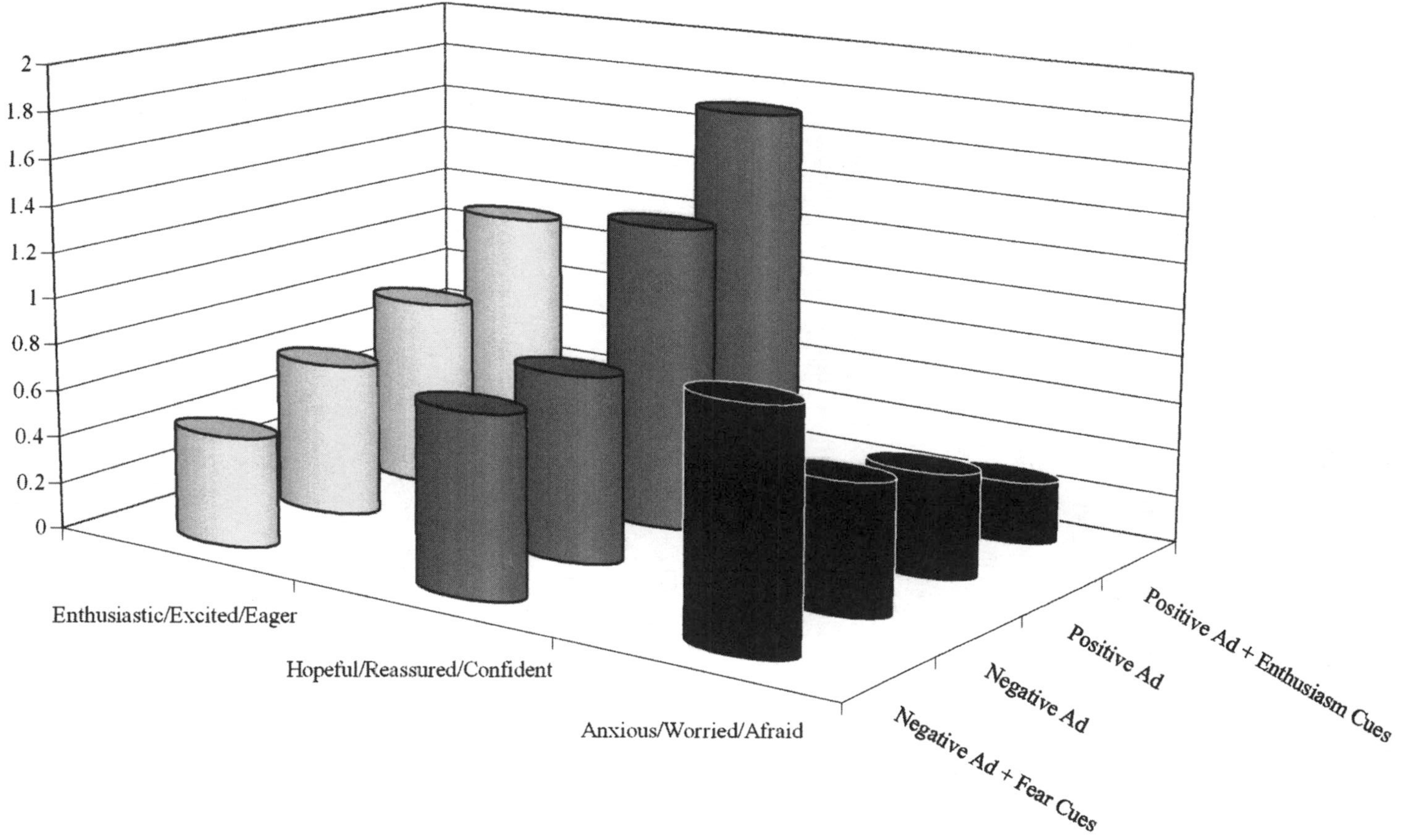

Note: Values are the mean responses on 5-point (0–4) scales. Emotional reactions were solicited as subjects completed their participation in the study. The values shown here are based only on the responses of those who correctly recalled seeing a campaign ad and who tried to recall their reactions to it. N = 185.

The First Look: Direct Experimental Comparisons

Let's first compare the differences in motivation across experimental groups. I begin with interest in the campaign. Participants, on average, described themselves as somewhere between "moderately" and "quite" interested in following the election campaigns that year (3.4 on a seven-point scale). Figure 4.4 displays the mean levels of interest across the advertising conditions. As predicted, those who saw enthusiasm-evoking ads reported greater interest in the campaign than those who saw an identical positive ad with less evocative cues ($t = 2.45, p < .008$).[26] A combination of uplifting music and colorful images seems to have drawn viewers into the campaign more effectively than the positive message alone could do. In contrast, fear cues apparently had no effect on interest in the campaign. The mean response of subjects exposed to negative messages remained identical even when tense music and harsh images were added.

Keeping citizens interested is a worthy goal, but campaigns often wish to encourage more active forms of participation such as volunteering to help with the election effort. We know that only a small share of Americans get involved by donating their time and energies to campaigns (Verba, Schlozman, and Brady 1995). On average, participants in this study reported that they were "unlikely" or "very unlikely" to volunteer on behalf of the candidate. Only 15 percent claimed they were likely to volunteer, while another 10 percent said there was only a "50/50 chance" they would pitch in. These percentages are broken down by experimental condition in figures 4.5a and 4.5b (leftmost set of columns). Willingness to volunteer jumped nearly ten percentage points with exposure to enthusiasm-eliciting cues. This substantial increase mirrors the boost to campaign interest, though it falls shy of statistical significance in this case ($t = 1.36, p < .088$). Fear cues produced a modest six-percentage-point rise in motivation to join a campaign, though the difference relative to the less emotional ad falls well short of significance ($t = 1.03, p < .153$).

For politicians, what matters most is what transpires on Election Day. I now turn to how advertising appeals affect intentions to vote in the primary and general elections. Feelings of civic duty seem to attach most firmly to general elections, and the ritual of November's Election Day helps to reinforce the habit of voting in many citizens. Party primaries tend to see far lower levels of voting, but they also show greater variation in turnout, suggesting campaigns and competition play a larger role. If nothing else, primary elections offer candidates and their campaigns even more room to improve on baseline levels of voting. Participants in the study reported their intention to vote in both the primary and general election. I treat the respondent as genuinely likely to vote only if she claims she "definitely will

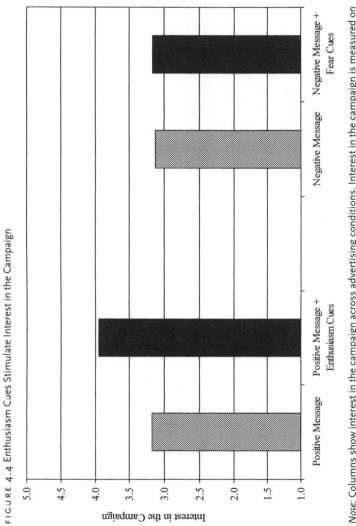

FIGURE 4.4 Enthusiasm Cues Stimulate Interest in the Campaign

Note: Columns show interest in the campaign across advertising conditions. Interest in the campaign is measured on a scale from 1 to 7.

FIGURE 4.5A Impact of Enthusiasm Cues on Motiviation to Participate in the Campaign and Election

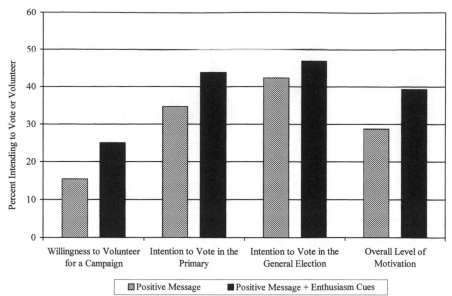

Note: Columns show the percentage of subjects reporting a willingness to volunteer for an election campaign, the percentage intending to vote in the primary or the general election, and the overall level of motivation, across advertising conditions. Overall level of motivation is an additive scale that combines intentions to vote, willingness to volunteer, and interest in the campaign (weighted equally) and has been rescaled here from 0 to 100.

vote," in an effort to compensate for gross overreporting. By this measure, 37 percent were likely to vote in the primary, while 48 percent were likely to turnout for the general election.[27] Once again, motivation levels appeared higher after exposure to enthusiasm-evoking music and images (see figure 4.5a). Forty-four percent of participants in the enthusiasm condition were likely voters in the primary, compared to 34 percent of participants in the baseline positive condition. This is an impressive boost in turnout intentions from a single ad, yet there is high enough variation that the difference fails to reach acceptable levels of significance ($t = 1.00, p < .161$). The story is similar for the more modest five-percentage-point increase in voting intentions for the general election. In the case of fear cues, figure 4.5b shows a four-point increase in likely voters for the primary and a three-point drop for the general election. Neither difference is significant.

To this point, we have seen a familiar pattern recur for interest, vote intentions, and willingness to volunteer. When enthusiasm cues are added to a positive ad message, the motivation to get involved—psychologically or

FIGURE 4.5B Impact of Fear Cues on Motivation to Participate in the Campaign and Election

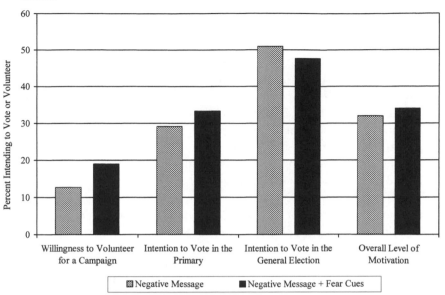

Note: Columns show the percentage of subjects intending to vote in the primary or the general election, the percentage reporting a willingness to volunteer for an election campaign, and the overall level of motivation, across advertising conditions. Overall level of motivation is an additive scale that combines intentions to vote, willingness to volunteer, and interest in the campaign (weighted equally) and has been rescaled here from 0 to 100.

physically—rises by a moderate to substantial amount. However, there is sufficient statistical leverage in only one of the four cases to be truly confident in the effect. Mindful of the larger pattern, we can check whether this general uptick in motivation merits greater confidence. For this purpose, I combine all four measures of involvement that have concerned us so far into a summary scale of overall motivation, which is reflected in the final pair of columns in figures 4.5a and 4.5b. Given that the new scale is simply a linear combination of the original items, the substantive results are not surprising: we see no effect from fear cues and a healthy increase from enthusiasm cues. However, in this case, the impact of enthusiasm on the overall level of motivation is significant ($t = 1.84, p < .034$).

For most citizens, the cardinal political act is voting. Civic norms imbue voting with a special status, generating social pressure to fulfill this "obligation" in a society that otherwise emphasizes political freedoms over responsibilities. Many more citizens claim to vote than actually do, and they often cite civic duty as the reason for their political participation. Groups rely on

appeals to civic-mindedness, as well as self-interest, to exhort potential voters to register if they have not. Having seen evidence that advertising appeals can stimulate interest and perhaps inclinations to vote, we might ask
if these appeals can promote the *belief* that voting is important. Although
this belief is clearly related to voting intentions (r = .39 to .51, depending on
the voting measure used), an inclination to take action is distinct from the
belief that one is obliged to take action. This sense of duty was measured by
a participant's agreement with the assertion that "people should vote whenever there is an election." The legacy of the Progressives is alive and well, as
83 percent of participants agreed with the preceding statement and over
half strongly agreed.

Emotional advertising appeals can influence the belief that people
should vote, but the exact results are somewhat different from those we have
seen so far. Subjects seeing an enthusiasm ad scored the highest level of
agreement of any group in the study, 4.45 on the five-point scale, but this is
only slightly, and insignificantly, higher than subjects who viewed a positive
ad with less evocative cues (4.35). However, for the first time, we see clear evidence of an effect for fear. Belief in the importance of voting increased from
4.04 to 4.38 when fear-evoking music and images were added to a negative
ad (t = 1.79, p < .038).

As a final check on the motivational power of emotional appeals, I turn
to what is undoubtedly a "hard case" for campaign advertising—namely,
encouraging voter registration among those who are not already registered.
The prevalence of registration requirements in most states is seen as one of
the major obstacles to voting in the U.S. (Powell 1986; Teixeira 1992). Most
citizens who are not registered can be safely classified as habitual nonvoters. Mobilizing them requires substantially more effort than motivating
registered voters, because it not only requires the added step of registration
but also requires mobilizers to convince those who, in many cases, are the
least disposed to vote among the entire electorate. Few regard this as a task
that can be accomplished through televised advertising; instead, it is left to
labor-intensive, face-to-face "registration drives" conducted by political
parties, unions, and interest groups.

Not surprisingly, most participants in the study claimed to be registered,
while only 23 percent confessed they were not. Those who admitted not being on the rolls were asked how likely they were to register before the election. Their answers were arrayed on a seven-point scale from "definitely
will not register" to "definitely will register." In keeping with their apparently higher-than-usual honesty for self-reports, 51 percent said they were
unlikely to register for the 1998 election and another 22 percent gave themselves only a "50/50 chance" of doing so. Nonetheless, given the serious motivational and structural barriers involved, I am inclined to regard any effect

more as a change in the recognition or feeling that one should act than as a reliable indicator of future action. However, stoking such feelings could be the first step toward eventual registration, for example if further encouragement or pressure were applied.

Can campaign ads influence the inclination to take that step? We cannot yet say so with confidence. In each case, there was a modest increase (a distance of roughly 0.2 to 0.3 on the seven-point scale) in intentions to register when either type of emotional cues was added to its respective baseline, but the changes are far from significant. Any shift would indeed need to be at least five times larger to show up as statistically significant given the small sample of sixty-seven unregistered subjects. Perhaps our confidence should be bolstered by how well it fits with everything else we have seen. As it turns out, further evidence later in this chapter will help to illuminate the relationship between emotional appeals and motivating unregistered citizens.

The Second Look: Multivariate Estimation

A first look at the evidence suggests a consistent pattern in which enthusiasm cues motivate greater involvement, but the effects in some of these cases are not large enough relative to individual variation to yield confident findings. As I mentioned earlier, we have the option of assessing the net impact of emotional appeals more precisely by taking account of an individual's preexisting disposition to get involved. In other words, we can estimate the impact of emotional appeals on motivation while controlling for a subject's answers on the pretest questionnaire. By holding constant an individual's proclivity to vote before seeing the ad, we can incorporate the logic of "within subjects" analysis (i.e., observing individual change) into our "between subjects" analysis of differences across groups.

Let me make a brief aside before proceeding with the analysis. At this point, some people, call them "experimental purists," are likely to ask "What's with all the multivariate hocus pocus?" Other people, including many political scientists, are just as likely to say "Finally, he's getting to the *real* results." The former group may rightly observe that the power of experiments, with controlled manipulation and random assignment, comes from allowing direct comparison and obviating the need for multivariate analyses meant to deal with potential confounds and selection problems. Indeed, results can be presented in a straightforward, easy-to-understand manner without the concerns about colinearity and endogeneity that complicate multivariate estimation. Why muddy the waters? Others, who have been raised on regression analysis and are often uncomfortable with experiments, may worry about what lurks behind all that simplicity.[28] By virtue of its very randomness, random assignment does not always distribute predisposing factors evenly across experimental groups; in fact, we should *expect* this to occur for some factors in any given study simply by chance! Such concerns aside, others may simply wish to improve the precision of estimated effects by taking into account other sources of variation, especially when we know a good deal about what produces that variation at the individual level.

I present both kinds of evidence in this chapter. I obtained pretest measures to allow for this sort of analysis, and closer inspection reveals that some predisposing factors (e.g., education) are not equal across all groups. Consistency across the two sets of results can only increase our confidence that we understand what is happening, at a small cost in redundancy. If inconsistencies arise, then readers will be able to choose for themselves which type of analysis they trust more. For my part, I prefer to see which relationships emerge most consistently and clearly across different modes of analysis. Researchers almost always know this about their data; to the extent practical, readers should too. Now, let's move on to the multivariate results.

I revisit each of the six main dependent variables discussed in the preceding section—interest in the campaign, intention to vote in the primary and general elections, willingness to volunteer for a campaign, belief in the importance of voting, and intention to register to vote.[29] For the multivariate analysis, I use a single estimation for the entire sample to obtain greater statistical power and because the relationship between the predisposing and dependent variables is presumed to be the same across experimental groups.[30] The equations include separate binary or "dummy" variables for each experimental manipulation, indicating, for example, whether a subject was exposed to fear cues and whether she was exposed to enthusiasm cues.[31] I use a seven-point scale of general voting intentions from the pretest as the main indicator of a subject's initial disposition.[32] The remaining predisposing factors consist of basic demographic factors, including education, income, gender, religion, occupation, and age.[33] I also control for two aspects of a subject's participation in the experiments—namely, the number of viewing companions who watched at the same time and the proximity (number of weeks) to the primary election. Finally, given the focus on stirring-up emotions, I control for the initial mood of participants based on a simple checklist administered at the start of their participation. Descriptions of the measures are in appendix A, and full results for the estimations are in appendix B.

Table 4.1 displays the *estimated* effects of enthusiasm and fear cues on each measure of political involvement. Overall, the results strengthen the patterns observed for mean group differences. Appeals to enthusiasm tend to stimulate greater involvement in the election across a number of measures, while appeals to fear also appear to have motivational power, though on a more limited basis. The single clearest effect is still for campaign inter-

TABLE 4.1 Effects of Emotional Cues on Interest in the Campaign, Motivation to Participate, and Belief in the Importance of Voting

Dependent Variables	Enthusiasm Cues	Fear Cues
Interest in the campaign	0.64***	−0.03
	(0.21)	(0.20)
Willingness to volunteer for a campaign	0.60**	0.45*
	(0.25)	(0.24)
Intention to vote in the primary	1.39**	0.35
	(0.53)	(0.48)
Intention to vote in the general election	0.87*	−0.12
	(0.53)	(0.48)
Agree that people should vote	0.17	0.33*
	(0.18)	(0.17)
Intention to register to vote	1.12*	0.07
(among those not registered)	(0.64)	(0.59)

Note: Entries are coefficients (and standard errors). Each row represents a separate estimation. The table displays the marginal effect of emotional cues on interest, participatory motivation, and belief in the important of voting, controlling for the advertising exposure and individial predispositions. Full results, including control variables, are in tables B.1 and B.2 in the appendices. $N = 286$, except for intention to register, for which $N = 65$.

***$p < .001$ **$p < .01$ *$p < .05$

est.[34] Enthusiasm cues noticeably excited interest in the campaign, moving psychological engagement a distance of roughly 10 percent of the scale on average.[35] Fear cues had no impact on interest.

For willingness to volunteer, the boost from both types of cues that was visible in the mean differences reappears with greater clarity. Appeals to enthusiasm showed a considerable potential to attract volunteers. We can translate the raw statistical results shown in table 4.1 into something more meaningful, such as the probability of participating.[36] The predicted probability that a subject is willing to volunteer increased by twelve percentage points when hopeful music and images were combined with the positive message of the ad. A subject's probability of saying she is willing to consider it ("50/50 chance") increased by slightly over six percentage points. Fear appeals also seemed to encourage a readiness to donate time, though the impact was not quite as pronounced as that of enthusiasm. In this case, the willingness to volunteer rose by over eight percentage points and the probability of giving it a "50/50" chance went up five percentage points.

The estimated effects of emotional appeals on intentions to vote also echo the earlier findings. Fear cues had no effect, but enthusiasm cues were extremely powerful, increasing the probability of intending to vote in the primary by twenty-five percentage points. The effect on general election voting intentions was slightly less but still substantial at twenty percentage points.[37] We also observe a much larger and clearer effect for intentions to register. Because the number of unregistered subjects is small, I use an abbreviated model for estimation composed only of the advertising variables, pretest voting inclinations, and a measure of political efficacy.[38] Enthusiasm cues stimulated the desire to register by over one full point on the six-point scale. In all, the boost to motivation from an enthusiasm-evoking campaign ad appears broad, extending across several measures and even spilling over to influence motivation levels for the general election as well as the primary.

Earlier we observed that fear cues had a significant effect on the extent to which a subject agrees that voting is a civic imperative. The multivariate analysis confirms that fear ads can strengthen belief in the importance of voting by 0.33 on the five-point scale. This is a modest increase compared to some of the other effects, but it is important to keep in mind that this belief is already so widely shared that there is not much room for improvement. In fact, the average subject was only 0.75 away from maximum agreement, so the effect of the fear appeal was equivalent to closing half of the remaining distance.

Before exploring any further, let us review the evidence on the motivational power of campaign ads. First and most importantly, enthusiasm cues exhibit the motivational power predicted by psychologists and the theory of affective intelligence. The effects are pretty consistent regardless of how we analyze the data, but they are usually stronger when we control for initial predispositions. The warm images and music reinforcing the campaign ad's message of a safe, improving community and a hopeful, confident candidate ignite viewers' desire to get involved, both as observer and participant. Enthusiasm's expected impact is substantial. Fear too has the potential to motivate, albeit less broadly. The harsh images and tense music, underscoring the campaign ad's message of communities at risk, spark greater willingness to donate time to election efforts and solidify belief in the importance of voting.

Knowing *and* Caring: Who Responds to Emotional Appeals?

Having tested the principal hypotheses on how emotional appeals affect motivation, I now turn to the possibility that not all citizens are equally responsive to these appeals. Specifically, I want to ask whether political "experts" respond differently from political "novices" (Fiske, Kinder, and Larter 1983). In asking who responds (more or less) to emotional appeals, there are many places for us to look for differences. However, there are at least three compelling reasons to examine whether political sophistication matters for the influence of emotion in campaign advertising.

First, there is a long tradition of dividing citizens into "classes" based on the depth of their knowledge and the sophistication of their beliefs regarding politics. Dividing Americans into categories according to their interest in, aptitude for, or awareness of politics appeared in early studies of election campaigns (Lazarsfeld, Berelson, and Gaudet 1944). But it is most strongly rooted in the work of Philip Converse (1964), who launched an extended debate within political science over the extent to which mass public opinion is well-informed, thoughtful, and ideological. He concluded these standards applied only to a thin stratum of American society. The forty years of reinforcement and revision are no doubt familiar to many readers of this book. Regardless of where one stands in the debate, its enduring legacy is the routine division of Americans, for purposes of analysis, into the more and less politically sophisticated. Moreover, there is now a considerable body of research showing that political sophistication shapes political cognition, or how people think about politics and especially how they process political information (Lau and Sears 1986; Lodge and McGraw 1995; Zaller 1992).

The second reason to examine this distinction is that it is a core element of conventional wisdom about emotional appeals (see chapter 2). Many reporters, consultants, and ordinary citizens believe that emotions hold dominion primarily over those lacking education, knowledge, or intelligence. Such claims rest comfortably on the old, but now contested, distinction between dispassionate rationality and emotion as superior and inferior guides, respectively, to human behavior (Damasio 1994; Marcus 2002). While not endorsing this extreme view, some scholars have based their models of political decisionmaking in part on the notion that less sophisticated citizens are more likely to rely on emotional considerations when making decisions (Redlawsk and Lau 2003; Sniderman, Brody, and Tetlock 1991).

The third reason is that psychological perspectives on emotion, discussed in chapter 3, lead us to expect that some individuals will respond differently to emotional appeals. On the one hand, the *fear and competence* corollary grows out of a recognition that researchers have observed mixed reactions to fear among humans and other animals: some take decisive action to confront the threat and others freeze up or withdraw. Scholars studying fear appeals in public health have proposed that feelings of efficacy play a role in determining which response prevails (Witte 1998). They argue that individuals with expertise or confidence in a particular domain respond more constructively to anxiety-inducing information and are likely to withdraw in the face of fear. On the other hand, psychological theories of emotion, despite the considerable work done on fear, have said little about the notion of individual factors that moderate responses to fear-evoking stimuli. They instead have emphasized the fundamental role emotions play in signaling the significance that stimuli or situations hold for the individual. This insight serves as the basis for the *relevancy* hypothesis, which holds that emotional appeals in campaign ads should have their greatest impact on those who see politics as most relevant. I propose this includes people who are the most involved in and knowledgeable about politics.

While providing an impetus to pursue the role of political sophistication, these various strands of work leave us with sharply contrasting expectations. The analyses so far have rested on the assumption that the effects are universal. One might characterize psychological research broadly as saying that emotion, as a basic facet of human psychology, should hold all citizens within its grasp. I treat the proposition that emotion appeals affect everyone equally as the *null* hypothesis. One could read the main body of public opinion work as simply anticipating *some* difference between more and less sophisticated citizens. Drawing on the work of Converse (1962, 1964, 1990), however, we could push the implications farther to argue that citizens who are typically "unreachable" with political information are also likely to be unreachable with political emotion. Likewise, those who have the greatest cognitive investment in politics should have the greatest emotional investment and be most responsive to emotional appeals. This view is consistent with the relevancy hypothesis, based on the idea that emotions are tied to the significance objects and events hold for an individual. Researchers studying fear appeals in other domains arrive at a similar prediction, but with distinct predictions about the direction of effects for different individuals. According to the *fear and competence* hypothesis, anxiety throws settled plans into disarray and can therefore make decisive action less likely, but those with greater competence are the most likely to see a way to resolve the situation and be motivated to take action accordingly. Finally, research that has explicitly considered how political sophistication affects reliance on emotion leads us to predict the opposite (Sniderman, Brody, and Tetlock 1991): politically sophisticated citizens should be less responsive to emotional appeals. This expectation also fits well with the conventional wisdom, sketched in chapter 2, that those who are poorly informed are most susceptible to emotional "manipulation," that arguments are wasted on them, and that winning over the "crowd" is simply a matter of playing to their emotions.

With these hypotheses in mind, we can now revisit the relationships uncovered in the preceding sections in search of different responses to emotional cues among political experts and novices. One can think about political sophistication in a multitude of ways (Luskin 1987). For this study, I conceive of it in terms of political awareness: a sophisticated citizen is in touch with the happenings of the political world, understands how politics works, and can thus put political information in perspective. This conceptualization fits well with claims about who is more and less susceptible to efforts at emotional manipulation. For simplicity, I rely on a measure of political knowledge to differentiate subjects as relatively less or more sophisticated. Participants are divided into two groups according to their answers to three factual questions about state politics.[39] I classify participants who failed to provide any correct answers as political novices or less sophisticated (55 percent) and those who provided one, two, or three correct answers as political experts or more sophisticated (45 percent).[40]

In testing the hypotheses, I repeat both the difference of means tests and the multivariate analyses in an effort to provide the reader with as much information as possible. For the means tests, I simply split the sample and perform the tests separately on each subsample and observe where significant differences emerge. For the multivariate analysis, I run the same estimations as before but include the dummy variable for sophistication and an interaction term of this variable with each advertising condition in the model (e.g., sophistication × enthusiasm cues).[41]

What should we see in the multivariate case? If the null hypothesis were true (i.e., emotional appeals work the same on everyone), the baseline emotional cues variable should have an impact but not the interaction term. If only experts are responsive, then the interaction term should show an effect in the predicted direction but not the baseline term. If only novices are more responsive, then the baseline term should show an effect and the interaction term should show a roughly equal effect in the opposite direction (i.e., essentially canceling the baseline effect).

Tables 4.2 and 4.3 display the results for enthusiasm cues and fear cues, respectively. On the left half of each table, we see the difference of means tests from both the original analysis of the entire sample and the new split-sample analysis. On the right half, we see the estimated effects of emotional cues from both the original multivariate analysis and the new analysis that includes interactions between emotional cues and political sophistication. I include the original results as a point of reference to aid our judgment about what is a substantial effect. We would expect the standard errors to grow in most cases simply as a result of splitting the sample between those with less and those with more knowledge about politics. Therefore, in judging whether both groups are equally responsive to a particular set of emotional cues earlier found to be significant, I rely primarily on the effect size relative to the original, full-sample effect.

When we consider the impact of ads appealing to enthusiasm (table 4.2), the evidence on differential responsiveness is divided in favor of two hypotheses. The more prevalent pattern seems to support the relevancy hypothesis: knowledgeable individuals are more responsive to the emotional version of the ad than individuals who know less about politics. The energizing effect of enthusiasm cues on willingness to volunteer, intention to vote in the primary, and intention to register appears to be contingent on

TABLE 4.2 Responsiveness to Enthusiasm Cues by Level of Political Sophistication

	Difference of Means Tests (Split Sample)			Multivariate Test (Interaction Effects)		
Dependent Variables	Difference in the Entire Sample	Difference for Subjects with Less Political Knowledge	Difference for Subjects with More Political Knowledge	Effect in the Original Model	Baseline Effect of Emotional Cues	Marginal Effect of Cues for Knowledgeable Subjects
Interest in the campaign	0.78**	0.50^	0.51	0.64***	0.58*	0.10
	(0.32)	(0.34)	(0.47)	(0.21)	(0.29)	(0.41)
Willingness to volunteer for campaign	0.19^	−0.21^	0.55**	0.60**	−0.33	1.57***
	(0.14)	(0.15)	(0.24)	(0.25)	(0.41)	(0.52)
Intention to vote in primary election	0.09	−0.05	0.11	1.39**	0.50	1.54^
	(0.09)	(0.10)	(0.14)	(0.53)	(0.78)	(1.02)
Intention to vote in general election	0.05	−0.01	−0.04	0.87*	0.81	−0.23
	(0.09)	(0.11)	(0.13)	(0.53)	(0.74)	(1.07)
Belief in importance of voting	0.11	0.05	0.01	0.17	0.21	−0.13
	(0.18)	(0.28)	(0.20)	(0.28)	(0.24)	(0.35)
Intention to register to vote	0.18	−0.75	3.17*	1.12*	0.45	2.31^
	(0.82)	(0.88)	(1.41)	(0.64)	(0.72)	(1.49)

Note: Entries for the left half of the table are differences in the means (and standard errors) between experimental conditions with and without emotional cues for (1) the entire sample, (2) subjects who have less knowledge about politics, and (3) subjects who have more knowledge, respectively. (Enthusiasm effects = mean of enthusiasm condition − mean of positive condition.) Entries for the right half of the table are coefficients (and standard errors) from multivariate estimation for (1) the impact of emotional cues in the original model, (2) the baseline effect of emotional cues in the interactive model, and (3) the effect of the interaction between emotional cues and political sophistication (i.e., more political knowledge). The models are the same as presented in table 4.1, except for the inclusion of a dummy variable for political knowledge and its interaction with the advertising conditions.

***$p < .001$ **$p < .01$ *$p < .05$ ^$p < .10$

TABLE 4.3 Responsiveness to Fear Cues by Level of Political Sophistication

Dependent Variables	Difference of Means Tests (Split Sample)			Multivariate Test (Interaction Effects)		
	Difference in the Entire Sample	Difference for Subjects with Less Political Knowledge	Difference for Subjects with More Political Knowledge	Effect in the Original Model	Baseline Effect of Emotional Cues	Marginal Effect of Cues for Knowledgeable Subjects
Interest in the campaign	0.03 (0.28)	-0.42 (0.38)	0.64* (0.39)	-0.03 (0.20)	-0.04 (0.27)	0.02 (0.41)
Willingness to volunteer for campaign	0.13 (0.12)	0.01 (0.16)	0.28^ (0.19)	0.45* (0.24)	0.35 (0.32)	0.28 (0.48)
Intention to vote in primary election	0.04 (0.09)	-0.18* (0.10)	0.34** (0.13)	0.35 (0.48)	-0.37 (0.76)	1.25 (1.03)
Intention to vote in general election	-0.03 (0.09)	-0.29** (0.11)	0.31** (0.12)	-0.12 (0.48)	-1.06^ (0.63)	2.22* (1.05)
Belief in importance of voting	0.34* (0.19)	0.02 (0.26)	0.77** (0.27)	0.33* (0.17)	0.13 (0.22)	0.47^ (0.34)
Intention to register to vote	0.34 (0.76)	-0.29 (0.80)	3.67^ (1.88)	0.07 (0.59)	-0.42 (0.67)	3.03* (1.51)

Note: Entries for the left half of the table are differences in the means (and standard errors) between experimental conditions with and without emotional cues for (1) the entire sample, (2) subjects who have less knowledge about politics, and (3) subjects who have more knowledge, respectively. (Fear effects = mean of fear condition − mean of negative condition.) Entries for the right half of the table are coefficients (and standard errors) from multivariate estimation for (1) the impact of emotional cues in the original model, (2) the baseline effect of emotional cues in the interactive model, and (3) the effect of the interaction between emotional cues and political sophistication (i.e., more political knowledge). The models are the same as presented in table 4.1, except for the inclusion of a dummy variable for political knowledge and its interaction with the advertising condition s.

***p < .001   **p < .01   *p < .05   ^p < .10

higher levels of political expertise. The impact on primary voting intentions is still clearly visible only in the multivariate analysis, but the effects on volunteering and registering are clear in both analyses. In the case of willingness to volunteer, there is also the hint of a polarizing effect of sorts, in which enthusiasm cues actually have a negative impact on the least knowledgeable, but the evidence is fairly tenuous on this point.

The pattern looks quite different, however, in two other cases. The power of enthusiasm cues to stimulate both interest in the campaign and the desire to vote in the general election appears to be universal. The evidence is extremely clear in the case of campaign interest. The strong effect observed in the full sample reemerges equally for both political experts and novices: effect sizes are 0.50 and 0.51, respectively, in the difference of means tests and 0.58 and 0.68, respectively, in the multivariate analysis.[42] A similar pattern of equality appears in the case of general election voting intentions, though evidence for the overall relationship between enthusiasm and general election voting comes only from the multivariate analysis. This set of findings supports the null hypothesis that responsiveness to emotional appeals does not depend on the sophistication of the viewer. Finally, there remains no evidence to suggest that enthusiasm appeals affect belief in the importance of voting.

An even clearer pattern in favor of the relevancy hypothesis emerges for ads appealing to fear (table 4.3). In the original difference of means tests at the beginning of this chapter, there was little evidence of the motivational power for fear appeals, aside from a positive impact on the belief that people should vote. Now, in the split-sample analysis, there is evidence that fear appeals have a broad power to motivate citizens who are knowledgeable about politics. Among more informed subjects, there are indications of an increase in *every* measure of political involvement. Results from the multivariate analysis point in the same direction but are not as strong, with solid evidence in support of the hypothesis in only half of the cases. There is even suggestive evidence, at least where intentions to vote are concerned, that fear causes political novices to withdraw from the general election, even as experts are inspired to act.

The strength and clarity of the findings for fear appeals varies across the measures of involvement. Evidence that fear cues stimulate the desire to vote in the general election, the desire to register, and a belief in the importance of voting among those who are more politically sophisticated is robust across the two modes of analysis. In the case of general election voting intentions, the negative effect on less sophisticated citizens holds up in both the difference of means and multivariate analyses. Difference of means tests yield evidence of a positive impact of fear on campaign interest and primary voting intentions among more knowledgeable subjects, but the evidence of the same effects is slight (in the case of voting intentions) or nonexistent in the multivariate tests. Finally, the original multivariate analysis revealed that fear cues increase the willingness to volunteer. However, the two new tests leave a divided verdict on who is more influenced in this way. According to the difference of means split-sample test, those more informed about politics respond positively to the fear-evoking version of the ad. According to the multivariate interaction test, the effect appears to be universal or "additive," meaning both groups respond but experts respond more strongly than novices. The evidence is not clear enough for us to draw a confident conclusion about differential responsiveness in the case of willingness to volunteer.

Overall, this investigation strongly suggests that political sophistication does affect responsiveness to emotional appeals. Moreover, the prevailing pattern is one of greater sensitivity on the part of politically savvy citizens. In eight of the eleven cases in which enthusiasm or fear cues show any signs of having a motivational effect, the effect exists exclusively for those who know more about politics. In short, the preponderance of the evidence favors the relevancy hypothesis. In the three remaining cases, the motivational effect appears universal or additive in nature, boosting the involvement of both less and more knowledgeable citizens. In a few cases, there are also signs of a demobilization effect from emotional appeals among political novices but, in contrast to what we might expect from previous research and the fear and competence hypothesis, there is some evidence of withdrawal in the face of both enthusiasm and fear appeals. Contrary to conventional wisdom, the investigation fails to turn up a single shred of evidence to suggest that less knowledgeable citizens are the most easily swayed by emotional appeals.[43]

In sum, the legacy Philip Converse has left for research on political information and cognition can now be extended to political emotion. He described a world in which political "haves" possess reliable psychological links to public affairs and political "have nots" largely lack them. In the results presented here, we see evidence of a world in which some people are "plugged in" to politics and therefore can be moved by appeals to emotion, while others are mostly "unplugged" and thus difficult to reach with such appeals. This notion is further supported by contemporary perspectives on emotion in psychology, which emphasize the role of emotions as indicators of the personal significance for an individual of another person, object, or situation. Knowing *and* caring seem to go hand-in-hand after all.

Do Emotional Appeals Have Civic Side Effects?

To this point in the chapter I have tested the impact of emotional appeals on the sorts of behavioral inclinations political campaigns typically try to influence. Consistent with theoretical predictions, enthusiasm appeals have broad power to motivate involvement in elections and fear appeals have more circumscribed powers of motivation. But what about other, unintended effects on political engagement? Perhaps, by appealing to these emotions, politicians unwittingly affect the confidence voters have in themselves, in others, or in public officials. The proliferation of campaign "air wars" featuring negative ads, attacks on opponents, emotional "manipulation," and similar tactics has generated substantial concern about the potential side effects for the citizenry and democracy (Ansolabehere and Iyengar 1995; Jamieson 1996; Kamber 1997). These concerns have grown amid broader worries about the poisonous consequences of that archvillain, the mass media (Sabato 1991; Patterson 1993; Putnam 1995; Bennett 1996; Lichter and Noyes 1996; Cappella and Jamieson 1997; Fallows 1997; Dautrich and Hartley 1999). In this final empirical section of the chapter, I investigate whether the effects of emotional appeals spill over to feelings of efficacy, cynicism, and trust.

Unlike participation and interest, we do not have clear theoretical predictions about the effects of enthusiasm and fear appeals on these civic attitudes. Prior research on the theory of affective intelligence has been silent on the issue (Marcus, Neuman, and MacKuen 2000). However, if enthusiasm reinforces commitment to and confidence in a person's pursuits, then we can hypothesize that ads appealing to enthusiasm boost feelings of competence (i.e., efficacy) in political affairs. The simpler notion of affect transfer might lead us to expect that appeals to enthusiasm or fear generate correspondingly positive or negative feelings about not only the candidates, but also the government and politicians in general. The broadest set of predictions stems not from a theory at all, but rather from conventional wisdom and the popular complaints cited above. From this point of view, politicians' efforts at emotional manipulation, especially their use of fear tactics, fuel rising levels of distrust, cynicism, and alienation from politics.

Scholars distinguish between two types of political efficacy: *internal,* a person's sense that she is competent enough to make a contribution, and *external,* her feeling that the government or leadership is responsive to the contributions she might try to make. I measured participants' feelings of efficacy by their agreement with the following two assertions: "Sometimes politics and government seem so complicated that a person like me can't really understand what's going on" (internal); and "People like me don't have any say about what the government does" (external). The evidence supports the sole prediction from affective intelligence theory: when ads appeal to enthusiasm, citizens feel more competent in dealing with politics ($t = 2.11, p < .019$). When campaign ads "prey on the fears" of citizens, however, there is no discernible effect. As figures 4.6a and 4.6b show, the evidence fails to support the other hypotheses. Contrary to the notion of affect transfer, the two emotional appeals do not push the belief that one has a say in the actions of government in opposite directions. Neither "preying on fears" nor appealing to

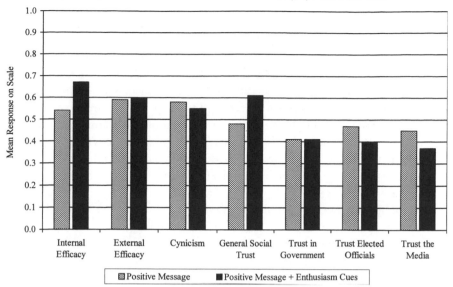

FIGURE 4.6A Impact of Enthusiasm Cues on Political Efficacy, Cynicism, and Trust

Note: Columns show the mean response on each scale by advertising condition. All variables have been rescaled to range from 0 to 1.

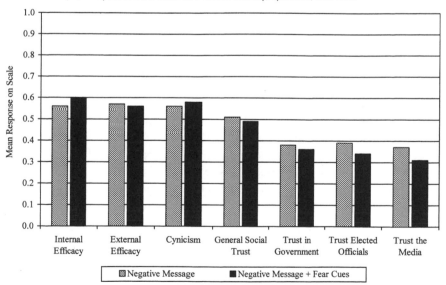

FIGURE 4.6B Impact of Fear Cues on Political Efficacy, Cynicism, and Trust

Note: Columns show the mean response on each scale by advertising condition. All variables have been rescaled to range from 0 to 1.

emotions generally conforms with popular expectations by increasing alienation or feelings of incompetence.

What about cynicism regarding the self-interested versus public-minded
motivations of politicians and political parties? I measured cynicism as a
scale that combines subjects' views on whether politicians and parties truly
care about their opinions and about the motives behind negative campaigning and public service in general.[44] Neither enthusiasm nor fear appeals affect cynicism about politicians, lending little support to conventional wisdom or the notion of affect transfer. If we examine the components of the
scale separately, we find similar results. The lone exception is suggestive evidence that enthusiasm appeals decrease cynicism as to whether public officials care what "people like me think" ($t = 1.48, p < .071$), which we could
regard as consistent with the notion of affect transfer.

Subjects answered a number of questions about the extent to which they
trust others, the government, elected officials, and the media. We again see
suggestive evidence in favor of affect transfer in the form of higher social
trust among those exposed to enthusiasm-evoking ads ($t = 1.38, p < .084$). In
contrast, conventional wisdom appears borne out by the fact that enthusiasm appeals diminish trust in the media ($t = 1.73, p < .04$) and, more tenta-
tively, elected officials ($t = 1.55, p < .06$). Evidence that fear appeals reduce
trust in the media, which would be consistent with both views, falls shy of
significance ($t = 1.28, p < .10$). There are no effects on trust in government.
In the end, neither hypothesis receives support in even half of the trust-
related tests.[45]

Evidence on the potential side effects of emotional appeals is weak and
decidedly mixed. I find support for the one theoretical prediction we can
make here: ads appealing to enthusiasm strengthen feelings of self-efficacy
regarding politics. For the much broader set of predictions related to affect
transfer or conventional wisdom, I find a scattering of results that are alternatively supportive and contradictory, and that range between barely and
not quite statistically significant. Overall, we ought to remain skeptical
about claims that emotional advertising brings woe or weal for civic attitudes until more conclusive evidence is before us. From this study, I can only
conclude that any residual harm or benefit from emotional appeals does not
spill over as much as it trickles down onto civic attitudes.

The Thirty-Second Brass Band?

In this chapter, I set out to investigate the capacity of campaign advertising,
and emotional appeals in particular, to stimulate interest and involvement
in politics. Experimental evidence demonstrates that exposure to advertising can exert a substantial influence on the political motivation of citizens.

As predicted in chapter 3, emotion plays a critical role. I conclude the chapter with a brief effort to put the principal findings in perspective.

Neuropsychological views of emotion specify distinct roles for enthusiasm and fear in governing behavior, but both have potential consequences for motivation. Signs of success trigger enthusiasm, which reinforces the desire to continue present pursuits and remain involved in the successful activity. Signs of danger trigger fear, which suspends current activities and focuses attention on the threat at hand. As a result, fear may stimulate action to address the threat or induce withdrawal when the path to resolution is unclear. Experimental evidence on emotion in campaign advertising supports these predictions.

Appeals to enthusiasm, cued with colorful scenes of children and stirring symphonic music, exhibit broad motivational power. Of six avenues by which participants could express a greater interest or commitment to getting involved, enthusiasm cues had a strong stimulating effect on four and suggestive effects on one of the others. These "feel-good advertisements," as consultants call them, provide a substantial boost to interest in the campaign, willingness to volunteer, and intentions to vote in both the primary and general election. In some cases these ads primarily demonstrate the ability to "activate" those already plugged into politics, but in other cases they show a deeper power for universal mobilization.

Appeals to fear, cued with dark scenes of violence and tense, discordant music, also have the potential to provoke involvement. The motivational power of fear cues seems narrower, arousing mostly those who are politically savvy. While the effect of fear is relatively weak in shaping such central aspects of involvement as interest in the campaign and intention to vote in the primary, it seems to work best in inspiring more dramatic action—increasing the willingness to donate time and prompting the unregistered to consider registering to vote. Fear ads also strengthen involvement in the two ways that left the least room for improvement: intentions to vote in the general election and belief in the importance of voting.

The short-term impact of these emotional appeals is hardly trivial; they rival the longer-term impact of social and political predispositions. We can confidently answer the question asked at the beginning of the chapter: candidates *can* use television advertising to achieve goals of political motivation. Emotional cues, especially enthusiasm, provide candidates with a powerful instrument for motivating more citizens to get involved in the campaign.

Are emotional appeals in campaign advertising the new brass bands for an age of electronic electioneering? Perhaps. Instead of waving posters in time to a rousing rendition of "Happy Days Are Here Again" at the local armory, we may find ourselves humming along to a symphonic score and the prospects of "Morning in America" from the living room. But these engaging campaign ads could turn out to be a weak substitute when one takes leave not just of the old band, but also the social camaraderie of the local rally. The emotional "half-life" is longer when the enthusiasm is shared by the crowd (Hatfield, Cacioppo, and Rapson 1994). While an electronic parade can march through 10 million homes, the road to resolving problems of collective action may be harder when starting from the Lazy-Boy recliner.

Although the evidence in this chapter does not offer guaranteed relief for turnout troubles, the findings are instructive about the process of political motivation. They tell us much about why parties and candidates used brass bands at all, as well as what the hoopla of the glory days of party politics and the hoopla of contemporary media politics have in common. We can begin to clear a place for the emotional dimensions of politics in our scientific understanding of politics. In fact, we can go where few political science theories have gone before to identify an explicitly motivational component to political action (see Verba, Schlozman, and Brady 1995; Fiorina 1999).

The evidence in this chapter also suggests potential sources of confusion in the present debate over negative advertising and thereby avenues for clarification. This study distinguishes positive and negative emotion from positive and negative information. Effects might well depend on whether an ad is "negative" because it attacks the opponent, emphasizes the failure of those in power, offers a gloomy view of conditions, or warns of a threat to the individual or community. As demonstrated earlier, fear ads actually have the potential to increase participation. In fact, theories of emotion predict that demobilization is more likely to be a consequence of cueing failure and disappointment than triggering fear.

Finally, experiments uncover causal relationships and their *potential* impact, but other methods and types of data, or even experiments extended over time, are required to learn about the duration and marginal effectiveness of emotional appeals. Clearly ads can affect motivation for better or worse in the short term, and candidates usually air advertising campaigns (not single advertisements) in order to sustain some of these effects. Such clues about causation do not tell us everything we need to know about the net effects of a real advertising campaign, but they are essential in equipping us to investigate those net effects with fewer tenuous assumptions about the connections we observe at the macro level. The results presented here testify—in a way only experiments can—that attempts to elicit enthusiasm, and sometimes fear, in political communication can motivate citizens. We are now ready to leave the topic of political motivation and turn to the role of emotional appeals in changing minds.

5

Emotion and the Persuasive Power of Campaign Ads

[P]ersuasion may come through the hearers, when the speech stirs their emotions. Our judgments when we are pleased and friendly are not the same as when we are pained and hostile. . . . [A]n emotional speaker always makes his audience feel with him, even when there is nothing in his arguments.

Aristotle (340 B.C.)

Political scientists remain ambivalent about the susceptibility of the American electorate to persuasion. The disillusioned consensus on participation, discussed in chapter 4, suggests a mass of voters whose weak grasp on public affairs leaves their minds pliable to political arguments, but whose low interest leaves their minds nearly unreachable by political appeals. When voters attend to politics at all, they rely overwhelmingly on partisan habits and well-worn criteria to choose a candidate, disregarding much of what campaigns have to say. If campaigns are instruments of communication designed to persuade and motivate citizens (Arterton 1992), and the attainability of these goals is in question, then why are so many resources expended, especially by the losers? Researchers have amassed considerable evidence on how voters make up their minds, but know far less about what politicians can do to change their minds. This chapter examines how candidates use emotional appeals to persuade citizens.

How do voters choose a candidate? No field of political science is more voluminous than research on the opinions and choices of the mass public. Early studies feared widespread gullibility in the face of mass-mediated propaganda, but concluded that campaigns principally reactivate deeply seated loyalties (Berelson, Lazarsfeld, and McPhee 1954; Lazarsfeld, Berelson, and Gaudet 1944). Political scientists have come to regard party identification as the most central of these predispositions (Campbell et al. 1960;

Converse 1969; Green, Palmquist, and Shickler 2002; Miller and Shanks 1995). Subsequently, many scholars have explained elections in terms of rational defections and swing votes that are motivated by economic conditions and government performance (Fiorina 1981; Erikson, MacKuen, and Stimson 2002; Key 1966). Working from these distinct perspectives, scholars have enriched our sense of political choices with an inventory of other ingredients. Political judgments are flavored by predispositions such as ideology, values, and group prejudice (Kinder 1998; Sniderman, Brody, and Tetlock 1991), by group identities (Conover 1984; Dawson 1994), by evaluations of policy positions (Aldrich, Sullivan, and Borgida 1989; Brody and Page 1972; Page and Shapiro 1992), and by assessments of candidate personalities (Kinder 1986; Rahn et al. 1990).

This list of factors does not leave much room for short-term changes, but rather implies electoral choices that are largely set before an election begins in earnest. What then is the role of campaigns? Some argue that campaigns merely increase awareness of such "facts" as the record of the incumbent or health of the economy and reacquaint voters with familiar choices (Gelman and King 1993; Zaller 2000). In other words, campaigns do matter, but only to help voters reach the decision clever modelers knew, well in advance, they would reach (Campbell and Garand 2000; Lewis-Beck and Rice 1992).[1] In these models, by the time the campaign season begins, voters are largely preconvinced, with a preexisting algorithm for making a choice; all they need is to be reminded of what matters. Candidates serve mainly as holders of issue positions, personalities, and political offices, by which they can be judged. This line of research leaves in doubt what candidates can do, if anything, during the election season to change voters' minds. Can they use campaigns, and television advertising in particular, to persuade citizens to support them?

Researchers face serious obstacles in documenting the consequences of campaigns and political communication generally, because the task often requires picking out subtle signals from a world of noise using less than ideal data. Nonetheless, scholars have recently made promising headway. Several influential studies document the effects of *information,* especially mass-mediated messages, at a broad level (Alvarez 1997; Bartels 1988, 1993, 1996; Popkin 1994; Zaller 1992). Although they leave uncertain what is in the hands of candidates, the studies show how the content and volume of information across political environments, including different election campaigns, shapes opinions and choices. Researchers also have found evidence that major events like debates and party conventions, as well as repeated campaign stops, may have a lasting impact on voters (Herr 2002; Holbrook 1996). Experimental work in political communication has finally uncovered hard evidence that political ads can affect voting decisions (Ansolabehere and Iyengar 1995), though the ensuing debate on negative advertising casts doubt on when or how often they have such effects (Lau et al. 1999). Recent advances in data collection have even opened up the possibility that we may be able to isolate better the effects of entire advertising campaigns (Goldstein and Freedman 2002a, 2002b).

At the same time, a new wave of research on emotion, highlighted in chapter 3, has suggested that it's not just the information that matters, it's what you do with it. These studies argue that emotional aspects of political communication and the emotional responses of citizens can alter how citizens process new information, form political attitudes, and make political choices (Huddy and Gunnthorsdottir 2000; Kinder and D'Ambrosio 2000; Lodge and Taber 2000; Marcus, Neuman, and MacKuen 2000; Way and Masters 1996b). This research offers hope for both resolving tensions between rational and partisan models of political choice and explaining the significance of different approaches to campaign politics. Marcus and colleagues (2000) argue that heterogeneity in the basis of voting choices and campaign styles may depend on affective intelligence, or the extent to which the current political environment elicits enthusiasm or anxiety from citizens. They show that citizens who feel calm about presidential candidates are more likely to act on partisan habits, but those who feel anxious are more likely to attend to new information, defect from partisanship, and vote on the basis of issue and trait assessments.

Despite the promise of this research, we are left with doubts. Voter anxiety and enthusiasm could stem from a variety of sources; the research to date simply assumes that responses are inspired directly by candidates or issues. Moreover, emotional responses could be an outcome of the same process that produces the observed behavioral changes. For example, the presence of a pro-choice Republican candidate may simultaneously cause Republican voters to defect from partisan loyalty and feel anxious about the candidate. The correlation in survey data does not allow us to conclude that anxiety played a causal role. Even worse, the anxiety toward the candidate could be a result of the behavioral changes—that is, the Republican voters might feel anxious *because* they are defecting. Again, correlations in survey data offer no sure escape from skeptics who claim emotion is epiphenomenal.

In this chapter, I test whether enthusiasm and anxiety can actually produce the changes in political judgment predicted by the theory of *affective intelligence* and suggested by survey research. I also attempt to explicitly verify the place of emotion in the dynamic process of political communication by determining the extent to which candidates can use emotional appeals in advertising to sway political judgment. I use the two experiments described in the preceding chapter to assess the persuasive power of emotional appeals. Classic approaches to the study of voting behavior offer distinct visions of election campaigns. In one view, campaigns primarily activate and reinforce existing loyalties; in the other, campaigns provide voters with information about issues and candidate qualities so that they may make a rational choice. The question of how well these competing visions describe the decisions of voters may depend on the emotional tenor of the campaign.

Does Appealing to Emotions Make Candidates More or Less Appealing? Affect Transfer versus Affective Intelligence

In chapter 3, I argued that ads can change impressions of candidates by appealing to voter enthusiasm or anxiety. In a sense, these ads cue one of the two systems of affective intelligence described by Marcus and colleagues (2000). From this theoretical perspective, emotional appeals change political attitudes or choices indirectly, as a result of causing individuals either to rely on existing dispositions or to actively process available information. However, conventional wisdom holds that positive ads work by making the sponsor more likable and that negative ads work by making the opponent less likable (see chapter 2).[2] According to this *affect transfer* hypothesis, ads try to associate the sponsor with positive emotions and the opponent with negative emotions. From this perspective, affect triggered by the images and music is "transferred" to the candidates being discussed in the ad.

To test these hypotheses, I turn first to evidence on changes in feelings toward the candidates. Subjects rated the candidates, along with other political figures, using feeling thermometers (i.e., 0 to 100 scales) on both the pretest and posttest questionnaires. We can observe changes in these *candidate affect* ratings to see whether subjects develop more or less favorable impressions of each candidate following exposure to campaign advertising. Consistent with work on political cognition (Holbrook et al. 2001), subjects began with slightly positive feelings about both candidates on average (55 for Harshbarger and 54 for McGovern). The conventional view leads us to expect a rise in affect toward the sponsor after viewing ads eliciting positive emotions such as enthusiasm, and leads us to expect a decline in affect toward the opponent after ads eliciting negative emotions such as fear. Figure 5.1 shows changes in candidate affect across the experimental groups.

The evidence does not support the conventional view. Subjects rated both the sponsor and the opponent less favorably after seeing the ad, regardless of tone or emotional appeal.[3] We should not be surprised that across all ads affect toward the opponent fell more than affect toward the sponsor, but even this difference is not significant. Contrary to expectations, enthusiasm appeals did not generate more warmth toward the sponsor, and fear appeals did not erode the favorability of the opponent. In fact, affect toward both the sponsor and the opponent seems to have fared the best after exposure to fear appeals. Subjects exposed to fear ads showed the only increase in candidate

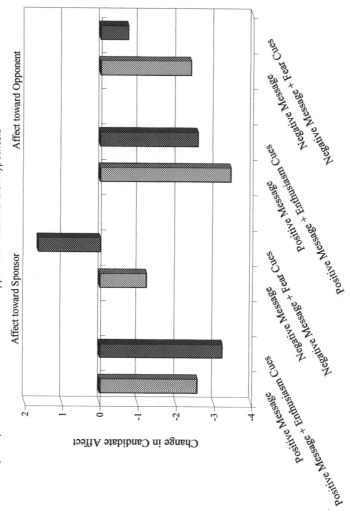

FIGURE 5.1 Experimental Evidence Does Not Support the Affect Transfer Hypothesis

Note: Values are the mean change in the feeling thermometer ratings of candidates, following advertising exposure.

affect, feeling slightly warmer on average toward the sponsor. Overall, there is no evidence to suggest that emotional appeals directly affect feelings toward each candidate, even though affect toward the sponsor appears modestly higher with the addition of fear cues ($t = 1.14, p < .136$).

Perhaps ads directly influence specific thoughts about a candidate rather than overall feelings. The posttest asked subjects to list any reasons they might have for liking or disliking each candidate. Subjects offered on average 1.2 reasons or "considerations" for liking the candidates and only half as many reasons for disliking them. Although subjects showed a predilection to stress positive reasons over negative ones ($t = 6.77, p < .001$), exposure to advertising does not automatically lead to significantly better appraisals of the sponsor than the opponent. Advertising tone (positive vs. negative message) also produced no systematic difference in the number of "likes" or "dislikes" for either candidate. There is weak evidence to suggest that enthusiasm cues increased the number of likes for the sponsor ($t = 1.56, p < .061$), but there is stronger evidence that the enthusiasm ads increased dislikes for the sponsor ($t = 2.51, p < .007$). At the same time, there is no evidence to suggest that fear cues increased the number of dislikes for the opponent ($t = 0.01$, $p < .503$) or decreased the number of likes ($t = 0.66, p < .256$). In sum, whether we look at candidate affect or cognitive considerations, there is almost no evidence in favor of the conventional view that positive and negative emotional appeals work by way of affect transfer.

Now we can test predictions based on affective intelligence theory. From this perspective, candidate impressions should occur indirectly as a function of the emotion cued, the individual's own predispositions, and the information and options with which she is confronted. We do *not* expect the changes to be a simple function of the emotion targeted by the ad. Appeals to enthusiasm should encourage voters to retain or intensify their initial dispositions toward the candidates. Those who, from the start, like one candidate more than the others should adhere to that conviction. Appeals to fear, on the other hand, should encourage voters to break loose from those dispositions, reorient their attention to new information, and reconsider their options. As a result, they should be more likely to change their relative assessments of the candidates in the direction suggested by the new information they consider.

These hypotheses concern changes in the comparative assessment of the candidates (cf. Rahn et al. 1990). *Comparative affect* takes on a positive value when the subject feels warmer toward the sponsor than the opponent, a negative value when she feels warmer toward the opponent, and a value of zero when she regards the candidates with equal warmth. Figure 5.2a shows whether viewers' comparative affect, after seeing the ad, changed in favor of the sponsor or the opponent. Fear appeals increase the share of viewers who feel more warmly toward the sponsor ($t = 1.91, p < .03$).

Affective intelligence theory predicts that the correspondence between the predispositions of the viewer and the ad being watched is relevant: fear ads should make those who are unconvinced of the sponsor's superiority more receptive to his or her message. If we divide the sample into three groups—those who originally preferred the sponsor, those who originally preferred the opponent, and those who were indifferent between them— we see that fear cues worked mainly on those who need to be persuaded. The probability of shifting toward the sponsor rose .08 for both those initially opposed or indifferent (t = 1.93, p < .028), but did not change among those who were initially supportive (t = 0.10, p < .539). The effect is nearly identical for *comparative considerations,* measured as the difference between the net likes-dislikes of the sponsor and the net likes-dislikes of the opponent.[4] The comparison moved one-half of a consideration in favor of the sponsor among those who were initially indifferent or opposed (t = 1.66, p < .05). Fear cues caused a slide in the opposite direction (i.e., away from the sponsor) among those who initially preferred the sponsor, but the change is not significant (t = 1.25, p < .111).

Enthusiasm appeals work differently. Figure 5.2b shows the probability that subjects held to their initial favorability rankings (i.e., there was no shift in which candidate the subject liked most, as measured by the feeling thermometers). Enthusiasm cues increased the probability of stable preferences by nearly 15 percentage points (t = 1.74, p < .043). The level of stability in comparative affect is constant across supporters, opponents, and those who were indifferent. For candidate likes and dislikes, we cannot observe change because the question was only asked after exposure. However, we can compare the responses of supporters and opponents after seeing positive or enthusiasm ads for evidence that the tally of reasons for liking and disliking the candidates is driven by initial feelings in the enthusiasm condition. When subjects saw an ad of the candidate they preferred, enthusiasm cues increased the number of likes mentioned about the sponsor by an average of 0.5 (t = 1.45, p < .078). When subjects saw an ad of the opposing candidate, enthusiasm cues increased the number of dislikes mentioned about the sponsor by 0.5 (t = 2.03, p < .026). Overall, those who preferred a candidate from the start shifted an average of one-half of a consideration in favor of the preferred candidate as a result of enthusiasm cues. As a result, the gap between each candidate's supporters in comparative considerations widened from 1.6, after exposure to positive ads, to 2.6, after exposure to enthusiasm ads. While this large effect suggests that enthusiasm ads polarize voters by strengthening their prior convictions, the relatively small number of cases prevents us from being fully confident in the effect.

The evidence on candidate impressions supports the theoretical argument advanced in this book. Emotional appeals affect the relative assessment

FIGURE 5.2A Evidence for Affective Intelligence: Fear Ads Create a Shift in Comparative Affect Favoring the Sponsor

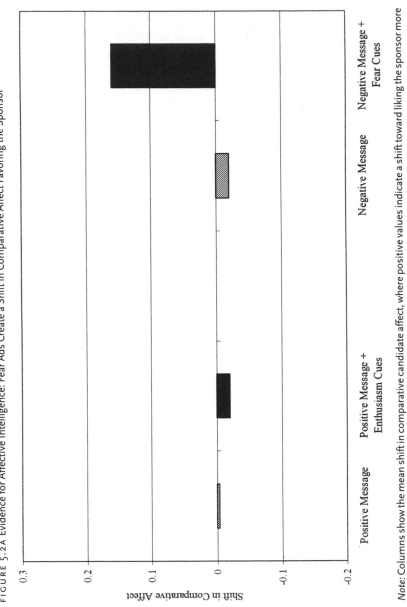

Note: Columns show the mean shift in comparative candidate affect, where positive values indicate a shift toward liking the sponsor more than the opponent on average and negative values indicate the reverse.

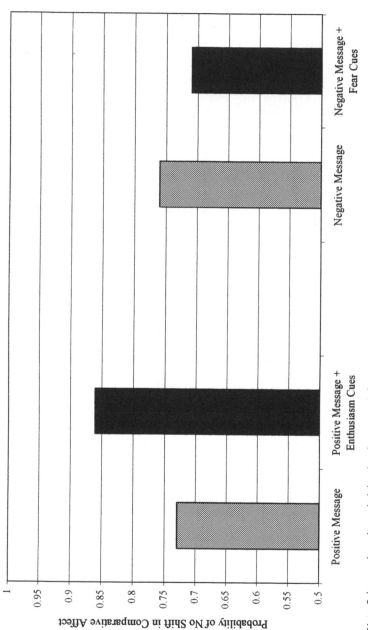

FIGURE 5.2B Evidence for Affective Intelligence: Enthusiasm Ads Discourage a Shift in Comparative Candidate Affect

Note: Columns show the probability that there is no shift in comparative candidate affect (i.e., that a subject's relative fondness for the two candidates does not change after advertising exposure).

of candidates by cueing distinct modes of political judgment. So far we have seen evidence that fear cues enable the ad to sway voters toward favoring the sponsor in terms of both feelings and thoughts. This effect is particularly visible among those most "in need" of persuasion—that is, those who do not initially support the sponsor. We have also seen evidence that enthusiasm cues reinforce existing preferences and discourage change.

These findings support predictions rooted in the neuropsychology of emotions. The evidence also allows us to reject conventional notions that the impact of positive or negative emotional appeals can be explained by the direct transfer of either cognitive considerations or affect to the viewer's impressions of the candidates. This popular and venerable belief about how campaign ads work appears to be simply wrong. Emotion in campaign advertising operates on a more subtle level. Rather than force-feeding the public, emotional appeals aim to win the hearts and minds of voters by alternatively whetting their appetite for an old favorite or for trying something new.

Scaring Up Support versus Shoring Up Support: Emotion and Candidate Choice

Although we have seen evidence that ads can change impressions of one seeking office, campaigns are not merely popularity contests. Candidates seek to win votes, not just admirers. If changing how an individual thinks and feels about the candidate is an important step in securing her support, it still does not guarantee that she will choose to cast her only vote in the contest for that, or any other, candidate. Citizens do not always vote for candidates they like the best. Some may see a particular flaw as important enough to disqualify an otherwise well-liked candidate for the job in question. Others may be so ambivalent about all of the candidates that they are not motivated to choose among them and instead refrain from voting at all. Still others may pass over the candidate they like best out of concern for electability or other strategic considerations, especially in primary elections (Bartels 1988).[5]

Subjects had the opportunity to express their voting preferences in both the pretest and posttest questionnaire. The question format, however, differed slightly. In order to reduce the risk that pretest questions would unduly prime subjects on campaign-related matters, the pretest asked subjects to name the person for whom they would vote in the gubernatorial primary, without providing a list of the candidates. This format requires subjects to recall, not just recognize, candidate names and therefore tends to increase the number of subjects who appear to have no preference. The posttest more closely simulated the ballot format by providing subjects with a list of the candidates. In both questionnaires, subjects were invited to indicate whether they "lean toward" or "strongly support" the candidate. The pretest measure offers us a good sense of initial voting preferences but, as a result of the format differences, I treat the pretest measure as a predictor through most of the analyses that follow, not as a baseline from which we can fully observe individual change.

Having said this, 31 percent of subjects appear to have changed their preference, underscoring the flexibility of voters in a low-salience primary such as this one. For many, the shift may grow out of participation in the study itself or from the changed format of the posttest. Indeed, two-thirds of the "changers" were originally indifferent but expressed a preference in the second questionnaire. Over 80 percent moved in or out of the undecided category, so those who flipped entirely from supporting one candidate to the other were in the minority.

Subjects exposed to campaign advertising were not more likely to switch their preferences than those in the control group (31% and 33%, respectively). As figure 5.3 shows, however, there are differences across the ads. Most importantly, for our purposes, the effects of enthusiasm and fear appeals match expectations. The probability of a shift in voting preferences dropped by 17 percentage points ($t = 1.97, p < .026$) with the addition of enthusiasm cues. Fear cues increased the probability of a shift in preferences by 11 percentage points ($t = 1.24, p < .108$), though statistical uncertainty puts this result on shaky ground. Did emotional appeals influence subjective feelings of certainty? Immediately after soliciting vote preference, subjects reported on the posttest whether they felt they knew enough "right now" to make their final decision. Only 23 percent expressed such certainty in their gubernatorial primary choice. While the level of certainty is similar across most conditions, a considerably larger 36 percent of subjects exposed to enthusiasm ads expressed certainty in their decision ($t = 2.00, p < .024$). Already, then, we have clear evidence that ads can firm up voting choices by appealing to enthusiasm.

Although the destabilizing capacity of fear and stabilizing capacity of enthusiasm are consistent with expectations, the hypotheses specify something more precise about the effects and the mechanism by which they are produced. Fear cues should persuade people to vote for the sponsor by causing them to give greater weight to new information than to their prior inclinations. Enthusiasm cues should encourage electoral fidelity by strengthening the impact of prior convictions. For purposes of testing these predictions, I use a simple specification that includes a single measure each for predispositions and new information. I then estimate the effects separately for each of the experimental groups. The measure of predispositions is pretest preferences, and the measure of new information is the message of the campaign ad, conceived in its simplest terms: "Vote for me, not my opponent."

Figure 5.4 shows the predicted impact of each factor on the probability of

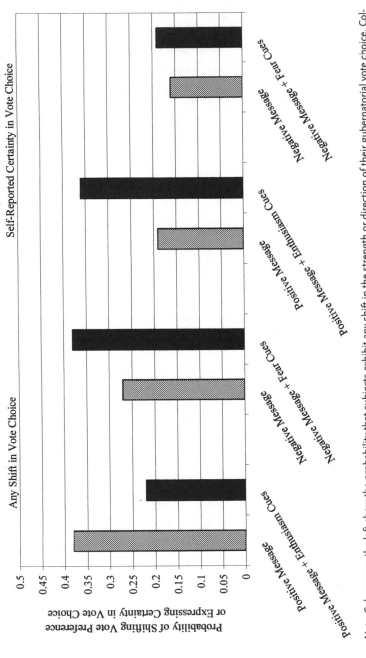

FIGURE 5.3 Fear Ads Unsettle Voting Choices, Enthusiasm Ads Stabilize Voting Choices and Increase Certainty

Note: Columns on the left show the probability that subjects exhibit any shift in the strength or direction of their gubernatorial vote choice. Columns on the right show the probability that subjects express certainty about their posttest vote choice.

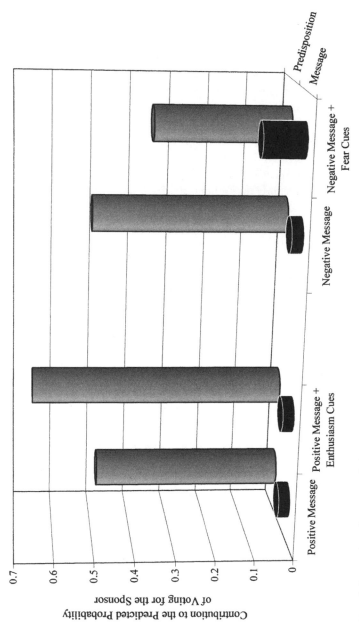

FIGURE 5.4 Advertising Message Influences Vote Choice Only for Fear Ads, Reliance on Predispositions Is Least for Fear Ads and Greatest for Enthusiasm Ads

Note: Columns show the impact of advertising message and initial dispositions to support the candidates on the predicted probability of voting for the sponsor, across the four experimental conditions.

choosing the sponsor across experimental conditions. This pattern mirrors the theoretical predictions set forth in chapter 3. Subjects in the fear condition placed noticeably less weight on their prior preference and a significant amount of weight on the ad's message. As we would expect, the impact of a single campaign ad does not rival the impact of previously accumulated judgment. Nonetheless, the magnitude of this effect—a boost of 11 percentage points for the sponsor—is politically quite meaningful. It is also comparable to the size of the persuasive effects observed by Ansolabehere and Iyengar (1995), albeit with an important difference: those researchers found that negative ads did not work well among Democrats, especially in the California primary elections. Here we see evidence that fear cues render negative ads persuasive in a Democratic primary election in Massachusetts. The advertising message was persuasive only in the fear condition and did not contribute significantly to candidate choice in any of the other conditions.[6]

Subjects in the enthusiasm condition appear to have relied on initial preferences more than subjects in any other condition, while those in the fear condition appear to have relied on initial preferences the least. Although variation in the strength of these factors is exactly consistent with predictions, the differences *across* conditions fall short of the standard threshold for statistical significance. Both the increased weight on predispositions from enthusiasm cues and the decreased weight from fear cues approach significance ($t = 1.44, p < .076$ and $t = 1.41, p < .080$, respectively). Differences in the contribution of prior preferences between the enthusiasm and fear conditions, whether due to emotional cues or to their conjunction with the verbal message, are significant ($t = 2.61, p < .005$). The advertising message has a clear persuasive effect only in the fear condition ($z = 1.82, p < .034$), though we cannot say reliably that the estimated impact of fear cues is significantly greater than other conditions ($t = 1.03, p < .150$). The overall pattern of weights given to these factors perfectly corresponds to the theoretical predictions, an outcome unlikely to have occurred by chance.

We can also test the interaction effects, and thus the predicted mechanism by which emotional appeals are posited to work, in a single model of vote choice using the full sample. This model includes the interactions between emotions and initial preferences, as well as recoded versions of the emotion variables so that they reflect which candidate the message of the ad is promoting. We also can run the same model to predict comparative candidate affect (i.e., relative feeling thermometers), substituting initial comparative affect for initial vote preferences as the predisposition. The estimated effects for the key variables of interest are shown in table 5.1, and full results with control variables are in appendix B (see table B.3). The results are remarkably similar for candidate affect and vote choice. There is strong evidence that fear ads persuade individuals to prefer the sponsor. The inter-

TABLE 5.1 Effects of Emotional Cues on Vote Choice and Comparative Affect

	Comparative Candidate Affect	Vote Choice
Enthusiasm cues	0.23	0.19
	(0.22)	(0.22)
Fear cues	0.53**	0.54**
	(0.21)	(0.20)
Enthusiasm cues × initial preferences	0.58	0.94**
	(0.39)	(0.34)
Fear cues × initial preferences	−0.50	−0.54*
	(0.37)	(0.30)
N	286	286

Note: Entries in the cells are coefficients (and standard errors) from maximum likelihood estimation of an ordered probit model. The table displays the marginal effect of emotional cues on vote choice and relative fondness for the candidates, controlling for the positive-negative tone of the message and prior preferences. It also shows the interaction effect of emotional cues and initial preferences or affect. Full results, including control variables, are in appendix B (see table B.3).

$**p < .01$ $*p < .05$

actions with initial preferences show up clearly in the case of vote choice: enthusiasm cues greatly increased the role of prior convictions and fear cues diminished their role. In the case of comparative likability, the otherwise similar interaction effects fall just shy of significance.

We acquire a more vivid sense of the potential implications of these results for campaign strategy by comparing the distribution of expected vote probabilities across the range of advertising conditions and voter predispositions. Using the full model, we can predict the probability that an individual chooses the sponsor, chooses the opponent, or remains undecided. We can then examine how advertising exposure affects these predicted probabilities for each of three distinct groups—those who initially prefer the sponsor, those who initially prefer the opponent, and those who are initially indifferent. Figure 5.5a shows the effects of fear cues on candidate choice. Fear works fairly well with those initially indifferent and opposed; the number who are willing to vote for the sponsor more than doubles among the indifferent and is five times higher among those initially opposed. However, it does not improve the standing of the sponsor at all among supporters. Still, fear not only helps to win converts, it also causes many of those initially opposed to back-off on their support for the opponent in favor of indecision.

The pattern for the effects of enthusiasm cues on candidate choice is notably different, as shown in figure 5.5b. On the left side of the graph, we see

FIGURE 5.5A Persuasion: Fear Ads Soften Opposition and Win Converts

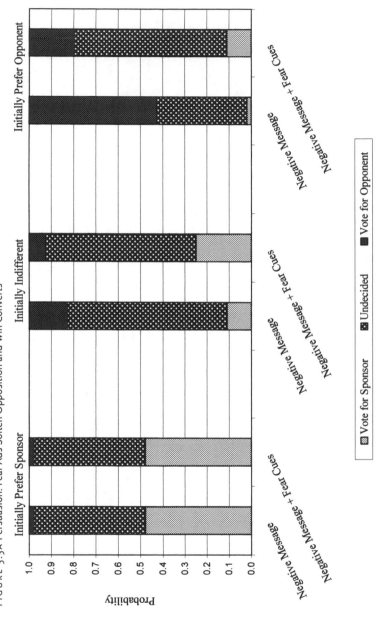

Note: Columns display the simulated probabilities of a subject saying she intends to vote for the sponsor, vote for the opponent, or remains undecided, across different conditions of advertising exposure and by initial candidate preference.

FIGURE 5.5B Activation and Polarization: Enthusiasm Ads Attract Supporters and Repulse Opponents

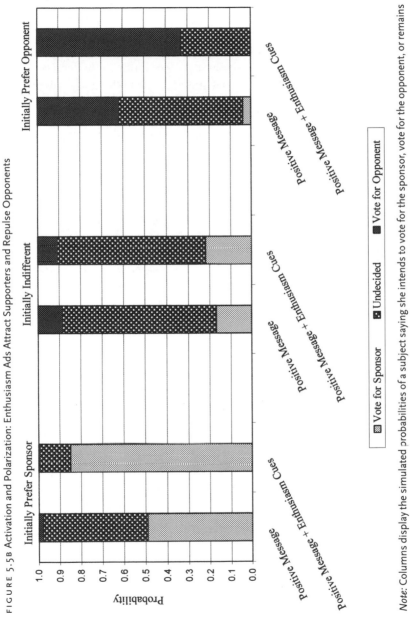

Note: Columns display the simulated probabilities of a subject saying she intends to vote for the sponsor, vote for the opponent, or remains undecided, across different conditions of advertising exposure and by initial candidate preference.

the role that enthusiasm plays in the classic activation function of election campaigns: enthusiasm dramatically transforms latent support into a stronger commitment to vote for the candidate. Because it reinforces prior convictions, enthusiasm also helps to activate voters among the opponent's base in support of their own candidate. As a result, we observe voters becoming entrenched on opposite sides of the contest. Enthusiasm cues offer no leverage with which to win over those who have not yet formed a preference. The distinct patterns in figures 5.5a and 5.5b suggest something of the targeted effectiveness of emotional appeals, an issue I revisit in chapter 6.

Emotional appeals—in this case embedded in the music and images of campaign ads—offer candidates leverage to reach and sway an otherwise inattentive audience with their message. A single type of appeal does not provide all the answers, however, as the effectiveness depends in part on the prior preferences of the citizen. Political ads that appeal to the distinct emotions of fear and enthusiasm have distinct consequences on candidate impressions and vote choice, which we can predict by applying neuropsychological views such as those embodied in the theory of affective intelligence. We can also tie each emotion to competing conceptions about the functions of election campaigns. Fear plays the most direct role in *persuasion* or the winning of support from those who were genuinely opposed or indifferent at the start. Enthusiasm undergirds the *reinforcement* and *activation* of support among those who are initially inclined to favor the candidate, but whose commitment to voting for the candidate may be weak. In sum, I find evidence that fear ads are useful tools for scaring up support in the unlikeliest of places and enthusiasm ads are useful for shoring up support closest to home.

Polarization Effect: Attraction, Repulsion, or Both?

Predictions for the impact of enthusiasm appeals on the aggregate pattern of electoral choice, captured vividly in figure 5.5b, reveal a striking pattern of polarization. An optimistic campaign message, coupled with stirring music and colorful images, seems to harden the convictions of supporters and opponents alike. There is some irony in the fact that appealing to positive emotions should so effectively widen the gulf between rival supporters of opposing political camps. Because this finding may have significant implications for how we understand the campaign process, it is worth taking a closer look at what happens.

Despite the apparent irony, polarization does follow rather logically from the prediction that enthusiasm reinforces existing commitments. Scholars also have long recognized that campaigns attempt to activate existing loyalties and, in doing so, tend to polarize partisans over the course of the election (Lazarsfeld, Berelson, and Gaudet 1944). Even so, prior to the conduct of these experiments, we did not know or have evidence demonstrating the role of enthusiasm and appeals to enthusiasm as a mechanism by which this reinforcement and polarization occur. Moreover, previous studies often saw this process as inextricably bound up with party identification. But we have just seen evidence that appeals to enthusiasm can produce divergence among those who merely hold different preferences in a primary election, where partisanship is nearly irrelevant.[7]

The concept of a polarizing force conjures up images of two sides pushing simultaneously in opposite directions. This is a pattern frequently observed in politics and implied by the results of the preceding section, yet polarization could be the end-product of separate one-sided efforts. After all, that is not an uncommon way to characterize campaigns. We tend to see campaigns as responsible for emboldening their own supporters, but perhaps they embolden each other's supporters as well. Do appeals to enthusiasm reinforce the convictions of supporters, renew the determination of opposing viewers, or both?

I previously uncovered a symmetrical pattern when looking at comparative considerations. After exposure to enthusiasm ads, the gap between supportive and opposing viewers was one consideration (or 67%) larger than it was after exposure to less evocative positive ads. These results, however, were merely suggestive. In the preceding analysis of vote choice, we saw more conclusive evidence for the interaction between enthusiasm cues and prior preferences. But the symmetrical results for vote choice in figure 5.5b are built into the model. Although the symmetrically coded interaction term is highly significant, this could be true even if the specification masked a much larger one-sided effect on supporters only or a lopsided effect in which the ad is twice as effective at rallying supporters than opponents.

We can better test the full extent to which enthusiasm appeals polarize voters by examining their impact on supportive and opposing viewers separately. I divided the sample into those who saw an ad by their preferred candidate and those who saw the opposing candidate. For each group, we must ask how much more likely are viewers who were exposed to enthusiasm cues to vote in accordance with their initial preferences. Polarization occurs by *attraction* if appeals to enthusiasm strengthen the convictions of those watching their preferred candidate. Polarization occurs by *repulsion* if such appeals strengthen the convictions of those watching the opposing candidate.

Figure 5.6 shows the effect of enthusiasm ads on the probability that an individual chooses her initially preferred candidate, depending on which candidate's ad was seen.[8] The results are clear: polarization is the product of both attraction and repulsion. Ads attempting to cue enthusiasm increased the probability that supporters choose the sponsor by 31 percentage points ($t = 2.03, p < .026$) and that opposing viewers choose the rival candidate by

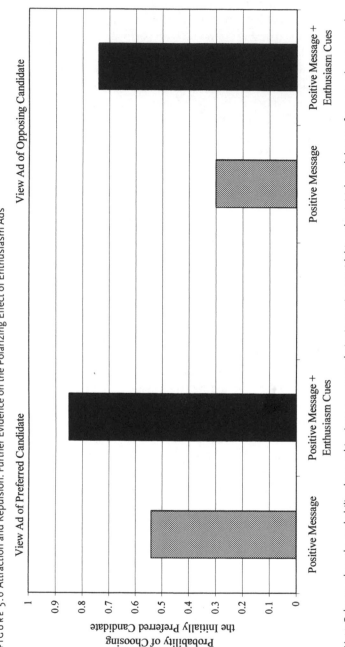

FIGURE 5.6 Attraction and Repulsion: Further Evidence on the Polarizing Effect of Enthusiasm Ads

Note: Columns show the probability that a subject's posttest vote choice is consistent with his or her initial candidate preferences, when exposed to an ad by the initially preferred candidate or that candidate's opponent.

44 percentage points (t = 2.42, p < .011). Thus, repulsion appears even stronger than attraction in this case, albeit as the result of starting from a lower baseline, but the magnitudes of these effects are not statistically distinguishable. The polarizing effects of enthusiasm appeals are both strong and symmetrical.

Priming the Foundations of Political Judgment

One of my central arguments in this book is that ads, by appealing to enthusiasm or fear, can trigger distinct modes of information processing and political judgment. We received some confirmation of this earlier in seeing that enthusiasm and fear ads seem to alter the weight viewers place on initial preferences and the advertising message. In addition, the preceding section sheds light on the mechanism by which enthusiasm appeals activate predispositions. A mechanism that involves reinforcing the status quo is likely to be relatively simple. People by nature act largely out of habit and, therefore, enthusiasm appeals are merely tapping a ready reflex for doing "more of the same."

But what about the mechanism by which fear appeals trigger a break with habit? As Marcus and colleagues (2000) have argued, people typically approach familiar situations in familiar ways (i.e., rely on habit), which allows them to disregard the overwhelming flood of details about the present situation in favor of reliance on old rules of thumb. The purpose of anxiety is to disrupt this reliance on routine and thereby encourage greater consideration of that flood of details or "contemporary evaluations." In an election campaign, this means that appeals to fear should break the hold of partisanship, ideology, and other preexisting summary judgments, and encourage attention to campaign messages, issues, economic conditions, and candidate traits.

We saw earlier that fear cues trigger less weight on prior preferences and more weight on the advertising message. Although the message of a campaign ad appealing to fear is the most readily available source of new information, voters may not naively and slavishly accept arguments made in paid advertising. Citizens are aware of the motivations of candidates and the tendency for campaign ads to contain partial truths and exaggerated claims. The existing literature offers ample proof that they will retain and learn some of what they hear from ads, but it also suggests they will not accept all of it uncritically (Ansolabehere and Iyengar 1995; Just et al. 1996; West 2001). Because campaign ads are seen as biased sources, prior research on media effects leads us to expect that ads may fare best when they either prime latent identities or cue our attention to information that has been or will be in the news (Ansolabehere and Iyengar 1994; Iyengar and Kinder 1987; Iyengar and Petrocik 2001; Mendelberg 2001; Valentino, Hutchings, and White 2002). Can fear cues shift attention beyond the ad itself to other sources of information? Can fear cause viewers to rely more on contemporary evaluations of issues and candidate traits? By looking at a wider range of determinants of electoral choice, I conduct a more thorough test of whether emotional appeals alter the process by which political decisions are reached.

Earlier I listed several types of long-term and short-term factors that are often relevant to voting decisions. These or similar considerations belong in a fuller model of voter choice. Building on the simple model analyzed earlier, I expand predispositions to include ideology as well as initial preferences and define contemporary evaluations to include evaluations of candidates in terms of issue positions and competence, assessments of leadership traits, and gut reactions toward the candidate's message. The gut reactions combine self-reported feelings of anger, excitement, and reassurance toward the sponsor and his or her campaign message.[9] Partisanship and evaluations of economic conditions are not salient considerations in the gubernatorial primary of the "out" party, so I set them aside. Finally, I do not include advertising message separately in this model because its impact is reflected in the more specific evaluations (i.e., issues, traits, and gut feelings).[10]

My goal, just as it was with the simple model earlier, is to see how much initial preferences, ideology, issue and trait evaluations, and gut reactions influence candidate choice in each of the experimental conditions. Figure 5.7a (p. 132) displays the results. Once again, fear ads changed the weight given to various factors in accordance with predictions. The presence of fear cues appears to have lessened the impact of initial preferences and ideology, but most of the difference is reflected here in the contribution of ideology ($t = 1.53, p < .065$). Fear cues produced dramatic increases in the weight that issues ($t = 1.59, p < .055$) and traits ($t = 2.40, p < .009$) were given in candidate choice, though the increase in the role of gut feelings by itself is not significant. When we consider the increased emphasis on contemporary evaluations as a whole, we see a striking change in the bases for candidate choice after exposure to fear ads (joint significance: $F = 9.74, p < .002$).

Enthusiasm cues also produced changes in the expected directions. Individuals based their decisions much more heavily on initial preferences ($t = 4.09, p < .001$). In this case, however, we do not see a comparable increase for ideology. Contemporary evaluations also appear to have had a smaller impact after exposure to enthusiasm cues: although we cannot be confident in the differences for individual factors, we can have some confidence in the overall pattern of less reliance on issues, traits, and gut feelings (joint significance: $F = 4.72, p < .032$).

Figure 5.7b (p. 133) provides a better sense of the changing bases of candidate choice by showing the *relative* contribution of the various factors in each advertising condition. The pie charts show the impact of each factor on choosing a candidate as a share of the total impact of all five factors. When ads appeal to enthusiasm, the weight on initial preferences nearly triples and choice is dominated by prior convictions. When ads appeal to fear, the weight on contemporary considerations mushrooms to squeeze out all but the smallest trace of influence from initial preferences.

The preceding comparisons are the critical ones for demonstrating that the addition of fear- or enthusiasm-evoking cues can in fact shift the bases of political judgment and specifically encourage more or less reliance on contemporary evaluations. I designed the experiments in this study to make those inferences separately for each set of cues. Nonetheless, the theoretical argument of this book highlights the contrast between decisionmaking in the face of fear and enthusiasm. We can compare candidate choice after exposure to the respective emotional ads only if we keep in mind they differ both in terms of audiovisual cues and the tone of the message. Individuals in the fear and enthusiasm conditions differ drastically in their reliance on initial preferences ($p < .001$), trait assessments ($p < .01$), and gut reactions ($p < .03$), while showing more tenuous differences in reliance on ideology ($p < .08$) and issue evaluations ($p < .10$). The near inversion in political judgment from fear and enthusiasm, captured in figures 5.7a and 5.7b, is remarkable (joint significance: $p < .001$ for each of predispositions and contemporary evaluations). Just as Marcus and colleagues (2000) observed with National Election Studies data, I find one set of voters making decisions largely on the basis of their political habits and another set of voters stepping out of habit to reason anew about the candidates and issues. But, in this case, I find evidence that candidates can use campaign advertising to shape whether habit or reason holds sway.

Fear and Critical Vigilance

In addition to claiming that fear cues alter the bases of political judgment, I have argued that a principal means by which they do so is to instigate a search for information that may be relevant to addressing the "threat." This implies, for example, a relationship between fear ads and news consumption that goes beyond the value of repetition and priming that has been implied in earlier work. If the theory of affective intelligence is correct, appeals to fear should increase the desire to attend to new information, and this desire should be focused somewhat selectively on information that could be seen as relevant to the threat raised by the ad. It might not be surprising if fear-targeting ads momentarily startled a viewer and grabbed his attention, but can such appeals shape the desire of viewers to seek out and pay atten-

FIGURE 5.7A Emotional Appeals Change the Criteria for Political Judgment

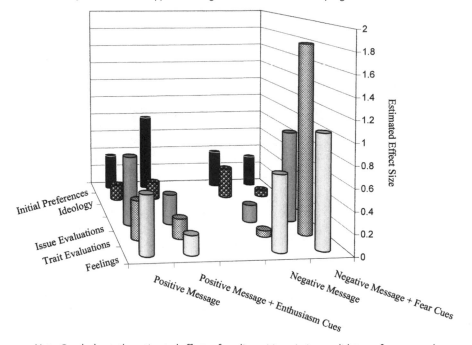

Note: Graph shows the estimated effects of predispositions (prior candidate preferences and ideology) and contemporary evaluations (views of candidate issue competence and leadership traits, and feelings about the advertising message) on posttest vote choice. In order to make these rough comparisons, the models were estimated using OLS (instead of ordered probit) and variables were recoded on a scale from 0 to 1 (Achen 1982).

tion to specific kinds of information? I test whether fear ads encourage this sort of political vigilance.

Although this study focuses more on motivation and persuasion than learning and attention, I collected several responses from subjects that might help shed light on the dynamics of attention. I did not collect direct measures of attention during viewing, for reasons of preserving both realism and deception, much the same as with the measurement of emotion. Subjects were unaware that the study concerned advertising until their participation was complete. At the end of the posttest, subjects indicated whether they recalled seeing a campaign ad and, if so, the name of the sponsor of the ad. Only 16 percent of subjects incorrectly recalled the presence or absence of a campaign ad. An additional 10 percent mis-recalled the sponsor. The focused environment and short duration of a lab experiment provide better than usual conditions for memory, but there is a difference between "noticing" and genuinely paying attention.

FIGURE 5.7B Enthusiasm Ads Increase Reliance on Predispositions, Fear Ads Increase Reliance on Contemporary Evaluations and Feelings

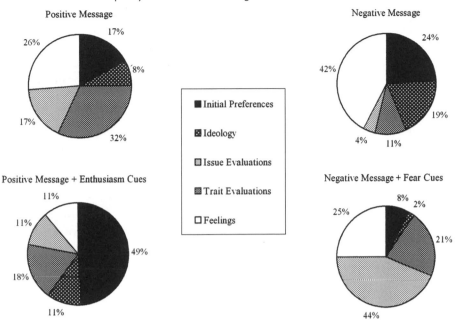

Note: Graphs show the relative contributions of predispositions (prior candidate preferences and ideology) and contemporary evaluations (views of candidate issue competence and leadership traits, and feelings about the advertising message) to posttest vote choice. In order to make these rough comparisons, the models were estimated using OLS (instead of ordered probit) and variables were recoded on a scale from 0 to 1 (Achen 1982). Percentages are calculated by dividing the estimated effects in each category by the sum of all estimated effects (cf. Marcus, Neuman, and MacKuen 2000, 115–20).

Political ads can do little to bring television viewers back to their seats during a commercial break, but, even in the lab, they must try to pierce the mental blinds that often descend when commercials come on. One approach is to make ads more interesting to the viewer. Communication scholars have found that certain visual, structural, and verbal techniques make political ads more memorable (Geiger and Reeves 1991; Kepplinger 1991; Lang 1991; Newhagen and Reeves 1991).[11] Perhaps what I have called "emotional cues" are merely audiovisual properties that serve to make the ads more vivid, compelling, or interesting—that is, more *entertaining*. If this were true, ads may be effective because they capture viewers' attention and the nature of their impact might be determined by the message of the ad.[12]

It is worth considering whether the so-called emotional ads in this study succeed on account of their "entertainment value" rather than their emotion-

eliciting qualities. If they did, we would expect viewers who were so entertained to show greater recall or memory for the ads. I also have argued that
cues aimed at eliciting anxiety serve to grab viewers' attention. If the theoretical argument of this book is correct, then we should expect greater recall
or memory, but only for those who may feel threatened.

The back row of figure 5.8 shows the probability of correctly recalling the
ad and its sponsor across each of the conditions. There are no significant differences in recall. Contrary to both affective intelligence theory and the entertainment value alternative, neither fear nor enthusiasm ads show signs of
being more memorable; if anything, they appear to be less so.

Another goal of campaign advertising, especially early during nomination campaigns, is increasing name recognition for the candidate. The
posttest asked subjects the extent to which they recognize the names of the
two major candidates in the race (among other names). The first two rows
of figure 5.8 display the mean level of recognition across the conditions for
these measures of memory and attention. Again, we see no evidence of differences at all.

What about the targeted nature of threats? Those who see a fear ad at-

FIGURE 5.8 Emotional Appeals Do Not Make the Ad or the Candidates More Memorable

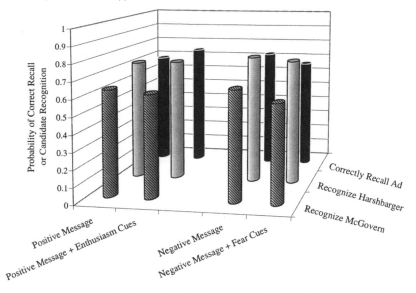

Note: The first two rows of columns show the probability of recognizing the names of the candidates by advertising exposure. The last row of columns shows the probability that a subject correctly recalls both seeing an ad and the name of the ad's sponsor.

tacking their preferred candidate may feel more threatened and, thus, find the ad more memorable. We see some suggestion of this across the three measures, though the difference is clear in only one case. For those who viewed an ad attacking their candidate, fear cues increased correct recall of the ad and sponsor by 24 percentage points ($t = 1.43, p < .082$), recognition of Patricia McGovern's name by 17 percentage points ($t = 1.00, p < .163$), and recognition of Scott Harshbarger's name by 27 percentage points ($t = 2.01$, $p < .027$). I find no such effects for enthusiasm cues. In sum, we see very little evidence that emotional cues make the ads themselves or the candidates who sponsor them more attention-fixing or memorable. The exception is suggestive evidence that candidates and ads are more memorable among those who see a fear ad from an opposing candidate. These results offer no support for the *entertainment value* hypothesis, but they also provide only modest support for the hypothesis of critical vigilance in response to fear.

I proposed earlier that the impact of fear cues could extend further than the content of the ad and indeed that voters may wish to look elsewhere in search of additional information.[13] In this study, as well as in the normal course of life, the most ready sources of information about politics aside from campaigns are the news media and other people (e.g., family, friends, coworkers). Although the study did not involve monitoring participants' conversational behavior, the posttest attempted to ascertain what participants took away from the local news broadcast they watched. If something about the ad prompted them to be more alert to relevant information, then we may see this reflected in their attention to certain news stories.

After viewing the news, subjects tried to recall the stories or topics they had heard about in the news. Responses are divided into three categories: (1) Subsequent relevant stories occurred after the commercial break and touch on topics such as politics, crime, or education (e.g., report on elementary school scholarships). (2) Prior relevant stories touch on the same set of topics but occurred before the commercial break (e.g., report on a high school student's pipe bomb threat). (3) Subsequent irrelevant stories occurred after the break and did not touch on any of these topics (e.g., a story about the seaworthiness of the U.S.S. *Constitution*).[14] If fear ads stoke a desire to seek out relevant information, then we should see improved recall of stories in the subsequent relevant category.

Figure 5.9 displays the mean proportion of recalled stories in each category. Fear cues nearly doubled the recall of subsequent relevant stories from 0.25 to 0.46 ($t = 1.90, p < .030$). Fear cues did not produce a significant improvement in recall of prior relevant or subsequent irrelevant stories. There is also suggestive evidence that enthusiasm cues actually distracted viewers. In this case, they reduced by one-half the recall of subsequent relevant stories ($t = 1.50, p < .068$) and modestly improved recall of irrelevant stories

FIGURE 5.9 Fear Ads Strengthen Attention to Relevant Information in the News, Enthusiasm Ads Turn Attention Elsewhere

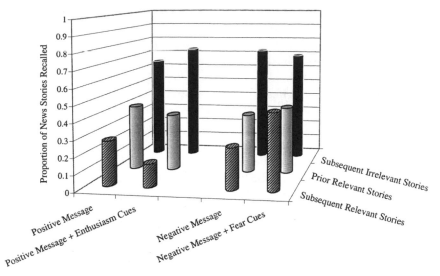

Note: Columns show the mean proportion of news stories recalled after viewing. News stories are categorized according to their relevance (i.e., focused on issues related to those discussed in the ad) and their timing (i.e., appeared before or after the ad).

($t = 1.45, p < .075$). These contrasting and selective effects of fear and enthusiasm are inconsistent with the hypothesis that the emotional versions of the ads are simply more vivid or entertaining. The findings are consistent, however, with our expectations for how appeals to these particular emotions should redirect attention.

The effect of fear cues on subsequent relevant news stories holds regardless of whether they saw an ad attacking or promoting their preferred candidate. There is evidence, however, that the interaction between fear cues, initial preferences, and ad sponsorship (seen previously for correct recall of the ad) is salient for recall of *prior* relevant news stories. Although there were generally no differences among viewers across advertising conditions, when the ad attacked a subject's preferred candidate, fear cues tripled the rate at which these earlier news stories were recalled ($t = 3.01, p < .003$). When the ad promoted the preferred candidate, fear cues diminished recall of these stories ($t = 1.47, p < .077$). This pattern looks similar to other fear effects we have observed, but it extends beyond the hypothesized consequences. It suggests ads may produce a priming effect among those especially targeted by the fear appeals, increasing the salience of related information that had been recently stored in memory. Although Lodge and Taber (2002) have found that emotionally laden cues prime similarly valenced concepts in memory, I am not aware of any evidence showing that fear primes related concepts or facts in memory. The possibility that fear directs not only a search for new information but also the retrieval of information from memory merits further investigation.

In addition to the sort of recall measures discussed so far, we can check whether emotional appeals affect self-reported inclinations to search for information. Elsewhere I have reported evidence that fear appeals triggered requests for information on related topics in response to an open-ended question on the posttest (Brader 2005). The posttest also asked subjects how likely they were to contact the campaigns for more information. Although contacting politicians is often understood as a form of participation, this question stressed a particular reason for such a contact—namely, to acquire additional information—that makes it directly relevant to what we are testing here. The posttest also asked subjects about their interest in watching several types of TV news stories, including those about politics, business and the economy, crime, and health. I assume that the primary purpose of watching the news is to acquire information. However, this battery of questions taps a general inclination to watch TV news more than a specific impulse to search for information. Responses to these questions are strongly related to regular consumption habits and, therefore, I control for prior dispositions to watch the news.

Fear stimulates a desire to search for new and relevant information. Findings for both sets of questions bear this out. Figure 5.10 shows the self-expressed likelihood of contacting campaigns for more information across advertising conditions. When fear cues were added to negative ads, the mean desire to contact campaigns increased by 67 percent, from 0.29 to 0.48 ($t = 1.43, p < .078$). Although this effect occurs more broadly, it is particularly powerful when the ad attacks a preferred candidate: subjects exposed to an opposing fear ad expressed a desire for contacting that is more than three times as great (.22 to .75) as those who saw an opposing negative ad without fear cues ($t = 1.94, p < .034$). Enthusiasm cues had no effect on the desire to contact campaigns.

We see a similar story with the desire to watch TV news. Table 5.2 shows the marginal effect of enthusiasm and fear cues on interest in watching different types of news. Ads that appealed to fear stimulated an increased interest in watching news about politics. The change is notable but not dramatic, as fear cues increased interest by nearly half a point or one-quarter of a standard deviation on a seven-point scale. However, as the bottom row of the table indicates, the change was again much larger for individuals who saw an ad attacking their preferred candidate. In addition, fear cues

FIGURE 5.10 Fear Ads Stimulate a Desire to Contact Campaigns for More Information

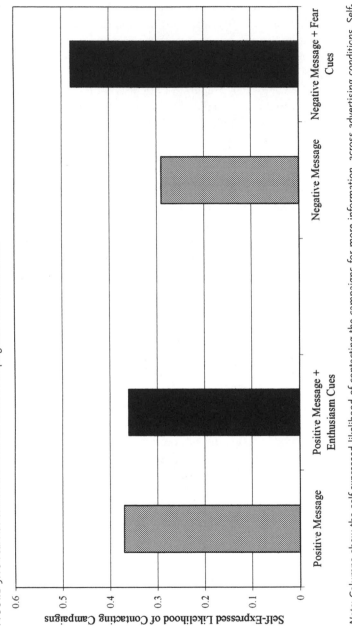

Note: Columns show the self-expressed likelihood of contacting the campaigns for more information, across advertising conditions. Self-expressed likelihood is measured on a scale from 0 to 2.

TABLE 5.2 Effect of Emotional Cues on Interest in Watching Television News

	Interest in Watching			
	News about Politics	News about the Economy	News about Crime	News about Health
Enthusiasm cues	0.14	0.30	0.08	0.00
	(0.25)	(0.26)	(0.32)	(0.31)
Fear cues	0.43*	−0.15	0.13	0.02
	(0.24)	(0.26)	(0.31)	(0.30)
Fear cues × prefer candidate attacked by the ad	1.97*	0.47	1.31	0.01
	(0.85)	(1.06)	(0.90)	(0.88)

Note: Entries in the cells are coefficients (and standard errors) from OLS regression. The table shows the estimated effects of emotional cues, controlling for news consumption habits, prior interest in the issue, and demographic characteristics. Full results are in appendix B (see table B.4). $N = 234$.

*$p < .05$

motivated viewers to seek information selectively, just as we observed in the recall of recently viewed news stories. Interest in watching grows for news about politics but not for news about the economy, crime, or health. For those seeing an opposing ad, there is some suggestion of an increased interest in crime news, which was one of the issues raised in the ads, but the effect does not reach statistical significance. Enthusiasm cues did not affect interest in watching news programming on any of these subjects.

I have now presented evidence on two related aspects of the mechanism by which emotional appeals are alleged to shift political judgment from habit to critical vigilance and reasoning (and back again). To paraphrase Samuel Johnson, nothing concentrates the mind like the prospect of hanging in the morning. Signs of threat refocus our attention and reorient our behavior on removing either the danger or ourselves. As part of that process in the domain of campaign advertising, appealing to fear does not simply induce viewers to consider the message of the ad, it encourages a broader reassessment of candidate choice on the basis of contemporary evaluations and reactions. Another key part of the cognitive and behavioral response is a search for information that is at once far-reaching (by extending well beyond the ad itself to the news and political sources) and selective (by focusing the search on relevant matters). These findings hint at a longer process of changes in what information citizens absorb, though we must await a more extended research design to explore the full nature of this process and to assess precisely how much citizens genuinely learn as a result.

Swaying the Sophisticated? Who Responds to Emotional Appeals, Revisited

We saw evidence earlier that emotional appeals tend to motivate more so-phisticated, not less sophisticated citizens, to take political action. Those findings are consistent with the *relevancy* hypothesis proposed in chapter 3, but contrary to a good deal of conventional wisdom. Perhaps we can make sense of the motivation findings in light of the already strong participatory inclinations among those with high levels of political knowledge. Their be-havior is not only governed by the same emotional processes as everyone else, their dispositions make them especially ready to react and act. Political "experts" are both cognitively and emotionally engaged with politics. But what about persuasion? The traditional assumption that emotions can be used to "manipulate" or sway the opinions of the "ignorant" masses seems to apply more firmly to questions of attitude change and political persuasion. Moreover, it seems the same qualities that make sophisticated citizens more amenable to motivation—greater knowledge and awareness, stronger and more developed beliefs, higher levels of interest—ought to make them *less* amenable to persuasion.

I revisit the findings of this chapter to see whether they hold equally across levels of political sophistication. I once again split the sample into two groups—political novices and experts—according to their factual knowl-edge of state politics. Because of the larger number of relationships examined in this chapter and the fact that several of them are already interaction effects, I focus only on the split-sample difference of means tests and present evi-dence only in those cases where we have already observed an effect. The multi-variate interaction test produces comparable results. The results are shown in table 5.3. The first two columns of the table list the major findings from the chapter and the original effect observed from adding enthusiasm cues to positive ads or fear cues to negative ads. The third and fourth columns show the effect among those with less or more political knowledge, respectively.

A quick glance at the table makes clear that the findings do not hold equally across levels of sophistication. Political experts are overwhelmingly more responsive to emotional appeals. The capacity of fear cues to change attitudes, persuade voting choices, and spark increased attention to new in-formation is strongest among the knowledgeable. The capacity of enthusi-asm cues to reinforce political habits, increase certainty in candidate choice, and discourage attention to new information is also strongest among those who know more. We can see the pattern even more clearly in this domain than in the case of political motivation. In almost every case, the hypothesis best supported by the evidence is that experts are more responsive to the attention-redirecting and persuasive effects of emotional appeals. There are two exceptions. Fear cues appear to have a universal effect on the recall of

TABLE 5.3 Responsiveness to Emotional Cues by Level of Political Sophistication

| | | Split Sample Test | |
Observed Effects of Emotional Cues	Difference in the Entire Sample	Less Political Knowledge	More Political Knowledge
Fear shifts comparative affect toward sponsor	0.18*	0.04	0.35**
Enthusiasm increases probability of no shift in affect	0.13*	0.08	0.19*
Enthusiasm decreases probability of any shift in vote	−0.17*	0.03	−0.39***
Enthusiasm increases self-expressed certainty	0.17*	−0.05	0.34**
Fear increases probability of persuasion (vote choice)	0.14	−0.08	0.43**
Enthusiasm attracts supporters	0.31*	0.50*	0.20
Enthusiasm repulses opponents	0.44**	0.17	0.56**
Fear improves recall of relevant news stories	0.21*	0.18	0.24
Enthusiasm worsens recall of relevant news stories	−0.13	−0.08	−0.21*
Fear increases the desire to contact campaigns	0.19*	0.06	0.35*
Fear increases desire to watch news about politics	0.29	0.01	0.67*
N	286	157	129

Note: Entries in the cells are differences in the means between experimental conditions with and without emotional cues for the entire sample, subjects who have less knowledge about politics, and subjects who have more knowledge, respectively. (Fear effects = mean of fear condition − mean of negative condition; Enthusiasm effects = mean of enthusiasm condition − mean of positive condition.)

$***p < .001$ $**p < .01$ $*p < .05$

relevant news stories, and novices seem to be more responsive to the ability of enthusiasm cues to attract supporters. However, it is noteworthy that the magnitude of the effect among experts in both of these cases is hardly trivial.

The results leave little doubt that responsiveness to emotional appeals in campaign advertising is strongly linked to political sophistication. These findings fly in the face of considerable folk wisdom about manipulating the masses with emotion, even more so than the findings of the preceding chapter. Psychologists argue that everyone's behavior is governed by emotional processes and caution against the well-worn separation between emotion and reason. That old-fashioned idea lurks behind the view that greater knowledge and cognitive ability allow control and suppression of influence by emotion, which is so clearly at odds with the present findings. But the same psychological theories appear to offer less guidance in understanding why we see nearly the opposite in this case. Why do appeals to emotion wield the most influence over those with the greatest knowledge?

As I suggested earlier, it may have something to do with the fact that knowing more about politics usually goes hand-in-hand with caring more about politics. No political scientist will be surprised to learn that knowledgeable participants in this study displayed more passionate connections to politics. The political "experts" are more interested in following politics ($+1.1\,SD$, $p < .0001$), more strongly inclined to vote ($+0.6\,SD$, $p < .0001$), more strongly partisan ($+0.4\,SD$, $p < .001$), more ideologically extreme ($+0.25\,SD$, $p < .02$), and voice stronger opinions on the job performance of the incumbent governor ($+0.32\,SD$, $p < .002$). However, while this leaves sophisticated citizens more inclined to pay attention to political arguments, their advantage in knowledge usually leaves them better equipped to assimilate new information with existing views, to counterargue against conflicting information, and generally to resist persuasion (Zaller 1992). Consistent with this point of view, experts were far more likely to correctly recall seeing an ad and the identity of its sponsor ($p < .002$) and yet far less likely to show any change in their voting preferences over the course of the study ($p < .007$). Why then were ads appealing to emotion particularly effective on them?

Returning to the theoretical argument of this book, I believe the answer lies in the continuous and subtle nature by which the brain processes information through the emotional systems. Cues like those in campaign ads often trigger emotional responses but not conscious awareness on the part of the individual. If enthusiasm or fear guide political judgment and attention beyond our awareness, then the capacity to counterargue is less useful. Moreover, because these emotional responses are based on the significance that signs of success or threat hold for the individual, those who care more about politics should show greater sensitivity to such cues. This is not to say that political appeals to enthusiasm and fear can never be rejected; indeed, the more explicit and open the appeal, the more we should expect that the capacity to assimilate or resist plays a role. However, responses to emotional cues of the sort often appearing in campaign ads occur automatically and, even when a person is aware of a change in feelings, she may not fully appreciate why that change occurred. She is still capable of both recognizing that she disagrees with the message of the ad and rejecting its arguments, but she may not be able to control easily the fact she feels less (or more) inclined to reject those arguments this time around.

In sum, campaign ads appealing to fear or enthusiasm tend to sway those who know and care more about politics. These results again support the relevancy hypothesis. A person's expertise in politics makes campaign advertising more relevant to his goals and behavior and, therefore, makes the emotional cues in such advertising more powerful in shaping his response. In such circumstances, the person retains well-developed tools for resisting persuasion but may lack the ability to control changes in his inclination to use those tools.

Should We Be Alarmed? Fearing Fear Itself

In this chapter, I tested campaign advertising's capacity, through the use of emotional appeals, to redirect attention and change political attitudes and choices. Experimental evidence demonstrates that exposure to emotionally evocative advertising can considerably influence electoral choices. Consistent with the theoretical predictions, emotional cues accomplish this by shaping the extent to which citizens rely on habit or increased reasoning and vigilance. We can conclude from the evidence that the persuasive power of advertising rests on this more subtle process, and *not* on either the direct transfer of affect or entertainment value often suggested in discussions of advertising. In short, the impact of emotions elicited by campaign advertising are both complicated and predictable.

Affective intelligence theory specifies distinct roles for enthusiasm and fear in social decisionmaking. Emotional responses to the external world play a key role in negotiating between our reliance on learned routines and our "decision" at times to evaluate the circumstances more closely and to reason about the proper course of action. Signs of success trigger enthusiasm, reinforcing the value of current pursuits and promoting habitual behavior. Enthusiasm encourages individuals to remain true to their convictions. Signs of threat trigger fear, which heightens attention to and consideration of new information in an effort to counter any danger. As a result, fear induces a temporary departure from habit to contemplate other options. Experimental evidence shows that campaign ads targeting these emotions produce the patterns of political judgment predicted by the theory of affective intelligence (Marcus, Neuman, and MacKuen 2000).

Fear plays a particularly decisive role in the process of persuasion. Appeals to fear, cued with harsh images and music, help to pry open the door to attitude change and unexpected choices. Fear does not guarantee a change of mind but, relative to either enthusiasm or less emotional appeals, it offers the best shot at doing so. Ads targeting voter anxiety are more effective at improving impressions of the sponsor relative to the opponent, in terms of both overall feelings toward the candidates and the balance of reasons for liking or disliking them. Fear ads can win converts or create uncertainty among those who were initially opposed, but they do not achieve this entirely or even mainly by increasing acceptance of the ad's message. The ads instead cause viewers to place less weight on prior preferences or ideology and more weight on contemporary assessments of the issue and character strengths of the candidates or their gut reactions to the campaign message. We see something similar for capturing the attention of viewers. Fear ads do not improve general recall of the ad or name recognition of the candidates, but they do motivate citizens to pay greater attention to related information in the news and to seek out more such information from political and nonpolitical sources. In most cases, these ads are especially effective on those who prefer the opposing candidate and those who are most knowledgeable about politics.

Enthusiasm can exert a powerful influence on political attitudes and choices, but it is tied more to the campaign processes of activation and reinforcement than to persuasion. Appeals to enthusiasm, with warm images and music, strengthen preexisting attitudes and reliance on them in the voter's choice of candidates. Thus, the evidence suggests that they are an excellent tool for "rallying the faithful." Given the attempt to stir up positive emotions, enthusiasm or "feel-good" ads ironically are likely to polarize the electorate through a combination of attraction and repulsion. These ads simultaneously renew the commitment of supporters and spur the determination of opponents. Like cueing fear, cueing enthusiasm is most effective on those with greater political knowledge.

The short-term impact of both types of appeals is often quite substantial. We can again confidently answer the question with which we began the chapter: candidates *can* use television advertising to persuade voters. Fear appeals provide candidates with an effective instrument for convincing citizens to change their minds, and enthusiasm appeals provide them with a powerful tool for invigorating supporters.

Emotional appeals may enhance the power of campaign communication, but are they legitimate and desirable means of communicating in a democracy? Should we be more alarmed than impressed at their effectiveness and with the use of fear as an instrument in democratic elections? Certainly many describe these practices disparagingly as "preying on" the fears of ordinary people. For some, the use of positive emotional appeals is acceptable, but appealing to negative emotions is a distasteful or even corrupt practice. Although rarely differentiating among fear appeals, attack ads, and other forms of negativity, political scientists and other observers routinely condemn the use of negative tactics (Jamieson 1992; Kamber 1997).

What is wrong with advertising that appeals to negative emotions? Critics do not always make this clear. Advocates of deliberative democracy may criticize attack ads for threatening the integrity of the process by discouraging a respectful exchange of ideas, though some have defended the adversarial nature of campaigns as important to competitive elections (Mayer 1996). Others treat their objection more as a matter of etiquette: negative emotions can be an unpleasant experience for people, and therefore it is impolite and distasteful to stir up "bad feelings." In this paradigm, legitimate arguments speak only to the "better nature" of the audience. There is a tendency to associate stirring up any negative emotion, such as fear or anger, with stirring up emotions that are more widely believed to be "wrongs" in themselves, such as hate or a lust for vengeance. Finally, for others, appeals to fear bespeak something sinister. They are tools befitting the demagogue and dictator more than the statesman and public servant. There is a hint of guilt by association, though such objections can be rooted in more substantive concerns that fear renders the mind overly pliable to manipulation.

That leads us to a broader objection. Many contend that arguments ought to be made and evaluated on the basis of logic and reason alone. From this perspective, any appeal to emotion—especially as a means of persuasion—is suspect. People should make up their own minds and have good reasons for the choices they make. Critics express concern that emotions lead people to make illogical choices and to change their mind against their will. This perspective clearly is grounded in the traditional division of rationality or reason from the emotions.

Observers who hold any of the preceding viewpoints have cause for alarm at the findings presented in this chapter. Emotional appeals can powerfully affect political attitudes and choices. Where persuasion is concerned, fear works, and we can expect rational politicians—especially those who would lose otherwise—to use the tools that help them succeed. Opponents of such tactics will find it hard to prevail on principle alone.

However, not everyone agrees about the illegitimacy of fear appeals. Some may see virtue in Aristotle's counsel that "fear sets us thinking what can be done" (*Rhetoric,* 1383a) or the lesson behind Samuel Johnson's observation that the appearance of a threat to one's life "concentrates the mind." They are not likely to argue that every, or even frequent, use of fear is laudable, but they might observe that many nonemotional arguments are also worthy of condemnation (e.g., those based on stereotypes, deception, or selfishness). Indeed, opponents of emotional appeals often cling to the powerful but misguided view of emotion and reason as antagonistic, when contemporary research suggests emotion is essential to adaptive social decisionmaking (Marcus 2002). From this perspective, cueing anxiety may allow politicians to appropriately alarm otherwise rationally inattentive and predisposed citizens to wake up to potential danger and reconsider what needs to be done. Progressives, for example, fretted more over the ignorance and partisan habits of the mass public.

Even if the complaints of critics have merit, competitive campaigns and an independent news media are likely to serve as a check on the worst abuses, just as they can for other forms of "manipulation." Moreover, the ability to stoke illegitimate fears (i.e., where there is no threat) must have real limits. These are arguments for understanding better the role of fear and other emotions in the political process. Future extensions of this research can provide insight into how political competition and actual conditions place constraints on the effectiveness of fear appeals—legitimate or not.

Although the normative issues are far from resolved, the findings of this chapter shed considerable light on the process of persuasion and opinion change. First, they reveal a potency in campaign advertising far greater than most previous research has documented. In the experimental setting, candidates possess substantial power to influence the choices of voters beyond simply activating predispositions and providing information about indisputable conditions. Second, building on the results in chapter 4, these findings should help to open our eyes to emotion as a predictable and explicable part of politics. Marcus and colleagues (2000) find similar relationships between emotional reactions to candidates and political judgment in presidential elections. This study uses experiments to help establish the causal claims behind those earlier results. It also extends them to the dynamic process of campaign communication. This study goes beyond showing that citizens who feel certain emotions make different choices to demonstrate that *candidates can change citizens' choices by appealing to their emotions through political advertising.* Finally, we are now in a better position to explain why campaigns may want to use different tactics to deliver the same message to different segments of the electorate. I pursue these implications further in chapter 6.

Experiments, such as those discussed here, illuminate the link between cause and effect, revealing a great deal about the potential influence of causal forces. However, we must pursue further experimental studies and other forms of data collection to learn about how long such effects last, how the effects accumulate, and what bounds the larger political and informational environment place on effectiveness. Clearly ads can affect political choices and behavior in the short term. These insights permit us to pursue research at other levels with greater confidence about the underlying causal processes at work. Again, the results presented here testify—in a way only experiments can—that campaign ads can use appeals to fear to persuade citizens and appeals to enthusiasm to reinforce their convictions.

6

Emotional Appeals in Ad Campaigns

Speaking and writing and canvassing are common to elections all over the world. What is peculiar to America is the amazing development of the "demonstration" as a means of raising enthusiasm. . . . The parade and procession business, the crowds, the torches, the badges, the flags, the shouting . . . keeps up the "boom," and an American election is held to be, truly or falsely, largely a matter of booming.

Lord James Bryce (1889)

Politicians routinely resort to the kinds of emotional appeals examined in preceding chapters, or so conventional wisdom suggests. Popular belief also holds that ads appeal to emotions in large part by packaging their message with imagery and music. My goal in this chapter is to shed further light on the extent to which and the ways in which politicians appeal to emotions in their ad campaigns. Indeed, as I finish this book, the sound and fury of another election has recently drawn to a close. Americans in 2004 were collectively exposed to over a million campaign ads on television. Many of those ads, it seemed to observers, targeted fear and anger with unparalleled vigor. In addition to all of the candidate and party advertising, numerous "527" organizations (named after a section in the Internal Revenue Code), such as MoveOn.org and Swift Boat Veterans for Truth, emerged almost exclusively to launch ad campaigns aimed at unleashing negative emotions toward George W. Bush and John Kerry. Thus, the peculiar, "booming" style of American campaigns described by Bryce over a century ago continues to stir up emotions, though the techniques have evolved somewhat. The electronic boom of the campaign parades through American homes for months on end, seeking to rouse not only fear and anger, but also hope, enthusiasm, and pride.

In this chapter, I take a closer look at the use of emotion in contemporary ad campaigns. I consider three sets of questions.[1] First, to which emotions do political ads appeal? I asserted earlier that the two types of appeals on which I focus in this book—fear and enthusiasm—are commonplace in elections. This chapter checks the veracity of that claim and considers what other emotions ads seek to elicit. In doing so, I pay particular attention to those emotions that are seen as central to dimensional or discrete theories of emotion and that are appropriate to electoral politics.

Second, in what ways do campaign ads attempt to appeal to distinct emotions? This chapter investigates the frequency with which candidates alter the music, images, color, and other facets of ads to appeal to emotions. I consider how well these cues correspond to what we would expect based on the functional specificity of emotions proposed by psychologists and the theory of *affective intelligence* (see chapter 3). Audiovisual features of an ad usually dovetail with its message. I examine the extent to which emotional appeals are associated with specific verbal messages and issue content. Yet another element of conventional wisdom suggests that reliance on emotional appeals comes at the expense of information, issues, and logic. I put this proposition to the test.

Third, are politicians strategic in appealing to emotions? Given what we have learned about the effects of different appeals, we might expect politicians to adopt these appeals selectively. The experimental evidence suggests that the relative advantage of using fear or enthusiasm appeals depends on the distribution of loyalties in the electorate and what information is available to voters if they consider departing from those loyalties. Guided by their intuitions and by trial-and-error, candidates and their consultants might (unknowingly) use emotional appeals in accordance with theoretical predictions, or they may simply follow the conventional wisdom of their profession. Although data for extensively testing such propositions are not yet available, I sort through preliminary evidence to reveal the circumstances under which politicians do and do not use specific types of emotional appeals.

A Study of the Emotional Content of Recent Advertising Campaigns

In an effort to provide answers to these questions, I report on the first large-scale, systematic study of emotion in contemporary ad campaigns.[2] In collaboration with colleagues, I initiated a project in 2002 to code and analyze the use of emotional appeals and related content in recent political ads.[3] This chapter reports the first results from that project. We obtained ads for the 2000 election from the *National Journal,* which tried to collect and store all ads aired in major markets, focusing heavily on major federal and state-wide races. The resulting sample includes a total of 1,565 ads from election campaigns in 2000, plus thirty ads from three gubernatorial elections held in 1999. It includes primary and general election spots aired by candidates seeking a wide array of offices—president, governor, U.S. senator, U.S. representative, state senator or representative, mayor, and state supreme court justice. It includes ads produced by candidates, political parties, and interest groups. The sample is drawn from contests in forty-six states.[4] In the analyses that follow, I focus on the slightly more than fourteen hundred ads specifically tied to major federal and statewide races.

Once the collection of ads was compiled and indexed, we began to build a dataset based on systematic content analysis. After a period of training, research assistants worked independently to record numerous features of each ad. This involved nine coders over the course of two years from 2002 to 2004. We assigned each coder to analyze a set of ads that had, for the most part, been compiled in no particular order. By the end, the team of coders had coded each ad at least twice and a subsample of ads a third or fourth time for reliability checks.

Coding instructions called on coders to record over a hundred variables for each ad. These variables naturally include the presence, type, and strength of emotional appeals. The list of items also covers many aspects of an ad's political content. Coders recorded information about the sponsor, message, and style of the ad. The coding scheme identifies the tone of an ad but also takes note of distinctions among types of negativity, emphases on character and issues, and use of biographical themes. It catalogs use of a wide range of political information or appeals, including party, ideology, character, issues, values, leadership, performance, endorsements, and links to social groups.

I designed the experimental study on the premise that nonverbal elements are often the key to cueing emotions, and this is reflected in the content analysis as well. Coders kept track of the visual portrayal of candidates, social groups, and people in general. Images can play an informational as well as an emotional role; therefore, the coding instructions contain a category for flagging ads that employ images as a form of visual evidence for the claims being made. Finally, coders monitored the use of color, music, sound effects, narration, production style, symbols, and other evocative imagery. The average intercoder reliability score across all variables is 0.87 (Holsti 1969). I describe the coding instructions where relevant in the text and provide complete details in appendix C. Before proceeding, however, I should explain how we coded emotional appeals.

Coding the Emotional Appeal of Campaign Ads

One could adopt a number of methods to code the emotional appeal of an advertisement. Recognizing the often personalized nature of emotional responses, one might ask coders to evaluate how the ad made *them* feel, especially if one were interested in the ad's ultimate impact on the public. In this approach, one tries to measure the actual emotion evoked by an ad, including unintended emotions, much like the manipulation check for the experiments (see chapter 4). Alternatively, concerned with theoretical precision, one could train a team of coders to recognize and record the antecedents of distinct emotions as specified by a particular psychological theory (e.g., Lazarus's [1991] *appraisal* theory).[5] This approach stresses more objective or universal aspects of emotion and sharpens the focus on discrete causes over global effects. For example, researchers have adopted this approach to study emotional expression in facial displays (Ekman and Rosenberg 1997; Sullivan and Masters 1988). Finally, in an approach that lies between the preceding options, one could ask coders to determine which emotion(s) the ad and its creators were trying to evoke. This maintains a focus on advertising as a form of candidate or group behavior by emphasizing intention and the emotion to which the ad was *appealing* rather than the emotion it in fact elicited. This calls on coders to make intersubjective judgments, reflecting a compromise of sorts between subjective responses and objective pattern recognition.

I adopt the last approach for this study in order to learn more about how politicians use ads to *target* voter emotions. The instructions ask coders to judge the extent to which an ad tried to elicit each of several emotions from its intended audience(s).[6] The *dimensional* and *discrete emotion* theories discussed in chapter 3 served as a guide for choosing the emotional categories and deciding which aspects of the verbal and audiovisual content of ads to code. To summarize, then, coders tried to discern the emotion(s) to which an ad appealed at the time it was aired. While such judgments involve subjectivity, they are based on cultural frames of reference and allow for intersubjective agreement in a way that reporting one's own emotional response does not.[7]

Having selected an approach to coding the appeals, one then faces the question of which emotions to include. In their "videostyle" protocol, Kaid and Johnston (2001) record the presence of fear appeals designed to scare voters and the use of humor. Kern's (1989) exploratory typology, based on interviews with consultants, included a set of nine positive and five negative categories.[8] Positive categories include compassion, ambition, nostalgia, reassurance, trust, intimacy, hope, national pride, and local pride. Negative categories include guilt, uncertainty, anger, and fear (the latter was divided into strong and weak forms). Although this is a reasonable approach, the results reveal the drawbacks of a system inspired primarily by consultants, who are not as concerned with theory. The scheme proved unwieldy: out of four coders, two or more reached agreement on whether an ad appealed to a given emotion in only half of the cases (Kern 1989, 75).[9] In particular, coders found it difficult to distinguish among several categories. These difficulties may have been exacerbated by conceptual confusion in the coding scheme, as the categories are actually a mix of common emotions (e.g., hope, pride, fear, and anger) and relational or personal qualities (e.g., intimacy, trust, ambition, and uncertainty).[10] Although Kern's study failed to produce reliable results, it served its intended purpose as an exploration—the first of its kind—into constructing a typology of emotional appeals.

For the present study, I developed a typology that includes seven emotions or clusters of related emotions. I based my choice of categories principally on the basic emotions identified in psychological theories (see chapter 3), as well as on previous research and recognition of the emotions most likely to be the target of political advertising appeals. My goal was to capture the range of emotions to which campaign ads might appeal while maintaining enough distinctiveness in the categories to permit reliable judging by coders. The categories include the two emotions at the center of this book—*fear* (anxiety/worry) and *enthusiasm* (hope/joy). They are tied to two fundamental affective response systems (Gray 1987), high arousal states of dimensional models of emotions (Watson, Clark, and Tellegen 1988), and the two key emotions in affective intelligence theory (Marcus, Neuman, and MacKuen 2000). *Anger* (outrage/disgust) also is tied to a fundamental response system (Panksepp 1998), a proposed third key emotion in the dimensional framework of affective intelligence (Marcus 2003), and seen as highly relevant to politics by those applying discrete or appraisal models (Conover and Feldman 1986; Kinder 1994; Lerner et al. 2003).[11] I include a separate category for *pride*. Although pride is often grouped with enthusiasm and was found to heavily overlap with hope and reassurance appeals by Kern (1989), appraisal theorists often treat it as distinct due to its retrospective and egocentric character (Lazarus 1991). In politics, pride appeals may also be distinctly associated with group, especially national, identities.

All four categories so far feature high-arousal emotions, play a prominent role in many theories of emotion, and are likely to engender few doubts about their relevance to political advertising. The three remaining categories include emotions that I also believe may be the target of political advertising appeals, but which are low-arousal states (thus, less likely to be the basis for a call to action) and/or play a less central role in affective intelligence theory and dimensional models despite their distinctiveness. *Sadness* (disappointment) sits opposite enthusiasm at the low-arousal end of the disposition system in affective intelligence theory (Marcus, Neuman, and MacKuen 2000) and is identified by appraisal theorists as a basic emotion elicited by the loss of something valued (Lazarus 1991). Some dimensional models see *amusement* as related to joy and enthusiasm, but it clearly has distinct antecedents and expressive outlets (Ekman and Rosenberg 1998; Frederickson and Branigan 2001) and has been regarded as an effective rhetorical appeal in political settings (Kaid and Johnston 2001; Richardson 2003).

Finally, *compassion* (sympathy) also serves as the basis for occasional political appeals and is distinct from those emotions already listed (Lazarus 1991), though its place in affective intelligence theory or other dimensional approaches is not obvious.[12]

The instructions ask coders: "Overall, to what extent is the ad trying to elicit [this specific emotion] from viewers?" Coders indicate whether the ad makes no such appeal, appeals somewhat to the emotion, or appeals strongly to the emotion. Intercoder reliability for the presence of each type of emotional appeal ranges from mediocre for pride to excellent for enthusiasm and amusement:[13]

Fear	0.81 (K = 0.60)
Enthusiasm	0.91 (K = 0.78)
Anger	0.82 (K = 0.64)
Pride	0.68 (K = 0.34)
Compassion	0.83 (K = 0.41)
Sadness	0.85 (K = 0.38)
Amusement	0.95 (K = 0.73)

These scores indicate the effort to code emotional advertising appeals was successful. In light of the subjectivity involved in assessing emotions, I deal with disagreements by combining coder evaluations into a single value for each ad.[14] Although my focus in this chapter remains on fear and enthusiasm, as it has been the entire book, I pay attention to the other categories in order to assess the relative prevalence of these two types of appeals and to be mindful of relationships across categories.[15]

*   *   *

A final word is in order about the nature of these data and the constraints they place on the claims being made here. My colleagues and I have tried to collect all of the ads produced and aired in contested presidential, gubernatorial, and congressional races during the 2000 election cycle. There may be a few missing, but we are confident that this collection is reasonably comprehensive and reflects well the universe of ads produced for TV in 2000. In the analyses ahead, therefore, when I present percentages, means, and other statistics, I am making claims about the *population of ads produced* for the 1999–2000 election season. Likewise, when I say that certain candidates are more likely to use this or that type of appeal, I am making a claim about the likelihood or extent to which those candidates include the appeal in their advertising arsenal. In presenting this evidence, I am not making claims about the population of *ad broadcasts* or *airings* that occurred, nor am I making claims about the types of ads candidates aired most frequently.[16] I wish to be clear about this now because it would be clumsy to rehearse these distinctions with every claim; instead, I will simply say something like the "percentage of all ads." However, it would be reckless for either the author or the reader to lose sight of what claims are and are not being made.[17]

Emotional Contours of Campaign Advertising in 1999–2000

We can now begin to get a sense of the distribution of emotional appeals among actual ads. In 1999 and 2000, almost all campaign ads appealed to the emotions of viewers and yet a substantial majority, 79 percent, also appealed to the viewers' capacity to reason by encouraging them to draw conclusions from evidence (i.e., logical appeal).[18] These two findings underscore the dangers of thinking of emotion and logic as mutually exclusive categories. Nonetheless, the reputation of political advertising as primarily emotional is well founded: in nearly 72 percent of ads, the appeal to emotions dominated the appeal to logic. For the most part, the patterns are similar across different types of races, as appeals to emotion dominate everywhere.[19]

Emotions predominate, but which ones? Table 6.1 displays the frequencies with which ads appealed to particular emotions. Fear, anger, enthusiasm, and pride were far and away the most common targets, each one being the focus of appeal more often than the remaining three emotions combined. Ads often appeal to more than one emotion. The first column of the table shows what share of ads make any attempt to tap a specific emotion, while the last column shows the share of ads appealing only to that specific emotion but no others. We can see that nearly half of all ads include some sort of appeal to fear, anger, and pride. Enthusiasm appeals are present in almost three out of every four ads, primarily as candidates attempt to stir hope and excitement for their own electoral cause. Very few ads, scarcely 10 percent, exclusively target a single emotion.

Although most ads appeal to multiple emotions, they exhibit considerable consistency and clarity in their primary emotional target. The middle two columns of table 6.1 tell this story. We can characterize two-thirds of all ads as having a single emotional appeal that is more prominent than any other appeal in the ad. In most cases, this dominant appeal is also a strong appeal.[20] For example, one-third of all ads in the sample feature a strong, dominant appeal to enthusiasm, whereas 7 percent of ads are dominated by strong fear appeals. There also is considerable overlap between pride and enthusiasm appeals, on the one hand, and fear and anger appeals, on the other.[21] Many psychologists indeed claim that pride and anger have similar antecedents to enthusiasm and fear, respectively (i.e., positive feedback about the success of one's goals; a threat to one's well-being), even though the for-

TABLE 6.1 Distribution of Emotional Appeals in the 1999 and 2000 Elections

| | Relative Strength/Dominance of the Emotional Appeal | | | |
Type of Emotional Appeal	Present	Dominant	Strong and Dominant	Exclusive
Fear	41%	8%	7%	< 1%
Anger	46	11	10	2
Enthusiasm	73	40	34	7
Pride	54	3	2	< 1
Compassion	21	2	2	< 1
Sadness	9	1	1	0
Amusement	9	3	3	< 1
Fear & anger (equal)	16	7	5	11
Enthusiasm & pride (equal)	18	12	10	28

Note: Entries are the percentage of ads containing any appeal to the emotion specified (first column), percentage of ads in which the specified emotional appeal is stronger than all others (second column), percentage of ads in which the specified emotional appeal is strong *and* stronger than all others (third column), and the percentage of ads in which this is the only emotion to which the ad appeals at all (fourth column). Entries in the first column do not reflect mutually exclusive categorization, but entries in remaining columns are mutually exclusive (i.e., any given ad can be represented in one row only). $N = 1,425$.

mer two emotions have a more retrospective quality (Gray 1994; Izard 1986; Lazarus 1991).[22] A significant fraction of ads contain equally strong, dominant appeals to these related pairs of emotions, as shown at the bottom of the table. In addition, these common pairings are much more likely to serve as the exclusive focus on an ad's emotional appeal; fully 40 percent of ads appeal equally to one of these pairs of emotions but no others. In all, twice as many ads appeal to positive emotions as negative emotions.

By summing the percentages in the third column of table 6.1, we see that 74 percent of ads in the sample fit one of nine emotional profiles as defined by a strong, dominant emotional appeal. What's missing? One in four ads makes either more thoroughly mixed or weak emotional appeals. Most of these fall in the latter category, which I referred to in chapter 1 as "unimpassioned" ads. The appropriateness of this term relative to other potential labels, such as "neutral" or "unemotional," is highlighted by the degree to which emotion is almost never entirely absent from ads. What if, true to their name, we defined unemotional ads as those lacking in appeals to any of the seven emotions in the typology? This definition characterizes just four of the 1,425 ads (0.28 percent) examined in this chapter. Therefore, I retain the more useful categorization of unimpassioned ads, defined as those lacking any strong appeal to emotion. By this definition, unimpassioned ads make up 24 percent of all ads. That leaves slightly more than 2 percent of ads in a residual category of "mixed emotions." Figure 6.1 summarizes the relative frequency with which ads in 1999 and 2000 matched one of the now eleven emotional profiles.

Although an ad's strongest appeal is usually to a single emotion or two closely related emotions, we should not dismiss the fact that 34 percent of ads contain appeals to both positive and negative emotions. This corresponds to what Kern (1989) refers to as the "get 'em sick, get 'em well" advertising concept, in which advertisers try to create anxieties and then reassure people they have the solution.[23] A look at how the presence of mixed appeals relates to advertising tone supports this notion. Forty-five percent of ads with both positive and negative appeals are comparative spots that contrast the virtues of the sponsor with the liabilities of the opponent.[24] Most of the remaining mixed cases (42 percent) are advocacy spots, in which candidates often offer their plans and themselves as solutions to certain problems. In other words, the type of ad most commonly referred to as "positive" in the academic literature is not necessarily all positive in terms of either the information it provides or the emotions it tries to elicit.

FIGURE 6.1 Classification of Campaign Ads by Dominant Emotional Appeal

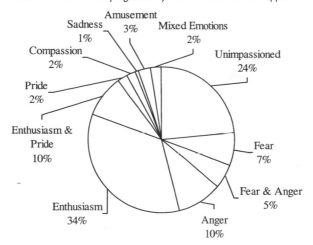

Note: The graph displays the percentage of ads from the 1999 and 2000 elections that match each of the eleven emotional profiles described in the text. Nine of the profiles indicate the emotion or pairing of emotions to which an ad appeals strongly and more strongly than any other emotion. These correspond to the third column of percentages in table 6.1. The category of "unimpassioned" includes ads that lack any strong emotional appeal. The category of "mixed emotions" includes ads with strong emotional appeals but in which none is dominant. *N* = 1,425.

This brings us to the relationship between message tone and emotional appeal, and, more generally, to the importance of recognizing the different ways in which ads can be positive or negative. Message tone and emotional valence often match, especially when it comes to the dominant emotional appeal: 83 percent of enthusiasm and pride ads promote the sponsor, while 69 percent of fear and anger ads focus on attacking the opponent. These same ads adopt the opposite tone in only 0.5 percent and 6 percent of the cases, respectively. At the same time, nontrivial fractions of attack (23 percent) and promotion (12 percent) spots make some sort of appeal to an emotion of the opposing valence. Although comparison spots are more likely than other ads to be classified as unimpassioned, most have a dominant emotional appeal. In fact, it would be difficult to guess the emotion targeted by a comparison spot in advance, as 32 percent are classified as unimpassioned, 36 percent as enthusiasm or pride appeals, and 26 percent as fear or anger appeals. By running through this list of numbers, I hope to stress that the need to distinguish between emotional appeal and informational tone is not simply a conceptual strategy for untangling advertising effects, but also a necessity for understanding real-world variation among campaign ads.[25]

In sum, three out of four campaign ads appeal strongly to a single dominant emotion or pairing of highly related emotions. The two emotions highlighted in this book, fear and enthusiasm, are the subject of three out of four of these strong, dominant appeals. The prevalence of emotional appeals is further revealed by the fact that almost all of the ads lacking a strong appeal make some appeal to emotion nonetheless. Finally, the data cast doubt on the conventional opposition of emotional appeals to logic and the tendency in previous scholarship to conflate message tone with emotional appeal.

Emotional Cues

I now revisit the conventional wisdom, discussed in the first two chapters of this book, about the way ads are used to elicit emotion. In particular, consultants, journalists, and academics seem to believe that the emotional appeal of an ad stems in large part from its audiovisual packaging. If anyone disagrees, they have been shy about saying so. For all that it may be obvious to casual observers, we now have an opportunity to take a more systematic look at how ads try to cue emotion.

In most cases, I pursue the analysis in this section by grouping together appeals to fear and anger, on the one hand, and appeals to enthusiasm and pride, on the other. My reason for doing so is that, unless otherwise noted, there are few meaningful differences within these pairs of emotions in terms of the presence of specific audiovisual cues. This suggests that these sorts of cues largely serve to evoke positive or negative affect in general, rather than elicit a more fine-grained emotional response on their own. This view is consistent with what psychologists have identified as a rapid preconscious system for affective response (Zajonc 1998) or "somatic markers" (Damasio 1994). According to this perspective, our brains respond extremely rapidly to sensory inputs, identifying them on the basis of past experience as good or bad (i.e., desirable or harmful), which lays the groundwork for subsequent, more refined reactions. Psychologists have also developed a vast inventory of images, the International Affective Picture System (IAPS), which have been standardized in terms of individuals' emotional responses; these responses have likewise been calibrated only at the level of positive and negative affect, rather than more specific emotions (Bradley, Cuthbert, and Lang 1996; Bradley and Lang 2000; Bradley et al. 2001). From this, it seems likely that the coupling of words and context with audiovisual cues is essential to eliciting more precise emotions, even if the audiovisual cues are the driving force behind experiencing an emotional response (but simply determine the valence of that response in most cases). However, Lerner and colleagues (2003) demonstrate that distinct video images from a known event (e.g., the September 11 attacks) can predictably elicit either fear or anger.[26]

Color often sends a clear and immediate, if unobtrusive, signal about emotion (Hemphill 1996; Valdez and Mehrabian 1994). Figure 6.2 demonstrates this for campaign ads. Distinct color schemes clearly differentiate among ads appealing to the primary emotions.[27] Black-and-white video images are ten times more likely to signal a fear or anger appeal than an enthusiasm or pride appeal ($t = 7.98, p < .001$).[28] A similar story holds true for the use of dim, dark, or gray color imagery in ads. Nine percent of fear or anger appeals use a darker color theme, which is used by less than a third of 1 percent of enthusiasm or pride appeals ($t = 7.68, p < .001$). Bright and colorful imagery provides an almost exact reversal of these percentages with enthusiasm and pride appeals on top ($t = 5.70, p < .001$). A large number of ads of all types adopt "normal," plain coloring, which does less to distinguish among emotional appeals, although it appears more frequently in conjunction with positive emotional appeals ($t = 3.50, p < .001$). In every case, unimpassioned ads fall more-or-less squarely in between the two sets of emotional appeals as far as color cues are concerned.[29]

Some observers and practitioners regard music as an especially potent instrument with which to elicit emotions. The power of a soundtrack stems in part from its ability to influence mood and emotional expectations while our attention is focused elsewhere—for example, on speech and pictures (Schwartz 1973; J. Smith 1999). Figure 6.3 displays how the use of music varies by emotional appeal. The fact that all but a modest fraction (17 percent) of ads have music may offer testimony to why so many ads are seen as making some sort of appeal to emotions. As we might expect, uplifting, sen-

FIGURE 6.2 Ads Often Use Color to Appeal to Distinct Emotions

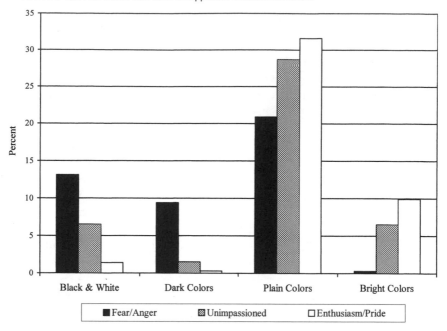

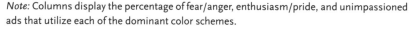

Note: Columns display the percentage of fear/anger, enthusiasm/pride, and unimpassioned ads that utilize each of the dominant color schemes.

timental, or patriotic music, rich in major chords, is commonly found in enthusiasm or pride ads but not fear or anger ads (t = 20.65, p < .001); the reverse is true when it comes to tense, somber, or discordant music (t = 24.03, p < .001). Once again, unimpassioned ads are middling relative to more emotional spots but make use of uplifting styles of music more often than tense styles.[30] It is not surprising that a significant share of unimpassioned ads contain no music, but it is noteworthy that fear and anger ads are three times as likely to be devoid of music as enthusiasm and pride ads (t = 7.59, p < .001). One reason for this may be the fact that ads appealing to negative emotions sometimes dispense with music to focus on sound effects. Twelve percent of ads contain sounds other than music and narration It is twice as common for negative appeals to be accompanied by sound effects as it is for positive appeals (18 percent vs. 9 percent; t = 3.97, p < .001).[31] As in the case of music, the nature of the sounds matches the emotional tone of the ad in most cases. Enthusiasm and pride appeals are more likely to be paired with sound effects that have a positive connotation (e.g., applause, shared laughter), while fear and anger appeals are paired with negative sound effects (e.g., screams, sirens, a baby crying).[32]

FIGURE 6.3 Ads Rely on Musical Cues to Appeal to Distinct Emotions

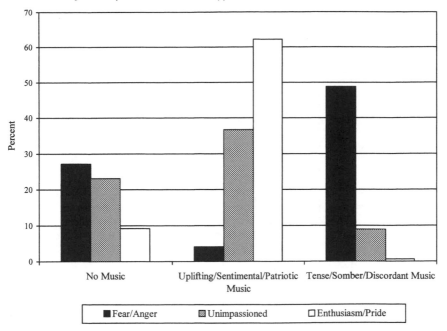

Note: Columns display the percentage of fear/anger, enthusiasm/pride, and unimpassioned ads that use particular types of music or have no music.

In the minds of many, imagery is the key to what makes political advertising, as well as commercial ads, emotionally evocative. By both nature and culture, humans tend to rely heavily on their sense of vision, making the dynamic pictures of television a compelling focus of attention (Barry 1997). Few visual objects captivate our attention more than fellow humans, especially their faces, toward which we have a strong orienting response (Masters 1988). As figures 6.4a and 6.4b show, campaign ads use images of people as well as a variety of scenes and symbols to cue distinct emotions. The content analysis included a count of the number of people who appear in each ad, other than the candidate and opponent. Most ads include images of people, but especially ads appealing to enthusiasm and pride. By comparison, fear and anger ads are four times as likely to leave people out of the picture ($t = 8.38, p < .001$), helping to suggest loneliness, loss, and desolation. In addition, when we consider only those ads containing images of people, enthusiasm and pride appeals feature more than twice as many people on average (21 vs. 9; $t = 8.95, p < .001$).

Numbers are not the only relevant issue—who populates an ad matters as well. Among ads with at least one person other than the candidates, pride

FIGURE 6.4A Ads Appealing to Enthusiasm and Pride Are Rich in Visual Cues Associated with Success and the "Good Life"

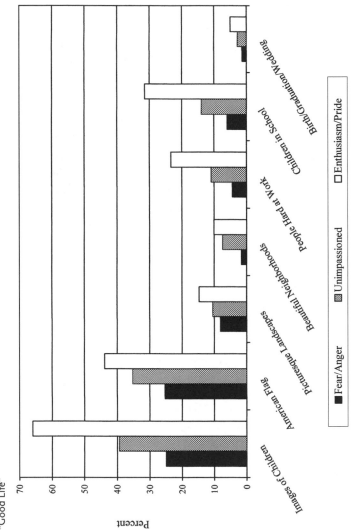

Note: Columns display the percentage of fear/anger, enthusiasm/pride, and unimpassioned ads that contain various types of positive visual imagery.

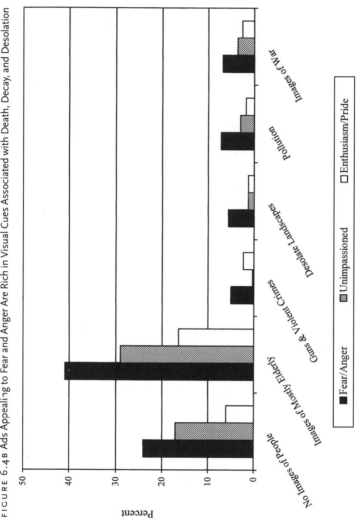

FIGURE 6.4B Ads Appealing to Fear and Anger Are Rich in Visual Cues Associated with Death, Decay, and Desolation

Note: Columns display the percentage of fear/anger, enthusiasm/pride, and unimpassioned ads that contain various types of negative visual imagery.

and enthusiasm ads are more likely to contain children (70 percent vs. 33 percent), senior citizens (56 percent vs. 45 percent), minorities (51 percent vs. 22 percent), families (38 percent vs. 14 percent), women (91 percent vs. 76 percent), as well as men (95 percent vs. 86 percent). Whites, the only other group measured in the content analysis, show up at equal rates in both types of ads. How can it be that no group appears less often in these ads? Ads with positive emotional appeals contain not only more people, but also a more diverse population. Ads targeting negative emotions are more likely to feature only people of the same race (78 percent vs. 47 percent), people of the same sex (30 percent vs. 7 percent), or seniors (11 percent vs. 3 percent).[33] Finally, it is more likely that most people shown in the ad will be elderly when the appeal is to fear or anger, but less likely that most of them will be children. These relative emphases help enthusiasm and pride ads cue associations with life and togetherness, while fear and anger ads cue decay and death.[34]

Ads also try to cue emotions with symbolic imagery of places and events. Figures 6.4a and 6.4b show a small selection of the possibilities in this domain. Ads appealing to the primary positive emotions more often feature patriotic images, such as the American flag and people in military uniform, and scenes of natural beauty. These ads also make greater use of scenes of success and rites of passage that convey common aspirations for the "good life"—well-groomed neighborhoods, people happy and hard at their work, children playing and learning at school, parents with a new baby, and graduation and wedding ceremonies. In the 2000 election, images of national or state buildings and monuments were used equally in the course of positive and negative emotional appeals.[35] Fear and anger ads are more likely to feature images associated with death, conflict, and misery, such as guns, violent crimes, barren landscapes, pollution, and warfare. These findings parallel research on the International Affective Picture System (IAPS), in which pictures of cute babies, sunrises, and so on have been tied reliably to positive emotional responses, whereas pictures of human mutilation, dangerous animals, and the like have been tied to negative emotions (Bradley et al. 2001).[36] In most cases, the use of imagery in unimpassioned ads falls somewhere in between the more emotional ads.[37]

Beyond the major components of color, music, and imagery, ads can resort to a number of other audiovisual elements as a source of emotional cues. I have already mentioned sound effects. Another emotional cue that travels by way of the audio channel is narration, by which I mean the tone of the narrator's voice rather than the words spoken. Given the special training that would be required of coders, we did not measure timbre, pitch, volume, and other qualities that might shed light on the emotional inflection of the voice-over.[38] However, we did record whether the ad used voice-over (from someone other than the candidate) and the gender of the narrator. Most ads use narration, but its use is more frequent among ads targeting fear and anger (92 percent vs. 74 percent; t = 6.94, p < .001). Looking only at cases in which voice-overs are used, fear and anger ads are also more likely to use a female narrator by a nearly two-to-one margin (36 percent vs. 20 percent; t = 5.13, p < .001). The relatively greater absence of narration in positive emotional spots can be explained by the fact that, as I discuss in the following section, the sponsor of the ad is much more likely to appear and do his or her own talking in enthusiasm and pride ads. Fifty percent of ads with no narration adopt a so-called talking head format. The reliance on female narrators to deliver fear and anger appeals is more difficult to explain. I suspect it is tied to gender stereotypes regarding source credibility, but pursuit of that question lies beyond the scope of this book.

On the video side, consultants can make use of a variety of production techniques during filming and editing with the potential to affect viewer perceptions and emotional reactions. One such tactic is the pace of video editing. In what is loosely referred to as the "MTV style" of fast-paced editing prevalent in contemporary commercials, movies, and TV shows, most political ads cut frequently from one scene to another throughout their thirty- or sixty-second run. Only 10 percent of ads use a single-shot format with no cuts. This latter style of editing is most common among unimpassioned ads (16 percent) and is also associated with a talking heads format. Enthusiasm and pride ads are more likely than fear and anger ads to feature a rapid series of scene transitions (79 percent vs. 66 percent; t = 4.70, p < .001), though this pacing is dominant for all ads regardless of emotional appeal.

Finally, we can consider the relationship of emotional appeals to the message of the ad. Choice of emotional appeal seems to be tied in predictable ways to political content. We have already seen that there is a clear, though far from perfect, link between the tone of the ad's argument (i.e., promoting, attacking, or comparing) and its emotional appeal. Although the contrast is not always dramatic, ads appealing to fear or enthusiasm also seem to differ in the extent to which they emphasize issues or personality. Most ads include at least some discussion of policy issues. While only 1 percent of fear ads avoid issues altogether, 7 percent of enthusiasm ads eschew them (t = 3.29, p < .001). Only about half of all ads invoke the personal qualities of the candidates, but ads appealing to enthusiasm are far more likely to do so than those appealing to fear (49 percent vs. 29 percent; t = 3.66, p < .001).[39]

Other evidence points in the same direction. Half of all ads mention the record or experience of one or both candidates. Sixty-one percent of fear ads invoke candidate records compared to 44 percent of enthusiasm ads (t = 4.05, p < .001). Similarly, 68 percent of fear ads explicitly cite evidentiary sources for factual claims, while only 21 percent of enthusiasm ads do so (t = 13.02, p < .001). Sixteen percent of ads frame candidate choice in terms of leadership, and 10 percent make reference to the personal history or biography of the candidate. In both cases, enthusiasm ads raise these candidate-centered considerations more frequently than fear ads: leadership framing occurs with 24 percent of enthusiasm appeals but with only 2 percent of fear appeals ($t = 6.75, p < .001$), while 14 percent of enthusiasm ads venture into biography but not a single fear ad does ($t = 5.37, p < .001$).[40] In sum, politicians are more likely to emphasize character, leadership, and biography when appealing to enthusiasm, but more likely to focus on issues or performance and to document the source of their claims when appealing to fear.

Consultants employ a wide array of techniques to cue the emotions of the electorate and often make use of redundant cues in the same ad to strengthen and clarify the appeal. A richer, more nuanced discussion of political ads along similar lines, with a greater focus on specific cases, can be found elsewhere.[41] My primary purpose has been to say something more systematic regarding the prevalence of certain types of emotional cues in contemporary campaign ads. The results provide support for the conventional belief that emotional appeals are strongly tied to music, images, and other audiovisual elements of an ad. Consistent with the antecedents of emotions specified by psychological theories (see chapter 3), ads appealing to enthusiasm tend to use cues associated with life and success, while ads appealing to fear use cues associated with death and danger. In contrast to their maligned image, however, fear ads focus much more heavily on issues and factual evidence than enthusiasm ads.

Evidence of Strategy in Appeals to Emotion

I now examine which politicians use specific appeals and under what circumstances. I particularly wish to take note of patterns that suggest the strategic use of emotional appeals. For the most part, candidates and consultants do not design political ads on the basis of scientific evidence, but rather tend to rely on their professional instincts and ad hoc focus group testing in each election. Nonetheless, the informal lessons they learn through experience and focus group "trial balloons" may lead some of them to produce and air ads in a manner consistent with the theoretical propositions that now have been supported by scientific evidence. It is also possible, however, that they simply fall back on the conventional wisdom and folk theories that dominate their craft. I complete the empirical analysis of this book by examining how well politicians' decisions about which appeals to produce in particular situations correspond with the experimental findings regarding effects.

For this purpose, I supplement the content analysis data with information about the election and sociopolitical context in which the ads were aired. In this way, we can get a richer sense of how (i.e., when and where) emotional appeals are used and not used. For example, we might ask whether politicians appeal more to certain emotions late or early in campaigns, as challengers or incumbents, or in closely contested races or with more comfortable margins. Given the theoretical propositions and experimental findings discussed earlier in the book, I hypothesize that candidates favor appeals to enthusiasm in those situations where they stand to gain more than their opponent from a mobilization of existing loyalties or reinforcement of the status quo. Likewise, candidates should favor appeals to fear when they would benefit from citizens taking a closer or second look at the available information.

Sponsorship, Incumbency, Competitiveness, and Phase of the Election

Before examining how electoral context affects the types of ads created, I begin with a couple of observations regarding sponsorship. Popular belief suggests that politicians should use surrogates to attack their opponents out of fear of a backlash against such negativity—in emotional terms, that the negative affect aroused will also be partially transferred to the sponsor. However, the evidence in this book provides no support for a backlash against use of fear appeals. I find that, where emotional appeals are concerned, politicians act in accordance with this bit of conventional wisdom. The proportion of fear ads created by political parties (31 percent) and interest groups (34 percent) is much greater than the proportion created by candidates (6 percent; $F = 90.68, p < .001$). The pattern reverses for sponsorship of enthusiasm ads: they constitute 52 percent of candidates' ads, but only 17 percent of party ads and 13 percent of interest group ads ($F = 82.08, p < .001$).[42] It is worth noting that these relationship hold even when controlling for advertising tone. While the pattern is consistent with prior findings on "negative" ads, the differential use of emotional appeals occurs over and above any pattern for attack and promotion.[43]

Turning to the political context, I begin by examining the impact of three factors commonly used by observers to classify elections: incumbency status, competitiveness of the race, and the phase of the election (i.e., primary or general election). Evidence of differential effects from enthusiasm and fear produce a clear expectation for incumbency status. Incumbents enjoy the advantage at reelection time of being the default choice. On average, therefore, they should reinforce the status quo by appealing to enthusiasm, and challengers should encourage voters to rethink default choices by appealing to fear. The theory and evidence presented in earlier chapters do not produce different expectations where timing and competitiveness are concerned. Both types of appeals are effective campaign tools. In addition, their distinct benefits do not necessarily make them differentially advantageous for different phases in a campaign or differing levels of competition. Conventional wisdom, however, tends to see fear appeals as especially potent, though their use is often frowned upon in the intraparty competition of primaries.

Results for incumbency status are consistent with what we would expect from evidence on effects. Challengers are more likely to use fear ads (9 percent vs. 5 percent), and incumbents are more likely to use enthusiasm ads (52 percent vs. 49 percent). However, only the finding for fear ads reaches statistical significance ($t = 1.89, p < .055$). Candidates in open seat races do not differ significantly in their use of emotional appeals from candidates in races with an incumbent.

Competitiveness substantially affects the prevalence of emotional appeals, especially appeals to fear. For House races, the *Hotline* report on "Races to Watch" provides a good preelection measure of competition. For senatorial and gubernatorial races, I define competitiveness retrospectively as those elections with a margin of victory of less than 6 percent of the two-party vote (i.e., 53 percent to 47 percent, or closer). Figure 6.5 shows the results. When a race is close, the share of ads targeting fear increases twofold for Senate candidates and threefold for House and gubernatorial candidates. In contrast, the share of ads trying to elicit enthusiasm drops by anywhere from six to fourteen percentage points. More intense electoral competition is strongly related to greater use of fear ads relative to enthusiasm ads.[44] Candidates appear to act on the widely held belief that fear appeals are more potent.[45]

The presidential race is singular and its competitiveness cannot vary in the same way. Its very distinct nomination and general election phases, both of which were rich in ads in 2000, provide an opportunity to analyze the impact of electoral phase. The differences here are the most striking yet. During the nomination process, only six percent of ads appealed to fear but 58 percent appealed to enthusiasm. Over the course of the general election, 31 percent of ads targeted fear and 27 percent targeted enthusiasm.[46] In short, the candidates created five times as many fear ads for the general election, whereas they cut the share of enthusiasm ads in half. Thus, candidates do appear less comfortable evoking fear when competing against fellow partisans. However, we could also explain some of the difference in light of the earlier finding that interest group and party ads, which are more likely to appeal to fear, become more plentiful during the general election. Nonetheless, controlling for tone (i.e., ads in which candidates attack their opponents) or ad sponsorship merely mutes the results for emotional appeals; it does not make them disappear. The difference may have something to do with the relative competitiveness of the phases of the presidential election. The more tightly fought general election results match the pattern seen for competitive races of other varieties.

Within the nomination phase itself, we can test another prediction implied by the theoretical claims and experimental evidence on effects. Front-runners benefit from the status quo and therefore should wish to appeal to

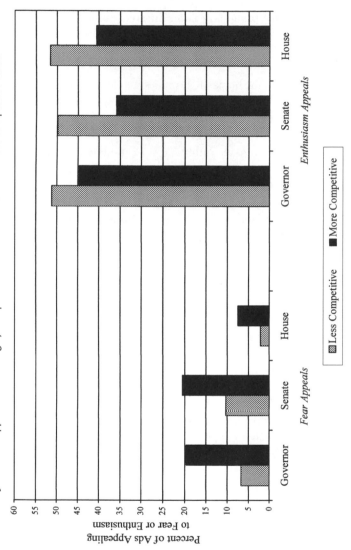

FIGURE 6.5 More Ads Appeal to Fear in Highly Competitive Races and Enthusiasm in Less Competitive Races

Note: Columns show the percentage of ads appealing to fear or enthusiasm in less competitive versus more competitive races for the office of governor, U.S. Senate, and U.S. House of Representatives.

enthusiasm; those trailing in the polls should prefer fear appeals. The pattern for presidential campaign ads in the 2000 primaries supports this prediction. The two front-runners George W. Bush and Al Gore were more likely to produce ads appealing to enthusiasm than their competitors (76 percent vs. 57 percent) and less likely to produce ads appealing to fear (1.7 percent vs. 2.9 percent), though the latter difference is obviously quite small.

Issue Salience

The findings earlier in the book suggest another element of context may be important. The ability of politicians to appeal to fear or enthusiasm in regard to a specific issue may be constrained by whether current conditions (as experienced by voters or reported in the news) indicate that such an appeal is warranted. For example, we might expect candidates to have an easier time tapping fears about crime when crime rates are high, or targeting enthusiasm about the economy during prosperous periods than during a recession. In addition, the effects of fear appeals on information search suggest they may achieve their greatest impact if those issues are in the news. I am able to use these data to take a preliminary look at how the conjunction of issue emphasis and emotional appeal in candidate advertising choices are influenced by the "issue context." Specifically, I compare the impact of violent crime rates on the use of emotional appeals in crime-related ads and the impact of manufacturing employment on the use of emotional appeals in jobs-related ads. In both cases, state issue context is divided between states in the top quartile for either violent crime rates or percentage of jobs in the manufacturing sector and states in the lower three quartiles. Figure 6.6 displays the comparisons.

I find that crime-related ads, including ads about the death penalty or gun control, are more likely to use fear appeals in high crime states than in low crime states (52 percent vs. 33 percent; $t = 1.76, p < .081$). Crime ads less frequently contain enthusiasm appeals in high crime states (44 percent vs. 54 percent), but the difference is not significant due to the small number of cases ($t = 0.89, p < .375$). The same pattern emerges in the use of emotional appeals in jobs-related advertising: ads raising that issue are more likely to appeal to fear in states with the largest manufacturing workforce and less likely to appeal to enthusiasm in the same states. However, these differences fall far short of statistical significance (fear: $t = 0.51, p < .610$; enthusiasm: $t = 1.09$, $p < .280$). In sum, the results for issue context are weak. In the two examples explored here, there are sizable differences in the expected directions, but the variation is too great and cases are too few to provide much confidence in the results at this time. These "findings" must remain merely suggestive

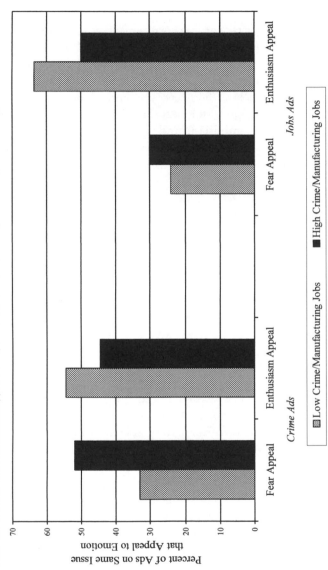

FIGURE 6.6 Fear and Enthusiasm Appeals on Specific Issues Are More Likely When They Fit Prevailing Conditions

Note: On the left, columns show the percentage of ads on crime-related issues that appealed to fear or enthusiasm in states with lower versus higher crime rates. On the right, columns show the percentage of ads on jobs-related issues that appealed to fear or enthusiasm in states with lower versus higher dependency on manufacturing jobs (i.e., the main sector of jobs experiencing long-term job loss in the late 1990s).

for future research, when data on ads from additional elections or on the volume of broadcast time purchased increase the number of observations.

Partisan Environment

Finally, I examine the impact of partisan environment on advertising choices. The predictions based on the findings for effects are perhaps clearest here: politicians should be more likely to use enthusiasm appeals in friendly partisan contexts, where they will benefit from reinforcing existing loyalties, and fear appeals in hostile contexts, where success requires undermining the existing loyalties of a larger share of the electorate. To test these hypotheses, I examine the prevalence of enthusiasm and fear appeals in statewide—gubernatorial and senatorial—races using two different measures of partisan context.[47] One measure of state partisanship is based primarily on voter registration data from 2000. However, because several states do not record party registration, I use the partisan balance of the lower and upper state legislative chambers as additional information in labeling states as Democratic or Republican. A second measure is based more simply on whether George W. Bush or Al Gore won the state in the 2000 presidential election. I use two measures as a guard against the results being unduly influenced by the assignment of individual states, as identifying the "true" partisan dispositions of a state or other geographical unit in the United States is often not a straightforward matter.[48] Underscoring this point, the two coding methods are hardly redundant measures, as twelve of fifty states change sides. I include details about particular state assignments in appendix C (see table C.1).

Figure 6.7 (p. 172) displays the results for fear appeals. Democrats are twice as likely to produce ads appealing to fear in states that lean to the advantage of Republicans. Likewise, Republicans are more likely to use fear when the political environment favors Democrats. All the differences are in the expected directions and three out of four are statistically significant (all except Republican ads using the first measure of state context). Figure 6.8 (p. 173) shows the analogous results for enthusiasm. Democrats produce more enthusiasm ads where their party is dominant than where the GOP reigns. Republicans in turn use more enthusiasm ads in Republican states than in Democratic states. Once again, all differences are in the expected direction and three out of four are statistically significant (the exception on significance is for Republican ads using the second measure of state context). The results in these two figures provide strong support for the notion that politicians and consultants behave as if they were familiar with the theory and experimental evidence. Politicians make greater use of fear appeals when they face a partisan disadvantage in winning voters and make greater use of enthusiasm appeals when they hold and wish to capitalize on that advantage.[49]

A couple of additional findings strengthen the overall picture on the relationship between partisanship and emotional appeals. First, minor party politicians are much less likely to create ads appealing to enthusiasm than major party politicians (6 percent vs. 49 percent; $t = 3.71, p < .001$). This is not simply a product of minor party candidates running as outsiders attacking the major party candidates; the results are strongest when holding the tone of the ad constant at advocacy or positive advertising. Minor party candidates do not have a deep reservoir of existing loyalties to tap, reinforce, and mobilize with enthusiasm appeals. They are only slightly more likely to use fear appeals (11 percent vs. 9 percent), however, and the difference is not significant.[50] Finally, ads that appeal to enthusiasm are more likely to mention the candidate's party affiliation than ads appealing to fear (10 percent vs. 6 percent; $t = 1.71, p < .088$). By a nearly identical margin, enthusiasm ads are more likely than fear ads to use ideological labels as well (10 percent vs. 4 percent; $t = 2.21, p < .028$). In short, politicians are twice as likely to explicitly mention predispositions such as partisanship and ideology when using the sort of emotional appeal—enthusiasm—that has the potential to reinforce and activate such orientations.

Comprehending the "Boom" in American Elections

In this chapter, I have presented the first fruits of an on-going study of emotional appeals in contemporary ad campaigns. The content analysis focuses on 1,425 ads produced by candidates, political parties, and interest groups in 1999 and 2000 for presidential, gubernatorial, and congressional elections. Beyond a modest exploratory effort by Kern (1989) fifteen years ago, nothing of this sort and certainly nothing of this scope has been attempted to study emotional appeals. In some sense, then, one purpose of this chapter is simply to provide a first look at the emotionality of campaign advertising. I have examined a wide array of empirical regularities: the kinds of emotions targeted, audiovisual cues and message characteristics associated with those emotions, and the situations in which politicians appeal to specific emotions. We can take away several broad lessons from these observations.

First, the conventional wisdom on the ubiquity of emotional appeals is correct. I sought to bring systematic evidence to bear on this and other common beliefs about emotion and advertising that I identified in chapter 2. The evidence supports the belief that politicians frequently appeal to the emotions of voters. Almost all campaign ads make at least a weak emotional appeal and nearly three in four have a strong, dominant emotional theme. The results of this study are consistent with Kaid and Johnston's (2001, 55) analysis of fifty years of presidential ads, in which emotional appeals emerge in 84 percent of ads. Similarly, in her study of a selection of 1984 ads, Kern

FIGURE 6.7 Candidates Produce More Fear Ads Where Their Political Party Is Weaker

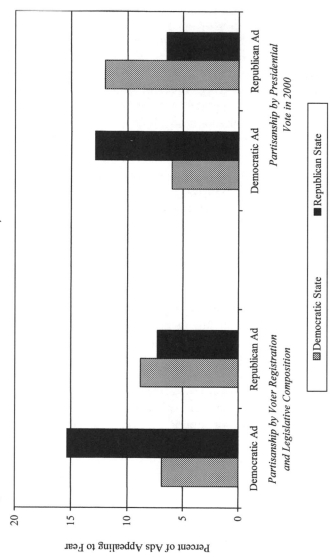

Note: Columns show the percentage of Democratic and Republican ads that appeal to fear in states where either Democrats or Republicans have the advantage. Columns on the left categorize state partisanship based on voter registration totals and partisan composition of the state legislature. Columns on the right categorize state partisanship on the basis of presidential vote in 2000.

FIGURE 6.8 Candidates Produce More Enthusiasm Ads Where Their Political Party Is Stronger

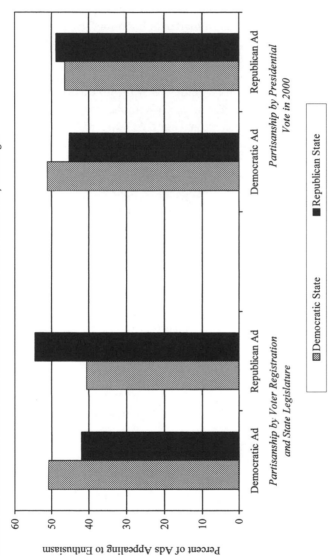

Note: Columns show the percentage of Democratic and Republican ads that appeal to enthusiasm in states where either Democrats or Republicans have the advantage. Columns on the left categorize state partisanship based on voter registration totals and partisan composition of the state legislature. Columns on the right categorize state partisanship on the basis of presidential vote in 2000.

(1989) noted it was nearly impossible to find "neutral ads," which she defined as commercials that compare the records and positions of candidates without affect-laden visuals and sounds (93–94). Although the tools have changed somewhat, one essential aspect of American elections has not changed much since Lord Bryce's observation more than a century ago, with which I began this chapter: campaigns are still "a matter of booming." It is now possible, however, to comprehend better the character, purposes, and significance of the boom.

Second, I also find support for the popular belief that the emotional impact of ads is rooted heavily in the audiovisual features used to "package" the message of an ad. Color, music, imagery, sounds, style of narration, and video editing can all serve as emotional cues. Ads appealing to enthusiasm and pride tend to be colorful, accompanied by uplifting music, full of children and people of diverse backgrounds, patriotic symbols, and images of successful, happy lives unfolding in a rapid cascade of changing scenes. In contrast, ads appealing to fear and anger tend to be dark, either devoid of music or accompanied by tense discordant instrumentation, replete with scenes of violence, decay, or desolation, threatening or irritating sound effects, and a foreboding voice-over. There is no single recipe for eliciting a particular emotion, but the evidence in this chapter shows that certain audiovisual features help to cleave sharp distinctions among emotional appeals. Of course, the appeal is also grounded measurably in the verbal message, and audiovisual elements dovetail with that message. In most but not all cases, the look and sound of an ad is similar for ads appealing to enthusiasm or pride and likewise for those appealing to fear or anger. Imagery, music, and other cues distinguish among ads most readily in terms of emotional valence (positive or negative) as well as arousal level. Words, context, and narrative structure (including narrative contained in the sequence of images) may be required to generate greater differentiation among negative and positive emotional appeals.

Third, as I claimed earlier in the book, appeals to enthusiasm and fear are staples of political advertising. Three out of four ads that strongly target emotions involve an appeal to enthusiasm or fear. This should not be surprising given the central function those particular emotions play in human motivation and judgment. I find that pride is also a frequent target of appeals but, consistent with affective intelligence theory (Marcus, Neuman, and MacKuen 2000), these appeals are rarely separable from enthusiasm. We might best view appeals to pride as a special subset of enthusiasm appeals. A fair number of campaign ads try to arouse anger, and they often do so in a manner similar to (or at the same time as) efforts to arouse fear. Unlike pride, however, anger appeals seem separable from fear appeals in many cases (i.e., the number of ads for which anger alone was the dominant appeal actually exceeded the number for which fear alone was dominant), underscoring the need for greater attention to anger in the future (Lerner et al. 2003; Marcus 2003). Ads do try to elicit other emotions such as compassion, sadness, and amusement, but much more sparingly than the four mentioned already.

Fourth, contrary to conventional wisdom, heavy reliance on emotion does not necessarily entail an absence of logical argument, factual evidence, or policy discussion. This is not to say that the arguments are strong or the discussion especially substantial; the weaknesses of thirty-second ads in this regard are well documented. The point is that candidates do not face an either/or choice between emotion, on the one hand, and logic, information, and political substance, on the other. While some candidates choose to emphasize one over the other, many clearly choose both, at least to the extent permitted by the overall structure of brief televised advertisements.

Fifth, politicians choose to appeal to enthusiasm or fear more often at times and in places that are consistent with their relative advantages as suggested by the experimental findings. Although candidates and their consultants show few signs of being consciously aware of these propositions regarding effects, they might behave *as if* they understood the propositions because prior experience and focus group tests provided them with equivalent feedback in an ad hoc form. Specifically, candidates are more likely to appeal to fear when they benefit less from the existing predispositions of the electorate than their opponent. Democrats use fear more in Republican states, and Republicans are apt to use fear in Democratic states. Similarly, challengers are more likely to use fear to shake up the status quo. On the flip side, candidates who do stand to benefit from dominant predispositions in the environment are more likely to appeal to enthusiasm and to invoke these predispositions explicitly while doing so. Democrats and Republicans focus on "rallying the faithful" when there are relatively more faithful to rally. Incumbents and front-runners also use enthusiasm appeals to a greater extent than challengers, though the evidence on incumbents is merely suggestive. Note also that the symmetrical nature of the findings in several of these cases does not follow automatically. Politicians could and did create ads that appealed to neither fear nor enthusiasm.

Sixth, and finally, in situations where theory or experimental findings suggest no clear advantage for enthusiasm or fear appeals, candidates seem to be guided by normative beliefs as well as by popular expectations that receive no support from the analyses in this book. For example, interest groups and parties are more likely than candidates to appeal to fear and less likely to appeal to enthusiasm. Candidates are also more likely to resort to fear appeals when the race is more competitive.

I began the book by asserting a rather broad, impressionistic view of campaign ads and the manner in which they appeal to the emotions of their intended audience. I draw it to a close with an effort to subject those ideas to scientific inquiry and arrive at a more precise understanding of emotionality in televised political ads. To do so, I collected and analyzed for the first time systematic evidence on the design and use of emotional advertising appeals in American election campaigns. As I hope I have demonstrated by now, emotions play a vital role in the intentions of consultants who make ads, in the content and usage of ads, and in the responses of potential voters. Given both the centrality of emotion and its relative absence from scientific research on political advertising, collection and analysis of data on this topic must continue.

7

Hearts and Minds: Rethinking the Place of Emotion in Political Life

Politics was everywhere, that is, except in the professional literature of American political science. . . . Apparently all the hullabaloo on the front pages and the evening news was just sound and fury — media overemphasis.

Morris Fiorina (scholar, 1981)

Fear is implanted in us as a preservative from evil; but its duty, like that of other passions, is not to overbear reason, but to assist it.

Samuel Johnson (1751)

Campaign politics is not a passionless enterprise. Candidates for major office and their supporters pour thousands of hours and millions of dollars into practically every electoral effort. They direct some resources to learning about the needs of the public and putting forth proposals to address those needs. Each candidate wishes to convince voters that she has the best ideas, values, and skills for the political office she seeks. The most casual observer of American politics recognizes, however, that this stylized textbook version of campaigning does not fully capture the "sound and fury" leading to Election Day.[1] The art of electioneering lies as much in personalized contact, spirited events, moving rhetoric, and slick advertisements. Television affords candidates the opportunity to use the medium's experiential intimacy and audiovisual basis to evoke emotional responses from members of the public whom they will never meet (Barry 1997; Hart 1999). Campaign consultants, whose profession has flourished with the rise of these electoral tactics, see the attempt to elicit emotions as an essential component of their advertising strategy (Boiney and Paletz 1991; Kern 1989; Perloff and Kinsey 1992; Schwartz 1973). Candidates' actions on the campaign trail leave little doubt that they set out to win both the hearts and minds of voters, probably in that order.

Indeed, candidates, parties, and groups spent over $1 billion on advertising for the 2004 presidential election, waging a televised war incessantly for nearly an entire year. They invested ten times the resources that had been expended just eight years earlier. President George W. Bush's campaign for re-election repeatedly reminded voters of the president's leadership in the wake of a collective tragedy on September 11, 2001, and invoked the spirit of the Olympics to celebrate the liberation of two countries (Afghanistan and Iraq). Senator John Kerry's campaign stressed his heroic service in the Vietnam War. However, while campaign stops and party conventions featured raucous music and fanfare designed to stir enthusiasm in large crowds, the ads mostly sounded notes of anxiety, anger, and even sorrow. The pro-Kerry group Real Voices produced testimonial ads, mostly in black-and-white, featuring tearful family members of soldiers who had been killed in Iraq. The pro-Bush group Progress for America told the story of a teenager who lost her mother in the 9/11 attacks and was comforted by an embrace from the president. Democratic ads reminded viewers visually and verbally of the daily deaths and disorder in Iraq, while Republican ads questioned Kerry's resolve as they showed images of armed terrorists and victims of attacks in Russia, Spain, and the United States. Strategists for the campaigns spent the year "looking for a good way to scare the American people" and debated just how scary to make the ads.[2] Journalists and other observers felt the 2004 election was unprecedented in its negative campaigning, its emotional appeals, and its emphasis on fear in particular.[3]

But, fear not, such activities do not matter, or so a review of political science texts will tell us. In analyzing elections, political scientists concentrate overwhelmingly on the state of the economy, policy differences, and group loyalties.[4] Scholars have cataloged a lengthy inventory of factors that influence voting behavior but attributed few of them to the campaign activities of candidates—or precisely those activities that absorb so much of the attention, effort, and resources of participants and observers. Researchers proceed as if they believe it is either impossible or improper to include emotional aspects of electioneering in the scientific study of politics. In more casual commentary, political scientists seem to agree that candidates target the hearts *and* minds of voters, but they have made little effort to spell out what difference, if any, we should make between hearts and minds.

A gulf persists between what matters in the conduct of campaigns according to practitioners and what matters in the models of politics created by political scientists. The gulf creates puzzles: Why do candidates devote so many resources to allegedly epiphenomenal aspects of campaigning? If major election campaigns only inform or remind voters of their true interests but do not affect the predictable outcome (Gelman and King 1993), then why does at least one candidate in each competitive election work so hard and pay so much to lose? Such behavior hardly seems rational.

In this book, I have sought to reconsider whether and how candidates can sway the electorate with campaigns and especially televised advertising. In doing so, I have taken seriously the notion that they are indeed campaigning for the hearts as well as minds of citizens. Candidates try to communicate their message to potential supporters but do not expect their audience to make a coldly calculated and fully informed judgment on the merits. They also attempt to elicit emotional responses that will facilitate either a change of preference or action on behalf of an existing preference. By the same token, candidates do not usually expect to "push the buttons" of voters in order to elicit a hot-headed, unthinking reaction, *regardless* of the merits or even existence of a message, although proponents of campaign reform may occasionally see it that way. In short, candidates rarely choose between waging a campaign based on substantive information or one based on emotional appeals; instead, they typically employ emotional appeals to ensure the effectiveness of their substantive message. The goal of the book has been to better understand how and why that happens.

With that in mind, I began the book by contrasting conventional wisdom about the predominance of emotional appeals with the relative neglect of emotion in systematic research on political advertising. Consultants, journalists, and even many academics seem to believe that emotional appeals (1) are a routine part of politics, (2) are key to the power of campaign ads, (3) derive their power from music and imagery, (4) work primarily by transferring the aroused feelings to the candidates, (5) are manipulative and irrational, and (6) work mainly on those who are uneducated and uninformed. I have argued that research in psychology and neuroscience can help us think more precisely about the role emotions play in political communication. Scholars have fruitfully applied some of these notions to improve our understanding of public opinion, and I have tried to build on such efforts to help explain the causal links between campaign advertising and the attitudes and behavior of voters. To this end, I presented results from a set of experiments and a large-scale content analysis of recent ad campaigns that were designed to test both the theoretical propositions and several elements of the conventional wisdom. The evidence provides considerable support for the theoretical perspective and confirmed some common beliefs about the ubiquity, power, and source of emotional appeals. However, the evidence also calls into question conventional notions about the effects and normative standing of such appeals.

In this final chapter of the book, I focus more closely on three ways in which this project invites us to rethink the place of emotion in political life.

First, this research offers news answers about the role of emotion in campaign politics as well as new evidence about old assumptions. I summarize the principal findings from both the experiments and content analysis. Second, new answers often lead to new questions or reshape the relevance of old ones. I discuss a number of new questions that emerge from this research and what future steps we might take to answer them. Third, the theoretical perspective and findings of this book suggest that a proper understanding of the role of emotion can help us take a fresh look at politics. I concentrate on four empirical and normative implications, including the need to move beyond a focus on information, take a middle course between vilifying and reifying emotion, revisit the ethical status of emotional appeals, and see competing visions of civic life through a new window.

New Answers

For a long time, the reigning view in the study of political communication was that the mass media and election campaigns have a minimal impact on the decisions of citizens. In recent years, this view has been overturned in the face of mounting evidence that news, political ads, and other campaign events can change the priorities and preferences of voters (Kinder 2003). Most of the research revealing such effects has focused on the content and tone of political information (Ansolabehere and Iyengar 1995; Bartels 1993; Goldstein and Freedman 2002a; Iyengar and Kinder 1987; Zaller 1992, 1996), though some of the work emphasizes the power of group-related cues (Gilliam and Iyengar 2000; Kahn 1996; Mendelberg 2001; Valentino, Hutchings, and White 2002). During this time, many scholars have recognized that campaign ads rely heavily on appeals to emotion (Boiney and Paletz 1991; Jamieson 1992; Kern 1989; Nelson and Boynton 1997; Richardson 2003; West 2001). Until now, widespread observations about the importance of emotion in political advertising—by journalists, practitioners, and scholars—have gone untested. We lacked evidence to verify what role, if any, emotions play in the effectiveness of campaign ads.

I set out to test how the emotional appeals prevalent in election campaigns affect the participation and choices of citizens, subjecting conventional wisdom about the power of emotional appeals to empirical investigation. Although the novelty of this effort makes it exploratory in one sense, I have attempted to put the inquiry on firm scientific ground by formulating and testing specific hypotheses based on the *affective intelligence* theory and the view that emotions emerge from fundamental systems for guiding goal-oriented behavior. The book's focus has been on two particularly common types of appeals and two basic emotions about which psychologists have learned a great deal—namely enthusiasm and fear.

Experimental Evidence on the Impact of Fear and Enthusiasm Appeals

As a first step in reconsidering the place of emotions in campaign politics, I employed an experimental design to establish what kind of causal role, if any, emotional appeals play in the process of campaign communication. Previous research has demonstrated strong ties between emotions and public opinion using survey data, but it has shed little light on the origins of those emotions or the causal process connecting the political environment, emotions, and individual voting behavior. The experiments described in this book illuminate these matters by testing whether politicians can influence citizens by using campaign ads to target specific emotions. Subjects in one set of experiments saw either a positive ad with relatively unevocative imagery or the identical ad with enthusiasm-evoking imagery and music. Subjects in another set of experiments saw either a negative ad with the same "neutral" imagery or the identical ad with fear-evoking imagery and music. In this way, we could observe *some* of the emotional impact of campaign ads while holding the political information and arguments constant.

Establishing causality is the hallmark strength of experiments. Failing to inspire confidence in the generality of the results is their notorious weakness. Some causes for skepticism about how effects work in the "real world" can be addressed in advance, through the design of the research. In this study, several steps were taken to more closely simulate actual experiences. Exposure to political ads is typically incidental and so, in the experiments, it occurred during a commercial break in a local television news program, which served as the ostensible purpose for viewing. The ads referred to actual candidates in an on-going election campaign, and the questionnaires asked about real political choices faced by potential voters. Subjects were not recruited from a captive student population, but rather constitute a diverse sample of the relevant electorate. In addition to relying on highly naturalistic experiments, this study's focus on fear and enthusiasm appeals allows us to compare the results to correlations observed between these two emotions and political behavior in national surveys. A final "reality check" on the experiments is provided by evidence on how politicians actually use campaign ads to appeal to emotions, provided one assumes political consultants often know what works (at least in the campaign at hand, if not at the level of abstract theory).

The findings confirm some general beliefs about emotional appeals shared by observers and practitioners, such as the belief that campaign ads derive considerable power from appealing to emotions and the belief that music and images are often a key to the power behind these emotional appeals. Emotional cues embedded in music and images can strengthen the effectiveness of a campaign ad in achieving two fundamental goals of electioneering. Although exposure was apparently incidental to viewing a local news program, a shift in emotionally evocative music and images substantially altered the extent to which citizens were motivated or persuaded by an otherwise identical campaign message. At the same time, the findings cast doubt on other elements of conventional wisdom, such as the belief that emotional appeals work primarily by transferring affect directly to candidate evaluations or by simply provoking greater attention to the ad. Consultants and other political observers believe that emotional appeals work by seeking to "*transfer* or *refer* positive and negative affect evoked by means of sight and sound from emotionally laden symbols to the candidate and his opponent" (Kern 1989, 32). Although I uncover many effects in this study, the findings lend no support to the notion that the effectiveness of emotional appeals can be explained by affect transfer.

The findings instead lend considerable support to propositions about the direct and indirect impact of appeals derived from psychological theories of emotion. Consistent with these hypotheses, attempts to elicit fear and enthusiasm alter the impact of political communication in distinct ways. Attempts to elicit enthusiasm, through warm images and uplifting music, lend positive ads the capacity to motivate viewers and embolden supporters. With exposure to enthusiasm appeals, citizens show greater interest in the campaign, greater desire to volunteer for one of the candidates, and greater inclination to vote in the election. They also are more likely to be certain about their choice of candidates and rely more heavily on prior convictions, regardless of whose ad they saw. Thus, somewhat ironically, enthusiasm appeals tend to polarize those voters already backing rival candidates, an effect driven both by attraction of supporters and repulsion of opponents.

Attempts to elicit fear or anxiety, through harsh images and tense music, lend negative ads the capacity to redirect the attention of viewers and persuade unbelievers. After exposure to fear ads, citizens experience greater uncertainty about their political choices and are more likely to change their political preferences and vote choice. Fear leads voters to place less weight on prior convictions and more weight on contemporary evaluations and feelings. As a result, these appeals exhibit the greatest persuasive power on the opponent's base of support. Fear ads also motivate citizens to contact campaigns for more information and to turn their attention toward news sources that hold greater potential for addressing the alleged reason for anxiety. Finally, fear appeals can strengthen belief in the importance of voting and stimulate greater involvement in election among some citizens. However, the motivational impact of fear appeals appears more circumscribed than for enthusiasm appeals and even shows some potential to demobilize those who are less informed about politics.

Experiments turned up no evidence to support the view that emotional appeals work simply by provoking greater attention to the ad. Neither type of emotional appeal increases the ability of subjects to recognize the names of the candidates or to recall correctly the ad and its sponsor. While these results undercut one conventional view, they also weaken support for the *vigilance* hypothesis derived from theories of emotion. This hypothesis predicts that fear will heighten attentiveness to the source of the threat. Although fear appeals instigate a search for additional information in the expected manner, they do not improve recall in a way that would suggest subjects paid greater attention to the ad.

Perhaps the most surprising finding of the entire study is that the most knowledgeable or "sophisticated" citizens are also the most responsive to emotional appeals. Recall from chapter 2 the conventional wisdom that "the more ignorant and less sophisticated tend to lean on their emotions" (Sniderman, Brody, and Tetlock 1991, 22). Experimental results strongly contradict the common belief that emotional appeals are tools for manipulating the least informed, educated, or intelligent citizens. The vast majority of motivational and persuasive effects uncovered in this research can be found exclusively or predominantly among those who know more about politics. Most of the remaining effects seem to work the same for all citizens regardless of political expertise. Research on fear appeals in other domains has suggested that responses to fear, either as action to address a threat or withdraw from a threat, depend on feelings of competence. Evidence that fear appeals induce more participation from political experts and discourage participation among novices appears consistent with this idea, but it cannot explain why experts are also more responsive to enthusiasm appeals. However, the fact that those who are politically savvy respond more clearly and strongly to emotional advertising appeals *is* consistent with my argument that emotions serve as "relevance detectors."

Evidence on the Prevalence, Design, and Use of Emotional Appeals

Another set of findings in the book emerges from a systematic content analysis of contemporary campaign ads aimed at generating more precise knowledge about how candidates design and use emotional appeals. The content analysis is based on over 1,400 presidential, gubernatorial, and congressional ads from the 1999 and 2000 elections across the United States. Results from this part of the study lend strong support to the common belief that politicians routinely use ads to appeal to emotions and to the belief that the emotional appeal of an ad is closely tied to its audiovisual content. Most ads make at least a limited appeal to emotions and a substantial majority make a strong emotional appeal. Moreover, the evidence supports earlier claims that the two emotions at the center of the project—enthusiasm and fear—

are among the emotions to which politicians most frequently appeal. The colors, images, and music used in ads appealing primarily to fear and enthusiasm match the types of emotional cues I earlier argued we should expect based on psychological theories regarding the antecedents of those emotions. In sum, the prevalence and design of ads appealing to specific emotions corresponds well to some general beliefs held by observers and the more specific expectations advanced in this book.

Candidates rely on fear and enthusiasm appeals in distinct ways. In some cases, they appear to act on well-worn beliefs such as the notion that fear appeals are most effective. For example, gubernatorial and congressional candidates churn out relatively more fear ads and relatively fewer enthusiasm ads during highly competitive races. Other distinctions provide support for the idea that candidates may use emotional appeals strategically in a way that is consistent with what we have learned about their effects. For example, challengers are more likely than incumbents to produce fear appeals, while front-runners are more likely than those trailing in the polls to use enthusiasm appeals. There is also suggestive evidence that candidates are more likely to use fear in connection with specific policy issues in states where the public has relatively greater cause for concern on those issues. Finally, there is strong evidence that partisans use more enthusiasm appeals where their party is dominant and more fear appeals where the opposing party is dominant. Similarly, third-party candidates rely less on enthusiasm appeals than major party candidates.

*　　*　　*

Experiments and content analysis analyzed in this book challenge a final bit of conventional wisdom. According to critics, "campaign ads that appeal by emphasizing emotion inherently depreciate rational processes" (Arterton 1992, 102), and the problem with ads is that they "appeal to emotion instead of reason, and those emotions appealed to are often our darker ones" (Kamber 1997, 36). Despite these complaints, neither emotional appeals in general nor fear appeals in particular are necessarily at odds with logic, information, and substance. Ads often contain appeals to both emotion and logic, and fear ads are more likely than enthusiasm ads to be based on issues and candidate records rather than personality. The impact of emotional appeals does not reflect the blind transfer of affect from irrelevant symbols to candidates, but rather stems from adaptive changes in how information is processed that conform with learned signals about what the environment holds in store for the individual. Appeals to fear have the potential to promote more active consideration of present circumstances and a search for new information.

We must give more thought to how emotion and information are related. Substance and arguments are often required to give the overall message, and therefore its response from the public, precise meaning and direction. The message must provide voters with a sense of what to feel scared or hopeful about and, in many cases, what voters should do with those feelings. Moreover, because emotions often have a rational basis, the ability to engender and sustain an emotional response regarding issues of public affairs should not be altogether independent of having a reasonable grounding in beliefs and facts. On the other hand, emotions are not mere extensions of argument. They lend force to the argument, not so much by making it more convincing, but rather by helping to redirect attention and motivate thought into action. Our emotions send us signals to say: "This is important!" And the rapidity of our emotional responses allows this process to bias what we make of the information we are receiving for both better and worse.

In this vein, the present study contributes to recent research in political psychology that suggests emotions play a vital part in shaping political behavior. This book uses experiments to provide more definitive evidence of the causal role of emotions, building on earlier work to show that candidates can use campaign ads to elicit emotional responses and produce predictable changes in the attitudes and motivation of viewers. The distinctive pattern of effects from emotional appeals is largely consistent with the relationships observed in survey studies of public opinion (Kinder and D'Ambrosio 2000; Marcus, Neuman, and MacKuen 2000). It also is consistent with experimental work on the use of emotionally evocative pictures in interest group fliers or emotional responses to leaders' facial displays (Huddy and Gunnthorsdottir 2000; Masters and Sullivan 1993; Way and Masters 1996b). Taken together, these studies complement each other and provide greater confidence that the connections between campaign communication, emotional responses, and attitude change are neither causally spurious nor artifacts of the lab. We may come away from this research with even more questions about the possibilities and limitations of using campaign ads to sway voters with emotional appeals, some of which I address in the next section of the chapter. The relevance and importance of these questions, however, emerges only after we have demonstrated that emotion can play a powerful and explicable role and therefore that these new questions are worth pursuing.

New Questions

I now want to shift the discussion to some caveats and qualifications regarding the preceding assessment of emotional appeals. Many questions remain that cannot be answered by the evidence gathered in this book. Therefore, I consider a few of the ways in which this research can and should be extended to tell us more.

Advertising Campaign Strategy and Consequences

Campaign ads, especially those utilizing emotional cues, can have a substantial impact on voter participation and choice. In this study, we observed effects from advertising appeals comparable in size to significant shifts in bedrock social and political factors such as education, age, partisanship, and sophistication. I have refrained from emphasizing the magnitude of the effects, however. The size of the effect is likely to depend on many details not observed in this study and influenced by the dynamic campaign process. In other words, research on the magnitude of effects must take better account of the real world of competitive campaigning over a period of weeks and months.

Many questions remain that we would need to answer in order to assess the overall effectiveness of campaign ads and ad campaigns. For example, what is the marginal effect of a single ad after a viewer's repeated exposure to similar or opposing ads, or amid exposure to other forms of political communication (e.g., news, political conversations, direct contact from campaigns)? In the context of "noisy" election campaigns, we expect diminishing returns and offsetting effects in the realms of both participation and choice. As we increasingly identify the discrete causal forces at work in campaigns, we must investigate the net contribution of each to electoral outcomes when all forces are at work. More elaborate experiments that vary the amount, form, and consistency of exposure to campaign ads or other forms of political communication can shed light on the consequences of exposure to multiple sources.

Equipped with better causal knowledge from experiments, we can try to disentangle effects through aggregate analysis of opinion and behavior over the course of entire election campaigns. To do so confidently, we must obtain and connect three sets of data: actual advertising stimuli, exposure to those stimuli, and citizen behavior. Until recently, the weakest link in this chain has been data on exposure. In recent years, a new source of data has offered the potential to increase significantly what we know about exposure to campaign advertising (Freedman and Goldstein 1999; Goldstein and Freedman 2002b).[5] The data consist of observations of each time an ad is aired on major broadcast and cable TV networks in most of the largest media markets in the United States. This offers researchers information on the frequency and volume of advertising for specific ads and the time and place (i.e., media market and channel) of its targeting. While individual-level exposure remains the great missing piece, these data at least provide researchers with a sense of *likely* exposure over time and across space. If such data can be matched to content analysis data on the emotions to which the ads appeal, then it offers improved potential for learning more about the intended and unintended impact of appeals at an aggregate level. It is unlikely that entire ad campaigns can be classified as appealing to distinct emotions, but there is reason to expect we can find sufficient variation in the extent to which certain emotions are targeted across time and space to permit such analysis.

Potential implications for campaign strategy, such as the timing and targeting of appeals, also merit further study. The findings in this book suggest politicians' reliance on specific emotional appeals depends on the status of their campaign as well as the larger social and political context. However, candidates and their consultants must choose not only which ads to produce, but also the timing of ad buys (e.g., early or late in the campaign), the frequency and duration with which each ad will be aired, and to which audiences the ad will be targeted. With the sort of media market data mentioned above, political scientists can begin to formulate and test more well-developed propositions about campaign strategy regarding the use of emotional appeals in the conduct of entire ad campaigns. Moreover, such propositions need to focus on the relationship of these strategies to both the political context (as I have done here) and on the strategic choices of rival candidates (cf. Simon 2002).

Cueing Emotions: Personal Experiences and Political Environments

This book is about emotional appeals in campaign ads, but many implications of the principal findings have a wider scope. Indeed, in presenting a theoretical basis for thinking about emotional cues in politics, I argued that we could see campaign advertising as merely one obvious and central application of a broader phenomenon. If emotions are a fundamental part of human reasoning, then emotion should shape the effects of communication on political behavior generally. Earlier work suggested that politicians also try to arouse emotions through printed propaganda, an idea echoed by the consultants in chapter 2. There is every reason to suspect that stirring enthusiasm is precisely the purpose of face-to-face political activities such as campaign stops and party conventions. Whether intentional or not, events and news reports of those events are likely to provoke emotions that influence how citizens perceive the information they are receiving. Emotional cues exist in abundance in campaign ads, where they have been placed deliberately to evoke a response, but such cues reside elsewhere throughout the political landscape. We have only begun to investigate the sources and consequences of citizens' emotional responses to their political environment.

Future research on the capacity of politicians and events to elicit emotions must consider individual variation. Emotional systems in the brain assess the significance of stimuli on the basis of prior experience. Therefore, we should expect heterogeneity in responses. Identical stimuli—a flag, a burning cross, a president's tear, a gay rights parade—may elicit different emotions or degrees of emotion from person to person. Likewise, a person's response to a particular stimulus may shift from one context to the next— for example, whether an American flag is shown flying over the ruins of the World Trade Center or as the backdrop to a campaign fundraiser. Recognition of the power of political symbols is hardly new (Edelman 1964; Sears 1993) but, equipped with a better grasp of how emotion works, we can make more precise predictions about the impact of symbolic communication. We should be able to anticipate the ways in which emotional responses differ across groups and circumstances and test these predictions using survey and experimental data.

The link between emotional appeals, substantive claims, and the current context is also important. Emotions arise from assessments of what external events portend for the individual, and thus we should expect contextual variation in response to stimuli. For example, we might ask whether fear and enthusiasm appeals work best when they resonate with current conditions or the existing feelings of viewers (cf. Roseman, Abelson, and Ewing 1986). The capacity to elicit particular emotions may be highly sensitive to prevailing conditions and concerns. For this reason, fear ads that are devastatingly effective tools of persuasion in one campaign may fall on deaf ears or backfire against the sponsor in other campaigns. Results in chapter 6 provide suggestive but ultimately inconclusive evidence that the advertising strategy of candidates may be sensitive to context in this manner. Future research using experiments and aggregate campaign data are necessary to explore contextual constraints on cueing emotions.

Affective Variations: Emotion as Mediator, Moderator, and Marker

Much work remains to be done to clarify the role of emotions themselves. In the first place, the universe of politically relevant emotions certainly extends beyond fear and enthusiasm. As we saw in chapter 6, although these two are common targets of campaign ads, politicians also appeal to pride, anger, compassion, amusement, and sadness. Kinder (1994) offers a rare example of trying to take a wider range of emotions and their distinct qualities seriously. Marcus (2003) has begun to wrestle with the way in which anger relates to affective intelligence theory. It may be that emotions such as pride, hope, and enthusiasm are only subtle variations on a theme and can largely be understood as part of the success-feedback or disposition system described in chapter 3 (cf. Marcus, Neuman, and MacKuen 2000). The more one delves into finer distinctions among emotions, the more one is required to move away from obvious features of both the environment and the individual, and toward subtle variations of situation and personal experience. When considering which one of a set of related emotions will be elicited, I suspect the answer has increasingly little to do with the stimulus itself and far more to do with what lies inside the individual.

From the theoretical perspective advanced in this book, emotions are a critical mediating force between an individual's environment and her response to it. Prior research suggests that people who experience specific emotions behave in ways consistent with theoretical predictions about the effects of those emotions (Kinder and D'Ambrosio 2000; Marcus, Neuman, and MacKuen 2000). Other research suggests that political stimuli can elicit emotions expected by theory (Huddy and Gunnthorsdottir 2000; Way and Masters 1996b). The present study shows that ads cueing specific emotions cause changes in attitudes and behavior consistent with eliciting those emotions. Nonetheless, research on emotion and politics rarely demonstrates all of the links necessary to fully establish the mediating role of emotions in a single study. Future research could tighten the link between political appeals, the emotional responses they elicit, and the effects we observe (e.g., see Brader, Valentino, and Suhay 2004).

Pursuing these goals requires grappling with methodological issues. Not surprisingly, given general neglect of the topic, the development of survey instrumentation for tapping emotional responses lags far behind development in other areas (Marcus, Neuman, and MacKuen 2000). Self-reports may at times be inadequate because emotions often emerge without conscious awareness and their influence occurs on-line (i.e., as information is processed), hindering subsequent detection. The best way to assess mediations may be to sacrifice generalizability by monitoring physiological responses. Political scientists will have to consider split-sample designs in which disciplinary preferences for a "natural" or comfortable interview environment are balanced with more intrusive techniques for monitoring emotion (Larsen and Frederickson 1999). Similarly, although the focus of this study is on nonverbal cues, verbal messages can also trigger strong emotional responses. Efforts to disentangle the contribution of emotional versus cognitive responses to verbal messages is also likely to require greater reliance on psychophysiological techniques. It is reasonable to ask whether it is worth the investment of time, money, and effort. Based on mounting evidence of the importance of emotion from these experiments and other recent studies, the answer is an unequivocal "yes."

Finally, there are not only many more emotions to consider, but "affect" takes on distinct conceptual forms other than emotions, such as moods and the evaluative dimension of attitudes. Political psychologists have started to consider most varieties of affect in their research. As they continue to do so, it will become increasingly important to clarify the relationship of these concepts to one another. For example, in addition to the work on emotions and feelings cited frequently in this book, scholars have studied how preexisting or induced mood states *moderate* rather than mediate responses to political candidates and messages (Isbell and Ottati 2002; Roseman, Abelson, and Ewing 1986; Way and Masters 1996b). In a different approach that treats mood as a mediating variable, Rahn (2000) adapts the affect-as-information approach from psychology to develop the concept of public mood as a diffuse affective state toward one's political community (see also Rahn and Hirshorn 1999; Rahn, Kroeger, and Kite 1996). The one form of affect that has not been neglected by political scientists in the past is affect as a component of political attitudes. Much of the work in this tradition has not sought to clarify what role, if any, affect plays besides indicating whether an object is liked or disliked. While this approach grows out of the social psychology of attitudes, there may be connections to the psychological theories of emotion presented earlier. For example, Damasio's (1994) notion of "somatic markers," which serves as the basis for my explanation of emotional cues, seem similar in many ways to the what social psychologists have meant by the "affective component" of attitudes. Some recent work by political psychologists strives to provide a more theoretical account of the role of affect as it relates to attitude objects, including work on *motivated reasoning* (Lodge and Taber 2000) and *conviction* (Burns and Kinder 2003).

Rethinking the Place of Emotion in Politics

Over the past two to three decades, research in psychology and neuroscience has made tremendous advances in our understanding of human emotions, their causes, and their consequences (Damasio 2000; Zajonc 1998). A steady stream of books popularizing scientific research on emotions has appeared on shelves since the early 1990s, and the last few years have seen an equally impressive flood of scholarly handbooks and edited collections on the topic. This work has brought a rehabilitation of emotion both conceptually and normatively. Work on emotions emerged from dormancy not only in the study of politics but across the social sciences. In addition, the new vision of emotions propagated in many of these books stresses their importance not just as part of human experience, but as part of human reasoning and adaptive social behavior. This represents an assault on centuries old dualisms of mind versus body and emotion versus reason, most famously attacked in Damasio's *Descartes' Error* (1994). As the body of research grows in political science, first on emotion in public opinion and now on emotion in political communication, the evidence points increasingly to the need to rethink the place of emotions in political life. In this last section of the book, I say a few words about some of the lines along which that rethinking should occur.

Moving Beyond Information and Advertising Tone

It is an exciting time in the study of political advertising. Lynda Lee Kaid and colleagues have pushed systematic inquiry into the content of political advertising not only in the contemporary United States, but also historically and cross-nationally. Ken Goldstein and colleagues have pioneered research into the volume and targeting of ad campaigns, and thus the potential exposure of voters, with actual broadcast data recently acquired from the private sector. Steve Ansolabehere, Shanto Iyengar, and others have sharpened study of the effects and underlying causal mechanisms through the use of high quality experimentation.

In the recent explosion of advertising research, the most prominent debate has centered on the consequences of adopting a positive or negative tone (Lau et al. 1999). Like other areas of political communication research, tone refers first and foremost in these studies to the kind of information presented in the ad. While these attributes of communication have been a fine place to begin, we must move beyond the near exclusive focus on information. I have tried to demonstrate here that what matters is not just what is said but how it is said. Messages come in packages, and the packaging matters.

Nonetheless, it would be a mistake to overstate this distinction and encourage a focus on either information and cognition *or* symbolism and emotion. Information can elicit emotional responses, and symbols can carry cognitive meaning. In our scholarship, we must be mindful of all of these factors and the ways they interact. Information is not simply something that is learned and stored in memory; it can provoke a reaction. Emotional responses are not merely expressions of preferences; they can change the way new information is perceived and processed. Advertising tone involves positive and negative emotions as well as positive and negative information. Although I have argued for the need to distinguish between the valence of information and emotion, this is insufficient. There is mounting evidence to suggest we need to consider looking beyond valence (i.e., positive versus negative) to specific types of positivity and negativity in both information and emotion.

Preying on Hopes and Fears? The Ethics of Emotional Appeals

The debate over negative advertising often assumes a normative tinge. More often than not, scholars approach the subject with the assumption that negative advertising is undesirable or unethical. Such assumptions echo the criticism of journalists, pundits, reformers, and many politicians. As we saw in chapter 2, observers are often equally critical of emotional appeals, which are widely condemned as insubstantial, irrational, manipulative, and subversive. In light of the research reported in this book, it is time to reconsider the ethics of emotional appeals, positive or negative: Are emotional appeals legitimate?

The persuasive power of fear appeals uncovered in this research may well reaffirm popular notions of the moral corruptness of negative advertising, yet concluding as much is premature for many reasons. First, critics and scholars alike tend to gloss over distinctions in types of negativity. For example, ads may be "negative" because they voice pessimism about the status quo or some public policy, criticize an opposing candidate's record, smear the reputation or personal image of the opposing candidate, or attempt to elicit a negative emotion such as fear, anger, or sadness. It could be that we would wish to condemn all forms of negativity in the end or that our objection is to negativity in general. However, in many cases, people make blanket condemnations when their criticism is in fact motivated by a particular version of negativity. Second, some have defended the value of negative information in public discourse (Mayer 1996; Zaller n.d.). They have argued that informed decisionmaking and democratic accountability depend on candidates, groups, and the news media raising information that is critical of some people and policies. Third, Marcus (2002) has argued convincingly that anxiety plays a vital and rational role in the political process. From the perspective of affective intelligence theory, fear appeals serve a function—promoting vigilance—that Thomas Paine argued long ago was the burden of a free people. Do we really wish to assert that it is a violation of norms to warn people about the existence of a genuinely perceived threat?

Although the censure of emotional appeals is often folded carelessly in with censure of negativity, some critics do in fact mean to question the legitimacy of emotional appeals. These observers deride what they see as politicians' efforts to manipulate the emotions of voters with campaign ads and rhetoric that "preys on the hopes and fears" of ordinary people. For these critics, emotional appeals are manipulative because they circumvent reason and lead a person to make decisions she would not make in her "right mind." Emotions, so it is believed, are a weakness. Politicians behave unethically when they take advantage of these weaknesses, much the same as if they bought votes from the needy or fooled a gullible child for their own purposes. In the Progressive spirit, others simply lament the elevation of style over substance. These latter-day reformers view emotional campaign advertising as the substitution of cheap thrills and superficial judgments for genuine, meaningful political discourse. As they see it, politicians who prioritize images over issues may not be unethical, but they are certainly irresponsible. These two related perspectives raise concerns beyond the use of emotional images and music in campaign advertising, but their complaints are surely aimed at such sensationalism.

Although these concerns are not without merit, a proper understanding of the empirical place of emotion should temper our judgments as to whether emotional appeals are necessarily manipulative or illegitimate. First, emotions are an essential part of our reasoning and social decisionmaking faculties, contrary to the dualism that sees emotion as antagonistic and inferior to reason. We must rethink any critique that suggests individuals ought to decide on the basis of reason instead of emotion, as healthy individuals will decide on the basis of reason only with the help of emotion. Second, as we have seen in this study, attempts to elicit enthusiasm and fear may help politicians motivate and inform otherwise apathetic citizens. If emotional appeals provide a key to a more participatory and informed populace, then their use may not be suspect but in fact laudable. Moreover, contrary to what is often assumed, appeals to positive emotions are not necessarily more desirable than appeals to negative emotions. Ads appealing to enthusiasm tend to reinforce existing loyalties and further polarize of the electorate. In practice, politicians also tend to focus less on issues and more on image when they make enthusiasm appeals, while their fear appeals tend to be more substantive.

In light of the preceding observations, we might begin by classifying emotional appeals as illegitimate or manipulative according to the same criteria we would use to classify arguments. In other words, politicians manipulate citizens when they knowingly present information in a way that leads citizens to behave contrary to their true interests. Both arguments and emotional appeals can be manipulative. Of course, defined in this way, judgments about what is manipulative are not easy. The "right decision" for any citizen is an issue at the very heart of political contestation, and political opponents tend to disagree as a matter of principle about even what information is relevant to a particular decision. One could argue that emotional appeals as operationalized in this study—emotional cues in images and music—are suspect because they are largely devoid of political substance. Others may still defend their use in achieving important goals for campaigns and political communication in a democracy. Full consideration of the ethics of emotional appeals is beyond the scope of what I can accomplish here, but I believe we need to reconsider our views based on scientific knowledge about what emotions and emotional appeals do.

Putting Emotion and Reason in Perspective: Between Vilification and Reification

We can expand this discussion to consider the normative place of emotion in political life more generally. As I mentioned earlier, the recent resurgence of scholarship on emotion has attempted to rehabilitate the concept of emotion from its second-class status in the Western tradition (Marcus 2002). From an evolutionary perspective, the emotional machinery of the brain has endured the test of time across animal species by providing a flexible means of adapting to changes in one's environment. Adaptation and survival are indeed good. From a social perspective, emotions seem necessary to reasoning and proper behavior, as evidenced by the fact that those with impairments of emotional functioning at best find themselves less able to make sound decisions or at worst become sociopaths and a menace to society. Dysfunction and sociopathy are surely bad.

In a similar vein, recent research on emotion in politics, the present study included, could be seen as an attempt to resuscitate emotion as not only a useful explanatory concept, but also as an aspect of political life to be valued. Some earlier work presented a vision of affect or emotion as a useful shortcut, good in the sense of serving as a crutch to help the politically feeble persevere (Abelson et al. 1982; Sniderman, Tetlock, and Brody 1991). More recent research has advanced a view of emotion that facilitates rational behavior by deftly allowing for a switch between reliance on learned routines and reasoned judgment, as the situation demands (Huddy and Gunnthorsdottir 2000; Marcus, Neuman, and MacKuen 2000). In this book, I underscore the motivational power of emotions and the fact that emotional appeals serve as cues to the politically strong more than crutches for the weak.

All of this may be true, but we should not get carried away in praise of emotion (cf. Clore and Isbell 2001). Doing so would be a disservice to understanding the proper place of emotion in political life. Like rationality, emotion is neither good nor bad in itself. It harbors liabilities as well as benefits. Emotions guide reason, enable rational behavior, and motivate thoughts into action, but they distort, distract, and deflate as well. People experience emotional trauma, suffer from emotional disorders, and become overwrought with emotion. While emotions greatly assist in our everyday decisions and actions, they also leave us susceptible to manipulation at the hands of others and at times to being overwhelmed by our circumstances. Our conceptions about the normative value of emotions are best shaped by continuing to learn more about the empirical function of emotions as signifiers of situational relevance that "prepare" us for different courses of action. In recognizing this function, we may come to appreciate connections among what were previously seen as oppositions.

For example, political scientists have wrestled with alternative conceptions of the American voter from unsophisticated party loyalist to rational decisionmaker to cognitive miser. Emotion offers us a bridge between these conceptions and the paradigms that produced them. We can set aside the question of whether Converse (1964) or Downs (1957) provides a better model and instead ask when is either a Conversian or Downsian model the best way to understand a voter's behavior. Absent signs of threat and thus anxiety, we expect citizens, on average, to rely on the habits formed through years of socialization and embodied in their predispositions. Moreover, we should see citizens embrace or retreat from political involvement as they receive positive or negative feedback, respectively, on the success of their own political causes or those of groups with which they identify. Under these conditions, the American voter more closely resembles the party identifier or inattentive independent described by Converse, his fellow Michigan scholars, and their successors.

However, when signs of threat appear and anxiety grows, we expect citizens, on average, to pay greater attention and attempt to learn more about the threat or ways of addressing it. In addition, citizens should rely more on new information than predispositions as they reason and choose among alternative courses of political action. Under these conditions, the American voter more closely resembles the rational voter described by Downs and his rational choice successors. The voter's emotional responsiveness to the political world provides her with a rational vigilance that allows her to act as a creature of habit on the basis of experience when all is well and to engage in reasoned or rational judgment on the basis of new information when danger demands. The rational American voter is an emotional voter.

Nonetheless, this rational voter is not perfect. There remains plenty of room for stereotypes, reliance on inadequate information, overreactions, selective perception, and other shortcomings. Responsiveness to emotional cues rooted in past associations ensures that voters will occasionally respond too strongly to bygone symbols and too weakly to novel circumstances. Political actors can attempt to stir anxiety falsely or otherwise manipulate voters. Emotion, like rationality, does not ensure desirable or good outcomes; emotion assists the democratic citizen in self-governance *and* can facilitate manipulation and error. With a proper understanding of emotion, political scientists can ask better questions and investigate more fully the strengths and weaknesses of citizen judgment.

Campaigning for Hearts and Minds: Past, Present, and Future

I began the chapter by asserting that campaign politics is not passionless. Political scientists may agree, but, for the most part, they have left emotion out of their models of the political world. Building on advances in psychology and the study of emotion and public opinion, this book has strived to bring emotion into our explanation of how political communication influences citizens. Although the goal of campaigns is to "get the message out," the art of campaigning lies as much in how the message is delivered. Candidates on the campaign trail leave little doubt that they set out to win both the hearts and minds of voters. The two processes—winning hearts and minds—are not independent. Imagery, music, and color are designed to elicit emotion and thereby shape the way in which, and the extent to which, the substantive message of the ad is effective. When the ad stirs enthusiasm, it draws voters into politics and hardens the convictions of friend and foe alike. When the ad taps fear, it loosens the grip of habit and encourages attention to new information from the ad and other relevant sources. This study confirms what observers and practitioners have long believed: emotion is central to how campaign ads work. But more than that, the study has transformed these intuitions into explicit predictions, grounded them in theory, and verified them scientifically.

Taking emotion seriously allows us to breathe life back into the world of campaign politics and political life more generally. We can look anew at election campaigns and other links between the political environment and responses of the mass public. Differences in mass politics across countries, political eras, elections, and other critical moments might be better understood if we keep in mind the emotional tenor of the times. The theory of affective intelligence advanced by Marcus and colleagues (2000) suggests that the extent to which times are ripe for mobilization or persuasion will depend considerably on public emotions. In troubled times, minds are more easily led; in good times, citizens are creatures of habit. This study suggests that politicians can have a hand in changing the emotional tenor of politics with potentially serious consequences for political behavior.

Paul Lazarsfeld and his colleagues at Columbia University (1944) initiated the first modern study of voter decisionmaking during the campaign for the 1940 presidential election. The scholars were particularly interested in the power of political communication via the mass media and were prepared to find that mass audiences are easily swayed. Their concern with the power of mass-mediated propaganda grew out of what they had observed in the 1930s: the rise to power of Adolf Hitler and Nazi Germany, apparently through manipulation of German masses by emotional rhetoric broadcast over radio. Scholarly interest also stemmed from the seeming rise of mass-mediated wartime propaganda. As students of American politics know, however, Lazarsfeld discovered American voters to be quite insulated from mass-mediated political messages, ushering in the view of minimal media effects. Having set out in search of widespread conversion, they found mostly reinforcement and activation of existing loyalties.

Reconsider the case now. Although merely a speculative exercise, we might reinterpret these discrepancies from the mid-twentieth century as the result of two different styles of politics set in motion by the contours of political emotion. In 1940, in Erie County, Ohio, the presidential election contest between two-term incumbent Franklin Roosevelt and challenger Wendell Wilkie was part of life as usual. The New Deal realignment had been consolidated, the country had made some progress in pulling itself out of the worst of the Depression, and the portentous events overseas were of some concern but remained remote. Absent issues or conditions to dramatically heighten public worries, American voters stuck with their predispositions, resisted new contrary information, and responded to the mobilization efforts of local party organizations. Nearly a decade earlier, Weimar Germans were mired in the worldwide Depression, their own situation even more hopeless due to the bankrupting reparations agreed to in the Versailles Treaty. Their government was crippled by political polarization and chaos. Life was full of economic and physical dangers, and the future was anything but certain. With mass anxieties through the roof, observers *thought* they witnessed an impassioned strongman turn many reluctant heads and persuade people to support a cause they otherwise might not.[6]

Having seen how levels of social anxiety in certain times and places shape the reach of political communication and opinion leadership, we can also consider how the distribution of political orientations in the public shapes the style of election campaigns. Campaign politics has varied considerably in the United States during the past two centuries In much of the nineteenth century, political parties were organizationally strong and their mass support was well defined by religious, ethnic, and sectional loyalties. Today, parties enjoy less organizational strength and compete to win the swing votes of the vast unaligned middle, while relying on their narrower ideological base of support. In light of these characterizations, we can make new sense of the differing campaign styles of these eras. When the partisan camps were large and well defined (with a narrow middle), parties practiced the politics of enthusiasm. They mobilized their supporters through parades, rallies, and weeks of revelry. Election Day was more like a drunken festival hosted by rival sports teams than a sober fulfillment of citizen duty. Today, parties increasingly practice a politics of anxiety. They attempt to capture swing voters through media campaigns that often take aim at the worrisome character, policies, and performance of the opponents. The remnants of enthusiasm politics live on in party appeals to their own supporters, manifested in the hullabaloo and hoopla of campaign events at local rallies and nationally televised political conventions.

With these brief sketches, I suggest just a couple of the ways in which we might return to familiar areas of our political knowledge and see connections we did not see before. The challenge ahead is to use this insight to better explain political communication and behavior. In this book, my purpose has been to show not just how taking emotion seriously opens new windows on our view of campaign advertising, but also how these open windows improve our view of other fields near and far. How might this lead us to reexamine what is familiar or what has remained elusive in the study of politics? We could consider what role emotions play in the "rally 'round the flag" phenomenon. We might revisit what happened in January 1998, when an atmosphere of crisis emerged over an unfolding sex scandal in the White House and heightened attention to the State of the Union address, which in turn stressed economic prosperity and seemingly salvaged the presidency. We could ask what role emotion played in the last-minute reversal of electoral fortunes in Spain, when terrorist bombs struck days before a national election in 2004.

More broadly, the findings of this book invite a fresh look at the dynamics of mass politics, especially when televised campaign ads are involved. It appears that a shift in the emotional flavor of political appeals can transform, for a time, the most basic manner in which citizens respond to politics. Absent anything out of the ordinary, we expect citizens to get by on habits formed through years of socialization and embodied in their political predispositions. When summoned with a call of pride and the promise of victory, they should answer with added vigor and determination to see their own cause prevail. But when roused by a cry of alarm, citizens should divert their attention to learning about the threat, reassess their current situation, and consider new options. At the micro level, this calls to mind dueling archetypes that have dominated the study of political behavior—namely, the inattentive partisan and the reasoning voter (Campbell et al. 1960; Popkin 1994). Perhaps both models describe citizens well, but under different emotional states. Greater attention to the role of emotion may fruitfully shift inquiries away from which model is better toward when each model works best. The lesson and challenge for future research is not to launch a special subfield on "emotion and politics," but rather to incorporate emotion into existing lines of research. Emotion is well integrated into the processes of political communication and behavior; it should be integrated equally as well into our studies and understanding of the same.

Experiments: Question Wording and Sample

Wording and Coding of Pretest and Posttest Questionnaires

This section of the appendix contains the wording of pretest and posttest questionnaires used in both experiments, as well as response options and variable coding. I explain modifications to particular items for analysis and more details about particular coding decisions of primary variables in chapters 4 and 5. This list includes only those items used for the analyses in this book.

LOCAL TV NEWS USAGE. How often do you watch the local television news? [pretest] (0 = Never, 1 = Once or twice a month, 2 = Once a week, 3 = A few times a week, 4 = Every day)

MOOD. Generally speaking, how would describe your mood today? Please put a mark next to *any* of the following words that come close to describing how you feel overall? (proud, worried, angry, happy, calm, confused, sad, affectionate, ashamed, excited, bored, amused, hopeful, disappointed, surprised, confident) [pretest]

EDUCATION. Please place a mark next to the option that best describes your education. [pretest] (0 = Never completed high school, 1 = Completed high school [or equivalent], 2 = Attended some college, 3 = Finished college, 4 = Obtained a graduate or professional degree [or currently pursuing such a degree])

INCOME. Please think about the total income for all members of your household in 1997. Please mark the range in which your family income falls. If you are uncertain, please give your best guess. [pretest] (0 = Less than $20,000, 1 = $20,000–$39,999, 2 = $40,000–$59,999, 3 = $60,000–$79,999, 4 = $80,000–$99,999, 5 = $100,000 and over)

LOCAL RESIDENCY. How many years have you lived in Massachusetts? [pretest] (This variable is recoded as the proportion of a subject's life lived in the state.)

OCCUPATION. What is your present occupation (job) or career? [pretest]

RELIGION. Thinking about religion, what do you consider yourself? (Catholic, Protestant, Jewish, Other [please indicate]) [pretest]

RACE. What is your race? (Asian American/Pacific Islander, Black/African American, Native American, White/Caucasian, Other/Mixed [please specify]). [pretest]

HISPANIC ETHNICITY. Are you of Spanish or Hispanic descent? (yes, no) [pretest]

PARTY IDENTIFICATION. Generally speaking, do you usually think of yourself as a Republican, Democrat, independent, or what? (If Republican or Democrat: Would you call yourself a strong Republican/Democrat or a not very strong Republican/Democrat? If Independent or Other: Do you think of yourself as closer to the Republican Party or to the Democratic Party?) [pretest]

SIZE OF GOVERNMENT (IDEOLOGY). Please tell us which of two statements below comes *closest* to your opinion. You might agree to some extent with both, but we want to know which one is *closer* to your views. [pretest] (0 = The less government, the better, 1 = There are more things that government should be doing)

ISSUE CONCERN. What would you say is the most serious issue facing the country these days? (Dummy variables for education and crime) [pretest]

ISSUE IMPORTANCE. There are many problems facing our nation today. But at certain times some things are more important than others and need more attention from the government. What priorities do you think the government should have? Please indicate how you would rate the *importance* of each issue, where "1" means it is not important for the government to tackle the issue right now and "7" means it is absolutely essential for the government to do something. (health care, the environment, drug abuse, education, crime, taxes, poverty) [pretest]

FEELING THERMOMETERS. Now we'd like to get your feelings toward some people. Please rate each person using something we call the feeling thermometer. Ratings between 50 degrees and 100 degrees mean that you feel favorable and warm toward the person. Ratings between 0 degrees and 50 degrees mean that you don't feel favorable toward the person. You would rate the person at the 50 degree mark if you feel neither warm nor cold toward the person. If you can't recall who the person is, mark "don't know." Otherwise write any number from 0 to 100, indicating how you feel about the person. [pretest & posttest]

OPEN CANDIDATE CHOICE. Regardless of whether you plan to vote, as of today, *if you were to vote* in the following elections, whom do you think you would vote for? Please write the name of the candidate you prefer and indicate whether you support that person strongly or not very strongly at this time. If you aren't sure yet or don't recall the names of the candidates, mark the line that says "not sure yet." (Democratic primary for governor) [pretest] (−1 = Patricia McGovern, 0 = Not Sure between McGovern and Harshbarger, and 1 = Scott Harshbarger)

FORCED CANDIDATE CHOICE. There are several Democrats competing to be that party's nominee for governor. As of today, if you were to vote in the Democratic primary, whom do you think you would vote for? [posttest] (Scott Harshbarger, Patricia McGovern, Not Sure Yet)

CERTAINTY OF CANDIDATE CHOICE. As of right now, do you feel you know enough about the candidates for governor to make your final decision? (yes/no)

CANDIDATE CONSIDERATIONS (LIKES/DISLIKES). Because this is an election year, you've probably heard some talk about the candidates running for governor of Massachusetts. Although many people have not made up their minds about the candidates yet, we'd like to know more about the general impressions you have formed *so far.* First we would like to ask you about the good and bad points of the candidates. For each candidate, you may list as many good and bad points as you like. Is there anything in particular about Patricia McGovern that makes you want to vote for her? Is there anything in particular about McGovern that makes you want to vote against her? Is there anything in particular about Scott Harshbarger that makes you want to vote for him? Is there anything in particular about Harshbarger that makes you want to vote against him? [posttest]

EVALUATION OF CANDIDATE ISSUE COMPETENCE AND TRAITS. We are interested in the kinds of words and phrases people sometimes use to describe candidates. Please tell us your opinion about how well the word or phrase describes each candidate below. We realize that not everyone is completely familiar with these candidates, but if you have heard *anything* at all about them, we would like to get your impression or "gut feeling" so far. Please try to answer each of the items below. If you have heard absolutely *nothing* about a candidate and therefore are incapable of answering the question, then mark "don't know at all." Think about Scott Harshbarger. How well do these words describe Harshbarger? ("Favors more education spending," "Favors tough sentences for criminals") Now think about Patricia McGovern. How well do these words describe McGovern? (Issue Competence = "Favors more education spending," "Favors tough sentences for criminals"; Traits = "Intelligent," "Provides strong leadership," "Compassionate," "Gets things done," "Honest") [posttest] (0 = Not well at all, 1 = Not too well, 2 = Quite well, 3 = Extremely well)

NAME RECOGNITION. Below is a list of public figures. Some of the people listed are well known, others are relatively unknown. We would like to know whether you have heard of any of the people in this list. Please mark the appropriate column to indicate whether the name sounds very familiar, somewhat familiar, or you don't recall ever hearing of this person. [posttest]

POLITICAL KNOWLEDGE/SOPHISTICATION. Here are some questions about Massachusetts and U.S. politics. If you are not sure of the answer at this time, feel free to write "don't know" in the blank. Who is currently vice president of the United States? How many members are elected to the Massachusetts Senate? What government position does Janet Reno currently hold? How many justices are there on the U.S. Supreme Court? Who holds the position of Speaker of the House in Massachusetts? Which political party controls the U.S. Senate right now? In the race for governor, who was officially nominated by the Massachusetts Democratic Party earlier this summer? [pretest] (The dummy variable for local political sophistication is coded 0 if no correct responses are given to the three state politics questions and 1 if one or more correct responses is given. Knowledge about national politics is a simple count of the number of correct answers, 0 to 4.)

FOLLOW POLITICS. Some people constantly follow what goes on in politics, while others are not interested in it. How often do you follow politics? [pretest] (0 = Never, 1 = Very rarely, 2 = Sometimes, 3 = Quite a bit, 4 = All the time)

INTEREST IN CAMPAIGN. We are in an election year. Some people don't pay much attention to election campaigns. How interested have you been in the campaigns so far this year? Please indicate by circling a number from 1 to 7, where "1" means not interested at all and "7" means completely interested. [posttest]

PRIOR INTENTION TO VOTE. We are in an election year. So far as you know now, do you expect to vote in this election? Please indicate how likely you think it is that you will vote in the election, where "1" means you definitely will not vote and "7" means you definitely will vote. [pretest]

INTENTION TO VOTE IN PRIMARY. So far as you know now, do you expect to vote in the state primary election this coming September? Please indicate how likely you think it is that you will vote in the primary, where "1" means you definitely will not vote and "7" means you definitely will vote. [posttest] (As indicated in the text, this is modified into a dummy variable for likely voters, set at 1 for those who answer 7 on the original scale and 0 for all others.)

INTENTION TO VOTE IN GENERAL ELECTION. So far as you know now, do you expect to vote in the general election this coming November? Please indicate how likely you think it is that you will vote in the general election this year, where "1" means you definitely will not vote and "7" means you definitely will vote. [posttest] (As indicated in the text, this is modified into a dummy variable for likely voters, set at 1 for those who answer 7 on the original scale and 0 for all others.)

VOTER REGISTRATION. Are you registered to vote in Massachusetts? (0 = No, 1 = Yes) If you answered "no" or "don't know," how likely is it that you will register to vote for this year's elections? [posttest] (0 = Definitely will not register, 6 = Definitely will register)

WILLINGNESS TO VOLUNTEER. In the remaining months until the November Election Day, how likely is it that you will volunteer for a candidate running for national, state, or local office? Please circle a number to indicate how likely you are to volunteer, where "1" means you definitely will not volunteer and "7" means you definitely will volunteer. [posttest]

EXTERNAL EFFICACY. Please indicate whether you agree or disagree with the following statement. "People like me don't have any say about what the government does." [pretest/posttest] (4 = Disagree strongly, 3 = Disagree somewhat, 2 = Neither agree nor disagree, 1 = Agree somewhat, 0 = Agree strongly)

DESIRE TO CONTACT CAMPAIGNS. How likely are you to contact one of the campaigns to ask for more information? [posttest] (0 = Definitely will not contact, 6 = Definitely will contact)

INTERNAL EFFICACY. Please indicate whether you agree or disagree with the following statement. "Sometimes politics and government seem so complicated that a person like me can't really understand what's going on." [posttest] (4 = Disagree strongly, 3 = Disagree somewhat, 2 = Neither agree nor disagree, 1 = Agree somewhat, 0 = Agree strongly)

GENERAL SOCIAL TRUST. Generally speaking, would you say that most people can be trusted, or that you can't be too careful in dealing with people? [posttest] (0 = Can't be too careful, 1 = Most people can be trusted)

IMPORTANCE OF VOTING. Please indicate whether you agree or disagree with the following statement. "People should vote whenever there is an election." [posttest] (0 = Disagree strongly, 1 = Disagree somewhat, 2 = Neither agree nor disagree, 3 = Agree somewhat, 4 = Agree strongly)

TRUST IN GOVERNMENT. People have different ideas about the government. These ideas don't refer to Democrats or Republicans in particular, but just to the government in general. How much of the time do you think you can trust the government to do what is right? [posttest] (0 = None of the time, 1 = Only some of the time, 2 = Most of the time, 3 = Just about always)

TRUST IN OTHER SOCIAL INSTITUTIONS. People often feel they can put more trust in some institutions than in others. In general, how much do you trust the institutions or people listed below? Please indicate by circling a number between 1 and 7, where "1" means distrust completely and "7" means trust completely. (the media, public schools, courts, police, elected officials) [posttest]

CYNICISM ABOUT PUBLIC OFFICIALS. Please indicate whether you agree or disagree with the following statement. "I don't think public officials care much what people like me think." [posttest] (0 = Disagree strongly, 1 = Disagree somewhat, 2 = Neither agree nor disagree, 3 = Agree somewhat, 4 = Agree strongly)

CYNICISM ABOUT PARTIES. Please indicate whether you agree or disagree with the following statement. "Parties are only interested in people's votes but not in their opinions." [posttest] (0 = Disagree strongly, 1 = Disagree somewhat, 2 = Neither agree nor disagree, 3 = Agree somewhat, 4 = Agree strongly)

CYNICISM ABOUT CAMPAIGN NEGATIVITY. Election campaigns are often quite negative in tone. Do you think this is because candidates are having a tough but fair debate about important issues, or do you think candidates are mostly lying about one another and engaged in unfair "character assassination"? [posttest] (0 = Candidates have a tough but fair debate about important issues, 1 = Candidates lie about one another and engage in unfair character assassination)

CYNICISM ABOUT THE MOTIVES OF POLITICIANS. Do you think politicians are primarily "in it for themselves" or do you think their primary concern is the "public good"? [posttest] (0 = In it for themselves, 1 = Public good)

NEWS RECALL. The video selection you watched contained news stories touching on a variety of topics. What topics do you recall hearing about? [posttest]

INTEREST IN NEWS BY TYPE. These days television news covers a wide variety of issues and people watch the news for a variety of reasons. How about you? What parts of news programs do you find most interesting? Please indicate on the following scale, where "1" means you are not at all interested in this part of the news and "7" means you are completely interested. (politics, economy/business, crime/court stories, health news) [posttest]

AD RECALL. Finally, candidates often like to run advertisements during television news programs. Some—but not all—of the videos we show people contain campaign ads. How about the video you watched? Do you recall seeing a campaign ad? [posttest] (0 = Correct, 1 = Incorrect)

REACTION TO THE AD. If you recall seeing one of the campaign ads, please think about the ad for a moment. Generally speaking, how did the ad make you *feel*? To what extent did you feel any of these emotions in response to the advertisement? [posttest] (hopeful/reassured/confident, anxious/worried/afraid, enthusiastic/excited/eager, angry/irritated/upset) (0 = Not at all, 1 = Slightly, 2 = Somewhat, 3 = Quite a bit, 4 = Completely)

TARGET OF ANGER. If you felt angry, what person, group, or situation did you feel angry at? Or did you just feel angry in general?

Additional Information on the Sample and Research Locations

This portion of the appendix contains additional details about the sample from the two experiments and the communities from which subjects came and in which they participated. Table A.1 compares the demographic profile of the combined experimental sample to similar statistics on the state population from the U.S. Census and Current Population Surveys. Below, I provide a complete list of communities in which subjects resided at the time, a list of the locations where I conducted the research, and the education and income profile of the cities surrounding those research sites (see table A.2).

Communities in Which Subjects Resided

Andover, Arlington, Barre, Belmont, Billerica, Boston, Brimfield, Brockton, Brookline, Cambridge, Chelsea, Dover, Dracut, Everett, Falmouth, Framingham, Hingham, Hyannis, Lawrence, Lexington, Lowell, Lynn, Malden, Mashpee, Medfield, Medford, Melrose, Milford, Milton, Natick, Needham, Newton, North Andover, Norton, Norwood, Quincy, Revere, Salem, Scituate, Somerville, Stoneham, Stoughton, Sunderland, Swampscott, Wakefield, Waltham, Watertown, Waverley, Wellesley, Westwood, Wilmington, Woburn

List of Research Sites in Massachusetts

Cambridge:	Dudley House, Lehman Hall, Harvard University (Harvard Yard)
Arlington:	Rollins Library (700 Massachusetts Avenue)
Waltham:	Waltham Public Library (735 Main Street)
Watertown:	St. John's United Methodist Church (80 Mt. Auburn Street)
Brookline:	Brookline Public Library (361 Washington Street)
Wellesley:	Wellesley Free Library (530 Washington Street)
Boston:	Francois Xavier Bagnoud Building, Harvard School of Public Health (Longwood Medical Area)
Belmont:	Belmont Public Library (336 Concord Avenue)
Needham:	Needham Public Library (1139 Highland Avenue)
Boston:	Old South Meeting House, Downtown Crossing (310 Washington Street)
Andover:	Memorial Hall Library (Elm Square)
Lowell:	Pollard Memorial Library (401 Merrimack Street)
Cambridge:	Littauer Center, Harvard University (North Harvard Yard)

TABLE A.1 Profile of the Sample and State Populations

	Profile of the Sample	Profile of Massachusetts
Age (mean among adults)	41	43
Gender		
Male	47%	48%
Female	53	52
Race		
White	89%	90%
Black	4	5
Other	7	5
Hispanic ethnicity	4	5
Religion		
Catholic	37%	54%
Protestant	23	21
Other Christian	6	8
Jewish	12	4
Other religion	7	2
Not religious	15	8
Income (median household)	$33,500	$38,500
Education		
Less than high school	4%	20%
High school	16	30
Some college	24	16
College	27	24
Graduate degree	29	11
Partisanship		
Democrat	46%	38%
Independent/Not enrolled	45	49
Republican	9	13

Note: Population figures are based on the 1990 U.S. Census (1997 Statistical Abstract) and Massachusetts State Data Center (www.umass.edu/miser). Religious affiliation is drawn from Kosmin and Lachman 1993. Massachusetts partisanship is based on voter registration totals in August 1998, as reported by the Massachusetts Secretary of State website. Sample respondents reported their household income within $20,000 intervals; the median falls in the $20,000–$39,999 range and, if ordered, would occupy a position two-thirds the way through that category's respondents (the dollar figure is interpolated accordingly).

TABLE A.2 Profile of the Research Site Communities

Community	Percent with College Degree	Median Household Income
Andover	59.5	$61,100
Arlington	48.0	43,300
Belmont	60.9	53,500
Boston	20.9	29,200
Brookline	68.3	45,600
Cambridge	57.8	33,100
Lowell	35.1	29,400
Needham	61.6	63,400
Waltham	32.9	38,500
Watertown	46.7	43,500
Wellesley	73.9	79,100

Note: Education and income data are from Massachusetts State Data Center (www.umass
.edu/miser).

Multivariate Statistical Analyses: Full Results

This appendix contains the full results from multivariate estimations discussed in chapters 4 and 5. Tables B.1 and B.2 display the estimated effects of advertising (i.e., experimental treatment) and control variables on various measures of motivation; the results were summarized in table 4.1. Table B.3 displays the estimated effects of advertising and control variables on comparative candidate affect and vote choice; the results were summarized in table 5.1. Table B.4 displays the estimated effects of advertising and control variables on interest in watching various types of television news; the results were summarized in table 5.2.

TABLE B.1 Multivariate Analysis of Effects of Emotional Cues on Motivation

Explanatory Variables	Interest in the Campaign	Willingness to Volunteer for a Campaign	Intention to Vote in the Primary
Enthusiasm cues	0.64***	0.60**	1.39**
	(0.21)	(0.25)	(0.53)
Fear cues	−0.03	0.45*	0.35
	(0.20)	(0.24)	(0.48)
Advertising exposure	−0.44*	−0.69**	−1.15*
	(0.22)	(0.25)	(0.56)
Weeks left in campaign	−0.08**	−0.05	−0.12
	(0.03)	(0.03)	(0.08)
Number of viewers	−0.05	0.05	−0.19
	(0.06)	(0.07)	(0.16)
Prior motivation to vote	0.29***	0.19***	1.02***
	(0.04)	(0.05)	(0.16)
Follow politics	0.70***		
	(0.08)		
Education	−0.24***	−0.11	0.10
	(0.07)	(0.08)	(0.18)
Income	−0.05	−0.06	0.28*
	(0.05)	(0.06)	(0.13)
Gender (female)	0.04	−0.16	0.45
	(0.16)	(0.18)	(0.39)
Retired	0.85**	0.61*	3.01***
	(0.26)	(0.26)	(0.83)
Religion (Protestant)	−0.20	−0.21	−1.51**
	(0.18)	(0.21)	(0.56)
Occupation (public employee)	1.00*	1.60***	3.76**
	(0.43)	(0.45)	(1.50)
Initial mood	0.06	0.10	0.27*
	(0.05)	(0.05)	(0.12)
Importance of crime		0.75**	
		(0.26)	
Importance of education		0.62*	
		(0.31)	
N	286	286	286

Note: The table displays full results from the estimations summarized in table 4.1. Entries are coefficients (and standard errors), derived from OLS regression, MLE ordered probit, and MLE logit models, respectively.

***$p < .001$ **$p < .01$ *$p < .05$

TABLE B.2 Further Multivariate Analysis of Effects of Emotional Cues on Motivation

Explanatory Variables	Intention to Vote in the General Election	Agree That People Should Vote	Intention to Register to Vote
Enthusiasm cues	0.87*	0.17	1.12*
	(0.53)	(0.18)	(0.64)
Fear cues	−0.12	0.33*	0.07
	(0.48)	(0.17)	(0.59)
Frame (negative/positive)	−0.41	0.11	−0.19
	(0.25)	(0.09)	(0.33)
Advertising exposure	−0.63	0.00	−0.30
	(0.48)	(0.15)	(0.50)
Weeks left in campaign	−0.11	−0.02	−0.11
	(0.07)	(0.02)	(0.07)
Number of viewers	−0.26	−0.05	
	(0.14)	(0.04)	
Prior motivation to vote	0.57***	0.20***	0.73***
	(0.09)	(0.03)	(0.11)
Political efficacy		0.11**	−0.28
		(0.04)	(0.15)
Education	0.32*	0.00	
	(0.16)	(0.05)	
Income	0.23*	0.04	
	(0.11)	(0.04)	
Gender (female)	0.42	0.18	
	(0.33)	(0.11)	
Retired	2.26***	0.45*	
	(0.70)	(0.19)	
Religion (Protestant)	−1.50***	−0.04	
	(0.44)	(0.13)	
Occupation (public employee)	2.52*		
	(1.27)		
Initial mood	0.18	0.04	
	(0.10)	(0.04)	
N	286	286	65

Note: The table displays full results from the estimations summarized in table 4.1. Entries are coefficients (and standard errors), derived from MLE logit, OLS regression, and OLS regression models, respectively. The occupation variable is dropped from the estimation in the second column due to a lack of variation (i.e., values of the dependent variable are constant).

***$p < .001$ **$p < .01$ *$p < .05$

TABLE B.3 Multivariate Analysis of Effects of Emotional Cues on Persuasion

Explanatory Variables	Comparative Candidate Affect	Vote Choice
Enthusiasm cues	0.23	0.19
	(0.22)	(0.22)
Fear cues	0.53**	0.54**
	(0.21)	(0.20)
Frame (negative/positive)	−0.15	0.14
	(0.13)	(0.12)
Enthusiasm cues × initial preferences	0.58	0.94**
	(0.39)	(0.34)
Fear cues × initial preferences	−0.50	−0.54*
	(0.37)	(0.30)
Frame × initial preferences	−0.27	−0.12
	(0.20)	(0.17)
Initial preferences	1.72***	1.06***
	(0.18)	(0.15)
Anger at sponsor	−0.54**	−0.36
	(0.20)	(0.19)
Weeks left in campaign	0.02	0.05
	(0.03)	(0.03)
Viewers	−0.05	−0.13*
	(0.06)	(0.06)
Ideology	0.03	0.01
	(0.06)	(0.06)
Importance of electing a woman	0.09	−0.12
	(0.07)	(0.07)
Importance of drugs	0.03	−0.11**
	(0.04)	(0.04)
Local residency	0.59**	0.64**
	(0.21)	(0.21)
N	286	286

Note: The table displays full results from the estimations summarized in table 5.1. Entries are coefficients (and standard errors), derived from MLE ordered probit models.

***$p < .001$ **$p < .01$ *$p < .05$

TABLE B.4 Multivariate Analysis of Effects of Emotional Cues on Interest in Watching Television News

Explanatory Variables	Political News	Economic News	Crime News	Health News
Fear cues	0.43*	−0.15	0.13	0.02
	(0.24)	(0.26)	(0.31)	(0.30)
Enthusiasm cues	0.14	0.30	0.08	0.00
	(0.25)	(0.26)	(0.32)	(0.31)
Frame (negative/positive)	0.05	−0.19	0.17	0.07
	(0.13)	(0.14)	(0.16)	(0.16)
Frequency watch local TV news	0.26***	0.21**	0.38***	0.29***
	(0.08)	(0.08)	(0.09)	(0.09)
Education	0.05	−0.05	−0.08	0.01
	(0.09)	(0.09)	(0.11)	(0.11)
Age	0.00	0.01	−0.01	0.02*
	(0.01)	(0.01)	(0.01)	(0.01)
Gender (female)	0.28	−0.21	0.16	0.32
	(0.18)	(0.19)	(0.23)	(0.23)
Income	−0.02	0.09	−0.09	0.00
	(0.06)	(0.06)	(0.08)	(0.07)
Minority (nonwhite)	0.68**	0.85**	0.22	0.71*
	(0.26)	(0.28)	(0.33)	(0.32)
Follow politics	0.71***	0.56***	−0.05	−0.19*
	(0.10)	(0.10)	(0.12)	(0.11)
Initial mood	0.15**	0.22***	0.05	0.08
	(0.06)	(0.06)	(0.07)	(0.07)
Knowledge about national politics	0.32***			
	(0.09)			
Importance of taxes		0.10*		
		(0.05)		
Importance of crime			0.31***	
			(0.08)	
Importance of health care				0.15*
				(0.07)

Note: The table displays full results from the estimations summarized in table 5.2. Entries are coefficients (and standard errors), derived from OLS regression models. $N = 234$.

***$p < .001$ **$p < .01$ *$p < .05$

Advertising Content Analysis: Coding Rules

This appendix provides information about the coding instructions for the content analysis of campaign ads described in chapter 6. It also describes the coding of supplemental data regarding the electoral, political, and social context. I obtained the contextual data from the *Almanac of American Politics* and official reports from the 2000 U.S. Census, the Federal Election Commission, the Bureau of Labor Statistics, and the Federal Bureau of Investigations.

Coding Rules for Content Analysis and Contextual Variables

SPONSOR. Name of the candidate or group sponsoring the ad.

TONE. 1 = Promotional, 2 = Comparative, 3 = Strictly attack.

TYPE OF CRITICISM. [for comparative and attack ads only] Seven-point scale, where 1 = Strictly issue-based criticism, 4 = Balance between issue and character/personal attack, and 7 = Strictly character attack (i.e., mudslinging).

MENTION OPPONENT BY NAME. 0 = No, 1 = Yes.

MENTION SPONSOR'S PARTY. [not including "paid for" acknowledgment] 0 = No, 1 = Yes.

MENTION OPPONENT'S PARTY. [not including "paid for" acknowledgment] 0 = No, 1 = Yes.

USE OF IDEOLOGICAL LABELS. 0 = No, 1 = Yes.

FOCUS ON ISSUES. 0 = No discussion of issues/policies, 1 = Some discussion of issues/policies, 2 = Heavy emphasis on issues/policies.

FOCUS ON GROUPS. [socioeconomic or interest groups] 0 = No discussion of groups or group-based appeals, 1 = Some discussion of groups or group-based appeals, 2 = Heavy emphasis on groups or group-based appeals.

FOCUS ON PARTIES. 0 = No discussion of parties or party-based appeals, 1 = Some discussion of parties or party-based appeals, 2 = Heavy emphasis on parties or party-based appeals.

FOCUS ON IDEOLOGY. 0 = No discussion of ideology or the role of government, 1 = Some discussion of ideology or the role of government, 2 = Heavy emphasis on ideology or the role of government.

FOCUS ON VALUES. [not including references to personal ethics] 0 = No discussion of shared/cultural values, 1 = Some discussion of shared/cultural values, 2 = Heavy emphasis on shared/cultural values.

FOCUS ON PERSONAL QUALITIES. 0 = No discussion of the personal qualities of the candidates, 1 = Some discussion of the personal qualities of the candidates, 2 = Heavy emphasis on personal qualities of the candidates.

INVOKE LEADERSHIP. 0 = Ad is not framed in terms of leadership/leadership not invoked, 1 = Ad is framed in terms of leadership/leadership is invoked.

MENTION RECORD OF CANDIDATES. 0 = No mention of a candidate's experience or record in office, 1 = Mention either or both candidates' experience or records in office.

PRIMARY/SECONDARY/TERTIARY ISSUE. [list of several general and specific issue categories; codes given only for those categories used in the text] 10 = Crime, 35 = Jobs/unemployment.

WHITE/BLACK/ASIAN/HISPANIC VISUALS. Count of the number of people (other than the candidates) of each racial group who appear in the ad.

CHILDREN/ELDERLY VISUALS. Count of the number of people (other than the candidates) of each age group who appear in the ad.

MALE/FEMALE VISUALS. Count of the number of people (other than the candidates) of each sex who appear in the ad.

FAMILY VISUALS. Count of the number of family units (defined as two or more related individuals belonging to at least two different generations) that appear in the ad.

MENTION BIOGRAPHY. 0 = No mention of the personal history/biography of the candidate, 1 = Mentions the personal history/biography of the candidate.

SPONSOR APPEARS. 0 = Sponsor does not appear in ad, 1 = Sponsor appears in the ad.

OPPONENT APPEARS. 0 = Opponent does not appear in the ad, 1 = Opponent does appear in the ad.

MILITARY VISUALS. 0 = No images of military personnel/veterans, 1 = Images of military personnel/veterans.

GUN VISUALS. 0 = No images of guns, 1 = Images of guns.

DRUGS VISUALS. 0 = No images of illegal drugs, 1 = Images of illegal drugs.

SYMBOLIC IMAGES. [list three most prominent] 1 = American flag, 2 = White House, 3 = U.S. Capitol Building, 4 = Supreme Court Building, 5 = Statue of Liberty, 6 = Military memorials, 7 = Other national monuments, 8 = Likeness of U.S. Constitution or Declaration of Independence, 10 = State capitol building or monument, 11 = State flag, 12 = Military awards/citations/insignia, 13 = Eagle, 30 = Foreign monument or flag, 50 = Other widely recognized symbol not listed above, 999 = No specific symbols.

VISUAL SCENES. [list three most prominent types of scenes portrayed in visual imagery] 1 = Children playing, 2 = Family togetherness, 3 = Wedding, 4 = Graduation ceremony, 5 = Parents with newborn baby, 6 = Beautiful neighborhood, 7 = Picturesque landscapes, 8 = People hard and happy at work, 9 = Children happy and learning in school/full classroom, 10 = Violent criminal acts, 11 = Nonviolent criminal acts (including drug use), 12 = Crime scenes, 13 = Jails or prisons, 14 = Immigrants crossing the border/border checkpoints, 15 = Empty classrooms or schools, 16 = Empty playgrounds, 17 = Abandoned or rundown buildings, 18 = Devastated or barren landscapes, 19 = Pollution/sewage, 20 = Burning cross, 30 = War/combat, 31 = U.S. military ships/planes/tanks/missiles, 32 = Foreign military ships/planes/tanks/missiles, 33 = Nuclear explosion, 40 = Nursing home/assisted care of elderly, 41 = Sick patients in hospital, 42 = Sick/starving/malnourished children, 43 = Homeless people, 44 = Victims of a disaster, 45 = Students struggling to learn (having difficulty), 46 = People struggling to pay bills or buy essential goods, 47 = Workers being laid off or struggling to find work, 48 = People with disabilities struggling, 50 = Office of a political official, 51 = Interior of a legislative chamber, 999 = None of these visual scenes.

CITE SOURCE OF EVIDENCE. [either in narration or text on screen] 0 = No sources are cited for factual claims, 1 = Cites sources for factual claims.

MUSIC. 1 = Ad contains uplifting/sweet/sentimental/patriotic music and major chords, 2 = Ad contains tense/somber music and minor chords, 3 = Balance of uplifting and tense music, 999 = No music.

SOUND EFFECTS. 1 = Ad contains positive sound effects (e.g., laughter, cheers, applause), 2 = Ad contains negative sound effects (e.g., screams, sirens, crying), 3 = Mix of positive and negative sound effects or neutral sound effects, 999 = No sound effects.

DOMINANT COLOR. 1 = Black and white, 2 = Dark or gray colors, 3 = Ordinary or muted colors, 4 = Bright colors ("colorful"), 5 = Mix of color schemes and none is dominant.

EMOTIONAL APPEAL. 0 = No appeal to viewer emotions, 1 = Appeal to viewer emotions.

LOGICAL APPEAL. 0 = No appeal to logic (i.e., logical arguments/inferences from evidence), 1 = Appeal to logic.

DOMINANT APPEAL. 0 = Emotional appeal dominant, 1 = Logical appeal dominant, 2 = Neither or other appeal dominant.

AMUSEMENT/HUMOR APPEAL. 0 = No attempt to elicit amusement (appeal to humor), 1 = Some appeal to amusement/humor, 2 = Strong appeal to amusement/humor.

FEAR APPEAL. 0 = No attempt to elicit fear/anxiety, 1 = Some appeal to fear/anxiety, 2 = Strong appeal to fear/anxiety.

ENTHUSIASM APPEAL. 0 = No attempt to elicit enthusiasm/hope/joy, 1 = Some appeal to enthusiasm/hope/joy, 2 = Strong appeal to enthusiasm/hope/joy.

ANGER APPEAL. 0 = No attempt to elicit anger/contempt/disgust, 1 = Some appeal to anger/contempt/disgust, 2 = Strong appeal to anger/contempt/disgust.

PRIDE APPEAL. 0 = No attempt to elicit pride (i.e., satisfaction in what's been accomplished or who we are), 1 = Some appeal to pride, 2 = Strong appeal to pride.

COMPASSION APPEAL. 0 = No attempt to elicit compassion/sympathy, 1 = Some appeal to compassion/sympathy, 2 = Strong appeal to compassion/sympathy.

SADNESS APPEAL. 0 = No attempt to elicit sadness/disappointment/regret, 1 = Some appeal to sadness/disappointment/regret, 2 = Strong appeal to sadness/disappointment/regret.

SEX OF NARRATOR. 0 = Male voice, 1 = Female voice, 2 = Can't tell sex of narrator, 5 = Both male and female voices, 999 = No narration.

PACE OF VIDEO EDITING/SEQUENCING. 0 = Single continuous shot, 1 = Low number/frequency of cuts from one scene to next (i.e., a couple of cuts), 2 = Moderate number/frequency of cuts (i.e., several cuts), 3 = High number/frequency of cuts (i.e., rapid cuts throughout ad).

DOMINANT STYLE/FORMAT OF AD. 0 = Talking head, 1 = Person on the street, 2 = Just the facts (i.e., mostly text, tables, and graphs), 3 = Cartoon/animation, 4 = Imagery and voiceover, 9 = Other style or mix of styles.

OFFICE SOUGHT. 1 = U.S. president, 2 = U.S. Senate, 3 = Governor, 4 = U.S. House of Representatives, 11 = State legislature (lower chamber), 12 = State senate, 13 = Mayor, 14 = Judge, 15 = Lieutenant governor, 16 = Attorney general, 17 = Other statewide office, 18 = Other local office, 20 = No office sought (i.e., nonadvocacy ad).

ELECTION. 0 = Primary/nomination, 1 = General election.

OPEN SEAT. 0 = Not an open seat race, 1 = Open seat race.

UNOPPOSED. 0 = Contested race, 1 = Uncontested race.

TYPE OF SPONSOR. 0 = Candidate, 1 = Political party, 2 = Interest group/PAC.

INCUMBENT. [nonopen seat races only and candidate ads only] 0 = Challenger, 1 = Incumbent.

INCUMBENT PARTY. [candidate and party ads only] 0 = Challenging party, 1 = Incumbent party.

PARTY. [candidate and party ads only] 0 = Democrat, 1 = Republican, 2 = Independent/minor party.

STATE. [congressional and gubernatorial ads only] Numerical code for the state in which the election occurred, using the Inter-University Consortium for Political and Social Research (ICPSR) coding system.

DISTRICT. [U.S. House races only] Number of the congressional district seat being sought.

MARGIN. Absolute value of the difference between the Democratic and Republican shares of the two-party vote.

HOTLINE COMPETITIVENESS RATING. [U.S. House races only] 0 = No rating/not competitive, 1 = Vulnerable district but opposing party not targeting, 2 = Long shots, 3 = Potential sleepers, 4 = Best pick-up opportunities.

VIOLENT CRIME RATE. Number of violent crimes per 1,000 residents in the state in 2000.

MANUFACTURING EMPLOYMENT. Percentage of the state workforce employed in manufacturing sector jobs.

UNEMPLOYMENT RATE. Unemployment rate for the state in 2000.

PRESIDENTIAL PARTISANSHIP. 0 = Al Gore won the state in 2000 presidential race, 1 = George W. Bush won the state in 2000 presidential race. [see table C.1]

STATE PARTISANSHIP. 0 = Democratic Party advantage, 1 = Republican Party advantage. Based on state voter registration (where applicable), party balance in the state legislature, and party balance in the congressional delegation. [see table C.1]

TABLE C.1 Coding of Partisan Advantage in All Fifty States

State	Presidential Measure	State Measure	State	Presidential Measure	State Measure
Alabama*	R	D	Montana	R	R
Alaska	R	R	Nebraska	R	R
Arizona	R	R	Nevada	R	R
Arkansas*	R	D	New Hampshire	R	R
California	D	D	New Jersey	D	D
Colorado	R	R	New Mexico	D	D
Connecticut	D	D	New York	D	D
Delaware	D	D	North Carolina*	R	D
Florida	R	R	North Dakota	R	R
Georgia	R	R	Ohio	R	R
Hawaii	D	D	Oklahoma*	R	D
Idaho	R	R	Oregon	D	D
Illinois	D	D	Pennsylvania	D	D
Indiana	R	R	Rhode Island	D	D
Iowa*	D	R	South Carolina	R	R
Kansas	R	R	South Dakota	R	R
Kentucky*	R	D	Tennessee*	R	D
Louisiana*	R	D	Texas	R	R
Maine	D	D	Utah	R	R
Maryland	D	D	Vermont	D	D
Massachusetts	D	D	Virginia	R	R
Michigan*	D	R	Washington	D	D
Minnesota	D	D	West Virginia*	R	D
Mississippi*	R	D	Wisconsin*	D	R
Missouri	R	R	Wyoming	R	R

Note: R = Republican advantage, D = Democratic advantage.

*Measures suggest different partisan advantage for the state.

Notes

Chapter One

1. For more on the cognitive revolution in psychology, see Gardner 1987 and Hunt 1993.

2. Since the inception of televised campaigning in the 1950s, political ads have appealed to emotions as well as logic (Kaid and Johnston 2001). By the 1980s and 1990s, ads had become shorter and more slickly packaged compared to previous decades and constituted the largest expenditure for most major federal and state elections (Bennett 1996; West 2001).

3. Jim Rutenberg, "Scary Ads Take Campaign to a Grim New Level," *New York Times,* October 17, 2004. See also John McChesney, "Politics of Fear Marks Latest Campaign Ads," *National Public Radio,* October 20, 2004; Don Gonyea, "Message of Fear Dominates as Vote Nears," *National Public Radio,* October 20, 2004; Fred Brown, "The Politics of Fear," *Denver Post,* October 31, 2004; David Montgomery, "Experts Say Fear-Mongering Making This the Ugliest Election in Memory," *Mercury News* (San Jose), October 29, 2004; Marian Wilkinson, "Crying Wolf, but Republicans' Scary Ads Bite," *Age* (Melbourne), October 26, 2004.

4. Katy Burns, "Appeal to Fear Is All Bush Has Left: Use of Scare Tactics Reaches New Low," *Concord Monitor,* October 31, 2004.

5. The words must be consistent with those elements and may help establish the mood by suggesting the country is "back on the right track," as well as by using the metaphorical language of "morning." The script, however, bears primary responsibility for making the argument and presenting the facts, whereas the pictures and music are mostly about stirring sentiment. Some words and narration are more emotionally evocative than others (think of the speeches of Martin Luther King Jr.), and some images can constitute visual presentation of "facts" (e.g., a signing ceremony for new legislation). In this sense, music and other sound effects are perhaps the purest examples of emotional elements. Even so, it is reasonable to differentiate the various components of ads according to their principal purpose, which is tied in part to the different ways in which language, music, and images are processed by the brain (see chapter 3). For example Graber (2001) points out that verbal information requires slower, serial processing (17) and that "[v]isuals excel in emotion arousal compared to most nonvisual stimuli" (35).

6. My intention in reviewing the sorts of scenes, symbols, and sounds used in feel-

good ads is to make clear that this is what I mean by the term "emotional appeals." Although there are many subtle variations in these ads that are suitable to different themes and audiences, this book focuses on their common goal of arousing hope and enthusiasm. Other scholars provide nuanced accounts of historical ad campaigns, analyze production techniques, and decode the meaning embedded in the rhetorical and narrative structure of ads (Diamond and Bates 1992; Jamieson 1996; Kern 1989; Nelson and Boynton 1997; Richardson 2003). My objective is to explain why and how these symbolic appeals to emotion matter for the decisions that voters make.

7. Evidence from focus groups suggests that voters who failed to catch the full allegorical meaning of the ad still grasped the "peace through strength" message and responded favorably (Diamond and Bates 1992).

8. Some ads also use "threatening" images of people from social groups disliked by the intended audience. To the extent these group cues are designed to trigger anxiety, they are encompassed in my definition of fear appeals. However, racial group cues also have more specialized effects, such as activating stereotypes and priming the role of prejudice in decisionmaking. For research demonstrating these effects, see Mendelberg 2001 and Valentino, Hutchings, and White 2002.

Chapter Two

1. To borrow the language of Alexander Hamilton and James Madison in *The Federalist* Nos. 1 and 10, respectively.

2. The distinctions between free and paid media can be overdrawn; for example, journalists often write stories about advertising, and ads often make use of material that appeared on the news and in debates.

3. The restoration is partial because TV permits only one-way communication of nonverbal behavior from leaders to citizens, but not vice versa.

4. Putnam contends that television is a primary cause of declining civic engagement and social interaction in the United States, particularly in redirecting vast amounts of leisure time to the relatively passive and asocial activity of viewing.

5. By the 1980s, it became feasible for people to make a career by providing strategic or technical expertise to candidates or political groups (Trent and Friedenberg 2000). The timing and pace of the transformation is illustrated by the growth of the professional organization for consultants, the American Association for Political Consultants (AAPC). Its first meeting in 1969 drew only a handful of members. In 1980, that number had risen only modestly to fifty members, but membership then sky-rocketed to over seven hundred by 1990 and continued to climb to eleven hundred members by 2004 (see AAPC's website: www.theaapc.org; see also Trent and Friedenberg 1991). In recent years, the AAPC's annual directory of firms providing consulting and related services has contained over twenty-five hundred entries. The symbolic status of 1980 as a turning point for the rise of consulting is underscored by the fact that the trade journal of the industry, *Campaigns & Elections,* was first published in that year.

6. Other scholars have done an excellent job at documenting the history of campaign advertising in considerable detail. For example, see Diamond and Bates 1992 and Jamieson 1996 for distinct and rich treatments of the subject.

7. In scholarly analysis, the concepts simply seem to fade from attention when researchers turn to systematically assessing patterns and effects of advertising.

8. David S. Broder, "Five Ways to Put Some Sanity Back in Elections," *Washington Post,* January 14, 1990, B1.

9. Matea Gold, "The Recall Campaign; Race Issues Color Views of State Recall Campaign; Some Candidates Make Ethnic Appeals While Shifting Demographics Stoke Resentment," *Los Angeles Times,* September 18, 2003, A24; David S. Broder, "Lifestyle Issues Top Maine Ballot," *Washington Post,* October 17, 2000, A11; "Ad Watch; Proposition 54," *Los Angeles Times,* September 28, 2003, A35. See also Howard Kurtz, "For Health Care Lobbies, a Major Ad Operation," *Washington Post,* April 12, 1993, A1; Jill Zuckman, "Campaign 2000/GOP Primaries; Bush and McCain: A Friendship Sours," *Boston Globe,* March 3, 2000, A17; "Davis vs. Simon; Remarkable GOP Primary Sets Up Fall Runoff," *San Diego Union-Tribune,* March 6, 2002, B12.

10. Rudy Maxa, "GOP's Jingle Man Prospers with TV; Robert Goodman," *Washington Post Magazine,* March 11, 1979, 4; Howard Kurtz, "When Rhetoric and Reality Intersect, Some Voters Find Jarring Dissonance; Position Papers Aren't Easily Translated into Emotional Appeals," *Washington Post,* January 26, 1992, A16.

11. "Grassroots 'Weeds' Need to Be Clipped, Say Angry Activists," *O'Dwyers PR Services Report,* June 1996, 1.

12. Andrew Rosenthal, "For the Idyllic Political Ad, a Fadeout," *New York Times,* June 21, 1987, A22; David S. Broder, "Lifestyle Issues Top Maine Ballot," *Washington Post,* October 17, 2000, A11; Louise Branson, "Dirty Ads to Sway US Voters," *Straits Times* (Singapore), November 6, 2000, 49; Karen Abbott, "Growth-Control Ads Tap into Emotions," *Rocky Mountain News,* October 27, 2000, 32A; Steve Shultze, "Wesley Clark," *Milwaukee Journal Sentinel,* January 22, 2004, 11A; Lloyd Grove, "Campaign Ads: Emotional vs. Cerebral; Bush Ads Feature Nominee and Granddaughter; Dukakis Opts for Flowing Facts and Figures," *Washington Post,* September 27, 1988, A6. See also Debra Gersh, "Regulating Political Campaign Advertising on Television, Cable; Congress Holds Hearings on Three Proposed Bills," *Editor & Publisher Magazine,* May 29, 1993, 26; Sally Jacobs, "Political Ads Borrow Credibility of Public," *Boston Globe,* October 11, 1994, Metro 1; Martha T. Moore, "Spin of 'Meister Murphy' Spearheads Alexander's Campaign," *USA Today,* March 5, 1996, 8A; John M. Broder, "Emotional Appeal Urges Blacks to Vote," *New York Times,* November 2, 2000, A26; "Davis vs. Simon; Remarkable GOP Primary Sets Up Fall Runoff," *San Diego Union-Tribune,* March 6, 2002, B12; Linda Feldmann, "With Ads, Bush Joins Fray," *Christian Science Monitor,* November 25, 2003, A1.

13. "Political Ads," *Boston Globe,* August 13, 1994, Metro 25.

14. Kevin McCauley, "Media, PR Battle Political 'Handlers,'" *O'Dwyer's PR Services Report,* September 1990, 1; Robert Whereatt, "Suspicion, Paranoia, Lies; All Factors in the Election Game," *Star Tribune* (Minneapolis), October 3, 1994, 1B.

15. Lizette Alvarez, "In Campaign Nationwide, Plans for Social Security Become a Focus of Ads," *New York Times,* October 10, 2002, A30; Karen Abbott, "Growth-Control Ads Tap into Emotions," *Rocky Mountain News,* October 27, 2000, 32A; Michael Cooper, "Your Vote or Your Life: Ads Focus on Old Crime Fears," *New York Times,* August 19, 2001, A41; Ed Buxton, "Spin Doctors Can't Cure Ailing Political Ads," *Ad Day,* October 18, 1998, 3. See also Dane Smith, "It's Not All Rosy on the Ad Front; While Candidates Have Accentuated the Positive in Campaign Commercials, Parties and Others Have Sometimes Gone on the Attack," *Star Tribune* (Minneapolis), November 4, 2002, 9A.

16. Ginny Holbert, "A & E Follows Trail of Campaign Ads," *Chicago Sun-Times,* August 21, 1992, 61; Joseph Hanania, "The Power of the Images Paid for by Politicians,"

New York Times, October 15, 2000, B29; Andrew Rosenthal, "Political Marketing; Kemp and Dole Ads Try 'Morning Again' Style," *New York Times,* October 27, 1987, A29; Peter Marks, "In New Hampshire Ads, an Audible Warmth," *New York Times,* December 6, 1999, A1; Allen Rabinowitz, "How Good Cinematography Brings Power to Political Ads," *Campaigns & Elections,* August 2000, 54; Michael Cooper, "Your Vote or Your Life: Ads Focus on Old Crime Fears," *New York Times,* August 19, 2001, A41; Dane Smith, "It's Not All Rosy on the Ad Front; While Candidates Have Accentuated the Positive in Campaign Commercials, Parties and Others Have Sometimes Gone on the Attack," *Star Tribune* (Minneapolis), November 4, 2002, 9A.

17. Rudy Maxa, "GOP's Jingle Man Prospers with TV; Robert Goodman," *Washington Post Magazine,* March 11, 1979, 4. See also Allen Rabinowitz, "How Good Cinematography Brings Power to Political Ads," *Campaigns & Elections,* August 2000, 54; Whit Ayres, "Can Campaign Advertising Be on the Level?" *Campaigns & Elections,* October 2001, 20; Deborah Caulfield Rybak, "TV's Anti-tobacco Ad 'Sunshine' Is Raising Questions, Emotions," *Star Tribune* (Minneapolis), January 19, 2003, 1B; Carey Cramer, "A Step by Step Approach to a Hard-Hitting GOTV Plan," *Campaigns & Elections,* October/November 2002.

18. Richard Schlackman and Jamie Douglas, "Going Negative; Attack Mail: The Silent Killer," *Campaigns & Elections,* July 1995.

19. Marguerite Arnold, "TV Spot Production: A Political Campaign Primer," *Campaigns & Elections,* September 1999.

20. Joe Hallett, "Candidates Turn to TV as Campaign Nears End," *Cleveland Plain Dealer,* October 11, 1998, 1A.

21. Ibid.

22. Joel Achenbach, "Drink No Wine After Its Time?," *Washington Post,* July 24, 1992, D5; paraphrased by journalists.

23. Robert Whereatt, "Suspicion, Paranoia, Lies; All Factors in the Election Game," *Star Tribune* (Minneapolis), October 3, 1994, 1B.

24. These general statements testifying to the prevalence of emotional appeals in campaign politics also hint at many of the related facets of conventional wisdom, especially that these sorts of appeals are seen as powerful and illegitimate.

25. The first belief (in the ubiquity of emotional appeals) stems as much from a general view about the nature of election campaigns as from an observation about TV advertising in particular. However, the second belief (in the efficacy of emotional appeals) seems to have been carried over from views of commercial or product advertising on TV. Creators and scholars of commercial advertising have long regarded emotion as a central determinant of ad effectiveness (Agres, Edell, and Dubitsky 1990; Biswas, Olsen, and Carlet 1992; Holbrook and Batra 1987; Hammond 1987; Hitchon and Thorson 1995; Huang 1998; Olney, Holbrook, and Batra 1991; O'Shaughnessy and O'Shaughnessy 2003; Pelsmacker and Geuens 1997; Scott and Batra 2003). Admakers from Madison Avenue have indeed been involved in the political advertising business, though there is usually considerable friction between commercial admakers and political media consultants (Diamond and Bates 1992). Although some see ad agency types as more emotion-oriented in their approach to political ads than consultants, the real difference appears to be in their relative predilection for appealing to positive and negative emotions, respectively. See Andrew Rosenthal, "For the Idyllic Political Ad, a Fadeout," *New York Times,* June 21, 1987, A22; Martha T. Moore, "Dole Team Looking for Messenger for Its Message," *USA Today,* June 20, 1996, 10A;

"Campaign Ads a Turn-off for Madison Avenue Execs," *USA Today,* November 4, 1996, 5E; Warren Berger, "Schlock the Vote," *Advertising Age's Creativity,* July 1, 2000, 35.

26. John Lancaster, "Attacking Md.'s Gun Law; L.A. Consultant's Ads Play on Fear, Emotion," *Washington Post,* October 16, 1998, A1; Whit Ayres, "Can Campaign Advertising Be on the Level?" *Campaigns & Elections,* October 2001, 20.

27. Jeff Millar, "Paid Political Ads Get to Decide How This Voter Will Cast Ballot," *Houston Chronicle,* October 28, 1999, Houston 2.

28. John Lancaster, "Attacking Md.'s Gun Law; L.A. Consultant's Ads Play on Fear, Emotion," *Washington Post,* October 16, 1998, A1; Bill Moss, "Races Mired in Mud Tactics," *St. Petersburg Times* (Florida), August 19, 1990, A19.

29. Arthur Cole, "A Simple Approach to Campaign-finance Reform," *Boston Globe,* October 15, 1997, A18.

30. Theo Stein, "Trappers Forging On With Appeals Amend. 14 Foes Want Law Sacked," *Denver Post,* April 3, 2001, B4.

31. Michael Barone, "These Dukakis Ads Just Don't Work," *Washington Post,* October 11, 1988, A19.

32. David S. Broder, "Five Ways to Put Some Sanity Back in Elections," *Washington Post,* January 14, 1990, B1. See also Colleen Patrick, "A Call for Action against Negative Political Ads," *Seattle Times,* September 20, 1990, A19.

33. J. Gordon, "Campaign Ads Insult Democracy," *New York Times,* November 8, 1984, A30.

34. Richard Schlackman and Jamie Douglas, "Going Negative; Attack Mail: The Silent Killer," *Campaigns & Elections,* July 1995. See also Michael Cooper, "Your Vote or Your Life: Ads Focus on Old Crime Fears," *New York Times,* August 19, 2001, A41; Matt Bai, "2003: The 3rd Annual Year in Ideas; Turnout Wins Elections," *New York Times,* December 14, 2003, F100.

35. Patricia Lopez Baden, "When You're Watching a Political Ad—Watch It," *Star Tribune* (Minneapolis), September 27, 1998, 1A.

36. Diane Carman, "Ad Design Buys Votes, Emotions," *Denver Post,* December 3, 1998, B1.

37. Craig Gilbert, "UW Expert Puts Positive Spin on Negative Political Ads," *Milwaukee Journal Sentinel,* January 5, 2003, 1A. See also Patricia Lopez Baden, "When You're Watching a Political Ad—Watch it," *Star Tribune* (Minneapolis), September 27, 1998, 1A.

38. Few, I believe, would say the words (or message-oriented images) cannot have emotional impact. Few also would doubt that words matter in defining the meaning of ads, giving them content. In order for the audiovisual packaging of an ad to influence responses to the content of its political message, the ad must have content (regardless of how superficial it may be). One can use the same images and music to sell soft drinks and presidents (Diamond and Bates 1992), but, in order to have the desired effect, any given ad must at least communicate whether it is a soft drink or a president that the viewer should feel good about.

39. Carey Cramer, "A Step by Step Approach to a Hard-Hitting GOTV Plan," *Campaigns & Elections,* October/November 2002.

40. Editorial, "A Truly Bad Idea," *Washington Post,* November 22, 1984, A26; John Lancaster, "Attacking Md.'s Gun Law; L.A. Consultant's Ads Play on Fear, Emotion," *Washington Post,* October 16, 1998, A1; William Pfaff, "Bar Political Ads from the Airwaves," *St. Louis Post-Dispatch,* March 28, 1990, 3C; Rose Elizabeth Bird, "On Flag Burning," *San Francisco Chronicle,* June 16, 1990, A16. See also Ed Bruske, "For Marshall

Coleman; Imaginative Look at Va. Campaign of Images," *Washington Post,* April 12, 1981, B1; J. Gordon, "Campaign Ads Insult Democracy," *New York Times,* November 8, 1984, A30; Jamie Beckett, "SF Voters Tune Out Rash of Political Ads," *San Francisco Chronicle,* November 12, 1990, C3.

41. Andrew Rosenthal, "For the Idyllic Political Ad, a Fadeout," *New York Times,* June 21, 1987, A22.

42. Whit Ayres, "Can Campaign Advertising Be on the Level?" *Campaigns & Elections,* October 2001, 20.

43. Susan Hendrix, "Writing Better Scripts for Television Ads," *Campaigns & Elections,* August 2002.

44. Jamie Beckett, "Why Political Ads Are Misleading; Laws Requiring Companies to Tell the Truth Don't Cover Politics," *San Francisco Chronicle,* October 19, 1992, C1.

45. Martha T. Moore, "Video Clips Have Become the Bookmarks of History," *USA Today,* September 21, 1998, 1A.

46. Mark Dolliver, "Political Campaign Ads Need to Be Energized; Spots Leave Voters Wondering What Candidates Are Selling," *ADWEEK,* October 22, 1990.

47. David S. Broder, "Politicians, Advisors Agonize over Negative Campaigning; Success of Tactics Discourages Policing," *Washington Post,* January 19, 1989, A1; James Bennet, "The Fear of Loathing on the Campaign Trail," *New York Times,* February 27, 2000, F52. See also Joel Brinkley, "Israeli TV Political Ads Lowering the Low Road," *New York Times,* October 9, 1988, A18; Lloyd Grove, "Campaign Ads: Emotional vs. Cerebral; Bush Ads Feature Nominee and Granddaughter; Dukakis Opts for Flowing Facts and Figures," *Washington Post,* September 27, 1988, A6; Patricia Lopez Baden, "When You're Watching a Political Ad—Watch It," *Star Tribune* (Minneapolis), September 27, 1998, 1A.

48. Rudy Maxa, "GOP's Jingle Man Prospers with TV; Robert Goodman," *Washington Post Magazine,* March 11, 1979, 4.

49. Dean Rindy, "Ads Don't Change—Candidates Do," *Campaigns & Elections,* July 1992.

50. Ron Faucheux, "Whether Its Fundraising, Volunteer Recruiting, Image Building, or Message Targeting, Videos Are Powerful Campaign Tools," *Campaigns & Elections,* August 1994.

51. Consultants believe that nontelevised forms of advertising can also have an emotional impact, especially with the help of pictures or sound. Joe Slade White, a consultant specializing in radio ads, says "radio is electronic human emotion," noting that it is best to hire singers to read radio ads because they "understand the nuances of emotion in a lyric and the rhythm and pacing necessary in a good script" ("Wavelength Winners; 12 Rules for Better Political Radio Ads," *Campaigns & Elections,* June/July 1993). Richard Schlackman and Jamie Douglas advise candidates that "main headlines and images will communicate your entire message" in direct mail. "Photographs work most effectively as an emotional symbol. . . . You have to break through with powerful, emotional images" ("Going Negative; Attack Mail: The Silent Killer," *Campaigns & Elections,* July 1995). See also Michael Vallante, "Postcards over the Edge—Overcoming Mailbox Clutter," *Campaigns & Elections,* April 1992; Peter Bynum, "Every Picture Tells a Story; Telling Your Tale through Persuasion Mail," *Campaigns & Elections,* June 1992. Streaming video on the Internet is in its infancy, says Michael Conway, but "as the technology matures, it will offer campaigns a powerful medium to create memorable imagery, emotional appeals, and, of course, spin" ("Streaming Video Hits the Big Time. . . . And the

Small Time," *Campaigns & Elections,* May 2001). See also Rand Ragusa, "The Rise of Banner Ads in Politics," *Campaigns & Elections,* July 2003.

52. Paula Tait, "Eight Myths of Video Cassette Campaigning," *Campaigns & Elections,* December/January 1994.

53. Jennifer G. Hickey, "Ads Treat Voters as Consumers," *Insight on the News,* November 12, 2002, 14. See also Chris Powell, "Media: Politicians Should Sound Off between Programs," *Independent* (London), March 5, 2002, 8.

54. Anthony Lewis, "Negative Campaign Ads Sap the Power of Reason in Our Republic," *Tampa Tribune,* November 8, 1994, Nation 9.

55. Lynda Guydon Taylor, "Staging of Negative Ads Can Confuse Voters," *Pittsburgh Post-Gazette,* May 26, 2002, W3. See also Ken Liebeskind, "Ad Launches Presidential Campaign," *Editor & Publisher Magazine,* October 12, 1996, 38A; Richard L. Berke, "The World: Pitching Peace; Imagine Politics Without TV. Now Think About Ireland," *New York Times,* May 17, 1998, D3; Martha T. Moore, "Video Clips Have Become the Bookmarks of History," *USA Today,* September 21, 1998, 1A.

56. Dean Rindy, "Ads Don't Change—Candidates Do," *Campaigns & Elections,* July 1992.

57. Andrew Rosenthal, "For the Idyllic Political Ad, a Fadeout," *New York Times,* June 21, 1987, A22. See also "A Truly Bad Idea," *Washington Post,* November 22, 1984, A26.

58. Joe Hallett, "Candidates Turn to TV as Campaign Nears End," *Cleveland Plain Dealer,* October 11, 1998, 1A.

59. Lloyd Grove, "Campaign Ads: Emotional vs. Cerebral; Bush Ads Feature Nominee and Granddaughter; Dukakis Opts for Flowing Facts and Figures," *Washington Post,* September 27, 1988, A6; Michael Cooper, "Your Vote or Your Life: Ads Focus on Old Crime Fears," *New York Times,* August 19, 2001, A41; Louise Branson, "Dirty Ads to Sway US Voters," *Straits Times* (Singapore), November 6, 2000, 49. See also Howard Kurtz, "In 1994 Political Ads, Crime Is the Weapon of Choice," *Washington Post,* September 9, 1994, A1.

60. Patricia Lopez Baden, "When You're Watching a Political Ad—Watch It," *Star Tribune* (Minneapolis), September 27, 1998, 1A; Joel Brinkley, "Israeli TV Political Ads Lowering the Low Road," *New York Times,* October 9, 1988, A18; Michael Cooper, "Your Vote or Your Life: Ads Focus on Old Crime Fears," *New York Times,* August 19, 2001, A41. See also Lloyd Grove, "Campaign Ads: Emotional vs. Cerebral; Bush Ads Feature Nominee and Granddaughter; Dukakis Opts for Flowing Facts and Figures," *Washington Post,* September 27, 1988, A6; Joe Hallett, "Candidates Turn to TV as Campaign Nears End," *Cleveland Plain Dealer,* October 11, 1998, 1A.

61. Sally Jacobs, "Political Ads Borrow Credibility of Public," *Boston Globe,* October 11, 1994, Metro 1; Joe Hallett, "Candidates Turn to TV as Campaign Nears End," *Cleveland Plain Dealer,* October 11, 1998, 1A; Howard Kurtz, "In 1994 Political Ads, Crime Is the Weapon of Choice," *Washington Post,* September 9, 1994, A1.

62. John Berry, "Asia Minors," *ADWEEK,* July 17, 1989.

63. For similar views to those cited above, see also Barry 1997; Devlin 1987; Kern 1989; Milburn and Conrad 1996; Nelson and Boynton 1997; Newman 1999; Richardson 2001, 2003; Sabato 1981; and Shea and Burton 2001.

64. Rudy Maxa, "GOP's Jingle Man Prospers with TV; Robert Goodman," *Washington Post Magazine,* March 11, 1979, 4. See also Howard Kurtz, "In 1994 Political Ads, Crime Is the Weapon of Choice," *Washington Post,* September 9, 1994, A1.

65. Mike Hume, "Just Watch the Adverts, and Don't Worry Your Little Heads about

Politics," *Times* (London), March 19, 2001, Features; Peter Bynum, "Every Picture Tells a Story; Telling Your Tale through Persuasion Mail," *Campaigns & Elections,* June 1992; "Political Ads," *Boston Globe,* August 13, 1994, Metro 25; Michael Cooper, "Your Vote or Your Life: Ads Focus on Old Crime Fears," *New York Times,* August 19, 2001, A41; Craig Gilbert, "UW Expert Puts Positive Spin on Negative Political Ads," *Milwaukee Journal Sentinel,* January 5, 2003, 1A.

66. One can see Schwartz's influence on public discourse about emotional appeals in references to the "emotional resonance" of specific issues raised in ads and the way ads try to "play on" existing emotions. "Ad Watch; Proposition 54," *Los Angeles Times,* September 28, 2003, A35; Joe Hallett, "Candidates Turn to TV as Campaign Nears End," *Cleveland Plain Dealer,* October 11, 1998, 1A; John M. Broder, "Emotional Appeal Urges Blacks to Vote," *New York Times,* November 2, 2000, A26; Dane Smith, "It's not all rosy on the ad front; While candidates have accentuated the positive in campaign commercials, parties and others have sometimes gone on the attack," *Star Tribune* (Minneapolis), November 4, 2002, 9A. See also Kern 1989 on the impact of Schwartz on later consultants.

67. Dottie Enrico, "Worried? This Ad's for You," *USA Today,* June 3, 1996, 7B; Tom Hamburger and Eric Black, "National Ads Molded for Local Audience," *Star Tribune* (Minneapolis), September 8, 1996, 1A; Patricia Lopez Baden, "When You're Watching a Political Ad—Watch It," *Star Tribune* (Minneapolis), September 27, 1998, 1A.

68. Rudy Maxa, "GOP's Jingle Man Prospers with TV; Robert Goodman," *Washington Post Magazine,* March 11, 1979, 4; Michael Oreskes, "Vicious Circles; What Poison Politics Has Done to America," *New York Times,* October 29, 1989, D1; Anthony Lewis, "Negative Campaign Ads Sap the Power of Reason in Our Republic," *Tampa Tribune,* November 8, 1994, Nation 9; Joe Hallett, "Candidates Turn to TV as Campaign Nears End," *Cleveland Plain Dealer,* October 11, 1998, 1A; "The Election," *ADWEEK,* January 1, 2001.

69. For similar views about political ads working through emotional transference or association, see Barry 1997, 253–300; Messaris 1997; Milburn and Conrad 1996, 136; Patterson and McClure 1976, 101–2; Scher 1997, 11; Sherr 1999, 47; Strother 1999, 179; and Trent and Friedenberg 2000, 141.

70. J. Gordon, "Campaign Ads Insult Democracy," *New York Times,* November 8, 1984, A30; Rose Elizabeth Bird, "On Flag Burning," *San Francisco Chronicle,* June 16, 1990, A16; Arthur Cole, "A Simple Approach to Campaign-Finance Reform," *Boston Globe,* October 15, 1997, A18.

71. Diane Carman, "Ad Design Buys Votes, Emotions," *Denver Post,* December 3, 1998, B1; Alexandra Marks, "In This Campaign, Image Really Is Everything," *Christian Science Monitor,* April 11, 2000, 2; Patricia Lopez Baden, "When You're Watching a Political Ad—Watch It," *Star Tribune* (Minneapolis), September 27, 1998, 1A. See also Lloyd Grove, "Campaign Ads: Emotional vs. Cerebral; Bush Ads Feature Nominee and Granddaughter; Dukakis Opts for Flowing Facts and Figures," *Washington Post,* September 27, 1988, A6; David S. Broder, "Five Ways to Put Some Sanity Back in Elections," *Washington Post,* January 14, 1990, B1; Anthony Lewis, "Negative Campaign Ads Sap the Power of Reason in Our Republic," *Tampa Tribune,* November 8, 1994, Nation; Meg Carter, "Party Posters Fall Flat with the Slough 'Switchers,'" *Independent* (London), January 21, 1997, 14; Lynda Guydon Taylor, "Staging of Negative Ads Can Confuse Voters," *Pittsburgh Post-Gazette,* May 26, 2002, W-3.

72. Joan Vennochi, "Wellstone's Terrific, Now That He's Gone," *Boston Globe,* October 29, 2002, A17.

73. George Will, "Political Ads Benefit Forbes, Inform Voters," *Chicago Sun-Times,* January 14, 1996, 38.

74. Ken Liebeskind, "Ad Launches Presidential Campaign," *Editor & Publisher Magazine,* October 12, 1996, 38A.

75. Joel Brinkley, "Israeli TV Political Ads Lowering the Low Road," *New York Times,* October 9, 1988, A18. See also Ed Buxton, "Spin Doctors Can't Cure Ailing Political Ads," *Ad Day,* October 18, 1998, 3; Colleen Patrick, "A Call for Action against Negative Political Ads," *Seattle Times,* September 20, 1990, A19.

76. "Attack Ads Are a Blight," *Gazette* (Montreal), November 7, 2000, B2.

77. James Bennet, "The Fear of Loathing on the Campaign Trail," *New York Times,* February 27, 2000, F52.

78. Richardson (2003) seems to take a slightly different tack two years later: "Political advertising is successful when it communicates a combination of affect (emotion) and cognition (thought) that can trigger action (such as voting). In the final analysis, we may be able to better understand emotional political appeals, but it is unlikely they will ever be eliminated—nor should they" (132).

79. Dave Eisenstadt, "Wunderkind or One-Hit Wonder?; After Hitting It Big with Paul Wellstone, Ad Man Bill Hillsman Contemplates His Future," *Campaigns & Elections,* May 1991. See also Peter Bynum, "Every Picture Tells a Story; Telling Your Tale through Persuasion Mail," *Campaigns & Elections,* June 1992.

80. William Pfaff, "Bar Political Ads from the Airwaves," *St. Louis Post-Dispatch,* March 28, 1990, 3C.

81. J. Gordon, "Campaign Ads Insult Democracy," *New York Times,* November 8, 1984, A30.

82. Lizette Alvarez, "In Campaign Nationwide, Plans for Social Security Become a Focus of Ads," *New York Times,* October 10, 1902, A30.

83. Nonetheless, the percentage of consultants who say the use of scare tactics is acceptable is significantly greater than use of several other tactics, including making untrue statements (less than 1 percent), taking statements out of context (13 percent), using push polls (7 percent), and suppressing voter turnout (22 percent). On the other hand, nearly 73 percent of consultants say focusing on character rather than issues is acceptable. See Thurber and Nelson 2000 for more details on this survey.

84. Kevin McCauley, "Media, PR Battle Political 'Handlers,'" *O'Dwyer's PR Services Report,* September, 1990, 1.

85. Ed Buxton, "Spin Doctors Can't Cure Ailing Political Ads," *Ad Day,* October 18, 1998, 3.

86. Kevin McCauley, "Media, PR Battle Political 'Handlers,'" *O'Dwyer's PR Services Report,* September, 1990, 1.

87. Kamber, however, distances himself from ad agency critics of political advertising, because he sees product advertising as far worse: "Some political ads may be sleazy, but nothing compares to the pernicious idiocy that pours out of Madison Avenue. From dancing cats to belching frogs, to cartoon camels teaching children how to smoke, Madison Avenue has created a culture of amoral salesmanship and mindless dreck that, by comparison, makes political ads seem like high-minded discourse" (171).

88. Diane Carman, "Ad Design Buys Votes, Emotions," *Denver Post,* December 3, 1998, B1. It is quite common for people to voice these claims in the process of denying emotional appeals have any effect on themselves, people like themselves, or voters in

general. However, those expressing such opinions always credit something like intelligence, sophistication, or the wisdom of experience. We should not confuse the belief that such factors insulate a person from the effect of emotional appeals with beliefs about who possesses the requisite insulation.

89. J. Gordon, "Campaign Ads Insult Democracy," *New York Times,* November 8, 1984, A30.

90. Michael Oreskes, "Vicious Circles; What Poison Politics Has Done to America," *New York Times,* October 29, 1989, D1.

91. Meg Carter, "Party Posters Fall Flat with the Slough 'Switchers,'" *Independent* (London), January 21, 1997, 14.

92. Mike Hume, "Just Watch the Adverts, and Don't Worry Your Little Heads about Politics," *Times* (London), March 19, 2001, Features.

93. Peggy Lowe, "Feeley Closes Gap against Beauprez; Congressional Race 'Fluid'; Candidates Attack Negative Ads," *Rocky Mountain News,* October 30, 2002, 20A.

94. "Campaign Ads a Turn-off for Madison Avenue Execs," *USA Today,* November 4, 1996, 5E.

95. Diane Ratvitch, "Decline and Fall of Teaching History," *New York Times,* November 17, 1985, F50.

96. Nicholas K. Geranios, "Students Vote to Keep Nuke Cloud as School Symbol," *Associated Press,* February 24, 1988.

97. Gary Duncan and Severin Carrell, "Blair Sticks with a Carefully Ambiguous Line," *Scotsman,* June 1, 1989, 6; "Public Pulse," *Omaha World Herald,* November 9, 1994, 40.

98. R. Lyle Fendrick, "School Funds Mishandled; Taxpayers Pick Up the Tab," *Columbus Dispatch* (Ohio), April 20, 1998, 8A.

99. Deborah Anna Vondrak, "Legislating by Litigating: America's Trial Lawyers Use Class-actions to Side-step Congress, Thwart Voter's Will," *Knight Ridder Tribune News Service,* May 20, 1999.

100. Richard Price and Julie Carver, "In Search of 'the Perfect Juror,'" *USA Today,* September 16, 1994, 5A.

101. Sniderman and colleagues do not, however, fully subscribe to the conventional wisdom. They contend that what separates more and less sophisticated citizens is the manner and extent to which they use emotion. Other partially dissenting views can be found among advertising scholars and consultants. Jamieson (1992) claims that "televised political ads can short circuit the normal defenses that more educated, more highly involved viewers ordinarily marshal against suspect claims" (50). Kamber (1997) argues that "the problem with *kitsch* [such as in the *Morning in America* ads] is that it works, not just on those unnamed others who are always susceptible to emotional manipulation, but also on just about anyone who is not dead from the neck down. As much as these ads may offend your taste, your political beliefs, even your political dignity, they are affecting. And that is the worst thing about them" (104).

102. For more thorough reviews of research on the effects of communication, see Kinder 1998, 2003.

103. In 2001, Kaid mentions that "the ability of ads to elicit an emotional response in voters may also account for some of the effectiveness of spot ads" and cites three studies. Two of the studies correspond to the first two described in the text. The third is Kern's (1989) book, which discusses the emotional impact of ads based on the beliefs of consultants and the self-evident aims of the ads. However, for all the Kern draws attention

to the importance of emotion, she tests neither the ability of ads to elicit emotions nor the impact of emotional appeals on viewers.

104. Several other studies confirm that political ads can engender emotional reactions but do not link the emotion-eliciting qualities of ads to changes in knowledge, attitudes, or behavior. Richardson (2003), in a self-described exploratory study, finds appropriate emotional self-reports appear to be cued by changes in ad "genre" or background music and images, yet finds almost no significant differences in his sample of seventy students. Marcus, Neuman, and MacKuen (2000, 66–68) briefly refer to a study they conducted on 290 students, in which subjects exposed to negative presidential ads were more likely to report anxiety than those exposed to neutral ads or excerpts from the debates. The debate clips, intended to mimic positive ad appeals, apparently did not increase levels of enthusiasm, with the notable exception of Democrats responding to excerpts of Clinton (68 n. 4). Kaid and colleagues have measured emotional reactions to ads and found that they correlate in expected ways with candidate evaluations (Kaid 1997, 2001; Kaid and Holtz-Bacha 1995; Kaid and Tedesco 1999). The nonexperimental nature of their studies, in which all respondents see the same set of real ads with known candidates, makes it difficult to disentangle emotional reactions from attitudes toward the candidates: Did they like a candidate because the ad made them feel happy, or did they feel happy because the ad showed a candidate they liked? A similar problem plagues a study by Masterson and Biggers (1986): using *separate* samples, they measured preelection attitudes toward congressional candidates, postelection attitudes in an exit poll, and emotional responses to the candidates' ads (assessed weeks after the election by students in a different electoral district), in order to see if attitudes changed over the campaign in a direction consistent with the emotional impact of the ads. One of the many problems of this design is that it infers the student group's emotional reaction to the ads (taken as a whole) mirrors the likely reaction of constituents during the election. That aside, the results of the study, taken at face value, are largely inconclusive.

105. The difficulty level of these studies as tests of memory effects is mixed. On the one hand, there is a lack of realism. Subjects' participation did not remotely resemble the experience of normal TV viewing. We would expect subjects to be more attentive under these conditions. On the other hand, the nature of the memory tasks was quite demanding. If subjects were paying close attention, they encountered a large number of discrete "bursts" of information over the course of a twenty-five- or forty-minute session and then answered a range of recall and recognition questions.

106. Favorability of response is primarily inferred from the third-person effect (i.e., perceiving oneself as less convinced by an unworthy message than others and more convinced by a worthy message) and ratings of social desirability. Under the circumstances, that is, with unfamiliar candidates outside an election and during self-conscious viewing, it seems likely that attitudinal or voting measures capture little more than the social desirability assessments themselves, especially absent party labels (all measures are correlated at a 0.7 or 0.8 level).

107. A third study examines emotional responses to print advertising by candidates, but it is difficult to know what we should conclude from this study. Students read two print ads, either positive or negative, from fictitious rivals (Chang 2001). Attack ads elicit negative feelings and advocacy ads elicit positive feelings. Emotional reactions, in turn, predict negative or positive evaluations of the candidates, respectively. However, it is unclear from the presentation of results whether this relationship stems from ad valence, as the author

claims, or the content of candidate messages. This confusion emerges from the design of the study and presentation of results. Each subject saw two ads with differing issue content but identical valence. If we adopt the author's interpretation, we must believe that subjects, when asked to choose between candidates about whom they previously knew nothing, based their decision mainly on the tone of the ad rather than on the arguments therein and that they evaluated both candidates positively or both negatively. It seems more likely that emotional reactions, though influenced by valence, were also products of agreement with the arguments. Our ability to choose between interpretations is further hampered by the presentation of results on the author's claim that emotional reactions *mediate* the impact of valence on candidate evaluations. The results indeed show that valence affects emotions, emotions affect evaluations, and valence is not a significant predictor of evaluations when controlling for emotions. But the author never shows that valence is a significant determinant of evaluations on its own, when not controlling for emotions. Given the goals of political advertising, it seems odd that the author never differentiates between evaluations of the sponsor and the opponent; in fact, it is impossible to tell whether reactions to the ad are influencing both candidates similarly or only reactions to one candidate.

108. Huddy and Gunnthorsdottir (2000) also find evidence that the emotional appeal works primarily on those who are highly involved in the issue. This finding is discussed further in the next chapter.

109. On the related role of emotional expressions by TV newscasters, see Friedman, DiMatteo, and Mertz 1980 and Mullen et al. 1986.

110. One publication in this line of work sounds like it is more relevant to the present study than its content bears out (Englis 1984). Its title, "The Role of Affect in Political Advertising," is deceiving. This study actually concerns images of leaders excerpted from news programs and does not investigate ads.

111. For similar analysis comparing the emotional framing of policy issues in a survey, see Nabi 2003.

Chapter Three

1. Although underconceptualized, these views on how emotion enters political behavior are not necessarily wrong. Identities like party identification are affective, and evaluations or preferences are based on emotional responses. Thinking theoretically about emotion is not an alternative approach in competition with these others, but a missing piece that can deepen our understanding and may even help us specify the conditional relevance of existing models. In particular, emotion sheds light on dynamic elements of political behavior, such as motivation and persuasion, that remain poorly understood. The study of emotion does not just take us "deeper inside the heads" of individuals and away from the world of politics. Properly conceived, it clarifies the relationship between the activities of political actors, the opinions and choices of ordinary citizens, and the political context. This warm-blooded conception of citizens brings the study of political communication and political behavior closer together.

2. Scott McLemee, "Getting Emotional: The Study of Feelings, Once the Province of Psychology, Is Now Spreading to History, Literature, and Other Fields," *Chronicle of Higher Education,* February 21, 2003, A14.

3. In the sections that follow, I offer a brief overview of the current state of knowledge on emotion from research in psychology and neuroscience. I try to render the ideas in-

telligible and interesting to students of politics without doing gross injustice to the careful work of researchers in other fields. I cite specific material where appropriate but draw on a number of sources for the general discussion, including Damasio 1994, 2000; Ekman and Davidson 1994; Lazarus 1991; LeDoux 1996; Marcus 2000, 2003; Panksepp 1998; Parrott 2001; Plutchik 2003; Scherer 2000; and Zajonc 1998.

4. The amygdala is a region in the brain associated with emotional reactions in general and fear in particular (Damasio 1994; LeDoux 1996).

5. Research on mood tends to emphasize valence rather than discrete emotions, even though mood is often measured with reference to specific emotional terms (Martin and Clore 2001). Wendy Rahn has applied one popular approach, the affect-as-information model (Gohm and Clore 2002; Schwarz 2001; Schwarz and Clore 1983), to politics with the concept of *public mood* (Rahn 2000; Rahn, Kroeger, and Kite 1996).

6. Kinder 1994 draws on the appraisal approach to demonstrate not only that emotions shape political attitudes, but also that specific emotions arise in different circumstances and exert different effects that are predictable from the nature of the emotion in question.

7. The practice of referring to nonemotional appeals as "rational" is particularly problematic, because it conflates emotion with a lack of rationality. The conventional view of emotion in opposition to rationality or reason has been seriously challenged and seems untenable in light of contemporary scientific understandings (Damasio 1994; Kinder 1994; Lazarus 1991; Marcus 2002).

8. Cognition is sometimes defined in terms of processes such as reasoning, memory, problemsolving, comprehension, and perception. Sensory perception and phenomena (i.e., smells, sounds, etc.) form a major area of study in cognitive neuroscience, but it may be useful to think of sensory processes as distinct from other cognitive activities. Sensory data serve as raw inputs into both affective and higher order cognitive processes.

9. As LeDoux (1996, 19) asserts, "emotions are things that happen to us rather than things we will to occur." This point is underlined not only by the fact that we often feel "overcome" with emotion, but also by the difficulty we have in faking them. The best we can do is employ thought and memory to imagine a situation that holds emotional meaning for us, an "as if" process that can yield an emotional response, albeit usually one far weaker than direct experience yields (Damasio 1994; Millar and Millar 1996). However, none of this implies that we cannot bring emotions and their influence over us under control. One evolutionary benefit of higher cognitive functions is the ability to engage in emotional regulation through reappraisal of our circumstances and greater control over our responses (Damasio 1994; LeDoux 1989, 1994a; also see Barrett and Salovey 2002 for recent scholarly work on the concept of *emotional intelligence*). Even so, attempting to exercise "too much" control over our emotions can also have pathological consequences (Izard 1991).

10. For the reader's benefit, I adopt the ordinary language distinction between mind and body. It is precisely this Cartesian dualism, however, that is called into question by the advances of neuroscience. Mental reactions (changes in attention, perception, etc.) are also *physiological* changes (Damasio 1994; Gazzaniga 1992; Panksepp 1998).

11. Fully adaptive decisionmaking in humans depends on emotion and reasoning working in tandem. The evolutionary advantages of human reasoning, with its capacity for abstract and systematic analysis, are built on top of the older evolutionary mechanisms of emotion, which provide rapid feedback about proximity to goals and danger (Damasio 2000).

12. This description bears more than a passing resemblance to the traditional approach-avoidance view. Gray (1994) in fact refers to the two emotional systems as the "behavioral inhibition" and "behavioral approach" systems, respectively. The key difference is that the neuropsychological view conceives of these as separate systems serving distinct functions: fear and enthusiasm are not opposites. This view is closer to structural models of affect that posit most or all emotions as falling somewhere in the space defined by two valence dimensions—one positive, one negative (Cacioppo and Bernston 1994; Cacioppo, Gardner, and Bernston 1997; Watson, Clark, and Tellegen 1988). Nonetheless, neuropsychological theories tend to fall between such structural models and theories of discrete emotions. Many concur on the presence of *at least* two systems and believe that there are systems other than those producing fear and enthusiasm (Damasio 1994; LeDoux 1996; Panksepp 1998). A focus on fear and enthusiasm does not imply that other emotions are insignificant or that all emotions can be explained by the same two systems. Fear is the emotional state best understood by researchers (LeDoux 1995), and psychologists have invested considerably less overall in the study of positive emotions (Fredrickson and Branigan 2001).

13. There is a wide range of terms for the emotions and feelings that stem from the enthusiasm system. Gray (1994) refers to "hope" and "elation." Panksepp (1998) mentions "eagerness" and "hope" among others. Egloff and colleagues (2003) prefer "joy," "enthusiasm," and "excitement." Lazarus (1991) lists over two dozen synonyms. I suspect some of this variety in nomenclature emerges from the subtle distinctions the human mind makes as it interprets these "happy" emotional states, while some of it simply arises from the imprecision of everyday language in describing phenomena that are often hard to describe. The critical thing to recognize is that the diversity of terms masks broad agreement on the functions of the underlying system. It is about putting the right name on processes that have been found to exist, not on finding the processes to explain that for which we already have a name (see LeDoux 1995).

The concept of *interest* is a different story. There is considerable debate over whether interest is distinct from the emotions of the enthusiasm system and whether interest is properly considered an emotion at all. The problem is that we associate the feeling of being "interested" with excitement, enjoyment, and eagerness, on the one hand, and with alertness, curiosity, and attentiveness, on the other. Egloff and colleagues (2003) show that excitement and enthusiasm are quite distinct empirically from alertness and attentiveness. My discussion of the enthusiasm system incorporates aspects of what some scholars conceive as the interest constellation of emotions (cf. Frederickson and Branigan 2001; Izard 1991; Panksepp 1998), but it is important to distinguish it from both arousal and attention, which can be affected by the enthusiasm system as well as other emotional systems (Bradley and Lang 2000).

14. See the citations for positive mood research above. Note, however, that this research program shows increased systematic processing not only during anxious states but also during sad or depressed mood states, which correspond more closely to low activation of the enthusiasm system. In general, much of the literature on "mood and information processing" or "mood and social judgment" focuses on positive and negative affect without differentiating among positive or negative emotions. This is true even when they measure "mood" with a battery of discrete emotion terms.

15. Political ads and campaign politics rarely elicit fear on a level sufficient to fully activate the fight-or-flight system. Although differing levels of fear involve similar shifts in

attention, information processing, and readiness for action, responses to threats that exceed some threshold of severity may be qualitatively different in one sense: whereas modest anxiety or fear preserves flexibility in choosing a course of action (see Scherer 1994a for the notion of the evolutionary advantages that our emotional systems provide in decoupling stimulus and response), intense terror or dread in the face of imminent harm can directly unleash "primitive" reactions such as cowering, fleeing, or lashing out. We know less about the threshold that triggers such responses in humans, in part due to practical and ethical limitations on research (Eagly and Chaiken 1993). Gray (1994) classifies fight-or-flight responses as belonging to a separate system from other fear responses, while Panksepp (1998) and LeDoux (1996) treat different types of fear responses as part of a single system. Lazarus (1991, 235) argues that there are advantages to treating "fright" and anxiety as different forms of the "same basic machinery" and to treating them as "different emotions altogether." Regardless of the approach one thinks best, the study of campaign advertising is clearly more concerned with responses to modest levels of fear.

16. Despite its apparent appropriateness, the literature on fear appeals does not serve as an adequate model for the study of emotional appeals in campaign advertising. First, the research has focused nearly exclusively on fear appeals and therefore has nothing to say regarding positive emotional appeals. Second, while the accumulated empirical results are indeed informative, researchers in the field have yet to develop a theory that is supported by the evidence (Eagly and Chaiken 1993; Witte and Allen 2000). Third, campaign ads are a distinct form of communication from the public health and safety campaigns that have been the focus of the field. Whereas the latter campaigns often ask people to break bad habits or undertake new (and perhaps burdensome) activities to prevent some danger, campaign ads ask people to choose between two or more alternatives ways (as represented by each candidate) of dealing with whatever threatens society. For campaign ads, the critical task is either persuading people of the "correct" alternative when they are already prepared to take action (i.e., they regularly vote, the question is for whom) or motivating people who agree that the candidate is best to vote despite the presence of a collective action problem (i.e., their vote is unlikely to make a difference and so they'll be stuck with the same outcome regardless of whether they vote).

17. For different perspectives on this growing literature, see the reviews in Glaser and Salovey 1998; Isbell and Ottati 2002; and Marcus 2000.

18. This analysis by Marcus, Neuman, and MacKuen (2000, 104–8) builds on an investigation by Kinder and D'Ambrosio (2000).

19. Nadeau, Niemi, and Amato (1995) also contend that the impact of anxiety is indirect, mediated by increasing the perceived importance of the issue. Although this is a plausible contention, it appears to be merely asserted, not demonstrated in the study. As in other studies using survey data of this sort, we can have only limited confidence in the causal claims. It is possible that perceived importance and acquisition of knowledge about the issue in fact fuel anxiety, rather than vice versa.

20. Damasio (1994) also describes the way in which these affective associations underlie the preferences that guide normal human decisionmaking, enabling our brains to sort through options quickly either to make an instinctive choice or focus on a small number of options that will receive closer scrutiny. He refers to the affective associations as "somatic markers" because they are formed "by connecting specific classes of stimuli with specific classes of somatic [i.e., bodily] state" (177). Damasio describes the essence

of these markers as follows: "When a negative somatic marker is juxtaposed to a particular future outcome the combination functions as an alarm bell. When a positive somatic marker is juxtaposed instead, it becomes a beacon of incentive" (174). This emotional sorting mechanism provides us with instinctual impulses to choose one way and not others, without consciously mulling over every option, its benefits or drawbacks, the opportunity costs, and so on. Absent emotions, the simplest decisions in social life would become bogged down in a quagmire of cognitive rational calculations. Instead, the emotional processing systems sift through new information and potential choices, relying on a constantly updating databank of prior associations to pursue the good, forgo the bad, and beware the threatening. Our emotional responsiveness to cues allows us to reason efficiently but also imperfectly, as we react sometimes too easily and uncritically to the promise of pain or pleasure.

21. Until such a repertoire of cues is known, exploratory behavior is necessary to build up the associations (e.g., children learn by touching a hot stovetop or being scolded when they near it). The unknown or novel is thus an ambiguous class of phenomena that stimulates curiosity, which is desirable because it facilitates learning and sheds light on potential avenues to success, but also fear, because it represents potential danger with uncertain consequences.

22. Panksepp (1998) observes that it is a characteristic property of emotions that it is easy, at least in theory, to identify their "onset" (start) but difficult to pinpoint their "offset" (end). There is also evidence that a critical adaptive function of some positive emotions, such as amusement, may be to accelerate "recovery" from negative emotions such as fear, anger, or sadness (Fredrickson and Branigan 2001).

23. There is in fact only limited evidence that subliminal advertising directly influences choices (Sears and Kosterman 1994), although popular misconceptions abound, as evidenced by the ruckus over the *RATS* ad in the 2000 presidential election (see Sid Perkins, "Dirty RATS: Campaign Ad May Have Swayed Voters Subliminally," *Science News* 163 [February 22, 2003], 116–17). On the other hand, there is ample evidence that subliminal visual cues can be used to prime affective responses and thereby influence the mode of decisionmaking (Krosnick et al. 1992; Way and Masters 1996a, 1996b; Zajonc 1998, 2000). If the advertisers actually intended to use subliminal affective cues in the *RATS* ad, then they may have been better served by using pictures of rats than just the word (though this option provides even less room for plausible deniability).

24. Recent research on the impact of racial cues in political communication shows that implicit racial appeals are more effective than explicit racial appeals, because the former prime racial stereotypes or prejudice without activating thoughts about contemporary norms of racial equality (Mendelberg 2001; Valentino, Hutchings, and White 2002). Thus, although racial priming and emotional appeals do not necessarily implicate the same psychological processes, they similarly suggest that often "less is more" in political communication.

25. If we stretched a bit, we might detect a couple of additional hypotheses among the beliefs of practitioners and observers. The first is not so much a hypothesis about how appeals work as about which type of appeals are most effective. Many people believe that negative emotional appeals are more effective than positive appeals. The *primacy of fear* hypothesis suggests that fear appeals will persuade and motivate voters more successfully than enthusiasm appeals. Consistent with this idea, scholars have argued there is an asymmetry in the way individuals incorporate positive and negative information when form-

ing attitudes (Cacioppo and Bernston 1994; Holbrook et al. 2001). They have noted a tendency for people to begin with a positive impression of new objects ("positivity offset") but then place greater weight on negative information in updating their opinions ("negativity bias"). Cacioppo and colleagues (1997) propose that positive ad campaigns leave citizens feeling good about their choices because "both candidates are associated with approach motivational forces," but negative ads "may have a stronger effect on electoral evaluations and behavior than positive campaign ads" (21). The primacy of fear hypothesis may also be supported by the existence of a long-standing research agenda highlighting the effectiveness of fear appeals in health communications (Witte and Allen 2000).

Another hypothesis implies something about the way emotional appeals work. A few people have suggested that emotional appeals work by resonating with the existing feelings of the viewer. The *resonance* hypothesis predicts that fear appeals will be effective with viewers who already harbor related fears and enthusiasm appeals will be effective with those who already share that enthusiasm at some level. Roseman, Abelson, and Ewing (1986) indeed find some evidence that people respond more favorably to emotional language that matches their feelings, though they also discovered that fearful individuals responded more favorably to hopeful appeals than fear appeals.

26. The *affect transfer* hypothesis is less ideally equipped to explain the impact of comparison spots that discuss both candidates, while targeting either positive or negative emotions throughout.

27. To the extent it has any merit, the vividness proposition may not be separable from emotion either, as scholars have implicated emotions in the definition of vividness (Nisbett and Ross 1980). It also is likely that advances in understanding emotion will improve our ability to explain what people find entertaining.

28. The hypotheses presented here are largely consistent with the theory proposed by Marcus and colleagues. However, one need not subscribe to their elegant model of affective intelligence as emerging from the interaction of these two emotional systems (and these two alone); instead, one could believe that there are additional emotional systems and/or that the systems come together in somewhat different ways and yet still make the predictions in this chapter about the effects of enthusiasm and fear appeals.

29. Because response efficacy is often not at issue in election campaigns, I will not test that hypothesis here. However, due to the recent rise in issue advocacy spots that are prohibited from making explicit recommendations about voting (West 2001), there may be greater call in the future to test the effectiveness of political fear ads that advocate voting (for or against some candidate) versus those that advocate calling a politician to express disapproval (as some issue ads do) or that advocate nothing at all.

30. The impact of attention and information search on knowledge or memory, especially as evidenced through recall tests, seems likely to depend on whether a person is engaged in the type of activity that promotes on-line or memory-based cognition (Hastie and Park 1986).

31. Nonetheless, we could form expectations about learning (knowledge acquisition) simply as a result of the preceding hypotheses. On the one hand, paying attention and a desire to acquire specific pieces of information seem likely to promote learning. On the other hand, people also can learn more about politics as a natural by-product of being interested and involved in it (Fiorina 1990). These observations lead us to the following corollary regarding learning: *enthusiasm and fear appeals should increase learning about the candidates and issues discussed in the ad (indirectly, as a result of heightened involvement or attention).*

Chapter Four

1. In the short term, incidental events, such as a rainy day or catching a ride home with a friend who plans to vote, can affect levels of turnout due to the low costs of voting and the nature of social organization (Aldrich 1993).

2. Subjects seem less likely to try to please the researcher (i.e., succumb to demand effects) when facing real choices. If choices are fictitious, abstract, or remote, then subjects may be even more conscientious about the fact that they are participating in a "laboratory" study and unconstrained by any true feelings about the options in front of them.

3. Nonetheless, it is possible for simulated or imagined circumstances to generate emotional reactions. We need only think about our responses to movies. But it would require a fairly "absorbing" lab exercise to encourage similar reactions to fictitious candidates and ads.

4. Resources permitted a focus on only one of the two party primaries. I selected the Democratic race because of the heavily skewed Massachusetts party system, in which registered Democrats outnumber Republicans three to one. The challenge was not to find Republican *candidates*. A popular Bill Weld (1991–97) had familiarized voters with choosing a moderate Republican governor, even though he never expended his personal political capital to build a state party organization for the GOP. When Weld stepped down in 1997, he left a moderate and less charismatic successor, Paul Cellucci, to carry the incumbency into the election year. Cellucci in fact won both a nasty primary battle with the conservative state treasurer, Joseph Malone, and the general election. Thus, the GOP primary itself would have made a satisfactory backdrop to the study. However, tremendous resources would have been required to recruit a sufficient number of Republican subjects. Even with a more lively Republican contest to attract many independents, the Democratic primary had a three to one imbalance in voter turnout for the two races.

5. The *Boston Globe,* reviewing the primary results on September 27, summed up the campaign as a "resounding ho-hum." The Republican gubernatorial primary was bitter, but a comfortable win for the incumbent. In the Democratic primary, 5 percent of primary voters did not cast a vote in the gubernatorial race—the highest office on the ballot!

6. We might ask how the "lab" setting affects the potential for persuasion. If the controlled environment encourages subjects to be unusually attentive to what they are watching, persuasion could be more likely than in natural settings. But artificially high attentiveness is discouraged by disguising the true purpose of the study and leaving subjects to watch unmonitored and in groups. In addition, the campaign ad represents only a small fraction of the viewing period and, thus, of the information encountered by subjects. Given the short period of time between soliciting preferences in the pretest and posttest (forty minutes, on average), subjects are likely to try to provide the same answer in order to appear consistent and not easily influenced. This tendency constrains the appearance of attitude change and makes tests of persuasion more conservative. The virtue of an experiment is that any such biases apply to all subjects but do not make it easier or harder to observe the expected differences between experimental groups.

7. The total number of participants was actually 307. We discovered, either in the course of participation or on subsequent review, that twenty-one individuals were not valid cases. Some did not meet the eligibility requirements despite our screening efforts. Others failed to complete the questionnaires because they lacked the mental concentration or command of English necessary to read questions and mark answers.

8. The median income for the sample is $33,500, but $38,500 for all residents. Whereas

56 percent of participants have a college degree, only 35 percent of Massachusetts adults possess one. As a result, the sample reflects the primary electorate, which tends to include a disproportionate number of educated and civically engaged citizens, better than the state residents as a whole. Most basic population figures are based on the 1990 U.S. Census and subsequent population surveys (see www.census.gov) or the Massachusetts State Data Center (www.umass.edu/miser). Subjects reported their household income in $20,000 intervals; the median falls in the $20,000–39,999 range and, using interpolation, would occupy a position two-thirds the way through that category's respondents.

9. Party enrollment rates are drawn from voter registration totals in August 1998, as reported by the secretary of state (www.magnet.state.ma.us/sec/elec) at the time. We made no effort to screen out Republicans, despite the study's focus on the Democratic primary contest. Screening for partisanship would have been an unnecessary drain on resources. The unusual partisan landscape of Massachusetts ensured that locating a sufficient share of Democrats and Independents as the main audience would not be a problem. In addition, the responses of Republicans are relevant because they may be concerned with the outcome of the opposing party primary and even wish to engage in cross-over voting. To the extent ads are irrelevant to Republicans, their presence injects a conservative bias in the study but, at 9 percent of the sample, not an overwhelming one.

10. The precise description read: "Television has become a very important source of news about our society, politics, and the world around us. The goal of our study is to learn more about what people take away from watching the news. We are especially interested in processes like "selective perception"—whether personal circumstances affect the news stories and facts a person finds most interesting and relevant."

11. This was done to minimize the possibility of sensitizing subjects to the advertising stimuli. The pretest inquired about intentions to vote in the upcoming election and asked subjects to name the candidate for whom they planned to vote in each of several races.

12. We generated a random ordering of video numbers in advance of the study, using a random number generator on a computer. The first subject to walk through the door saw the first video on the list, the second subject saw the second, and so on. Assignment continued each day from the same list, picking up where the previous day's assignments had ended.

13. The broadcast had originally aired in June of that year. Several segments such as weather and sports were deleted in order to keep the focus on "hard news." I deleted one news segment—on the Louise Woodward ("nanny") trial—that would have unduly dated the broadcast. With these segments, the total viewing time was roughly twelve minutes.

14. After beginning with $10 compensation across the board, I offered $15 or $20 in later weeks to increase our rate of recruitment.

15. Variation stemmed mainly from how long a subject spent completing the questionnaires. The record, I believe, was set by an especially thoughtful senior citizen who gave us two and a half hours of her time.

16. Viewing rooms often had windows in the doors or elsewhere that allowed my assistants or me to occasionally check on participants.

17. This study tests the impact of emotional appeals by observing the effect of manipulating the emotionality of only the nonverbal features of campaign ads, while holding the script constant. The strongest objection to this inference is that it assumes viewers only respond emotionally to the images and music but not at all to the message of the ad. Emotional responses to the message itself are indeed possible. Negative information

may elicit anxiety, and positive information may generate enthusiasm. However, it is difficult, if not impossible, to disentangle cognitive and emotional responses to the message of the ad. What risks do we run in relying on this design? If the script also contributes to the emotional appeal, then the design understates the total impact of emotion. The overall goal is to see how, if at all, cueing fear or enthusiasm alters the way political messages are processed. We can achieve this most easily by observing how individuals respond to ads that contain identical messages with or without a distinct set of emotional cues.

18. For example, it is difficult to imagine an ad that claims "things are going well" against a backdrop of threatening images and disconcerting music. A researcher might include such an ad in an experiment for esoteric reasons such as providing a complete test of all "logical" possibilities. However, even if we did so, we might have a hard time making inferences from the results. If the ads failed to influence subjects, should we infer this is a result of mixed signals from the ad's narration and imagery or a result of the ad striking subjects as "strange," as it no doubt would?

19. I produced the video stimuli for the experiments with the valuable assistance of a colleague, Victor Mendiola. We used digital video editing equipment to create the campaign ads, edit the news program, and insert the campaign ads into the commercial break of the news program. All of the digital editing and production work took place at the Technology Showcase at Harvard University using a Macintosh multimedia workstation and Adobe Premiere 5.0 software. In creating the ads, we laid the video track, music track, and narration tracks separately. Thanks to the digital editing software, we could seamlessly insert the ads into the commercial break of the news program. I recorded the news program and many of the images used in the ads from live television broadcast using S-VHS recording equipment to maintain image integrity. I received additional images for the ads from David Willis, who at the time managed Shanto Iyengar's media laboratory at UCLA. We compiled the news program and images for the ads using digital capture from the S-VHS tapes. We captured music for the soundtrack from compact disc recordings.

20. The final product of news and advertisements looked professional and realistic. The campaign ads were not the best "Madison Avenue" has to offer presidential candidates, but the same may be said of the ads used by the candidates in the actual Massachusetts races in 1998. Use of professional narration and digital editing ensured a respectable production value in keeping with local and state political contests. To underscore this point, when asked for reactions to the ad at the end of participation, only two participants (i.e., less than 1 percent) claimed to believe the campaign ad was not genuine. A female Harvard administrator with a postgraduate education said she assumed the ad she saw was "pretend." A male attorney for a legislative committee in the Massachusetts Statehouse remarked that the ad he saw was "not a real ad." He was familiar enough with the campaign to know which ads each candidate had actually run. Suspicion seemed to arise primarily from the fact we were conducting a study, not from anything unusual about the video.

21. In order to be believable, the ads must not only include a compelling composite of words, images, and music, but also a convincingly delivered script. I was fortunate to have the help of a narrator whose voice resonates with considerable professional experience on television. Marvin Kalb served three decades as a chief diplomatic correspondent for CBS News and NBC News. He also moderated the news analysis program *Meet the Press*. At the time of this study, Kalb was serving as director of the Joan Shorenstein Center on the Press, Politics, and Public Policy, and Edward R. Murrow Professor of Press, Politics, and Public Policy at the Kennedy School of Government at Harvard University.

22. Figures 4.1 and 4.2 show scripts that emphasize crime. A positive script emphasizing education reads: "There's good news in your neighborhood. The future looks bright for a generation of young people. Schools are less crowded and new programs make it easier to keep drugs and guns out. Test scores are rising and Massachusetts children are doing better than ever. [Scott Harshbarger/ Patricia McGovern] has championed efforts to hire new teachers and to make schools safe. When it comes to education, [Patricia McGovern/Scott Harshbarger] has done nothing at all. [Scott Harshbarger's/Patricia McGovern's] record has been praised by leading educators. Our children need a Governor like [Scott Harshbarger/ Patricia McGovern]." A negative script emphasizing education reads: "It's happening right now in your neighborhood. A generation of young people is in danger. Schools, already troubled by crowding, fight to keep drugs and guns out. Test scores are falling and Massachusetts children are falling behind. [Scott Harshbarger/Patricia McGovern] has a plan to hire hundreds of new teachers and to make schools safe. When it comes to education, [Patricia McGovern/Scott Harshbarger] has no plan at all. [McGovern's/ Harshbarger's] record has been criticized by leading educators. Our children cannot afford a Governor like [Patricia McGovern/Scott Harshbarger]. Vote for [Scott Harshbarger/Patricia McGovern]."

23. The "music," if one wishes to call it that, is a modern unharmonious symphony titled "Coptic Light," composed by Morton Feldman and performed by the Deutsches Symphonie-Orchester Berlin.

24. Self-report measures pose two problems: (1) emotions can occur without awareness, precluding accurate self-report (Damasio 2000); and (2) the very act of calling attention to an emotional state may alter subsequent evaluations (Schwarz and Clore 1983). Psychophysiological methods (monitoring galvanic skin response, heart rate, facial expressions, etc.) can detect responses that escape awareness (Larsen and Frederickson 1999), but strip away any semblance of realism. Both strategies make it harder to maintain deception and therefore to limit demands effects.

25. I obtained responses to these emotion questions from only some of the participants: only 185 of the 286 subjects in the final sample completed the cued recall manipulation check.

26. I use one-tailed tests of statistical significance because of the strong theoretical predictions for many effects of emotional cues. While two-tailed tests would be appropriate for many control variables, I try to use one-tailed tests consistently to avoid confusion from switching back and forth between standards. Wherever possible, I report standard errors, t-ratios, or equivalent statistics so readers may judge for themselves whether they are confident that the results do or do not provide evidence of an effect.

27. Using the full scale, 63 percent of the participants said they were more likely than not to vote in the primary and 73 percent said so for the general election. Actual turnout was estimated at 26 percent (*Boston Globe,* September 27, 1998, A1) and 55 percent (*Boston Globe,* November 4, 1998, B10), respectively.

28. However, for an example of a regression analyst who yearns for greater simplicity in regression analysis, see Achen 2002.

29. For each estimation, I use a statistical model that is appropriate for the dependent variable: ordinary-least-squares (OLS) regression analysis for the interest, belief, and registration scales; maximum likelihood estimation (MLE) of an ordered probit model for the three-category measure of volunteering; and MLE logit models for both dichotomous measures of intentions to vote.

30. We would not want to make this assumption, at least not for all factors, if we were testing for the ability of the ads to *prime* or *activate* certain predispositions. Scholars typically study the impact of priming on evaluations or choice (Iyengar and Kinder 1987; Kinder 2003). We will get to this kind of analysis in the next chapter.

31. A single control for the baseline ad conditions is included only when the impact of positive and negative scripts is found to be symmetrical (i.e., when positive scripts have a positive effect and negative scripts have a negative effect, or vice versa). In cases where the impact of positive and negative scripts is similar—e.g., if effect is 0.55 for positive tone and 0.34 for negative tone—this effect is captured by a general ad exposure variable. I estimated the models each way and, where the script valence variable is *not* included, the results for emotional cues are unaffected by its inclusion or exclusion.

32. In general, I tried to avoid using identical repeated measures given the relatively short time frame of the experiment. A subject may feel pressured to change her posttest response in a either socially desirable or researcher-pleasing manner (once she thinks she knows what the experiment is about) or to provide an identical posttest response to appear consistent. Using pretest items that are similar but not identical can help mitigate such biases.

33. I use retirement status to capture the higher participatory habits among older generations. Although life-cycle factors are also at work (see Verba, Schlozman, and Brady 1995), the wide generation gap separating the political and civic involvement of today's younger and older generations is well documented (Miller and Shanks 1995; Putnam 2000). Occupation indicates whether the subject works as a public employee (the bivariate correlation with measures of participation reaches .25). Religion is measured as Protestant affiliation (the bivariate correlation with participation reaches .15).

34. The pretest contained a question asking how much the subject follows politics in general. This five-point scale is a reasonable measure of general political interest and, therefore, I add it as a second baseline to the estimation of campaign interest. The general findings are the same regardless. However, if we omit this control, the substantive impact of enthusiasm cues on interest in the campaign rises by nearly 50 percent from 0.64 to 0.93, with corresponding further enhancement of its statistical significance.

35. In the full results, we also see evidence of the actual campaign serving its ritual purpose of waking the electorate from political slumber. From the first to the last week of the study, participants' interest in the election rose an average of 0.75 or about one-eighth of the scale ($p < .009$). This raises an interesting question about the temporal dynamics of campaigns. Are voters motivated most effectively by emotional appeals during the early, quiet portions of a campaign, or do appeals work best when they capitalize on the mounting excitement of the last few weeks? If the sample is split into two five-week periods, the relationship between enthusiasm cues and interest in the campaign appears stronger in the period immediately before the election. While the cell sizes in this study are too small to permit full investigation of such temporal changes, testing for shifts in the public's responsiveness to emotional appeals over the course of campaign seasons seems like an important avenue for future research.

36. All predicted probabilities and expected values reported in this book are generated via Monte Carlo simulation (ten thousand simulations) using Clarify 2.1 for Stata (see Tomz, Wittenberg, and King 2001).

37. In interpreting these dramatic numbers, we should be mindful that we are measuring motivation in terms of intentions and over a very short period of time. Nonethe-

less, this recognition does not hamper our interpretation of the *relatively* greater boost to motivation among those who saw an ad appealing to enthusiasm.

38. Political efficacy is a five-point scale measuring agreement with the following statement: "People like me don't have any say about what the government does."

39. The questions asked participants to name the Speaker of the Massachusetts House of Representatives, indicate the total number of members elected to the state Senate, and to identify which of the gubernatorial primary candidates had been officially nominated by the Democratic Party convention earlier in the summer. Roughly 37 percent correctly named the speaker, only 7 percent knew the size of the Senate, and 30 percent named the right candidate. Although these percentages are low, questions regarding local politics are more difficult than standard political knowledge items. A single correct response indicates a resident who has at least some grasp on state politics. Participants also answered four questions on national politics and, for the most part, only those who displayed reasonable knowledge of national politics could begin to answer correctly questions about state politics.

40. It is not vital to know whether this particular dividing line truly captures the threshold between political expertise and naiveté. Most researchers think of political sophistication not as a quality that people either possess or lack, but rather as one they possess to varying degrees. The most important consideration is placing people in the appropriate half of the distribution, which I suspect this measure does nicely (see the preceding note). Converse (1964), using his more stringent standards, concludes that a tenth or less of the American electorate approaches genuine sophistication. To the extent the best dividing line is somewhere higher (or lower) than I set it and true differences exist, the analysis in this chapter mutes the findings in the direction of the null hypothesis. As a practical matter, breakdowns that did not come as close to a 50–50 split would make it difficult to run separate analyses or use interaction terms reliably on a sample of this modest size. In this respect, the fact that the experiments oversampled highly educated individuals turns out to have the fortunate by-product of allowing us to pursue this analysis.

41. The alternative way to redo the multivariate analysis is to split the sample in two and run the original model separately for each group. I checked the results using this approach, and the pattern of key findings does not differ. That being said, the two approaches are not equivalent. Running the model separately for each group allows for the possibility that sophistication alters the relevance of *all* variables, including prior motivation and demographic controls. This is equivalent to running a single model with interaction terms for all of the original variables. The approach presented in the text assumes that the moderating effect of sophistication is limited to advertising variables and strains the statistical power of the data only to the extent necessary to test the hypotheses of interest.

42. In the multivariate analysis, the overall effect size for more knowledgeable individuals is the sum of the baseline effect and the interaction effect (i.e., $0.58 + 0.10 = 0.68$).

43. This study does not necessarily contradict the findings of earlier work on sophistication and *affect,* but it does suggest revisiting some of the conclusions drawn from those earlier findings. Research showing greater reliance on affect or "gut feelings" (relative to issue opinions and ideology) among political novices does not warrant sweeping claims that the political behavior of experts is guided less by emotion. The capacity of political communication to trigger emotional responses that in turn shape political reasoning and action should be distinguished from the tendency of individuals to make po-

litical choices on the basis of different factors (some more "cognitive" and some more "affective"). In general, this highlights the need for political scientists to move beyond their tradition of treating emotions as just another type of attitude.

44. More specifically, the four components of the measure are (1) agreement with the statement "I don't think public officials care much what people like me think"; (2) agreement with the statement "Parties are only interested in people's votes but not in their opinions"; (3) answer to the question "Do you think politicians are primarily 'in it for themselves' or do you think their primary concern is the 'public good'?"; and (4) answer to the question "Election campaigns are often quite negative in tone. Do you think this is because candidates are having a tough but fair debate about important issues, or do you think candidates are mostly lying about one another and engaged in unfair 'character assassination'?"

45. We observe an interesting pattern of results if we examine the social institutions implicated in the message of the ads. Ads in the study emphasized crime, drugs, and education. Participants reported the extent to which they trusted schools, on the one hand, and the courts and police, on the other. Fear appeals seemed to undermine trust in the institutions particularly linked to the issue focus of an ad. Ads evoking fear and warning of a decline in education quality and school safety cut into feelings of trust about schools ($t = 2.43, p < .01$). Ads evoking fear and alerting citizens to growing dangers to children from crime lessened the trust viewers place in the courts and police ($t = 1.48, p < .07$), as well as schools ($t = 1.39, p < .09$). However, one anomaly appears. There is suggestive evidence that fear ads focused on education *increased* trust in the courts and police ($t = 1.34$, $p < .09$). The evidence is modest but, if it proved to be genuine, it is troubling in two respects. On the one hand, it is troubling given the incentives politicians have, especially challengers or members of the minority party, to exaggerate problems with the failings of various social institutions (e.g., law firms, companies, unions, and the health care system, to name a few). On the other hand, even when true, accusations could be problematic if the performance of the institution depends on some level of trust from the public, because the ad may only make the problem worse.

Chapter Five

1. Nonetheless, who knows what and when seems to be open to interpretation (Bartels and Zaller 2001; Campbell 2001; Holbrook 2001; Norpoth 2001; Wlezien 2001).

2. These expectations can also be based on the cognitive content of advertising. Positive ads often contain glowing statements about the policy stands, achievements, and personal qualities of the sponsoring candidate. We should not be surprised then that viewers come away from the ad on average with more good things to say about that candidate and a more favorable impression of him overall. Similarly, negative ads often contain critical statements about the policy stands, achievements, and personal qualities of the opponent. We again should think it natural for viewers to come away with more bad things to say about the opponent and a more unfavorable impression of him overall. The cognitive account accords best with particular varieties of positive and negative ads known as "promotion" and "attack" spots, respectively, but not as well with comparison style ads that contain elements of both.

3. Given the comparison format of the ad and the fact that many observers classify comparison spots as quintessentially attack ads, a generally negative reaction toward

both candidates may lend credence to the idea that attack ads turn voters off from politics (Ansolabehere and Iyengar 1995).

4. As with candidate affect, the focus switches to the relative assessments of the candidates, because the theory of emotional appeals predicts a change in the "bottom line" rather than the symmetric influence of positive ads on positive considerations and negative ads on negative considerations. The measure of comparative considerations is calculated by subtracting net considerations for the opponent from net considerations for the sponsor.

5. It indeed would be interesting to test whether emotional appeals affect the relevance of strategic considerations and electability in particular. Unfortunately, I did not include the measures necessary to fully examine that question in this study.

6. It is worth noting that we simply cannot tell whether the message has a persuasive effect in the other advertising conditions. The estimated effect is positive in all cases and the predicted impact at 0.03, while small, is not trivial in politics. The basic message of these ads, as designed, may be modestly persuasive in general, but the sample sizes leave this study without the statistical power to detect effects of such magnitude.

7. In certain times and places, American political parties have been split into well-entrenched factions that resemble partisanship between parties. However, the 1998 gubernatorial nomination contest in Massachusetts between Harshbarger, McGovern, and others was not the product of firmly embedded Democratic Party factions. Harshbarger and McGovern had support from differing elements within the Democratic Party, as is typical, but they were not the champions of well-defined factions.

8. This analysis is based on actual mean differences across groups and experimental conditions. It does not depend on the results of a multivariate model, such as those shown previously in table 5.1.

9. This has been a more typical way for political scientists to treat affect or conscious feelings—as a sort of information used in political choice (Marcus and MacKuen 1993; Rahn 2000).

10. When advertising message is included in the model, along with the other factors, I find that any earlier evidence of its persuasive effect has been washed out by the posttest measures. However, there is some evidence of what might be called a "boomerang" effect in the negative ad condition: when controlling for prior preferences and posttest candidate evaluations that may have been influenced by the advertising message, there is a residual impact from negative ads (without fear cues) that makes individuals *less* likely to choose the sponsor. It is tempting to infer that this is a sign of the much-discussed backlash against negativity in political advertising. However, the exact interpretation is open to question, especially given the inclusion of posttest measures in the model. Regardless, the finding falls beyond the scope of this book.

11. However, reliance on fancy camera work and novel presentation styles is likely to require continuous adaptation in the fast-evolving, post-MTV world (Kern 1989).

12. Note, however, that this alternative hypothesis lacks both theoretical underpinnings and an explanation for the full range of differential effects we have seen from fear and enthusiasm ads.

13. Individuals can be simultaneously suspicious of advertising claims and yet respond with subtle anxiety to the cues or message of the ad. Recall from chapter 3 that emotional responses usually escape conscious awareness. Moreover, it is possible to be conscious of the emotional manipulation and still feel its effects, even though awareness

of a dubious source mitigates the effectiveness somewhat. You can be alert to the ways in which a horror film tries to scare you and yet still be tense or even frightened on cue.

14. I included all responses regardless of accuracy. For example, if subjects recalled a story about crime or election campaigns that did not actually appear, I coded it under recall of subsequent relevant stories. If they recalled a story about health care or automobiles that did not appear, I coded it under recall of subsequent irrelevant stories. Our main interest here is not the effect of fear on accuracy per se, but rather its effect on focusing the mind on relevant topics.

Chapter Six

1. I would have liked to take up a fourth issue here—namely, the aggregate impact of emotional appeals on voters over the course of entire ad campaigns and how those effects correspond to theoretical predictions. Unfortunately, the data necessary for an analysis of this nature are not presently available. When this project began many years ago, it did not seem possible even to conceive of carrying out a macro-level analysis except in the crudest fashion and then still requiring Herculean efforts at data collection. However, in the intervening time, new sources of data on both ad campaigns and voters have been generated. If linked to data on the emotional content of the ads, these new sources could, in time, provide a basis for revealing more about both strategy in the frequency, timing, and placement of ads and the impact of ad campaigns on voters or electoral outcomes.

2. Although studies have frequently remarked on the widespread use of emotional appeals, only two previous studies have incorporated emotional content into their systematic analyses of campaign ads. In their continuing research, Kaid and Johnston (2001; 2002) have applied the videostyle approach to over thirteen hundred presidential ads from 1952 to 2000. The videostyle coding instructions include three items on emotion: the first asks whether an emotional appeal is present in each ad, the second asks whether the dominant form of appeal is emotional (as opposed to logical or ethical), and the third asks whether the ad specifically uses a fear appeal. Although this approach is limited by not recording the emotional specificity of appeals other than fear, it can offer valuable historical perspective. For example, they find that emotion has been the dominant form of appeal in presidential ads from the 1960s through the 1990s. Kern's (1989) investigation of political advertising in the 1980s offers the most extensive look at the role of emotion of previous research. She relies mostly on interviews with consultants, impressionistic observations of ads, and case studies of three elections. She also undertakes an exploratory content analysis in an effort to develop a typology of specific emotional appeals. She collected a sample of 122 different ads from federal and state races in the 1984 election. It includes all ads that appeared on network television during prime time over the last ten days before the election in four media markets. Although quite limited in scope, the content analysis confirms the centrality of emotion-laden ads in several 1984 races.

3. My colleagues, Nicholas Valentino and Vincent Hutchings, are interested in studying other aspects of campaign advertising. Collaboration allowed us to more efficiently invest our time and money in compiling and coding ads.

4. The four states for which there are no ads in the sample are Alaska, Oregon, Vermont, and Wyoming.

5. This approach is particularly useful if one wishes to formulate predictions about the emotional impact of the ad (e.g., in designing stimuli for experiments) rather than

assess the aims of the ad. This alternative also could assist a more thorough inquiry into the precise elements of ads that correspond to either admaker intentions, voter reactions, or both, somewhat in the fashion of studies by Boynton and Nelson (1997) or Richardson (2003). These studies did not use psychological theories of emotion as a guide nor did they conduct systematic content analysis. However, they did display a more thoroughgoing concern for dissecting the specific features of actual ads that might serve as antecedents to viewer reactions.

6. It is important to emphasize that coders did not record the extent to which the ad provoked such feelings in *them*. Because emotional responses are tied to the significance cues hold for each person, there is certain to be a disjunction between what targeted voters feel during an election and what others feel when reviewing the same ad that does not (and perhaps never did) hold relevance for them. Thus, it is inappropriate to use this approach when analyzing ads from previous or distant elections. Even when studying ads in the time and place for which they are relevant, the approach has limitations. Whatever the intentions of the ad's creators, the emotional impact may vary considerably across individuals or groups of voters. The match between admaker intentions and voter reactions is an interesting topic for empirical investigation, but that investigation is precluded by using reactions to define the ad itself. Similarly, obtaining self-reports of feelings elicited by an ad is more likely to measure qualities of the viewer than the ad or, more accurately, the relationship between the ad and viewer, as perceived by the viewer.

7. Note that a gap can also emerge between the emotional response intended by an ad's creators and the actual response of any individual or group of voters. Therefore, it is important to recognize that it is a quality of the ad and not of the viewer that is being labeled. A study of actual emotional responses, especially if conducted during an on-going election, would provide a fascinating window into the fit between creator intentions and voter reactions, as well as individual variation in emotional response. But that is a very different kind of study.

8. Instructions asked coders whether they believed each ad was directed to a feeling and, if so, "to which feeling do you believe the ad was directed?" (Kern 1989, 72).

9. Kern does not indicate explicitly whether coders were limited in the number of emotions they could record for each ad, but references to overlapping results and ads coded as both positive and negative imply that coders may have been free to assign multiple emotional appeals to a single ad.

10. The categories of intimacy and ambition contributed heavily to the failure of coders to produce reliable results. Trust was the most common category marked, but it overlapped substantially with many other feelings. The two pride categories overlapped heavily with hope and reassurance. On the negative side of the spectrum, coders found it hard to distinguish mild fear from uncertainty/anxiety. These last two outcomes are not surprising in light of the theories I discuss in chapter 3. Finally, Kern reports that guilt was easy to distinguish in the pretest phase but makes no mention of guilt in the discussion of the full sample results.

11. Some draw a conceptual distinction between anger and disgust, arguing the latter is a reaction of revulsion at something distasteful, as distinct from an aggressive response to threat or injustice (Lazarus 1991). Indeed, with such definitions in mind, one can isolate distinct bodily expressions of these emotions in humans (Ekman and Rosenberg 1988). In this narrower sense, one can imagine some voters feeling disgust at what they consider unseemly behavior by politicians (e.g., sexual relations with younger women in

the White House), the implications of certain policies (e.g., mutilation of animals in medical testing or aborted fetuses), or the thought of embracing detested social groups (e.g., homosexuals). However, in emotional self-reports about political candidates, issues, and groups, disgust and anger are highly correlated (Marcus, Neuman, and Mac-Kuen 2000). Although I believe the instances in which campaign ads appeal to disgust but not anger are very limited, one might wish to create a separate category if pursuing a broader study of political propaganda.

12. Which emotions did I exclude? The most glaring omission is the remaining "pole" of the dimensional model underlying affective intelligence theory: the low-arousal state of the surveillance system is characterized by a state of calm or relaxation (Marcus, Neuman, and MacKuen 2000). Although people consciously use words, imagery, and music to elicit this emotion, it is very unlikely that a campaign ad would try to generate calm (essentially, an appeal to inaction) without translating it into hope or pride. Leaders may use guilt in a political manner when seeking to enlist aid on behalf of the disadvantaged (e.g., Martin Luther King Jr.'s piercing reminder that the greater threat to freedom and equality for African Americans rests with the inaction of the many, more than the hateful actions of bigots). However, I believe guilt is an extremely unlikely target for campaign ads unless paired with an appeal for compassion. Finally, I did not include a set of emotions more relevant in interpersonal relations than the public life of political campaigns, such as love (affection), jealousy, and shame.

13. The number in parentheses is Cohen's K, widely recognized as an extremely conservative index of reliability (Clark-Carter 1997; Lombard, Snyder-Duch, and Bracken 2002). The *Kappa* statistic indicates the proportion of agreement that would not have been expected by chance, where expected agreement is based on the assumption that the distribution of values in the population mirrors the multiplicative marginals of the crosstabulation. For example, if coders agreed in 70 percent of cases and the expected level of agreement was 40 percent, Cohen's K would be 0.50 (i.e., $(0.7 - 0.4)/(1 - 0.4)$).

14. These combined values run from 0 (no appeal) to 4 (a strong and clear appeal).

15. I included additional emotional categories and discussed them briefly here in recognition that fear and enthusiasm are not the only appeals available to politicians. I wish to cast an eye beyond these two so that we may be mindful of the ways in which this work needs to be extended in the future. As the content analysis will reveal, political scientists would do well to devote more attention to anger and its relationship to fear and enthusiasm in future research (cf. Marcus 2003). Despite the centrality of fear and enthusiasm to affective intelligence theory and the broader theoretical approaches emphasized in this book, the proponents of these models do not contend that other emotions are irrelevant.

16. In recent years, political scientists have begun to gain access to data indicating when and where every ad airs in major media markets around the country. These data make it possible to learn far more about the volume and targeting of ad campaigns. The Wisconsin Advertising Project (WAP), run by Ken Goldstein, has been preparing these data for release to the public. Data for the 2000 election became available in 2003, and I have initiated a massive project to link the content analysis data presented in this chapter with the WAP data. The fact that candidates sometimes make several versions of the same ad and that ads do not come with a unique name or identifying number makes this task challenging. However, it should be possible in the future to use the combined datasets for investigating claims about the prevalence of emotional appeals among ad broadcasts. Data for the 2002 and 2004 elections have not yet been made public.

17. For more on the importance of making a clear distinction between number of ads produced and volume of ads aired, see Goldstein and Freedman 2002b.

18. This does not imply that the ads made sophisticated or well-supported arguments.

19. For readers acquainted with the *Federalist Papers,* there may be one modest difference worthy of note. In their arguments on behalf of the new constitution, Alexander Hamilton and James Madison defended the U.S. Senate as a more deliberative legislative body than the U.S. House of Representatives, whose proceedings were seen as vulnerable to popular passions. Over two hundred years later, we find that ads for politicians seeking the Senate were more likely to rest on logical appeals (31 percent vs. 22 percent), while ads for those seeking the House were indeed more likely to target popular passions (77 percent vs. 68 percent). This difference is highly significant (t = 3.20, p < .001). If Hamilton and Madison were with us, they might take some small comfort from the slightly more deliberative tone, should one wish to call it that, struck by senatorial candidates during elections largely awash in emotion.

20. In 74 percent of these cases, the strength of the emotional appeal is rated at the maximum value of 4 on the 0-to-4 scale that combines judgments from both coders (i.e., both coders characterized it as a strong appeal). In the remaining cases, the appeal is rated at 3, indicating that one coder evaluated the ad as appealing to the emotion strongly and the other evaluated it as appealing to the emotion somewhat.

21. The scales for the strength of pride and enthusiasm are correlated at r = 0.55. Scales for fear and anger are correlated at r = 0.64.

22. Some psychologists also suggest that pride implicates greater ego involvement or identification than enthusiasm, whereas source of blame and locus of control influence the distinction between anger and fear (Lazarus 1991).

23. Kern (1989) found that 39 percent of ads in her 1984 sample appealed to both positive and negative emotions (75).

24. Given their dual aim, it is not surprising that 72 percent of comparison spots include both kinds of emotional appeals.

25. In this section, I provide a view of the national landscape, but there were a few regional contours in the use of emotional appeals in 1999 and 2000. In the heartland of the Midwest, campaigns produced ads with, well, more heart: They appealed more heavily to enthusiasm (t = 3.67, p < .001), pride (t = 3.08, p < .002), and compassion (t = 3.65, p < .001), but less heavily to anger (t = 2.91, p < .004). Politics was a little scarier on the coasts, as campaigns created ads targeting fear more strongly than in the Midwest or South (t = 3.32, p < .001). On a lighter note, southern campaign ads were twice as likely to try to amuse their audiences as ads in other regions of the country (t = 2.67, p < .008).

26. I set aside analysis of sadness, compassion, and amusement appeals for the rest of the chapter, because there are two few ads of each type to support reliable comparisons in most cases. As ads from 2002 and 2004 are coded, I hope to be able to say more about these types of appeals in the future.

27. Intercoder reliability on the full color variable is mediocre (0.58), as coders found it difficult to differentiate muted colors from dark colors. Coding of other color themes proved easier and resulted in higher reliability scores when considered separately (e.g., 0.97 for black-and-white). Therefore, I base my analysis in the text solely on cases for which the two coders achieved agreement on color.

28. Unless otherwise indicated, all reports of significance tests in this chapter are from two-tailed tests.

29. The difference between unimpassioned ads and the emotional appeals is statistically significant in all cases. For black-and-white, t = 2.88 (p < .004) and t = 4.45 (p < .001) for the difference from negative and positive emotions, respectively. For dark colors, t = 4.58 (p < .001) and t = 2.10 (p < .036). For bright colors, t = 4.38 (p < .001) and t = 1.80 (p < .071).

30. For no music, t = 1.22 (p < .225) and t = 6.11 (p < .001). For uplifting music, t = 11.23 (p <.001) and t = 7.90 (p < .001). For somber music, t = 12.64 (p < .001) and t = 6.94 (p < .001).

31. By far, the ads relying most heavily on sound effects are those using humor (39 percent).

32. The combined emotional categories obscure a few distinctions. Fewer fear ads lack music than anger ads (21 percent vs. 35 percent; t = 2.65, p < .009), and the same is true for pride relative to enthusiasm (4 percent vs. 11 percent; t = 2.59, p < .010). Ads trying to tap voter pride make greater use of uplifting, sentimental, or patriotic music than ads trying to elicit enthusiasm (72 percent vs. 59 percent; t = 3.16; p < .002).

33. The result for same-race images is driven almost entirely by the presence of all whites. There is also a slightly higher proportion of same-race images in fear/anger ads featuring blacks and Hispanics, but these differences are not large enough to be significant on their own. Same-race ads featuring minorities are scarce; only sixteen ads in the entire sample for 1999 and 2000 fit this description. The differences for same-sex images hold for both men and women.

34. All of the reported differences between types of emotional appeals in this paragraph are statistically significant at p < .005 or lower.

35. Images of the U.S. Supreme Court, however, appear at a higher rate in ads appealing to fear, due mostly to interest groups warning about the effects of presidential choice on the judiciary.

36. In fact, some of the most reliable positive emotional images in the IAPS are erotic in nature. However, such pictures are not generally appropriate for campaign ads in the United States. That being said, it is apparently not unusual for Finnish politicians to appear discreetly naked on television entertainment programs, consistent with the sauna culture of that country (Moring 1995).

37. All differences between the two sets of emotional appeals reported in this paragraph are statistically significant at p < .005 or lower, except for images of violent crimes and guns (t = 2.27, p < .024).

38. I have begun collaborating with a colleague in neuropsychology to assess the objective auditory properties of the music and narration used in campaign ads, properties associated in previous studies with distinct emotions. We hope to compare these auditory properties to coders' global judgments about the emotional appeal of ads and to the use and impact of these ads in actual ad campaigns.

39. Intercoder agreement on whether an ad made reference to the personality or character of candidates is lower than desirable (0.64). Therefore, this analysis is based only on those ads for which the two coders agreed. The finding is the same if the full sample is used.

40. If we look at other emotions, we see that differences go beyond simple valence. For example, discussion of personal qualities is much more likely among ads appealing primarily either to anger (68 percent) or amusement (73 percent) than among all other types of ads.

41. For example, see Jamieson 1992, 1996; Nelson and Boynton 1997; and Richardson 2003.

42. The results are similar for anger and pride, except that parties are even more likely to create ads appealing to anger than interest groups ($p < .060$) and interest groups are more likely to appeal to pride ($p < .021$). These significance levels are based on post-hoc comparison tests. The higher incidence of pride appeals among interest groups is largely, though not entirely, a function of ads from two sponsors. The Alliance for Quality Nursing Home Care and the American Health Care Association, two umbrella groups for nursing home operators, ran a series of ads thanking and commending various incumbent members of Congress for their leadership in voting to preserve "vital Medicare funding." Their ads account for almost half the interest group pride appeals. The Republican Leadership Council, an organization formed by centrist Republican leaders, produced another quarter of these ads in support of specific congressional candidates.

43. Interest groups in 2000 were also significantly more likely to produce ads appealing to amusement than either parties or candidates.

44. These results are not merely an artifact of unopposed or relatively unchallenged candidates using positive emotional appeals because they have no need to make a strong case for themselves or worry about competition. Such candidates indeed have little reason to spend money on television advertising period, and usually do not. Moreover, the findings reported in the text are strongest when we compare the most competitive races with the next most competitive set (say, where the margin of victory ranges from 6 to 10 percent) rather than with the least competitive races that have victory margins of 15, 20, or more percent.

45. If this is true, then why don't politicians use fear appeals all of the time? Indeed, why do they appeal to positive emotions far more often? I believe this stems from both the popular belief that negative appeals increase the likelihood of backlash (i.e., they are riskier) and the prevailing norm that fear appeals are a morally suspect form of campaigning. Therefore, candidates treat fear appeals as a tactic they should use only when they feel it is truly necessary.

46. For the change in fear appeals between nomination and general election phases, $t = 5.83$ ($p < .001$). For the change in enthusiasm appeals, $t = 5.45$ ($p < .001$).

47. I do not use presidential ads for this analysis because this requires data on the relative frequency with which the ads aired across states. I do not use ads from U.S. House races because I possess less adequate measures for local partisanship at this time.

48. The closest thing to an ideal measure, given my interests, would be data from fifty simultaneous surveys, each taking a large random sample of adult citizens in a state and asking the standard National Election Studies party identification question.

49. The results are as follows. For Democratic fear ads when state context is measured by voter registration, $t = 3.18$ ($p < .002$), and when measured by presidential election results, $t = 2.65$ ($p < .008$). For Republican fear ads and the registration measure, $t = 0.61$ ($p < .542$), and for the presidential election measure, $t = 1.93$ ($p < .054$). For Democratic enthusiasm ads and the registration measure, $t = 1.96$ ($p < .050$), and for the presidential election measure, $t = 1.75$ ($p < .081$). For Republican enthusiasm ads and the voter registration measure, $t = 3.07$ ($p < .001$), and for the presidential election measure, $t = 0.43$ ($p < .667$).

50. Minor party candidates are more likely than major party candidates to use humor in their ads (17 percent vs. 2 percent; $t = 4.46, p < .001$). There is some suggestion they are also more likely to use unimpassioned ads, but the difference falls short of significance (39 percent vs. 24 percent; $t = 1.49, p < .135$).

Chapter Seven

1. This so-called textbook view of democratic politics, heavy on the "civics," actually proves elusive *even in civics textbooks* of the Progressive Era, when the conception probably held the most sway (cf. Schudson 1998). You are likely to encounter this idealized take on candidate selection in, of all places, the campaign literature put out by candidates, whose actions belie these very pronouncements. In this way, they reinforce the norms by which their own less-than-ideal campaign strategies are critically judged.

2. Evan Thomas, "The Inside Story: How Bush Did It," *Newsweek,* November 15, 2004, 123.

3. Jim Rutenberg, "Scary Ads Take Campaign to a Grim New Level," *New York Times,* October 17, 2004; Don Gonyea, "Message of Fear Dominates as Vote Nears," *National Public Radio,* October 20, 2004; David Montgomery, "Experts Say Fear-Mongering Making this the Ugliest Election in Memory," *Mercury News* (San Jose), October 29, 2004.

4. While campaigns may be about issues and candidate characteristics to a large extent, research on campaigns has not suggested what, if anything, candidates can do to win besides pick the best issue positions from the beginning or possess the best personality. They can do this without waging expensive campaigns.

5. The original source of these data is the Campaign Media Analysis Group (CMAG), a private sector company. The Brennan Center for Justice at New York University purchased the CMAG data on advertising in the 2000 election cycle with financial support from the Pew Charitable Trusts. The Wisconsin Advertising Project (WAP), under the direction of Ken Goldstein at the University of Wisconsin-Madison, was contracted to provide a basic content analysis of the ads in the CMAG dataset and prepare the data for analysis by researchers. This process has continued with subsequent election cycles. In 2003, WAP made the 2000 CMAG data available for use by other scholars at a negligible cost. At the time of this writing, data from other elections is not yet available. I have acquired the 2000 CMAG data from WAP and begun a massive project to link our content analysis with the CMAG observations. This takes a great deal of time not only due to the large number of ads involved (i.e., over sixteen hundred ads in our content analysis and nearly one million observations of "ad broadcasts" in the CMAG dataset) but also due to the fact that any one ad often has been given different names or labels by various sources. In addition, content of the ads in the CMAG data file is verifiable only using black-and-white storyboards that provide the full script of the ad but only intermittent snapshots of its visual content (once every few seconds). To link the data files, these storyboards must be matched with actual video files of the original ad, which were used for our content analysis. Although a long and difficult process, I believe the rewards for research will merit the effort.

6. This is obviously *not* intended as a complete or satisfying account of how Hitler came to power. My point here is simply to highlight how we might think differently about the public mood in different times and places, as well as its implications for susceptibility to mass persuasion.

References

Abelson, Robert P., Donald R. Kinder, Mark D. Peters, and Susan T. Fiske. 1982. "Affective and Semantic Components in Political Person Perception." *Journal of Personality and Social Psychology* 42:619–30.

Achen, Christopher. 1982. *Interpreting and Using Regression.* Newbury Park, CA: Sage Publications.

———. 2002. "Toward a New Political Methodology: Microfoundations and ART." *Annual Review of Political Science* 5:423–50.

Adolphs, Ralph, and Antonio R. Damasio. 2000. "Neurobiology of Emotion at a Systems Level." In *The Neuropsychology of Emotion,* edited by Joan C. Borod, 194–213. New York: Oxford University Press.

———. 2001. "The Interaction of Affect and Cognition: A Neurobiological Perspective." In *Handbook of Affect and Social Cognition,* edited by Joseph P. Forgas, 27–49. Mahwah, NJ: Lawrence Erlbaum.

Agranoff, Robert, ed. 1972. *The New Style in Election Campaigns.* Boston: Holbrook Press.

Agres, Stuart J., Julie A. Edell, and Tony M. Dubitsky. 1990. *Emotion in Advertising: Theoretical and Practical Explorations.* New York: Quorum Books.

Aldrich, John H. 1993. "Rational Choice and Turnout." *American Journal of Political Science* 37:246–78.

———. 1995. *Why Parties? The Origin and Transformation of Political Parties in America.* Chicago: University of Chicago Press.

Aldrich, John H., John L. Sullivan, and Eugene Borgida. 1989. "Foreign Affairs and Issue Voting: Do Presidential Candidates 'Waltz Before a Blind Audience.'" *American Political Science Review* 83:123–42.

Altshuler, Glenn C., and Stuart M. Blumin. 2001. *Rude Republic: Americans and Their Politics in the Nineteenth Century.* Princeton: Princeton University Press.

Alvarez, R. Michael. 1997. *Information and Elections.* Rev. ed. Ann Arbor: University of Michigan Press.

Ansolabehere, Stephen, and Shanto Iyengar. 1994. "Riding the Wave and Claiming Ownership over Issues." *Political Communication* 11:413–29.

———. 1995. *Going Negative: How Attack Advertising Shrinks and Polarizes the Electorate.* New York: Free Press.

―――. 1996. "The Craft of Political Advertising: A Progress Report." In *Political Persuasion and Attitude Change,* edited by Diana Mutz, Paul Sniderman, and Richard Brody, 101–22. Ann Arbor: University of Michigan Press.

Ansolabehere, Stephen, Shanto Iyengar, and Adam Simon. 1999. "Replicating Experiments Using Aggregate and Survey Data: The Case of Negative Advertising and Turnout." *American Political Science Review* 93 (4): 901–9.

Ansolabehere, Stephen, Roy Behr, and Shanto Iyengar. 1993. *The Media Game: American Politics in the Media Age.* New York: Macmillan.

Ansolabehere, Stephen, Shanto Iyengar, Adam Simon, and Nicholas Valentino. 1994. "Does Attack Advertising Demobilize the Electorate?" *American Political Science Review* 88:829–38.

Aristotle. 1991. *Rhetoric.* Edited by George A. Kennedy. Oxford: Oxford University Press.

Arterton, F. Christopher. 1992. "The Persuaive Art in Politics: The Role of Paid Advertising in Presidential Campaigns." In *Under the Watchful Eye: Managing Presidential Campaigns in the Television Era,* edited by Mathew D. McCubbins, 83–126. Washington, DC: CQ Press.

Bachorowski, Jo-Anne, and Michael J. Owren. 2001. "Not All Laughs Are Alike: Voiced but Not Unvoiced Laughter Readily Elicits Positive Affect." *Psychological Science* 12 (3): 252–7.

Bandura, Albert. 1977. "Self-Efficacy: Toward a Unifying Theory of Behavioral Change." *Psychological Review* 84 (2): 191–215.

Bargh, John A., and Tanya L. Chartrand. 1999. "The Unbearable Automaticity of Being." *American Psychologist* 54:462–479.

Barrett, Lisa Feldman, and Peter Salovey, eds. 2002. *The Wisdom of Feeling: Psychological Processes in Emotional Intelligence.* New York: Guilford Press.

Barry, Ann Marie Seward. 1997. *Virtual Intelligence: Perception, Image, and Manipulation in Visual Communication.* Albany: State University of New York Press.

Bartels, Larry M. 1988. *Presidential Primaries and the Dynamics of Public Choice.* Princeton: Princeton University Press.

―――. 1993. "Messages Received: The Political Impact of Media Exposure." *American Political Science Review* 87:267–84.

―――. 1996. "Uninformed Votes: Information Effects in Presidential Elections." *American Journal of Political Science* 40:194–230.

Bartels, Larry M., and John Zaller. 2001. "Al Gore and George Bush's Not-So-Excellent Adventure." *PS: Political Science and Politics* 34:8–20.

Basil, Michael, Caroline Schooler, and Byron Reeves. 1991. "Positive and Negative Political Advertising: Effectiveness of Ads and Perceptions of Candidates." In *Television and Political Advertising.* Vol. 1, *Psychological Processes,* edited by Frank Biocca. Hillsdale, NJ: Lawrence Erlbaum.

Bauer, Raymond A., and Donald F. Cox. 1963. "Rational versus Emotional Communications: A New Approach." In *Television and Human Behavior,* edited by Leon Arons and Mark A. Way, 140–54. New York: Appleton-Century Crofts.

Beck, Kenneth H., and Arthur Frankel. 1981. "A Conceptualization of Threat Communications and Protective Health Behavior." *Social Psychology Quarterly* 44 (3): 204–17.

Bennett, W. Lance. 1996. *The Governing Crisis: Media, Money, and Marketing in American Elections.* 2d ed. New York: St. Martin's Press.

Berelson, Bernard R., Paul F. Lazarsfeld, and William N. McPhee. 1954. *Voting: A Study of Opinion Formation in a Presidential Campaign.* Chicago: University of Chicago Press.

Biswas, Abhijit, Janeen E. Olsen, and Valerie Carlet. 1992. "A Comparison of Print Advertisements from the United States and France." *Journal of Advertising* 21:73–81.

Bless, Herbert. 2000. "The Interplay of Affect and Cognition: The Mediating Role of General Knowledge Structures." In *Feeling and Thinking,* edited by Joseph P. Forgas, 201–22. New York: Cambridge University Press.

———. 2001. "The Consequences of Mood on the Processing of Social Information." In *Blackwell Handbook of Social Psychology: Intraindividual Processes,* edited by Abraham Tesser and Norbert Schwarz, 391–412. Malden, MA: Blackwell.

Boiney, John, and David L. Paletz. 1991. "In Search of the Model Model: Political Science versus Political Advertising Perspectives on Voter Decision Making." In *Television and Political Advertising.* Vol. 1, *Psychological Processes,* edited by Frank Biocca. Hillsdale, NJ: Lawrence Erlbaum.

Brader, Ted. 2005. "Striking a Responsive Chord: How Political Ads Motivate and Persuade Voters by Appealing to Emotions." *American Journal of Political Science* 49:388–405.

Brader, Ted, Nicholas A. Valentino, and Elizabeth Suhay. 2004. Seeing Threats versus Feeling Threats: Group Cues, Emotions, and Activating Opposition to Immigration. Paper presented at the annual meeting of the American Political Science Association, September 4, in Chicago.

Bradley, Margaret M., Bruce N. Cuthbert, and Peter J. Lang. 1996. "Picture media and emotion: Effects of a sustained affective content." *Psychophysiology* 33:662–70.

Bradley, Margaret M., and Peter J. Lang. 1999. "Fearfulness and Affective Evaluations of Pictures." *Motivation and Emotion* 23:1–13.

———. 2000. "Measuring Emotion: Behavior, Feeling, and Physiology." In *Cognitive Neuroscience of Emotion,* edited by Richard D. Lane and Lynn Nadel, 242–76. New York: Oxford University Press.

Bradley, Margaret M., Maurizio Codispoti, Bruce N. Cuthbert, and Peter J. Lang. 2001. "Emotion and Motivation I: Defensive and Appetitive Reactions in Picture Processing." *Emotion* 1:276–298.

Brody, Richard A., and Benjamin I. Page. 1972. "Comment: The Assessment of Policy Voting." *American Political Science Review* 66:450–8.

Bryce, James. 1889. *The American Commonwealth.* London: Macmillan.

Buck, Ross W. 2000. "The Epistemology of Reason and Affect." In *The Neuropsychology of Emotion,* edited by Joan C. Borod, 31–55. New York: Oxford University Press.

Bucy, Erik P. 2000. "Emotional and Evaluative Consequences of Inappropriate Leader Displays." *Communication Research* 27 (2): 194–226.

Burns, Nancy, and Donald R. Kinder. 2003. Conviction and Its Consequences. Unpublished manuscript, University of Michigan, Ann Arbor.

Burns, Nancy, Kay Lehman Schlozman, and Sidney Verba. 2001. *The Private Roots of Public Action: Gender, Equality, and Political Participation.* Cambridge: Harvard University Press.

Cacioppo, John T., and Gary G. Bernston. 1994. "Relationship between Attitudes and Evaluative Space: A Critical Review, with Emphasis on the Separability of Positive and Negative Substrates." *Psychological Bulletin* 115 (3): 401–23.

Cacioppo, John T., and Wendi L. Gardner. 1999. "Emotion." *Annual Review of Psychology* 40:191–214.

Cacioppo, John T., Wendi L. Gardner, and Gary G. Berntson. 1997. "Beyond Bipolar Conceptualizations and Measures: The Case of Attitudes and Evaluative Space." *Personality and Social Psychology Review* 1 (1): 3–25.

Campbell, Angus, Philip E. Converse, Warren E. Miller, and Donald E. Stokes. 1960. *The American Voter.* New York: Wiley.

Campbell, James E. 2001. "The Referendum That Didn't Happen: The Forecasts of the 2000 Presidential Election." *PS: Political Science and Politics* 34:33–38.

Campbell, James E., and James C. Garland, eds. 2000. *Before the Vote: Forecasting American National Elections.* Thousand Oaks, CA: Sage Publications.

Cappella, Joseph N., and Kathleen Hall Jamieson. 1997. *Spiral of Cynicism: The Press and the Public Good.* New York: Oxford University Press.

Chang, Chingching. 2001. "The Impacts of Emotion Elicited by Print Political Advertising on Candidate Evaluation." *Media Psychology* 3:91–118.

Clark-Carter, David. 2002. *Doing Quantitative Psychological Research; From Design to Report.* Hove, UK: Psychology Press.

Clore, Gerald L. 1994. "Why Emotions Are Felt." In *The Nature of Emotion,* edited by Paul Ekman and Richard J. Davidson, 103–111. New York: Oxford University Press.

Clore, Gerald L., and Linda M. Isbell. 2001. "Emotion as Virtue and Vice." In *Citizens and Politics,* edited by James Kuklinski, 103–123. New York: Cambridge University Press.

Clore, Gerald, and Timothy Ketelaar. 1997. "Minding Our Emotions: On the Role of Automatic, Unconscious Affect." In *The Automaticity of Everyday Life,* edited by Robert S. Wyer Jr., 105–20. Mahwah, NJ: Lawrence Erlbaum.

Clore, Gerald L., and Andrew Ortony. 2000. "Cognition in Emotion: Always, Sometimes, or Never?" In *Cognitive Neuroscience of Emotion,* edited by Richard D. Lane and Lynn Nadel, 24–61. New York: Oxford University Press.

Conover, Pamela J. 1984. "The Influence of Group Identifications on Political Perception and Evaluation." *Journal of Politics* 46:760–85.

Conover, Pamela J., and Stanley Feldman. 1986. "Emotional Reactions to the Economy: I'm Mad as Hell and I'm Not Going to Take It Any More." *American Journal of Political Science* 30:50–78.

Converse, Philip E. 1962. "Information Flow and the Stability of Partisan Attitudes." *Public Opinion Quarterly* 26:578–99.

———. 1964. "The Nature of Belief Systems in Mass Publics." In *Ideology and Discontent,* edited by David Apter, 206–61. New York: Free Press.

———. 1969. "Of Time and Partisan Stability." *Comparative Political Studies* 2:139–71.

———. 1990. "Popular Representation and the Distribution of Information." In *Information and Democratic Processes,* edited by John Ferejohn and James Kuklinski, 367–88. Urbana: University of Illinois Press.

Cornelius, Randolph R. 1996. *The Science of Emotion: Research and Tradition in the Psychology of Emotions.* Upper Saddle River, NJ: Prentice-Hall.

Crigler, Ann N., Marion Just, and W. Russell Neuman. 1994. "Interpreting Visual versus Audio Messages in Television News." *Journal of Communication* 44:132–49.

Dalton, Russell J., and Martin P. Wattenberg. 1993. "The Not So Simple Act of Voting." In *Political Science: State of the Discipline II,* edited by Ada Finifter, 193–218. Washington, DC: American Political Science Association.

Damasio, Antonio R. 1994. *Descartes' Error: Emotion, Reason, and the Human Brain.* New York: G. P. Plenum.

————. 2000. "A Second Chance for Emotion." In *Cognitive Neuroscience of Emotion,* edited by Richard D. Lane and Lynn Nadel, 12–13. New York: Oxford University Press.

Dautrich, Kenneth, and Thomas H. Hartley. 1999. *How the News Media Fail American Voters.* New York: Columbia University Press.

Dawson, Michael. 1994. *Behind the Mule.* Princeton: Princeton University Press.

de Pelsmacker, Patrick, and Maggie Geuens. 1997. "Emotional Appeals annd Information Cues in Belgian Magazine Advertisements." *International Journal of Advertising* 16:123–47.

Delli Carpini, Michael X., and Scott Keeter. 1996. *What Americans Know about Politics and Why It Matters.* New Haven: Yale University Press.

Devlin, L. Patrick. 1987. "Campaign Commercials." In *Political Persuasion in Presidential Campaigns,* edited by L. Patrick Devlin, 205–16. New Brunswick, NJ: Transaction.

————. 1995. "Political Commercials in American Presidential Elections." In *Political Advertising in Western Democracies,* edited by Lynda Lee Kaid and Christina Holtz-Bacha, 186–205. Thousand Oaks, CA: Sage Publications.

Diamond, Edwin, and Stephen Bates. 1992. *The Spot: The Rise of Political Advertising on Television.* 3d ed. Cambridge: MIT Press.

Doppelt, Jack C., and Ellen Shearer. 1999. *Nonvoters: America's No-Shows.* Thousand Oaks, CA: Sage Publications.

Downs, Anthony. 1957. *An Economic Theory of Democracy.* New York: Harper.

Druckman, James. 2001. "On the Limits of Framing Effects: Who Can Frame?" *Journal of Politics* 63 (4): 1041–66.

Eagly, Alice, and Shelly Chaiken. 1993. *The Psychology of Attitudes.* Fort Worth, TX: Harcourt.

Edelman, Murray. 1964. *The Symbolic Uses of Politics.* Urbana: University of Illinois Press.

Egloff, Boris, Stefan C. Schmukle, Lawrence R. Burns, Carl-Walter Kohlmann, and Michael Hock. 2003. "Facets of Dynamic Positive Affect: Differentiating Joy, Interest, and Activation in the Positive and Negative Affect Schedule (PANAS)." *Journal of Personality and Social Psychology* 85 (3): 529–40.

Ekman, Paul. 1992. "An Argument for Basic Emotions." *Cognition and Emotion* 6 (3/4): 169–200.

Ekman, Paul, and Richard J. Davidson, eds. 1994. *The Nature of Emotion: Fundamental Questions.* New York: Oxford University Press.

Ekman, Paul, and Erika K. Rosenberg. 1998. *What the Face Reveals: Basic and Applied Studies of Spontaneous Expression Using the Facial Action Coding System.* New York: Oxford University Press.

Eliasoph, Nina. 1998. *Avoiding Politics: How Americans Produce Apathy in Everyday Life.* New York: Cambridge University Press.

Ellsworth, Phoebe. 1994a. "Levels of Thought and Levels of Emotion." In *The Nature of Emotion,* edited by Paul Ekman and Richard J. Davidson, 192–96. New York: Oxford University Press.

————. 1994b. "Some Reasons to Expect Universal Antecedents of Emotion." In *The Nature of Emotion,* edited by Paul Ekman and Richard J. Davidson, 150–54. New York: Oxford University Press.

Englis, Basil G. 1994. "The Role of Affect in Political Advertising: Voter Emotional Responses to the Nonverbal Behavior of Politicians." In *Attention, Attitude, and Affect in*

Response to Advertising, edited by Eddie Clark, Timothy Brock, and David Stewart, 223–47. Hillsdale, NJ: Lawrence Erlbaum.

Erikson, Robert S., Michael B. MacKuen, and James A. Stimson. 2002. *The Macro Polity.* New York: Cambridge University Press.

Fallows, James. 1997. *Breaking the News: How the Media Undermine American Democracy.* New York: Vintage Books.

Ferejohn, John A., and James H. Kuklinski, ed. 1990. *Information and Democratic Processes.* Urbana: University of Illinois Press.

Ferguson, Eva Dreikurs. 2000. *Motivation: A Biosocial and Cognitive Integration of Motivation and Emotion.* New York: Oxford University Press.

Fiedler, Klaus. 2001. "Affective Influences on Social Information Processing." In *Handbook of Affect and Social Cognition,* edited by Joseph P. Forgas, 163–85. Mahwah, NJ: Lawrence Erlbaum.

Finkel, Steven E., and John G. Geer. 1998. "Spot Check: Casting Doubt on the Demobilizing Effect of Attack Advertising." *American Journal of Political Science* 42:573–95.

Fiorina, Morris P. 1981. *Retrospective Voting in American National Elections.* New Haven: Yale University Press.

———. 1990. "Information and Rationality in Elections." In *Information and Democratic Processes,* edited by John Ferejohn and James Kuklinski, 329–42. Urbana: University of Illinois Press.

———. 1999. "Extreme Voices: A Dark Side of Civic Engagement." In *Civic Engagement in American Democracy,* edited by Theda Skocpol and Morris P. Fiorina, 395–425. Washington, DC: Brookings Institution.

Fiske, Susan T., Donald Kinder, and Michael Larter. 1983. "The Novice and the Expert: Knowledge-Based Strategies in Political Cognition." *Journal of Experimental Social Psychology* 19:381–400.

Fiske, Susan T., and Shelley E. Taylor. 1991. *Social Cognition.* 2d ed. New York: McGraw-Hill.

Forgas, Joseph P., ed. 2000. *Feeling and Thinking: The Role of Affect in Social Cognition.* New York: Cambridge University Press.

Fredrickson, Barbara, and Christine Branigan. 2001. "Positive Emotions." In *Emotions,* edited by Tracy J. Mayne and James Ramsey, 123–51. New York: Guilford Press.

Freedman, Paul, and Ken Goldstein. 1999. "Measuring Media Exposure and the Effects of Negative Campaign Ads." *American Journal of Political Science* 43 (4): 1189–1208.

Frey, Kurt P., and Alice H. Eagly. 1993. "Vividness Can Undermine The Persuasiveness of Messages." *Journal of Personality and Social Psychology* 65 (1): 32–44.

Friedman, Howard S., M. Robin DiMatteo, and Timothy I. Mertz. 1980. "Nonverbal Communication on Television News: The Facial Expressions of Broadcasters during Coverage of a Presidential Election Campaign." *Personality and Social Psychology Bulletin* 6:427–35.

Frijda, Nico H. 1986. *The Emotions.* New York: Cambridge University Press.

———. 1994a. "Emotions Require Cognitions, Even If Simple Ones." In *The Nature of Emotion,* edited by Paul Ekman and Richard J. Davidson, 197–202. New York: Oxford University Press.

———. 1994b. "Universal Antecedents Exist, and Are Interesting." In *The Nature of Emotion,* edited by Paul Ekman and Richard J. Davidson, 155–62. New York: Oxford University Press.

————. 1999. "Emotions and Hedonic Experience" In *Well-Being,* edited by Daniel Kahneman, Ed Diener, and Norbert Schwarz, 190–210. New York: Russell Sage Foundation.

————. 2000. "The Psychologists' Point of View." In *Handbook of Emotions,* 2d ed., edited by Michael Lewis and Jeannette M. Haviland-Jones, 59–74. New York: Guilford Press.

Gardner, Howard. 1985. *The Mind's New Science: A History of the Cognitive Revolution.* New York: Basic Books.

Garramone, Gina M. 1983. "Issue versus Image Orientation and Effects of Political Advertising." *Communication Research* 10 (1): 59–76.

Garramone, Gina M., Charles K. Atkin, Bruce E. Pinkleton, and Richard T. Cole. 1990. "Effects of Negative Political Advertising on the Political Process." *Journal of Broadcasting and Electronic Media* 34:299–311.

Gaut, Berys. 1999. "Identification and Emotion in Narrative Film." In *Passionate Views: Film, Cognition, and Emotion,* edited by Carl Plantinga and Greg M. Smith, 200–16. Baltimore: Johns Hopkins University Press.

Gazzaniga, Michael S. 1992. *Nature's Mind: The Biological Roots of Thinking, Emotions, Sexuality, Language, and Intelligence.* New York: Basic Books.

Geer, John G. 2003. Attacking Democracy: A (Partial) Defense of Negativity in Presidential Campaigns, 1960–2000. Paper presented at the annual meeting of the American Political Science Association, August 28–31, in Philadelphia.

Geiger, Seth F., and Byron Reeves. 1991. "The Effects of Visual Structure and Content Emphasis on the Evaluation and Memory for Political Candidates." In *Television and Political Advertising.* Vol. 1, *Psychological Processes,* edited by Frank Biocca, 125–43. Hillsdale, NJ: Lawrence Erlbaum.

Gelman, Andrew, and Gary King. 1993. "Why Are American Presidential Election Campaign Polls So Variable When Votes Are So Predictable?" *British Journal of Political Science* 23:409–51.

Gerber, Alan S., and Donald P. Green. 2000a. "The Effects of Canvassing, Direct Mail, and Telephone Contact on Voter Turnout: A Field Experiment." *American Political Science Review* 94:653–63.

————. 2000b. "The Effect of a Nonpartisan Get-Out-The-Vote Drive: An Experimental Study of Leafletting." *Journal of Politics* 62 (3): 846–57.

Gilens, Martin. 1999. *Why Americans Hate Welfare: Race, Media, and the Politics of Antipoverty Policy.* Chicago: University of Chicago Press.

Gilliam, Frank, and Shanto Iyengar. 2000. "Prime Suspects: The Influence of Television News on the Viewing Public." American Journal of Political Science 43:560–573.

Glaser, Jack, and Peter Salovey. 1998. "Affect in Electoral Politics." *Personality and Social Psychology Review* 2 (3): 156–72.

Gohm, Carol L., and Gerald L. Clore. 2002. "Affect as Information: An Individual-Differences Approach." In *The Wisdom of Feeling,* edited by Lisa Feldman Barrett and Peter Salovey, 89–113. New York: Guilford Press.

Goldstein, Ken, and Paul Freedman. 2002a. "Campaign Advertising and Voter Turnout: New Evidence for a Stimulation Effect." *Journal of Politics* 64:721–40.

————. 2002b. "Lessons Learned: Campaign Advertising in the 2000 Election." *Political Communication* 19 (1): 5–28.

Gordon, Ann, David M. Shafie, and Ann N. Crigler. 2003. "Is Negative Advertising Effective for Female Candidates? An Experiment in Voters' Uses of Gender Stereotypes." *Harvard International Journal of Press/Politics* 8:35–53.

Graber, Doris A. 1988. *Processing the News: How People Tame the Information Tide.* New York: Longman.

————. 2001. *Processing Politics: Learning from Television in the Internet Age.* Chicago: University of Chicago Press.

Gray, Jeffrey A. 1987. *The Psychology of Fear and Stress.* 2d ed. New York: Cambridge University Press.

————. 1994. "Three Fundamental Emotion Systems." In *The Nature of Emotion,* edited by Paul Ekman and Richard J. Davidson, 243–47. New York: Oxford University Press.

Green, Donald, Bradley Palmquist, and Eric Schickler. 2002. *Partisan Hearts and Minds: Political Parties and the Social Identities of Voters.* New Haven: Yale University Press.

Hamilton, Alexander, James Madison, and John Jay. [1788] 1961. *The Federalist Papers.* Edited by Clinton Rossiter. New York: Mentor.

Hammond, Meryl. 1987. "Measuring Emotion." *Marketing and Media Decisions* 22:54–55.

Hart, Roderick. 1999. *Seducing America: How Television Charms the Modern Voter.* Rev. ed. Thousand Oaks, CA: Sage Publications.

Hartmann, George W. 1936. "Field Experiment on the Comparative Effectiveness of 'Emotional' and 'Rational' Political Leaflets in Determining Election Results." *Abnormal Psychology* 31:99–114.

Hastie, Reid, and Bernadette Park. 1986. "The Relationship between Memory and Judgment Depends on Whether the Judgment Task Is Memory-Based or On-Line." *Psychological Review* 93 (3): 258–68.

Hatfield, Elaine, John T. Cacioppo, and Richard L. Rapson. 1994. *Emotional Contagion.* New York: Cambridge University Press.

Hemphill, Michael. 1996. "A Note on Adults' Color-Emotion Associations." *Journal of Genetic Psychology* 157 (3): 275–80.

Herr, J. Paul. 2002. "The Impact of Campaign Appearances in the 1996 Election." *Journal of Politics* 64:904–13.

Hertel, Guido, Jochen Neuhof, Thomas Theuer, and Norbert L. Kerr. 2000. "Mood Effects on Cooperation in Small Groups: Does Positive Mood Simply Lead to More Cooperation?" *Cognition and Emotion* 14 (4): 441–72.

Hitchon, Jacqueline C., Chingching Chang, and Rhonda Harris. 1997. "Should Women Emote? Perceptual Bias and Opinion Change in Response to Political Ads for Candidates of Different Genders." *Political Communication* 14:49–69.

Hitchon, Jacqueline C., and Esther Thorson. 1995. "Effects of Emotion and Product Involvement on the Experience of Repeated Commercial Viewing." *Journal of Broadcasting and Electionic Media* 39:276–89.

Holbrook, Allyson L., Jon A. Krosnick, Penny S. Visser, Wendi L. Gardner, and John T. Cacioppo. 2001. "Attitudes toward Presidential Candidates and Political Parties: Initial Optimism, Inertial First Impressions, and a Focus on Flaws." *American Journal of Political Science* 45 (4): 930–50.

Holbrook, Morris B., and Rajeev Batra. 1987. "Assessing the Role of Emotions as Mediators of Consumer Responses to Advertising." *Journal of Consumer Research* 14:404–20.

Holbrook, Thomas. 1996. *Do Campaigns Matter?* Thousand Oaks: Sage Publications.

————. 2001. "Forecasting with Mixed Economic Signals: A Cautionary Tale." *PS: Political Science and Politics* 34:39–44.

Holsti, Ole R. 1969. *Content Analysis for the Social Sciences and Humanities.* Reading, MA: Addison-Wesley.

Hovland, Carl I., Irving L. Janis, and Harold H. Kelley. 1953. *Communication and Persuasion: Psychological Studies of Opinion Change.* New Haven: Yale University Press.

Huddy, Leonie, and Anna H. Gunnthorsdottir. 2000. "The Persuasive Effects of Emotive Visual Imagery: Superficial Manipulation or the Product of Passionate Reason?" *Political Psychology* 21 (4): 745–78.

Huang, Ming-Hui. 1998. "Exploring a New Typology of Advertising Appeals: Basic, versus Social, Emotional Advertising in a Global Setting." *International Journal of Advertising* 17:145–68.

Hunt, Morton. 1993. *The Story of Psychology.* New York: Anchor Books.

Isbell, Linda M., and Victor C. Ottati. 2002. "The Emotional Voter: Effects of Episodic Affective Reactions on Candidate Evaluations." In *The Social Psychology of Politics,* edited by Victor C. Ottati et al., 55–74. New York: Kluwer.

Iyengar, Shanto. 1991. *Is Anyone Responsible? How Television Frames Political Issues.* Chicago: University of Chicago Press.

Iyengar, Shanto, and Donald R. Kinder. 1987. *News That Matters: Television and American Opinion.* Chicago: University of Chicago Press.

Iyengar, Shanto, and William J. McGuire. 1993. *Explorations in Political Psychology.* Durham, NC: Duke University Press.

Iyengar, Shanto, and John R. Petrocik. 2001. "'Basic Rule' Voting: Impact of Campaigns on Party- and Approval-Based Voting." In *Crowded Airwaves,* edited by James Thurber, Candice Nelson, and David Dulio, 113–48. Washington, DC: Brookings Institution.

Iyengar, Shanto, and Adam F. Simon. 2000. "New Perspectives and Evidence on Political Communication and Campaign Effects." *Annual Review of Psychology* 51:149–69.

Izard, Carroll E. 1991. *The Psychology of Emotions.* New York: Plenum Press.

———. 1994. "Cognition Is One of Four Types of Emotion Activating Systems." In *The Nature of Emotion,* edited by Paul Ekman and Richard J. Davidson, 203–7. New York: Oxford University Press.

Izard, Carroll E., and Brian P. Ackerman. 2000. "Motivational, Organizational, and Regulatory Functions of Discrete Emotions." In *Handbook of Emotions,* 2d ed., edited by Michael Lewis and Jeannette M. Haviland-Jones, 253–64. New York: Guilford Press.

Jamieson, Kathleen Hall. 1988. *Eloquence in an Electronic Age: The Transformation of Political Speechmaking.* New York: Oxford University Press.

———. 1992. *Dirty Politics: Deception, Distraction, and Democracy.* New York: Oxford University Press.

———. 1996. *Packaging the Presidency: A History and Criticism of Presidential Campaign Advertising.* 3d ed. New York: Oxford University Press.

Jamieson, Kathleen Hall, Paul Waldman, and Susan Sherr. 2000. "Eliminate the Negative? Categories of Analysis for Political Advertisements." In *Crowded Airwaves,* edited by James Thurber, Candice Nelson, and David Dulio, 65–95. Washington, D.C.: Brookings Institution.

Janis, Irving L., and Seymour Feshbach. 1953. "Effects of Fear-Arousing Communications." *Journal of Abnormal and Social Psychology* 48 (1): 78–92.

Johnston, Anne, and Lynda Lee Kaid. 2002. "Image Ads and Issue Ads in U.S. Presidential Advertising: Using Videostyle to Explore Stylistic Differences in Televised Political Ads from 1952 to 2000." *Journal of Communication* 52 (2): 281–300.

Joslyn, Mark. 2001. Review of *Affective Intelligence and Political Judgment,* by George Marcus, W. Russell Neuman, and Michael MacKuen. *American Political Science Review* 95:1003–4.

Joslyn, Richard. 1980. "The Content of Political Spot Ads." *Journalism Quarterly* 57:92–98.

Jowett, Garth S., and Victoria O'Donnell. 1999. *Propaganda and Persuasion.* 3d ed. Thousand Oaks, CA: Sage Publications.

Juslin, Patrik N. 2000. "Cue Utilization in Communication of Emotion in Music Performance: Relating Performance to Perception." *Journal of Experimental Psychology* 26 (6): 1797–1813.

———. 2001. "Communicating Emotion in Music Performance: A Review and a Theoretical Framework." In *Music and Emotion,* edited by Patrik N. Juslin and John A. Sloboda, 309–37. New York: Oxford University Press.

Juslin, Patrik N., and John A. Sloboda, eds. 2001. *Music and Emotion: Theory and Research.* New York: Oxford University Press.

Just, Marion, Ann Crigler, Dean Alger, Timothy Cook, Montague Kern, and Darrell West. 1996. *Crosstalk: Citizens, Candidates, and the Media in a Presidential Campaign.* Chicago: University of Chicago Press.

Kahn, Kim Fridkin. 1996. *The Political Consequences of Being a Woman.* New York: Columbia University Press.

Kahn, Kim Fridkin, and Patrick J. Kenney. 2000. "How Negative Campaigning Enhances Knowledge of Senate Elections." In *Crowded Airwaves,* edited by James Thurber, Candice Nelson and David Dulio, 65–95. Washington, DC: Brookings Institution.

———. 2004. *No Holds Barred: Negativity in U.S. Senate Campaigns.* Upper Saddle River, NJ: Pearson Prentice-Hall.

Kaid, Lynda Lee. 1991. "Ethical Dimensions of Political Advertising." In *Ethical Dimensions of Political Communication,* edited by Robert Denton Jr., 145–99. New York: Praeger.

———. 1997. "Effects of the Television Spots on Images of Dole and Clinton." *American Behavioral Scientist* 40:1085–94.

———. 2001. "TechnoDistortions and Effects of the 2000 Political Advertising." *American Behavioral Scientist* 44 (12): 2370–78.

Kaid, Lynda Lee, and Christina Holtz-Bacha. 1995. "Political Advertising across Cultures: Comparing Content, Styles, and Effects." In *Political Advertising in Western Democracies,* edited by Lynda Lee Kaid and Christina Holtz-Bacha, 206–27. Thousand Oaks, CA: Sage Publications.

Kaid, Lynda Lee, and Anne Johnston. 1991. "Negative versus Positive Television Advertising in Presidential Campaigns, 1960–1988." *Journal of Communication* 41:46–53.

———. 2001. *Videostyle in Presidential Campaigns: Style and Content of Televised Political Advertising.* Westport, CT: Praeger.

Kaid, Lynda Lee, and John C. Tedesco. 1999. "Tracking Voter Reaction to Television Advertising." In *The Electronic Election,* edited by Lynda Lee Kaid and Dianne Bystrom, 233–45. Mahwah, NJ: Lawrence Erlbaum.

Kamber, Victor. 1997. *Poison Politics: Are Negative Campaigns Destroying Democracy?* New York: Insight Books.

Kent, Frank R. 1928. *Political Behavior.* New York: William Morrow.

Kepplinger, Hans Mathias. 1991. "The Impact of Presentation Techniques: Theoretical Aspects and Empirical Findings." In *Television and Political Advertising.* Vol. 1, *Psychological Processes,* edited by Frank Biocca, 173–94. Hillsdale, NJ: Lawrence Erlbaum.

Kern, Montague. 1989. *30-Second Politics: Political Advertising in the Eighties.* New York: Praeger.

Key, V. O., Jr. 1966. *The Responsible Electorate: Rationality in Presidential Voting, 1936–1960.* Cambridge, MA: Harvard University Press, Belknap Press.

Kinder, Donald R. 1986. "Presidential Character Revisited." In *Political Cognition,* edited by Richard Lau and David Sears, 233–55. Hillsdale, NJ: Lawrence Erlbaum.

———. 1994. "Reason and Emotion in American Political Life." In *Beliefs, Reasoning, and Decision Making,* edited by Roger Schank and Ellen Langer, 277–314. Hillsdale, NJ: Lawrence Erlbaum.

———. 1998. "Opinion and Action in the Realm of Politics." In *The Handbook of Social Psychology,* vol. 1, edited by Daniel Gilbert, Susan Fiske, and Gardner Lindzey, 778–67. 4th ed. New York: McGraw-Hill.

———. 2003. "Communication and Politics in the Age of Information." In *Oxford Handbook of Political Psychology,* edited by David Sears, Leonie Huddy, and Robert Jervis, 357–93. New York: Oxford University Press.

Kinder, Donald R., and Lisa D'Ambrosio. 2000. "War, Emotion, and Public Opinion." University of Michigan. Unpublished manuscript.

Kinder, Donald R., and Thomas R. Palfrey, ed. 1993. *Experimental Foundations of Political Science.* Ann Arbor: University of Michigan Press.

Klapper, Joseph. 1960. *The Effects of Mass Communication.* New York: Free Press.

Kosmin, Barry A., and Seymour P. Lachman. 1993. *One Nation under God: Religion in Contemporary American Society.* New York: Harmony Books.

Krosnick, Jon A., Andrew L. Betz, Lee J. Jussim, and Ann R. Lynn. 1992. "Subliminal Conditioning of Attitudes." *Personality and Social Psychology Bulletin* 18:152–62.

Kuklinski, James, and Norman Hurley. 1994. "On Hearing and Interpreting Political Messages: A Cautionary Tale of Citizen Cue-Taking." *Journal of Politics* 56:729–51.

Lane, Richard D., and Lynn Nadel, eds. 2000. *Cognitive Neuroscience of Emotion.* New York: Oxford University Press.

Lang, Kurt, and Gladys Engel Lang. 1968. *Politics and Television.* Chicago: Quadrangle.

Lang, Annie. 1991. "Emotion, Formal Features, and Memory for Televised Political Advertisements." In *Television and Political Advertising.* Vol. 1, *Psychological Processes,* edited by Frank Biocca, 221–43. Hillsdale, NJ: Lawrence Erlbaum.

Lang, Annie, John Newhagen, and Byron Reeves. 1996. "Negative Video as Structure: Emotion, Attention, Capacity, and Memory." *Journal of Broadcasting and Electronic Media* 40:460–77.

Lanzetta, John T., Denis G. Sullivan, Roger D. Masters, and Gregory J. McHugo. 1985. "Emotional and Cognitive Responses to Televised Images of Political Leaders." In *Mass Media and Political Thought,* edited by Sidney Kraus and Richard Perloff, 85–116. Beverly Hills: Sage Publications.

Larsen, Randy, and Barbara L. Fredrickson. 1999. "Measurement Issues in Emotion Research." In *Well-Being,* edited by Daniel Kahneman, Ed Diener, and Norbert Schwarz, 40–60. New York: Russell Sage.

Lau, Richard R., and David P. Redlawsk. 2001. "An Experimental Study of Information Search. Memory, and Decision Making during a Political Campaign." In *Citizens and Politics,* edited by James Kuklinski, 136–59. New York: Cambridge University Press.

Lau, Richard R., and David O. Sears, eds. 1986. *Political Cognition.* Hillsdale, NJ: Lawrence Erlbaum.

Lau, Richard R., Lee Sigelman, Caroline Heldman, and Paul Babbitt. 1999. "The Effects of Negative Political Advertisements: A Meta-Analytic Assessment." *American Political Science Review* 93 (4): 851–76.

Lazarsfeld, Paul F., Bernard Berelson, and Hazel Gaudet. 1944. *The People's Choice: How the Voter Makes Up His Mind in a Presidential Campaign.* New York: Columbia University Press.

Lazarus, Richard S. 1981. "A Cognitivist's Reply to Zajonc on Emotion and Cognition." *American Psychologist* 36:222–23.

———. 1982. "Thoughts on the Relations between Emotion and Cognition." *American Psychologist* 37:1019–24.

———. 1984. "On the Primacy of Cognition." *American Psychologist* 39:124–29.

———. 1991. *Emotion and Adaptation.* New York: Oxford University Press.

———. 1994a. "Appraisal: The Long and Short of It." In *The Nature of Emotion,* edited by Paul Ekman and Richard J. Davidson, 208–15. New York: Oxford University Press.

———. 1994b. "Universal Antecedents of the Emotions." In *The Nature of Emotion,* ed. Paul Ekman and Richard J. Davidson, 163–71. New York: Oxford University Press.

LeDoux, Joseph E. 1989. "Cognitive-Emotional Interactions in the Brain." *Cognition and Emotion* 3 (4): 267–89.

———. 1994a. "Cognitive-Emotional Interactions in the Brain." In *The Nature of Emotion,* edited by Paul Ekman and Richard J. Davidson, 216–23. New York: Oxford University Press.

———. 1994b. "Emotional Processing, but Not Emotions, Can Occur Unconsciously." In *The Nature of Emotion,* edited by Paul Ekman and Richard J. Davidson, 291–92. New York: Oxford University Press.

———. 1995. "In Search of an Emotional System in the Brain: Leaping from Fear to Emotion and Consciousness." In *The Cognitive Neurosciences,* edited by Michael S. Gazzaniga, 1049–61. Cambridge: MIT Press.

———. 1996. *The Emotional Brain: The Mysterious Underpinnings of Emotional Life.* New York: Simon and Schuster.

LeDoux, Joseph E., and Elizabeth A. Phelps. 2000. "Emotional Networks in the Brain." In *Handbook of Emotions,* 2d ed., edited by Michael Lewis and Jeannette M. Haviland-Jones, 157–72. New York: Guilford Press.

Leege, David C., and Lyman A. Kellstedt, eds. 1993. *Rediscovering the Religious Factor in American Politics.* Armonk, NY: M. E. Sharpe.

Lerner, Jennifer S., Roxana M. Gonzalez, Deborah A. Small, and Baruch Fischhoff. 2003. "Effects of Fear and Anger on Perceived Risks of Terrorism: A National Field Experiment." *Psychological Science* 14 (2): 144–50.

Lerner, Jennifer S., and Dacher Keltner. 2000. "Beyond Valence: Toward a Model of Emotion-Specific Influences on Judgement and Choice." *Cognition and Emotion* 14 (4): 473–93.

Leventhal, H., and Klaus Scherer. 1987. "The Relationship of Emotion to Cognition: A Functional Approach to a Semantic Controversy." *Cognition and Emotion* 1:3–28.

Lewis-Beck, Michael S., and Tom W. Rice. 1992. *Forecasting Elections.* Washington, DC: Congressional Quarterly Press.

Lichter, S. Robert, and Richard E. Noyes. 1996. *Good Intentions Make Bad News: Why Americans Hate Campaign Journalism.* Lanham, MD: Rowman and Littlefield.

Lippmann, Walter. 1922. *Public Opinion.* New York: Free Press.

Lodge, Milton, and Kathleen M. McGraw, eds. 1995. *Political Judgment: Structure and Process.* Ann Arbor: University of Michigan Press.

Lodge, Milton, Kathleen M. McGraw, and Patrick Stroh. 1989. "An Impression-Driven Model of Candidate Evaluation." *American Political Science Review* 83:399–419.

Lodge, Milton, and Charles Taber. 2000. "Three Steps toward a Theory of Motivated Political Reasoning." In *Elements of Reason,* edited by Arthur Lupia, Mathew McCubbins, and Samuel Popkin, 183–213. New York: Cambridge University Press.

Lombard, Matthew, Jennifer Snyder-Duch, and Cheryl Campanella Bracken. 2002. "Content Analysis in Mass Communication: Assessment and Reporting of Intercoder Reliability." *Human Communication Research* 28:587–604.

Lupia, Arthur. 2002. "New Ideas in Experimental Political Science." *Political Analysis* 10 (4): 319–24.

Lupia, Arthur, and Mathew McCubbins. 1998. *The Democratic Dilemma.* New York: Cambridge University Press.

Luskin, Robert C. 1987. "Measuring Political Sophistication." *American Journal of Political Science* 31:856–99.

Marcus, George E. 2000. "Emotions in Politics." *Annual Review of Political Science* 3:221–50.

———. 2002. *The Sentimental Citizen: Emotion in Democratic Politics.* University Park, PA: Pennsylvania State University Press.

———. 2003. "The Psychology of Emotion and Politics." In *Oxford Handbook of Political Psychology,* edited by David Sears, Leonie Huddy, and Robert Jervis, 182–221. New York: Oxford University Press.

Marcus, George E., and Michael B. MacKuen. 1993. "Anxiety, Enthusiasm, and the Vote: The Emotional Underpinnings of Learning and Involvement during Presidential Campaigns." *American Political Science Review* 87:672–85.

———. 2001. "Emotions and Politics: The Dynamic Functions of Emotionality." In *Citizens and Politics,* edited by James Kuklinski, 41–67. New York: Cambridge University Press.

Marcus, George E., W. Russell Neuman, and Michael MacKuen. 2000. *Affective Intelligence and Political Judgment.* Chicago: University of Chicago Press.

Marcus, George E., W. Russell Neuman, Michael MacKuen, and John L. Sullivan. 1996. "Dynamic Models of Emotional Response: The Multiple Roles of Affect in Politics." In *Research in Micropolitics,* vol. 5. Greenwich, CT: JAI Press.

Martin, Leonard L., and Gerald L. Clore. 2001. *Theories of Mood and Cognition: A User's Guidebook.* Mahwah, NJ: Lawrence Erlbaum.

Masters, Roger D. 1991. *The Nature of Politics.* New Haven: Yale University Press.

———. 1994. *Beyond Relativism: Science and Human Values.* Hanover, NH: University Press of New England.

———. 2001. "Cognitive Neuroscience, Emotion, and Leadership." In *Citizens and Politics,* edited by James Kuklinski, 68–102. New York: Cambridge University Press.

Masters, Roger D., and Denis G. Sullivan. 1989. "Nonverbal Displays and Political Leadership in France and the United States." *Political Behavior* 11 (2): 123–56.

———. 1993. "Nonverbal Behavior and Leadership: Emotion and Cognition in Political Information Processing." In *Explorations of Political Psychology,* edited by Shanto Iyengar and William J. McGuire, 150–82. Durham: Duke University Press.

Masters, Roger D., and Baldwin Way. 1996. "Experimental Methods and Attitudes toward Leaders: Nonverbal Displays, Emotion, and Cognition." In *Research in Biopol-itics,* vol. 4, edited by Steven Peterson and Albert Somit, 61–98. Greenwich, CT: JAI Press.

Masterson, John T., and Thompson Biggers. 1986. "Emotion-Eliciting Qualities of Televi-sion Campaign Advertising as a Predictor of Voting Behavior." *Psychology* 23 (1): 13–19.

Mayer, William G. 1996. "In Defense of Negative Campaigning." *Political Science Quar-terly* 111 (3): 437–55.

McCubbins, Mathew D., ed. 1992. *Under the Watchful Eye: Managing Presidential Cam-paigns in the Television Era.* Washington, DC: CQ Press.

McGinnis, Joe. 1969. *The Selling of the President.* New York: Penguin.

McGuire, William J. 1985. "Attitudes and Attitude Change." In *The Handbook of Social Psychology,* vol. 1, edited by Gardner Lindzey and Elliot Aronson, 233–346. New York: Random House.

McHugo, Gregory J., John T. Lanzetta, and Lauren K. Bush. 1991. "The Effect of Atti-tudes on Emotional Reactions to Expressive Displays of Political Leaders." *Journal of Nonverbal Behavior* 15:19–41.

McHugo, Gregory J., John T. Lanzetta, Denis G. Sullivan, Roger D. Masters, and Basil Englis. 1985. "Emotional Reactions to Expressive Displays of a Political Leader." *Journal of Personality and Social Psychology* 49:1512–29.

Meirick, Patrick. 2002. "Cognitive Responses to Negative and Comparative Political Advertising." *Journal of Advertising* 31 (1): 49–62.

Mendelberg, Tali. 2001. *The Race Card: Campaign Strategy, Implicit Messages, and the Norm of Equality.* Princeton: Princeton University Press.

Milburn, Michael A. 1991. *Persuasion and Politics: The Social Psychology of Public Opin-ion.* Pacific Grove, CA: Brooks/Cole.

Millar, Murray G., and Karen U. Millar. 1996. "The Effects of Direct and Indirect Expe-rience on Affective and Cognitive Responses and the Attitude-Behavior Relation." *Journal of Experimental Social Psychology* 32:561–79.

Miller, Warren E., and J. Merrill Shanks. 1996. *The New American Voter.* Cambridge: Harvard University Press.

Mogg, Karin, and Brendan P. Bradley. 1998. "Selective Attention and Anxiety: A Cognitive-Motivational Perspective." In *Handbook of Cognition and Emotion,* edited by Tim Dalgleish and Mick Power, 145–70. New York: Wiley. s

Moring, Tom. 1995. "The North European Exception: Political Advertising on TV in Finland." In *Political Advertising in Western Democracies,* edited by Lynda Lee Kaid and Christina Holtz-Bacha, 161–85. Thousand Oaks, CA: Sage Publications.

Mulilis, John-Paul, and Richard Lippa. 1990. "Behavioral Change in Earthquake Pre-paredness Due to Negative Threat Appeals: A Test of Protection-Motivation The-ory." *Journal of Applied Social Psychology* 20 (8): 619–38.

Mullen, Brian, David Futrell, Debbie Stairs, Dianne M. Tice, Roy F. Baumeister, Kath-ryn E. Dawson, Catherine A. Riordan, Christine E. Radloff, George R. Goethals, John G. Kennedy, and Paul Rosenfeld. 1986. "Newscasters' Facial Expressions and Voting Behavior of Viewers: Can a Smile Elect a President?" *Journal of Personality and Social Psychology* 51:291–95.

Murphy, Sheila T., and Robert B. Zajonc. 1993. "Affect, Cognition, and Awareness: Af-fective Priming with Optimal and Suboptimal Stimulus Exposures." *Journal of Per-sonality and Social Psychology* 64:723–39.

Nabi, Robin L. 2003. "Exploring the Framing Effects of Emotion: Do Discrete Emotions Differentially Influence Information Accessibility, Information Seeking, and Policy Preference?" *Communication Research* 30 (2): 224–47.

Nadeau, Richard, Richard G. Niemi, and Timothy Amato. 1995. "Emotions, Issue Importance, and Political Learning." *American Journal of Political Science* 39:558–74.

Nelson, John S., and G. R. Boynton. 1997. *Video Rhetorics: Televised Advertising in American Politics.* Urbana: University of Illinois Press.

Nelson, Thomas, Rosalee Clawson, and Zoe Oxley. 1997. "Media Framing of a Civil Liberties Conflict and Its Effect on Tolerance." *American Political Science Review* 91:567–83.

Nelson, Thomas, and Donald Kinder. 1996. "Issue Frames and Group Centrism in American Public Opinion." *Journal of Politics* 58 (4): 1055–78.

Nesbit, Dorothy. 1988. *Videostyle in Senate Campaigns.* Knoxville: University of Tennessee Press.

Neuman, W. Russell, Marion R. Just, and Ann N. Crigler. 1992. *Common Knowledge: News and the Construction of Political Meaning.* Chicago: The University of Chicago Press.

Newhagen, John E., and Byron Reeves. 1991. "Emotion and Memory Responses for Negative Political Advertising: A Study of Television Commercials Used in the 1988 Presidential Election." In *Television and Political Advertising.* Vol. 1, *Psychological Processes,* edited by Frank Biocca, 197–220. Hillsdale, NJ: Lawrence Erlbaum.

Nimmo, Dan. 1970. *The Political Persuaders: The Techniques of Modern Election Campaigns.* Englewood Cliffs, NJ: Prentice-Hall.

Nisbett, Richard E., and Lee Ross. 1980. *Human Inference.* Englewood Cliffs, NJ: Prentice-Hall.

Norpoth, Helmut. 2001. "Primary Colors: A Mixed Blessing for Al Gore." *PS: Political Science and Politics* 34:45–8.

Norris, Pippa. 2000. *A Virtuous Circle: Political Communications in Postindustrial Societies.* NY: Cambridge University Press.

Oatley, Keith. 1992. *Best Laid Schemes: The Psychology of Emotion.* New York: Cambridge University Press.

Oatley, Keith, and Jennifer M. Jenkins. 1996. *Understanding Emotions.* Cambridge, MA: Blackwell Publishers.

Ochsner, Kevin N., and Lisa Feldman Barrett. 2001. "A Multiprocess Perspective on the Neuroscience of Emotion." In *Emotions,* edited by Tracy J. Mayne and James Ramsey, 38–81. New York: Guilford Press.

Öhman, Arne. 2000. "Fear and Anxiety: Evolutionary, Cognitive, and Clinical Perspectives." In *Handbook of Emotions,* 2d ed., edited by Michael Lewis and Jeannette M. Haviland-Jones, 573–93. New York: Guilford Press.

Olney, Thomas J., Morris B. Holbrook, and Rajeev Batra. 1991. "Consumer Responses to Advertising: The Effects of Ad Content, Emotions, and Attitude toward the Ad on Viewing Time." *Journal of Consumer Research* 17:440–53.

Ortony, Andrew, Gerald L. Clore, and Allan Collins. 1988. *The Cognitive Structure of Emotions.* New York: Cambridge University Press.

Osgood, Charles E., George J. Suci, and Percy H. Tannenbaum. 1957. *The Measurement of Meaning.* Urbana: University of Illinois Press.

O'Shaughnessy, John, and Nicholas Jackson O'Shaughnessy. 2003. *The Marketing Power of Emotion.* New York: Oxford University Press.

Ottati, Victor C., and Robert S. Wyer Jr. 1993. "Affect and Political Judgment." In *Explorations of Political Psychology,* edited by Shanto Iyengar and William J. McGuire, 296–315. Durham: Duke University Press.

Page, Benjamin I., and Robert Y. Shapiro. 1992. *The Rational Public.* Chicago: University of Chicago Press.

Page, Benjamin I., Robert Y. Shapiro, and Glenn R. Dempsey. 1987. "What Moves Public Opinion?" *American Political Science Review* 81 (1): 23–43.

Pallak, Suzanne R., Enid Murroni, and Juliann Koch. 1983. "Communicator Attractiveness and Expertise, Emotional versus Rational Appeals, and Persuasion: A Heuristic versus Systematic Processing Interpretation." *Social Cognition* 2 (2): 122–41.

Panksepp, Jaak. 1994a. "Basic Emotions Ramify Widely in the Brain, Yielding Many Concepts That Cannot Be Distinguished . . . Yet." In *The Nature of Emotion,* edited by Paul Ekman and Richard J. Davidson, 86–88. New York: Oxford University Press.

———. 1994b. "The Basics of Basic Emotions." In *The Nature of Emotion,* edited by Paul Ekman and Richard J. Davidson, 20–24. New York: Oxford University Press.

———. 1994c. "A Proper Distinction between Affective and Cognitive Process Is Essential to Neuroscientific Progress." In *The Nature of Emotion,* edited by Paul Ekman and Richard J. Davidson, 224–26. New York: Oxford University Press.

———. 1998. *Affective Neuroscience: The Foundations of Human and Animal Emotions.* New York: Oxford University Press.

———. 2000. "Emotions as Natural Kinds within the Mammalian Brain." In *Handbook of Emotions,* 2d ed., edited by Michael Lewis and Jeannette M. Haviland-Jones, 137–56. New York: Guilford Press.

Parrott, W. Gerrod. 2001. "The Nature of Emotion." In *Blackwell Handbook of Social Psychology: Intraindividual Processes,* edited by Abraham Tesser and Norbert Schwarz, 375–90. Malden, MA: Blackwell.

Patrick, Christopher J., and Stacey A. Lavoro. 1997. "Ratings of Emotional Response to Pictorial Stimuli: Positive and Negative Affect Dimensions." *Motivation and Emotion* 21 (4): 297–321.

Patterson, Thomas. 1993. *Out of Order.* New York: Vintage.

———. 2002. *The Vanishing Voter.* New York: Vintage.

Patterson, Thomas, and Robert McClure. 1973. *Political Advertising: Voter Reactions to Televised Political Commercials.* Princeton, NJ: Citizens' Research Foundation.

———. 1976. *The Unseeing Eye: The Myth of Television Power in National Politics.* New York: G. P. Putnam's Sons.

Perloff, Richard M., and Dennis Kinsey. 1992. "Political Advertising as Seen by Consultants and Journalists." *Journal of Advertising Research* 32 (3): 53–60.

Petty, Richard E., and John T. Cacioppo. 1981. *Attitudes and Persuasion: Classic and Contemporary Approaches.* Boulder: Westview Press.

Pfleiderer, Rolf. 2002. "Using Market Research Techniques to Determine Campaign Effects." In *Public Information Campaigns and Opinion Research,* edited by Hans-Dieter Klingemann and Andrea Römmele, 167–84. Thousand Oaks, CA: Sage Publications.

Plutchik, Robert. 1980. *Emotion: A Psychoevolutionary Synthesis.* New York: Harper and Row.

———. 2003. *Emotions and Life: Perspectives from Psychology, Biology, and Evolution.* Washington: American Psychological Association.

Popkin, Samuel L. 1992. "Campaigns That Matter." In *Under the Watchful Eye: Manag-*

ing Presidential Campaigns in the Television Era, edited by Mathew D. McCubbins, 153–70. Washington, DC: CQ Press.

———. 1994. *The Reasoning Voter: Persuasion and Communication in Presidential Campaigns.* 2d ed. Chicago: University of Chicago Press.

Powell, G. Bingham Jr. 1986. "American Voter Turnout in Comparative Perspective." *American Political Science Review* 80:17–43.

Pratkanis, Anthony, and Elliot Aronson. 1992. *Age of Propaganda: The Everyday Use and Abuse of Persuasison.* New York: W. H. Freeman.

Putnam, Robert. 1995. "Tuning In, Tuning Out: The Strange Disappearance of Social Capital in America." *PS: Political Science and Politics* 28:664–83.

———. 2000. *Bowling Alone.* New York: Simon and Schuster.

Rahn, Wendy M. 2000. "Affect as Information: The Role of Public Mood in Political Reasoning." In *Elements of Reason,* edited by Arthur Lupia, Mathew McCubbins, and Samuel Popkin, 130–50. New York: Cambridge University Press.

Rahn, Wendy M., John H. Aldrich, Eugene Borgida, and John L. Sullivan. 1990. "A Social-Cognitive Model of Candidate Appraisal." In *Information and Democratic Processes,* edited by John A. Ferejohn and James H. Kuklinski, 136–59. Urbana: University of Illinois Press.

Rahn, Wendy M., and Rebecca M. Hirshorn. 1999. "Political Advertising and Public Mood: A Study of Children's Political Orientations." *Political Communication* 16:387–407.

Rahn, Wendy M., Brian Kroeger, and Cynthia M. Kite. 1996. "A Framework for the Study of Public Mood." *Political Psychology* 17 (1): 29–58.

Redlawsk, David P., and Richard R. Lau. 2003. Do Voters Want Candidates They Like or Candidates They Agree With? Affect vs. Cognition in Voter Decision Making. Paper presented at the Shambaugh Conference on Affect and Cognition in Political Action, March 6–9, at University of Iowa, Iowa City, IA.

Richardson, Glenn W. Jr. 2001. "Political Advertising and Popular Culture in the Televisual Age." In *Communication in U.S. Elections,* edited by Roderick Hart and Daron Shaw, 203–20. Lanham, MD: Rowman and Littlefield.

———. 2003. *Pulp Politics: How Political Advertising Tells the Stories of American Politics.* Lanham, MD: Rowman and Littlefield.

Rippetoe, Patricia A., and Ronald W. Rogers. 1987. "Effects of Components of Protection-Motivation Theory on Adaptive and Maladaptive Coping with a Health Threat." *Journal of Personality and Social Psychology* 52 (3): 596–604.

Rogers, Ronald W. 1975. "A Protection Motivation Theory of Fear Appeals and Attitude Change." *Journal of Psychology* 91:93–114.

———. 1983. "Cognitive and Physiological Processes in Fear Appeals and Attitude Change: A Revised Theory of Protection Motivation." In *Social Psychophysiology,* edited by John Cacioppo and Richard Petty, 153–76. New York: Guilford Press.

Rolls, Edmund T. 1999. *The Brain and Emotion.* New York: Oxford University Press.

Roseman, Ira J. 2001. "A Model of Appraisal in the Emotion System: Integrating Theory, Research, and Applications." In *Appraisal Processes in Emotion,* edited by Klaus R. Scherer, Angela Schorr, and Tom Johnstone, 68–91. New York: Oxford University Press.

Roseman, Ira, Robert P. Abelson, and Michael F. Ewing. 1986. "Emotion and Political Cognition: Emotional Appeals in Political Communication." In *Political Cognition,* edited by Richard Lau and David O. Sears, 279–94. Hillsdale, NJ: Lawrence Erlbaum.

Rosenstone, Steven J., and John Mark Hansen. 1993. *Mobilization, Participation, and Democracy in America.* New York: Macmillan.

Rosselli, Francine, John J. Skelly, and Diane M. Mackie. 1995. "Processing Rational and Emotional Messages: The Cognitive and Affective Mediation of Persuasion." *Journal of Experimental Social Psychology* 31 (2): 163–90.

Rudolph, Thomas J., Amy Gangl, and Dan Stevens. 2000. "The Effects of Efficacy and Emotions on Campaign Involvement." *Journal of Politics* 62:1189–97.

Russell, James A. 1980. "A Circumplex Model of Affect." *Journal of Personality and Social Psychology* 39:1161–78.

Sabato, Larry. 1981. *The Rise of Political Consultants: New Ways of Winning Elections.* New York: Basic Books.

———. 1991. *Feeding Frenzy: How Attack Journalism Has Transformed American Politcs.* New York: Free Press.

Schenck-Hamlin, William J., David E. Procter, and Deborah J. Rumsey. 2000. "The Influence of Negative Advertising Frames on Political Cynicism and Politician Accountability." *Human Communication Research* 26 (1): 53–74.

Scher, Richard K. 1997. *The Modern Political Campaign: Mudslinging, Bombast, and the Vitality of American Politics.* Armonk, NY: M. E. Sharpe.

Scherer, Klaus R. 1994a. "Emotion Serves to Decouple Stimulus and Response." In *The Nature of Emotion,* edited by Paul Ekman and Richard J. Davidson, 127–30. New York: Oxford University Press.

———. 1994b. "Evidence for Both Universality and Cultural Specificity of Emotion Elicitation." In *The Nature of Emotion,* edited by Paul Ekman and Richard J. Davidson, 172–75. New York: Oxford University Press.

———. 1994c. "Toward the Concept of 'Modal Emotions.'" In *The Nature of Emotion,* edited by Paul Ekman and Richard J. Davidson, 25–31. New York: Oxford University Press.

———. 2000. "Psychological Models of Emotion." In *The Neuropsychology of Emotion,* edited by Joan C. Borod, 137–62. New York: Oxford University Press.

Scherer, Klaus R., Angela Schorr, and Tom Johnstone. 2001. *Appraisal Processes in Emotion: Theory, Methods, and Research.* New York: Oxford University Press.

Schier, Steven. 1999. *By Invitation Only: The Rise of Exclusive Politics in the United States.* Pittsburgh: University of Pittsburgh Press.

Schudson, Michael. 1998. *The Good Citizen: A History of American Civic Life.* New York: Free Press.

Schwartz, Tony. 1973. *The Responsive Chord.* Garden City, NY: Anchor Books.

Schwarz, Norbert. 2000. "Emotion, Cognition, and Decision-Making." *Cognition and Emotion* 14 (4): 433–40.

———. 2001. "Feelings as Information: Implications for Affective Influences on Information Processing." In *Theories of Mood and Cognition,* edited by Leonard L. Martin and Gerald L. Clore, 159–176. Mahwah, NJ: Lawrence Erlbaum.

Schwarz, Norbert, and Gerd Bohner. 2001. "The Construction of Attitudes." In *Blackwell Handbook of Social Psychology: Intraindividual Processes,* edited by Abraham Tesser and Norbert Schwarz, 436–57. Malden, MA: Blackwell.

Schwarz, Norbert, and Gerald L. Clore. 1983. "Mood, Misattribution, and Judgments of Well-Being: Informative and Directive Functions of Affective States." *Journal of Personality and Social Psychology* 45:513–23.

Scott, Linda M., and Rajeev Batra, eds. 2003. *Persuasive Imagery: A Consumer Response Perspective.* Mahwah, NJ: Lawrence Erlbaum.

Sears, David O. 1993. "Symbolic Politics: A Socio-Psychological Theory." In *Explorations in Political Psychology,* edited by Shanto Iyengar and William J. McGuire, 113–49. Durham, NC: Duke University Press.

Sears, David O., and Rick Kosterman. 1994. "Political Persuasion." In *Persuasion: Psychological Insights and Perspectives,* edited by Sharon Shavitt and Timothy Brock, 251–78. Boston: Allyn and Bacon.

Shaw, Daron R. 1999. "The Effect of TV Ads and Candidate Appearances on Statewide Presidential Votes, 1988–1996." *American Political Science Review* 93 (2): 345–61.

Shaw, Daron R., and Brian E. Roberts. 2000. "Campaign Events, the Media, and Prospects for Victory: The 1992 and 1996 Presidential Elections." *British Journal of Political Science* 30:259–89.

Sherr, Susan A. 1999. "Scenes from the Political Playground: An Analysis of the Symbolic Use of Children in Presidential Campaign Advertising." *Political Communication* 16:45–59.

Shyles, Leonard. 1983. "Defining the Issues of a Presidential Election from Televised Political Spot Advertisements." *Journal of Broadcasting* 28:405–21.

———. 1984. "Defining the 'Images' of Presidential Candidates from Televised Political Spot Advertisements." *Political Behavior* 62 (2): 171–81.

Simon, Adam F. 2002. *The Winning Message: Candidate Behavior, Campaign Discourse, and Democracy.* New York: Cambridge University Press.

Smith, Greg M. 1999. "Local Emotions, Global Moods, and Film Structure." In *Passionate Views: Film, Cognition, and Emotion,* edited by Carl Plantinga and Greg M. Smith, 103–26. Baltimore: Johns Hopkins University Press.

Smith, Jeff. 1999. "Movie Music as Moving Music: Emotion, Cognition, and the Film Score." In *Passionate Views: Film, Cognition, and Emotion,* edited by Carl Plantinga and Greg M. Smith, 146–67. Baltimore: Johns Hopkins University Press.

Sniderman, Paul, Richard A. Brody, and Philip E. Tetlock. 1991. *Reasoning and Choice: Explorations in Political Psychology.* New York: Cambridge University Press.

Strother, Raymond D. 1999. "Preparing Candidates for Television." In *The Manship School Guide to Political Communication,* edited by David D. Perlmutter, 176–85. Baton Rouge: Louisiana State University Press.

Sullivan, Denis G., and Roger D. Masters. 1988. "Happy Warriors: Leaders' Facial Displays, Viewers' Emotions and Political Support." *American Journal of Political Science* 32:345–68.

Sutton, Stephen R. 1982. "Fear-Arousing Communications: A Critical Examination of Theory and Research." In *Social Psychology and Behavioral Medicine,* edited by J. Richard Eiser, 303–37. London: Wiley.

Sutton, Stephen R., and Robert Hallet. 1989. "The Contributon of Fear and Cognitive Factors in Mediating the Effects of Fear-Arousing Communications." *Social Behaviour* 4 (2): 83–98.

Taber, Charles S. "Information Processing and Public Opinion." In *Oxford Handbook of Political Psychology,* edited by David Sears, Leonie Huddy, and Robert Jervis, 433–76. New York: Oxford University Press.

Teixeira, Ruy A. 1992. *The Disappearing American Voter.* Washington, DC: Brookings Institution.

Thorson, Esther, William G. Christ, and Clarke Caywood. 1991. "Effects of Issue-Image Strategies, Attack and Support Appeals, Music, and Visual Content in Political Commercials." *Journal of Broadcasting and Electronic Media* 35:465–86.

Thurber, James, and Candice Nelson, eds. 2000. *Campaign Warriors: The Role of Political Consultants in Elections.* Washington, D.C.: Brookings Institution.

Tomz, Michael, Jason Wittenberg, and Gary King. 2001. CLARIFY: Software for Interpreting and Presenting Statistical Results. Version 2.1. Cambridge: Harvard University. Available at www.gking.harvard.edu

Trent, Judith S., and Robert V. Friedenberg. 1991. *Political Campaign Communication.* 2d ed. New York: Praeger.

———. 2000. *Political Campaign Communication.* 4th ed. Westport, CT: Praeger.

Valdez, Patricia, and Albert Mehrabian. 1994. "Effects of Color on Emotions." *Journal of Experimental Psychology* 123 (4): 394–409.

Valentino, Nicholas A. 1999. "Crime News and the Priming of Racial Attitudes during Evaluations of the President." *Public Opinion Quarterly* 63:293–320.

Valentino, Nicholas A., Vincent L. Hutchings, and Ismail White. 2002. "Cues That Matter: How Political Ads Prime Racial Attitudes during Campaigns." *American Political Science Review* 96 (1): 75–90.

Valentino, Nicholas A., Michael W. Traugott, and Vincent L. Hutchings. 2002. "Group Cues and Ideological Constraint." *Political Communication* 19 (1): 29–48.

Verba, Sidney, and Norman Nie. 1972. *Participation in America.* New York: Harper and Row.

Verba, Sidney, Kay Lehman Schlozman, and Henry E. Brady. 1995. *Voice and Equality: Civic Voluntarism in American Politics.* Cambridge: Harvard University Press.

Watson, David, Lee A. Clark, and Auke Tellegen. 1988. "Development and Validation of Brief Measures of Positive and Negative Affect: The PANAS Scales." *Journal of Personality and Social Psychology* 54 (6): 1063–70.

Wattenberg, Martin P. 1992. *The Rise of Candidate-Centered Politics.* Cambridge: Harvard University Press.

Wattenberg, Martin P., and Craig Leonard Brians. 1999. "Negative Campaign Advertising: Demobilizer or Mobilizer?" *American Political Science Review* 93 (4): 891–99.

Way, Baldwin, and Roger Masters. 1996a. "Emotion and Cognition in Political Information Processing." *Journal of Communication* 46 (3): 48–65.

———. 1996b. "Political Attitudes: Interactions of Cognition and Affect." *Motivation and Emotion* 20:205–36.

West, Darrell M. 1999. "A Brief History of Political Advertising on Television." In *The Manship School Guide to Political Communication,* edited by David D. Perlmutter, 27–32. Baton Rouge: Louisana State University Press.

———. 2001. *Air Wars.* 3d ed. Washington, DC: CQ Press.

Witte, Kim. 1992. "Putting the Fear Back into Fear Appeals: The Extended Parallel Process Model." *Communication Monographs* 59 (4): 329–49.

———. 1998. "Fear as Motivator, Fear as Inhibitor: Using the Extended Parallel Process Model to Explain Fear Successes and Failures." In *Handbook of Communication and Emotion,* edited by Peter A. Andersen and Laura K. Guerrero, 423–50. San Diego: Academic Press.

Witte, Kim, and Mike Allen. 2000. "A Meta-Analysis of Fear Appeals: Implications for Effective Public Health Campaigns." *Health Education and Behavior* 27 (5): 591–615.

Wleizen, Christopher. 2001. "On Forecasting the Presidential Vote." *PS: Political Science and Politics* 34:24–31.

Wolfinger, Raymond E., and Steven J. Rosenstone. 1980. *Who Votes?* New Haven: Yale University Press.

Zajonc, Robert B. 1980. "Feeling and Thinking: Preferences Need No Inferences." *American Psychologist* 35:151–75.

———. 1984. "On the Primacy of Affect." *American Psychologist* 39:117–23.

———. 1994. "Evidence for Nonconscious Emotions." In *The Nature of Emotion,* edited by Paul Ekman and Richard J. Davidson, 293–97. New York: Oxford University Press.

———. 1998. "Emotions." In *The Handbook of Social Psychology,* vol. 1, edited by Daniel T. Gilbert, Susan T. Fiske, and Gardner Lindzey, 591–632. 4th ed. New York: McGraw-Hill.

———. 2000. "Feeling and Thinking: Closing the Debate over the Independence of Affect." In *Feeling and Thinking,* edited by Joseph P. Forgas, 31–58. New York: Cambridge University Press.

Zaller, John R. 1992. *The Nature and Origins of Mass Opinion.* New York: Cambridge University Press.

———. 1996. "The Myth of Massive Media Impact Revived: New Support for a Discredited Idea." In *Political Persuasion and Attitude Change,* edited by Diana Mutz, Paul Sniderman, and Richard Brody, 17–78. Ann Arbor: University of Michigan Press.

———. n.d. "A Theory of Media Politics." Unpublished manuscript, University of California-Los Angeles.

Index

Page numbers in boldface refer to figures and tables.